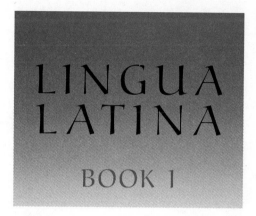

LINGUA LATINA

BOOK 1

LINGUA LATINA

BOOK I

JOHN C. TRAUPMAN, Ph. D.
St. Joseph's University
Philadelphia

AMSCO SCHOOL PUBLICATIONS, INC.
315 HUDSON STREET NEW YORK, N.Y. 10013

Books by John C. Traupman published by Amsco School Publications:
Latin Is Fun Book I;
Latin IsFun Book II;
The New College Latin & English Dictionary;
The New College German & English Dictionary

Cassettes
A cassette program is in preparation
and will be available from the publisher.

When ordering this book, please specifiy **R 117 P**
or LINGUA LATINA BOOK I

Cover and text design by Pedro A. Noa
Typesetting by Dominic Roberti
Illustrations by Anthony D'Adamo

Cover photographs:
Left: Roman Bath, Bath, England © David Ryan, PNI
Top right: Colosseum, Rome, Italy © Bob Abraham, The Stock Market
Below right: Roman Bridge © Steve Elmore, The Stock Market

ISBN 1-56765-425-8
NYC Item 56765-425-7

Printed in the United States of America
1 2 3 4 5 6 7 8 9 10   04 03 02 01 00 99 98

Contents

PART II ADJECTIVES AND ADVERBS

PART III PRONOUNS; ROMAN NUMERALS

PART IV VERBS

APPENDIX

Preface

Features of LINGUA LATINA BOOK 1

Coverage

This book covers the grammatical and syntactical material that is normally studied in the first year in both the more traditional textbooks and the newer generation of books that employ the inductive method. The heavy concentration on military terms has been replaced by terms from everyday Roman life, both public and private.

This book can be used throughout the year for review of sections of grammar as neeeded.

Roman Culture

Roman culture is integrated with language learning. Short and, it is hoped, interesting mini-essays on aspects of both the public and private life of the Romans provide background that renders the readings and exercises of the chapters more meaningful. These essays often provide the Latin words for the various concepts and items that are being discussed. These Latin words are then used in the reading passage and exercises.

Centralized Topics

Each chapter deals with a specific topic, so that grammatical structures, vocabulary, and cultural background can be integrated. The illustrative drawings are functional, not merely decorative. They help the student to visualize the Roman scenes and thus help the student to understand the Latin passages and exercises.

Contextual Exercises

Rather than merely having exercises consisting of lists of Latin words to be identified grammatically, the exercises, with rare exceptions, are contextual; that is, sentences have at least minimal context. An attempt has been made to make the sentences of the exercises realistic and meaningful. As far as possible, the sentences of the exercises serve to reinforce not only grammar but also Roman history and culture.

Variety of Exercises

There is a great variety of exercises to promote interest. Many of the exercises call for reading comprehension for their completion rather than simply making mechanical substitutions and parsing lists of words in isolation. Almost all of the short sentences of the exercises deal with Roman history and culture so that language and culture are reinforced simultaneously. Questions based on the readings may be in English, in Latin, multiple choice, or true-and-false. There are exercises consisting of scrambled sentences which must be put into reasonable Latin word order; the object of such exercises is to make the student aware of the importance of endings. There are exercises in which the student must pick out the grammatical or cultural "misfit" from sets of words. The analogy exercises, some based on grammar, others on culture, require higher-order thinking and prepare the student for the types of questions that will be encountered in standardized tests.

Writing Latin

The chief purpose of studying Latin is to read Latin, based on the acquisition of a large reading vocabulary. However, some writing in Latin will draw the students' attention to the exact forms of Latin words. There are some English-to-Latin translation exercises; they are based on the topic, grammar, and vocabulary of the chapter and at times are variations of the sentences used in the reading passage of the chapter. Many of them are in the form of completion exercises or of Latin answers to Latin questions based on the reading passages.

Etymology

Almost every chapter features practice in derivations. In addition to etymology, there are also exercises aimed at extending the students' Latin vocabulary through the study of cognates. Extensive use has been made of prefixes to show how families of verbs function. These verb clusters help the student to remember vocabulary more readily.

Reading Passages with Running Vocabulary

To facilitate the reading of the Latin passages and to provide the student with a sense of accomplishment, in addition to Latin words occurring in the introductory essay, an ample running vocabulary is provided in the right-hand margin. Thus a student is able to read a whole passage with comprehension and ease rather than laboriously decoding a few lines in a sitting. Important words in the reading passage are repeated in the exercises for reinforcement. When necessary, vocabulary is also provided directly above the exercises in which that vocabulary will be used, rather than piled at the beginning of the lesson. It is important that students meet new and unfamiliar words in context.

Grammatical Terms

Both English and Latin grammatical terms are explained in user-friendly language throughout the chapters. In addition, an extensive glossary of grammatical terms, with examples, is to be found in the back of the book.

English Spelling

The Latin source word will often provide a clue for the spelling of English derivatives. Explanations and exercises are included to make the student aware of this relationship between English and Latin.

Appendices

There is an appendix of English and Latin grammatical terms. An appendix on Latin word order draws together the remarks on Latin word order found throughout the book. An appendix on oral Latin for the classroom provides for the possibility of using spoken Latin in a realistic situation. There is also an appendix on Latin in use today, on Latin mottoes, as well as a chronology of Roman history.

The TEACHER'S MANUAL AND KEY provides the answers to all the exercises and a variety of tests.

Acknowledgments

The author wishes to express his deep appreciation of the many helpful suggestions that have come from teachers and students who have used various chapters of the book in experimental form. Special thanks are due to Carolyn White of the Columbia School for Girls, Columbus, Ohio, for not only reading the entire manuscript but also consulting with other teachers and testing the materials with her students. Special thanks are also due to Kevin G. Finnigan of the Fairport Central School district in Fairport, New York, for his many helpful comments on the various chapters. The author also wishes to express his appreciation to Rose Yost of Nazareth, Pennsylvania, and to Lorraine Bennett of the Cox Senior High School, Virginia Beach, Virginia, for their comments of several chapters.

J.C.T.

PART 1
NOUNS

CHAPTER 1

Nouns of the First and Second Declensions

The Nominative and The Accusative Case

Nunc aut numquam. Now or never.

I. DECLENSIONS

1. When dealing with Latin nouns (and with adjectives and pronouns), we will be speaking of **declensions and declining nouns**. We decline a noun when we change its endings to indicate how the noun is used in a sentence. All nouns declined in the same way belong to the same noun class, called declension. There are five of these declensions in Latin. We will study part of the first and second declensions in this chapter. Nouns consist of two parts:

a) the *base*, that is, the part of the noun that remains unchanged as it is being declined. The base gives the meaning of the noun.

b) the *endings* that are added to the base to indicate how a noun functions in a sentence. The endings do this by showing the number, gender, and case of the noun.

Example   **īnsul·a**   island

2. The base īnsul- indicates the meaning, and the ending **-a** tells you that this noun is feminine, singular, nominative. You will always know where the base ends, because in the tables and in the vocabularies in this book a centered period separates the base from the ending, and the ending in the tables is shown in a different type. The endings show the following:

a) *number*, that is, singular or plural,

b) *gender*, that is, masculine, feminine, or neuter,

c) *case*. In English we speak of the subjective (or nominative) case, the objective (or accusative) case, and the possessive case. Latin has five basic cases: nominative, genitive, dative, accusative, ablative. We will first treat the nominative and accusative cases. The other cases will be treated in the next few chapters.

| | FIRST DECLENSION | SECOND DECLENSION | |
	FEMININE	MASCULINE	NEUTER
	via *f* street, road	**amīcus** *m* friend	**oppidum** *n* town
SINGULAR			
NOM.	**vi·a** street, road	**amīc·us** friend	**oppid·um** town
ACC.	**vi·am** street, road	**amīc·um** friend	**oppid·um** town
PLURAL			
NOM.	**vi·ae** streets, roads	**amīc·ī** friends	**oppid·a** towns
ACC.	**vi·ās** streets, roads	**amīc·ōs** friends	**oppid·a** towns

PITFALL Notice that the feminine singular nominative **via** has the same ending as the neuter plural nominative and accusative **oppida**. Furthermore, the accusative form of neuter nouns is always the same as the nominative, both in the singular and the plural.

NOTES

1) Latin does not have the definite article *the* or the indefinite article *a*. Therefore **oppidum** can mean *the town* or *a town*. The sense of the Latin sentence will indicate which article is to be used when translating into English.

2) Nouns of the first declension end in **-a,** like **vi*a*** *f* road, street, **cas*a*** *f* cottage, **īnsul*a*** *f* island, **Itali*a*** *f* Italy. Most nouns of the first declension are feminine; a few nouns indicate males and are therefore masculine, e.g., **āthlēt*a*** *m* athlete, **naut*a*** *m* sailor; some can be masculine or feminine: **incol*a*** *m/f* inhabitant. Also masculine are a few personal or family names, e.g., **Num*a*** *m* Numa, **Catilīn*a*** *m* Catiline.

3) Most nouns of the second declension end in **-us** and are masculine, like **amīc*us*** *m* friend, **camp*us*** *m* plain, **mūr*us*** *m* wall. Some, such as the names of trees, are feminine, like **mōr*us*** *f* mulberry tree; also feminine are the names of some towns, like **Corinth*us*** *f* Corinth, and the names of a few countries, like **Aegypt*us*** *f* Egypt. Some nouns of the second declension end in **-er**, like **pu*er*** *m* boy, as we will see in the next chapter. When in doubt, check in the dictionary.

4) All nouns of the second declension ending in **-um** are neuter, like **oppid*um*** *n* town, **tēct*um*** *n* roof, **templ*um*** *n* temple, **aedifici*um*** *n* building.

II. THE NOMINATIVE CASE

1. The subject of the sentence is in the nominative case (also called the subjective case).

Example   ***Italia* habet multa oppida.**   Italy has many towns.

Here the noun **Italia** is the subject of the verb **habet** and therefore is in the nominative case.

2. A predicate noun, coming after a verb form such as *am, is, are, were,* is in the nominative case. The verb *to be* is also called a linking verb and acts like an equals sign in math. It merely says: subject = predicate noun or predicate adjective.

Example   **Italia est *paenīnsula*.**   Italy is a peninsula.

Here the noun **paenīnsula (paene** = almost; **īnsula** = an island*)* is a predicate noun and therefore is in the nominative case. Of course, **Italia** is also in the nominative case because it is the subject of the verb **est.**

3. A predicate adjective, linked to the subject by a form of the verb **esse** *to be*, e.g., **est, sunt,** is in the nominative case.

Example   **Via est** *longa.*   The road is long.

In this sentence the adjective **longa** comes after the linking verb **est**, and so it is a predicate adjective and must be in the nominative case.

PITFALL

The whole predicate of a sentence is everything that is said about, or *predicated* of, the subject. In the sentence **Via est longa,** the subject is **via** and the whole predicate is **est longa.** Since **longa** is part of the predicate, it is called predicate adjective. But be careful. Latin word order can be tricky. Take a good look at these two sentences: **Rōma antīqua est. Rōma est antīqua.** They both mean exactly the same thing: "Rome is ancient." Although **antīqua** comes before the verb **est** in the first sentence and after the verb **est** in the second sentence, in each case **antīqua** is a predicate adjective. You'll be hearing a lot more about Latin word order.

4. A noun in apposition with the subject or predicate noun will also be in the nominative case.

Example   **Īnsula** *Sicilia* **est īnfrā Rōmam.**   The island (of) Sicily is south of Rome.

Here, **Sicilia** is in apposition with the subject **īnsula** and therefore **Sicilia,** like **īnsula,** is in the nominative case. Notice that the Romans would say "the island Sicily," while we say "the island *of* Sicily." A realistic instance of a noun in apposition in English would be "Cicero, the consul, presided over the senate." Here *consul* is in apposition with Cicero. The word apposition comes from the Latin verb **appōněre** *to place next to.*

III. THE ACCUSATIVE CASE

1. The direct object of the verb is in the accusative case (also called the objective case).

Example   **Italia habet multa *oppida* parva.**   Italy has many small towns.

In this sentence **oppida,** a neuter plural noun, is the direct object of the verb **habet** and therefore must be in the accusative (or objective) case. The adjectives **multa** and **parva** modify **oppida** and therefore must also be neuter plural accusative because in Latin an adjective must agree with the noun it modifies in number, gender, and case.

WORD ORDER

In the writings of Latin authors, the verb often, but not always, comes at the end of the sentence. Therefore, the above sentence could have been arranged: **Italia multa oppida parva habet** and would have meant the same thing "Rome has many small towns." The word order could also have been: **Multa oppida parva habet Italia.** In this sentence there is a slight shift of emphasis; the idea "many small towns" is emphasized.

Another point about word order. When two adjectives modify the same noun, e.g., **multa** and **parva,** the Romans either separated the two adjectives with **et** "and" (**multa et parva oppida**), or, as was done here, one adjective is placed before the noun and one is placed after the noun.

2. A noun in apposition with the direct object will also be in the accusative case.

Example   **Īnsulam *Siciliam* vīsitō.**   I am visiting the island (of) Sicily.

Here, **Siciliam** is in apposition with the direct object **īnsulam,** and therefore both are in the accusative case.

3. A noun that is the object of certain prepositions is in the accusative case.

Example   **Nāvigium *ad Italiam* nāvigat.**   The ship is sailing toward Italy.

Here the preposition is **ad** and its object in the accusative case is **Italiam.** The two words together form a prepositional phrase. Some of the common prepositions that take (or govern) the accusative case are:

     ad (+ *acc*)   to, toward; at
     īnfrā (+ *acc*)   below; south of
     suprā (+ *acc*)   above; north of

4. The accusative is used to show **extent of time**, that is, how long an action goes on.

Example **Rōmulus *multōs annōs* rēgnāvit.** Romulus reigned (for) many years.

Although we may use the preposition *for* in English to express duration of time, Latin does not use a preposition to express this idea.

A LOOK AT THE GEOGRAPHY OF ITALY AND THE FOUNDING OF ROME

Italy is not a very big country. It's a peninsula (**paenīnsul·a -ae** *f*) about 750 miles long and between 100 and 150 miles wide. If you were to fly south in a plane down the center of Italy on a clear day, you could see the Adriatic coastline out of the left window and the Mediterranean coastline out of the right window. Italy would fit very nicely into the State of California, with even some room to spare.

The Apennine mountain range (**Āpennīn·us -ī** *m*) is like a big dorsal fin extending from northern Italy all the way to the south. And so, much of Italy is mountainous. On either side of the Apennines are rolling foothills and then small coastal plains. An Italian plain (**camp·us -ī** *m*) is really small compared with our Great Plains.

The biggest rivers are the Po (**Pad·us -ī** *m)* in the north and the Tiber (**Tiber·is -is** *m*) in central Italy. The Po in northern Italy flows from west to east and empties into the Adriatic Sea. More important and more interesting for us is the Tiber, which rises from cool, sparkling springs in the Apennines. It flows from north to south, separating Etruria in the west from Umbria in the east, and then separating the district of Latium in the west from the land of the Sabines on the east. After flowing south for some 185 miles, it reaches Rome, where it is about 300 feet wide (the length of a football field) and from 12 to 18 feet deep.

It was here that Romulus and his twin brother Remus were put into a box and set afloat on the Tiber by their nasty great-uncle Amulius. Amulius wanted to be king of Alba Longa, a mountain town some fifteen miles south of Rome. He exiled his older brother Numitor, who was king of Alba Longa. To make sure that brother Numitor would never have grandchildren to claim the throne at Alba Longa, he made Numitor's daughter, Rhea

Romulus and Remus
floating on the Tiber

Silvia, a Vestal Virgin (Vestal Virgins were priestesses consecrated to the goddess Vesta; they were not allowed to marry during their thirty years of service to Vesta). Somehow Silvia managed to have twins anyway. She claimed that Mars, god of war, was their father. Amulius, obviously unimpressed by the alleged divine lineage, set the twins adrift in the Tiber in a box.

Luckily, the box washed ashore. A she-wolf, coming down from the Aventine Hill **(Aventīn·us -ī** *m*) near the Tiber, found the bawling babes and nursed them by the river bank. (This is one of the few stories in which the wolf turns out to be a good guy.) A shepherd named Faustulus, who lived on the nearby Palatine Hill, discovered them and took them home to his wife Larentia to be raised. At that time the Palatine Hill was covered with shrubs and trees and occupied by a few shepherds' huts. (Modern archaeologists have actually discovered the foundations of a such a hut on

Faustulus finds
Romulus and Remus.

the Palatine.) Centuries later, in place of shepherds' huts, the mansions of the wealthy and the palaces of emperors would crown the hill.

When Romulus grew up, he founded a little town on the Palatine Hill where he had been raised and built a wall around it. The year was 753 B.C. According to some Roman historians, the date was April 21. Modern Romans still celebrate the birthday of Rome on April 21. Nowadays on April 21 many stores in Italy dress their windows with representations of the wolf with the twins.

Oh, in case you're wondering, Romulus and Remus slew their nasty granduncle Amulius and restored kind granddad Numitor to the throne at Alba Longa.

NOTES

1) Look at the map and you will see that Latin names of towns and cities can be masculine plural (like **Coriolī**), feminine singular (like **Rōma**), feminine plural (like **Cannae**), neuter singular (like **Mīsēnum**). Masculine singular names of towns would end in **-us,** but there are no towns ending in **-us.**

2) A town or city with a plural ending in Latin will take a plural verb, even though we use a singular verb in English. An adjective modifying such a noun is also plural. Take note of this fact in the exercises that follow.

Example   **Coriolī erant oppidum Latīnum.**   Corioli was a Latin town.

(The adjective **Latīnum** here modifies the neuter noun **oppidum** and therefore is neuter. It is a Latin town because it is in the district of Latium (pronounced *Lay-shum* in English). **Coriolī** is a plural noun of the second declension.)

Example   **Coriolī erant Latīnī.**   Corioli was Latin.

(**Latīnī** here is a predicate adjective (**Latīn·us -a -um**), modifying the subject **Coriolī**, and is therefore in the nominative case and plural, and so has the same ending as **Coriolī**. By the way, an adjective of the first and second declension has three endings: **-us** when modifying a masculine noun, **-a** when modifying a feminine noun, and **-um** when modifying a neuter noun.)

Map of Italy

Athēnae sunt oppidum Graecum.   Athens is a Greek town.

(**Graecum,** an adjective (**Graec·us -a -um**), here modifies **oppidum** and therefore is neuter.) Notice again that **Athēnae** is plural in form, although referring to only one town, and takes a plural verb.

Example   **Athēnae sunt Graecae.**   Athens is Greek.

(**Graecae** here is a predicate adjective and modifies the subject **Athēnae.** It is therefore nominative, feminine, plural.)

EXERCISES

All the exercises in this chapter are devoted to geography. Therefore, you will be learning Latin grammar and the geography of Italy as well. The places mentioned in this chapter will crop up again in subsequent chapters.

A. Read the sentences carefully and then add the proper endings, nominative or accusative, singular or plural, as the sentences require. Remember that, if the verb of a sentence is a form of the verb **esse** *to be* like **est** *(is)* or **sunt** *(they are),* the nouns must be in the nominative case. The object of a transitive verb like **habet** *(has)* and the object of a preposition like **ad** *(to, toward)* must be in the accusative case.

Examples   Sicili____ est magn____ īnsul____.
Sicilia est magna īnsula.
Sicily is a big island.

Italia nōn habet magnōs camp____.
Italia nōn habet magnōs campōs.
Italy does not have big plains.

VOCABULARY

camp·us -ī *m* plain	**long·us -a -um** long	**mult·ī -ae -a** many *(plural only)*
fluvi·us -ī *m* river	**magn·us -a -um** big	**nōn** *adv* not
habet has	**montān·us -a -um** moun-	**parv·us -a -um** small
lāt·us -a -um wide	tainous	

1. Sicilia est īnsul____, sed Italia est paenīnsul____.
2. Itali____ est long____ sed nōn lāt____.
3. Via ad Campāni____ est long____.

4. Italia habet parvōs camp____.
5. Itali____ habet multa oppid____.
6. Multa oppid____ sunt parva, sed multa oppid____ sunt magn____.
7. Italia est montān____.
8. Ardea est oppid____ parvum.
9. Ardea est parv____.
10. Mīsēnum est parv____.
11. Italia habet mult____ fluvi____.
12. Tiberis est fluvi____ longus.

B. Take a good look at the map above. Then complete the following statements about the geography of Italy. Remember that the preposition **īnfrā** means *south of* and **suprā** means *north of*. Both take the accusative case. This exercise deals only with the districts of Italy. They are all on the map in capital letters and are important in the study of Roman history.

Example | **Galli*a* Cisalpīn*a* est suprā Etrūri*am* et Umbri*am*.**
Cisalpine Gaul is north of Etruria and Umbria.

(Here **Etrūriam** and **Umbriam** are not predicate nouns and therefore do not agree with the subject, but objects of the preposition **suprā,** which governs the accusative case, and for that reason they must be in the accusative case. "Cisalpine" means *on this side* (Roman side) *of the Alps.*)

1. Latium est suprā Campāni____.
2. Pīcēn____ est suprā Samni____.
3. Samni____ est īnfrā Umbri____.
4. Lati____ est īnfrā Etrūri____.
5. Etrūri____ et Lati____ sunt suprā Campāni____.

C. Now that you're getting the hang of it, look at the map and from it supply the information in Latin about the towns and cities of Italy. Some of the Latin names of towns are very similar in form to the modern names. You will easily recognize Rome and Florence. The Latin names of other towns have not been Anglicized. For instance, the town of **Pompēiī** is called Pompeii by us today.

Example | **Rōm*a* est suprā Campāni*am*.**
Rome is north of Campania.

1. Mīsēn____ est īnfrā Rōm____.
2. Ōsti____ est suprā Arde____.
3. Mīsēn____ est īnfrā Capu____.
4. Coriol____ sunt īnfrā Rōm____.
5. Vēi____ sunt suprā Rōm____.
6. Alb____ Long____ est īnfrā Rōm____.
7. Arde____ est īnfrā Ōsti____.
8. Capu____ est suprā Pompēi____.

D. This time you'll really have to study the map since you're going to supply both the endings of the names of districts and towns and also the correct prepositions (**suprā** *north of;* **infrā** *south of*).

Example | **Etrūria est *suprā* Latium.**
Etruria is north of Latium.

1. Coriol____ sunt ____ Ōsti____.
2. Pompēi____ sunt ____ Capu____.
3. Lūcāni____ est ____ Sicili____.
4. Campāni____ est ____ Lūcāni____.
5. Capu____ est ____ Alb____ Long____.
6. Arde____ est ____ Campāni____.
7. Rōm____ est ____ Flōrenti____.
8. Alb____ Long____ est ____ Rōm____.

E. Try to understand the sentences as you read them. Then add the nominative or accusative endings as the sentences require. The sentences tell the story of early Rome and its seven kings. Five kings are mentioned by name, but the other two are not as significant, and so we'll just skip them. They are listed in the TIME LINE at the back of this book.

VOCABULARY

alt·us -a -um high	**geminī** *(mpl)* twins	**rēx** *m* king *(pl* **rēgēs)**
erant were	**habēbat** had	**Rōmānī** *(mpl)* the
erat was	**itaque** and so	Romans
etiam also	**mūr·us -ī** *m* wall	**sacra** *npl* sacred rites
Etrūsc·us -a -um	**prīm·us -a -um** first	**sēcūr·us -a -um** secure
Etruscan	**quārt·us -a -um** fourth	**septem** seven
fundāvit founded	**quīnt·us -a -um** fifth	**ultim·us -a -um** last

1. Rōmulus oppid____ Rōm____ fundāvit.
2. Rōma erat oppid____ parv____.
3. Rōma habēbat mūr____ alt____.
4. Itaque Rōmānī erant sēcūr____.
5. Rōmul____ erat rēx prīm____.
6. Rōmul____ et Rem____ erant gemin____.
7. Rōm____ septem rēgēs habēbat.
8. Numa Pompilius erat secund____ rēx.
9. Numa Pompilius mult____ templ____ fundāvit.
10. Num____ Pompili____ etiam sacr____ fundāvit.
11. Ancus Marcius, quārt____ rēx, oppid____ Ōstiam fundāvit.
12. Tarquinius Prīsc____ erat rēx quīnt____.
13. Tarquini____ Prīsc____ erat Etrūsc____.
14. Tarquinius Superb____ etiam erat Etrūsc____.
15. Tarquini____ Superb____ erat ultim____ rēx.

F. We said earlier that the feminine singular nominative and the neuter plural in the nominative and accusative have the same ending. In the following list, pick out the words that are *neuter plural* in form and check them off.

1. via
2. casa
3. oppida
4. īnsula

5. templa
6. nauta
7. sacra
8. paenīnsula

G. Translate into Latin.

1. Rome is a big town.
2. Rome is north of Alba Longa.
3. Italy is a long peninsula.
4. Sicily is a big island.
5. Romulus founded Rome.
6. Rome had a high wall.
7. Romulus was the first king of Rome.
8. Tarquinius Superbus was the last king of Rome.

WORD POWER

H. Supply the Latin source word for the following English derivatives. If the source is a noun, give the nominative; if it is an adjective, give the masculine form only; if it is a verb, give the infinitive.

1. longitude ____
2. latitude ____
3. primary ____
4. ultimate ____
5. secondary ____
6. to found ____
7. campus ____
8. multitude ____

9. security ____
10. mountainous ____
11. insulate ____
12. mural ____
13. altitude ____
14. quarter ____
15. Montana ____

CHAPTER 2

Nouns of the First and Second Declensions
The Genitive, Dative, Ablative, and Vocative Cases

THOUGHT FOR TODAY

Errāre hūmānum est. To err is human.

| | FIRST DECLENSION | | SECOND DECLENSION | |
	FEMININE		MASCULINE	NEUTER
	via *f* road, street		**amīcus** *m* friend	**oppidum** *n* town
		SINGULAR		
NOM.	**vi·***a*	the road	**amīc·***us*	**oppid·***um*
GEN.	**vi·***ae*	of the road	**amīc·***ī*	**oppid·***ī*
DAT.	**vi·***ae*	to, for the road	**amīc·***ō*	**oppid·***ō*
ACC.	**vi·***am*	the road	**amīc·***um*	**oppid·***um*
ABL.	**vi·***ā*	from, by, with the road	**amīc·***ō*	**oppid·***ō*
		PLURAL		
NOM.	**vi·***ae*	the roads	**amīc·***ī*	**oppid***a*
GEN.	**vi·***ārum*	of the roads	**amīc·***ōrum*	**oppid·***ōrum*
DAT.	**vi·***īs*	to, for the roads	**amīc·***īs*	**oppid·***īs*
ACC.	**vi·***ās*	the roads	**amīc·***ōs*	**oppid·***a*
ABL.	**vi·***īs*	from, by, with the roads	**amīc·***īs*	**oppid·***īs*

MASCULINE NOUNS OF THE SECOND DECLENSION IN *-er* AND *-ir*			
puer *m* boy		**ager** *m* field	**vir** *m* man

SINGULAR			
NOM.	**puer**	the boy	ager	vir
GEN.	**puer·ī**	of the boy	agr·ī	vir·ī
DAT.	**puer·ō**	to, for the boy	agr·ō	vir·ō
ACC.	**puer·um**	the boy	agr·um	vir·um
ABL.	**puer·ō**	from, by, with the boy	agr·ō	vir·ō

PLURAL			
NOM.	**puer·ī**	the boys	agr·ī	vir·ī
GEN.	**puer·ōrum**	of the boys	agr·ōrum	vir·ōrum
DAT.	**puer·īs**	to the boys	agr·īs	vir·īs
ACC.	**puer·ōs**	the boys	agr·ōs	vir·ōs
ABL.	**puer·īs**	from, by, with the boys	agr·īs	vir·īs

ENDINGS OF THE FIRST AND SECOND DECLENSIONS						
FIRST DECLENSION		**SECOND DECLENSION**				
FEMININE		MASCULINE		NEUTER		
	SINGULAR	PLURAL	SINGULAR	PLURAL	SINGULAR	PLURAL
NOM.	*-a*	*-ae*	*-us (-er, -ir)*	*-ī*	*-um*	*-a*
GEN.	*-ae*	*-ārum*	*-ī*	*-ōrum*	*-ī*	*-ōrum*
DAT.	*-ae*	*-īs*	*-ō*	*-īs*	*-ō*	*-īs*
ACC.	*-am*	*-ās*	*-um*	*-ōs*	*-um*	*-a*
ABL.	*-ā*	*-īs*	*-ō*	*-īs*	*-ō*	*-īs*

NOTE

The base of a noun is found by dropping off the ending of the genitive case. Thus, the base of the noun **ager** is **agr·**.

I. THE GENITIVE CASE

1. The genitive case is used **to show possession**, like the English possessive case. In English we show possession by an apostrophe and *s* (*'s*), for example, *the boy's kindness,* or by using an *of* phrase, for example, *the kindness of the boy.* Latin does not use a preposition with the genitive case.

Examples	**tēctum** *casae*	the roof of the cottage
	benevolentia *puerī*	the kindness of the boy/the boy's kindness

2. The genitive is used **with certain adjectives**.

Examples	**Via est plēna** *puerōrum.*	The street is full of boys.
	Virī sunt dignī *glōriae.*	The men are deserving of glory.

3. The genitive is used to indicate **the material of which something is made**.

Example	**mūrus** *saxī*	a wall of stone

4. The genitive is used to show **a quality**, but only when the quality is **modified by an adjective**.

Example	**Rhēa Silvia erat fēmina** *magnae benevolentiae.*	Rhea Silvia was a woman of great kindness.

Here the adjective **magnae** modifies the noun **benevolentiae**.

EXERCISE

A. Read the sentences carefully and then add the genitive endings, singular or plural, as the sentences require.

Example Oppidum Rōmān____ *(pl)* ōlim erat parvum.
Oppidum Rōmān*ōrum* **ōlim erat parvum.**
The town of the Romans was once small.

aedificāvit built
benevolenti·a -ae *f*
kindness
cas·a -ae *f* cottage, hut
dign·us -a -um worthy
Etrūsc·ī -ōrum *mpl*
Etruscans
Faustul·us -ī *m* Faustulus
fundāment·um -ī *n*
foundation

glōri·a -ae *f* glory
Lārenti·a -ae *f* Larentia
(*wife of Faustulus*)
Latīn·ī -ōrum *mpl* the
Latins
magn·us -a -um great;
big, large
māter mātr·is *f* mother
ōlim once
Rem·us -ī *m* Remus

Rhē·a -ae Silvi·a -ae *f*
Rhea Silvia (*mother of
Romulus and Remus*)
Rōmul·us -ī *m* Romulus
Rōmān·ī -ōrum *mpl*
Romans
templ·um -ī *n* temple
valid·us -a -um strong

1. Casa Faustul____ et Lārenti____ erat parva.
2. Rōmulus erat prīmus rēx Rōmān____ *(pl)*.
3. Mūrus oppid____ Rōm____ erat altus et validus.
4. Rōmulus erat dignus glōri____.
5. Terra Etrūsc____ *(pl)* erat suprā terram Latīn____ *(pl)*.
6. Fundāmenta templ____ *(pl)* sunt valida.
7. Faustulus erat vir magn____ benevolenti____.
8. Māter Rōmul____ et Rem____ erat Rhēa Silvia.
9. Rōmulus mūrum sax____ aedificāvit.
10. Oppidum erat plēnum vir____ *(pl)*.

II. THE DATIVE CASE

1. The dative **as indirect object**. The most common use of the dative is to indicate the person *to whom* something is given, said, or done. Frequently we use the preposition *to* in English to express the dative.

Examples	**Faustulus cibum *Rōmulō* et *Remō* dat.**	Faustulus gives food to Romulus and Remus.
		or Faustulus gives Romulus and Remus food.
	Vir nihil *puerō* dīcit.	The man says nothing to the boy.
	Faustulus geminōs *Lārentiae* dēmōnstrat.	Faustulus shows the twins to Larentia.
		or Faustulus shows Larentia the twins.

2. The dative is used **with intransitive Latin verbs**. Some Latin verbs take the dative case instead of the accusative case; these verbs are therefore called intransitive verbs, although they are transitive in English, since in English they take the objective case. "Transitive" in Latin means "going across" because the action goes directly across from the subject to the direct object.

Example **Lupa *puerīs* appropinquat.**　　The wolf approaches the boys.

　　　　　Cibus *virō* placet.　　　　　The food pleases the man.

In the first sentence, **puerīs** is dative because the verb **appropinquāre** takes the dative. In the English sentence, "boys" is the direct object of the verb "approaches" and therefore in the objective (or accusative) case. In the second sentence, **virō** is dative because the verb **placēre** always takes the dative case, even though the English verb "please" takes a direct object. A common way of translating the second sentence is "the man likes the food".

How do you know which verbs take the dative case? The dative case will always be indicated with such verbs in the vocabulary lists and, of course, in the dictionary.

3. The dative is used **with certain adjectives signifying** *friendly, unfriendly, similar, equal, near, related to*, etc.

Examples **Graecī erant *inimīcī Trōiānīs*.**　　The Greeks were unfriendly to the Trojans.

　　　　　Rōmulus erat *cārus Faustulō*.　　Romulus was dear to Faustulus.

　　　　　Rōma est *proxima fluviō*.　　　Rome is next to a river.

　　　　　Numa Pompilius templa *apta dēīs* aedificāvit.　　Numa Pompilius built temples fit for the gods.

4. **Possession** is expressed with ***esse* and the dative.**

Examples ***Faustulō* est casa parva.**　　Faustulus has a small cottage. (literally: To Faustulus is a small cottage.)

　　　　　***Mihi* nōmen est *Mārcus*.**　　My name is Marcus. (literally: To me the name is Marcus.)

NOTE

With **nōmen est** the name, too, is often put into the dative.

Example   ***Mihi Mārcō nōmen est.***   My name is Marcus.

We don't have the same expression in English. The closest to the Latin
is, for example, the English expression "There is no end to his troubles,"
meaning: "His troubles have no end."

EXERCISES

B. Looking over the full declensions at the beginning of this chapter, did
you notice that in some instances the forms of the dative and ablative are
identical? Indicate by a "yes" the form in the list below which can be
both dative and ablative. Explain the reason for your answer.

Examples

puerīs	Yes	(dative plural and ablative plural)
virō	Yes	(dative singular and ablative singular)
īnsulā	No	(ablative singular only)

1. oppidō
2. viā
3. geminīs
4. casae
5. amīcō

6. mūrīs
7. puerī
8. casārum
9. oppidum
10. templa

C. Read the sentences carefully and then add the dative endings, singular
or plural, as the sentences require.

Example

Lārentia multās fābulās Rōmul____ nārrat.
Lārentia multās fābulās Rōmulō nārrat.
Larentia tells Romulus many stories.

VOCABULARY

appropinquant approach	**dat** gives	**placet** pleases
cār·us -a -um dear	**dēmōnstrat** shows	**proxim·us -a -um** next to, near
cib·us -ī *m* food	**inimīc·us -ī** *m* enemy	**valid·us -a -um** strong

1. Faustulus lupam Lārenti____ dēmōnstrat.
2. Lārentia Rōmul____ et Rem____ cibum dat.
3. Lupa Faustul____ et Lārenti____ appropinquat.
4. Casa Faustulī est proxima fluvi____.

5. Casa magna Faustul____ nōn est.
6. Lupa est cāra gemin____ *(pl)*.
7. Mūrus altus et validus est Rōm____.
8. Casa parva Faustul____ et Lārenti____ placet.
9. Amūlius est inimīcus Rhē____ Silvi____.
10. Quid *(what)* dīcit rēx Tarquinius vir____ Rōmān____ *(pl)*?
11. Geminī lup____ appropinquant.
12. Lupa gemin____ *(pl)* placet.

D. In each of the following sentences, possession is shown by a form of the verb **habēre** *to have*, **habet** *(has)* or **habent** *(they have)*. Change each sentence, making the direct object the subject of the new sentence, and make the subject the dative of possession. The verb of the second sentence will be a form of the verb **esse** *(to be)*, either **est** or **sunt** depending on whether the new subject is singular or plural. Make the verb agree with the new subject.

Example

Geminī casam parvam habent.
Casa parva geminīs est.
The twins have a small cottage.

1. Faustulus amīcum bonum habet.
2. Lārentia casam parvam habet.
3. Casae tēcta habent.
4. Oppidum multās viās habet.
5. Vir amīcum nōn habet.
6. Rōmulus et Remus amīcōs habent.
7. Forum multa templa habet.
8. Puerī multōs amīcōs habent.

III. THE ABLATIVE CASE

The ablative case could be called the prepositional case because prepositions frequently occur with the ablative case. Here are some of the most common uses of the ablative case.

1. Ablative of accompaniment. The ablative case, used with the preposition **cum,** answers the question *"with whom?"* It is used with people and animals. Verbs indicating fighting also require **cum** with the ablative.

Examples

Rōmulus et Remus *cum Faustulō* diū habitant.　Romulus and Remus live a long time with Faustulus.

Rōmulus *cum Remō* pugnat.　Romulus fights with Remus.

2. **Ablative of means or instrument**. The ablative case can be used to indicate the means or instrument *with which* something is done. However, although in English we use the preposition "with," in Latin no preposition is used. Note the difference between these two sentences:

Examples

(means)
Rōmulus mūrum *saxīs* aedificat.   Romulus builds a wall with stones.

(accompaniment)
Rōmulus mūrum *cum Remō* aedificat.   Romulus builds a wall with Remus.

3. **Ablative of manner** answers the question *how* something is done. The ablative of manner functions like an adverb. The preposition **cum** must be used when the ablative noun is not modified by an adjective; the preposition may be absent when the ablative is modified by an adjective.

Examples

Rōmulus *cum glōriā* rēgnāvit.   Romulus reigned with glory.

Rōmulus *magnā (cum) glōriā* rēgnāvit.   Romulus reigned with great glory.

4. **Ablative of quality**. The ablative case, modified by an adjective, is used to denote quality.

Example

Catō erat (homō) *magnā prūdentiā*.   Cato was (a man) of great wisdom.

5. **Ablative of place *where***. The ablative case, when used with the preposition **in**, answers the questions *where? in which?* The preposition **in** can mean *in* or *on*.

Examples

Populus *in oppidō* habitat.   The people live in the town.

Remus *in mūrō* sedet.   Remus is sitting on the wall.

NOTES

1) With names of cities and small islands, the Romans did not use **in** with the ablative but a special case called the *locative*. In form it is similar to the genitive in singular nouns of the first and second declensions.

Examples	**Rōmulus *Rōmae* habitābat.**	Romulus lived in Rome.
	(**Rōm·a -ae** is feminine singular)	
	Rēx Tarquinius *Clūsiī* ōlim habitābat.	King Tarquinius once lived in Clusium.
	(**Clūsi·um -ī** is neuter singular)	

2) With plural names of towns and small islands, the locative is similar in form to the ablative case.

Examples	**Ōrāculum *Delphīs* erat clārum.**	The oracle at Delphi was famous.
	(**Delph·ī -ōrum** is masculine plural*)*	
	Ōrāculum *Cūmīs* etiam erat clārum.	The oracle at Cumae was also famous.
	(**Cūm·ae -ārum** is feminine plural.)	

6. **Ablative of place *from which*.** The ablative with the prepositions **ā, ab** or **ē, ex** answers the question *from which*. The forms **ā** and **ē** are used when the following word begins with most consonants; **ab** and **ex** are used before a vowel or *h*.

Examples	**Cicerō modo *ā forō* vēnit.**	Cicero just came from the forum.
	Turnus *ex oppidō parvō* vēnit.	Turnus came from a small town.

NOTE

No preposition is used with names of towns and small islands.

Example	**Aenēās *Trōiā* vēnit.**	Aeneas came from Troy.

7. **Ablative of time *at which* or *within which*.** No preposition is used in Latin to denote the time at which. A preposition is sometimes used to denote time within which.

Examples	*(time at which)*	
	tertiā hōrā	at the third hour
	quīntō annō	in the fifth year
	(time within which)	
	decem annīs	within ten years

8. **Other common Latin prepositions govern the ablative case:**

dē (+ *abl*)   down from; about, concerning
sine (+ *abl*)   without
sub (+ *abl*)   under (when motion is shown, **sub** takes the accusative)

9. **The adjectives dignus and indignus take the ablative.** (We saw earlier in this chapter that they can also take the genitive case.)

Examples   **Numitor erat dignus** *rēgnō.*   Numitor was worthy of the kingdom.

Amūlius erat indignus *rēgnō.*   Amulius was unworthy of the kingdom.

Exercises

E. From the words in parentheses select the noun(s) that have the correct endings. In some instances, more than one noun may have correct endings. Don't forget that the final **-a** is short in the feminine nominative singular, and long in the ablative.

1. ā, ab (Campānia, Etrūriā, Umbriam)
2. ad (oppida, via, mūrum)
3. ex (rēgnō, casīs, campōs)
4. cum (geminīs, Numā Pompiliō, Rhēae Silviae)
5. dē (Graecīs, Trōiam, bellō)
6. in (paenīnsulā, agrō, Asiae)
7. īnfrā (Etrūria, Latium, Capuam)
8. sine (amīcīs, āthlētās, aquā)
9. sub (equō, terrā, templō)
10. suprā (Rōmam, Rōmā, oppidum)

F. Complete the Latin sentences by translating the English phrases in parentheses into Latin.

1. Faustulus (*with Larentia and the boys*) habitat.
2. Geminī sunt dignī (*of kindness.*)
3. Faustulus Rōmulō (*about the wolf*) nārrat.
4. Amūlius (*without friends*) est.
5. Aenēās (*to Italy*) vēnit.
6. Etrūscī (*in Etruria*) habitant.

IV. THE VOCATIVE CASE

The vocative case of a noun is used in addressing a person or persons. The form of the vocative is the same as the nominative case, singular and plural, for all nouns except for masculine singular nouns of the second declension. Nouns ending in **-ius** in the nominative, such as **fīlius** and **Cornēlius**, end in a single **-ī** the vocative.

NOMINATIVE	**Mārcus**	**fīlius**	**Cornēlius**
VOCATIVE	**Mārce**	**fīlī**	**Cornēlī**

NOTE

The vocative of **meus** is **mī**. **Deus** has no special vocative form; in the plural, both **dī** and **deī** are used in the vocative as well as in the nominative, although **dī** occurs more frequently than **deī**.

EXERCISES

G. Give the vocative case of the following nouns, even when the vocative form is the same as the nominative form.

1. Amūlius
2. Lārentia
3. Rōmānī
4. Remus
5. Tarquinius
6. puer
7. virī
8. meus amīcus

H. READING FOR COMPREHENSION. In this exercise you will have practice in all the cases that you have reviewed thus far. Select the correct word or phrase in parentheses to complete each sentence. Try to understand each sentence as you are reading it. Then translate into English.

Dē Bellō Trōiānō
About the Trojan War

1. Homērus et Vergilius fābulam dē (Trōiā; Trōiam) nārrant. 2. Ōlim erat oppidum in (Asiam; Asiā) ubi Trōiānī habitābant. 3. Priamus tum erat rēx (Trōiānīs; Trōiānōrum) 4. Oppidum (mūrōs; mūrī) altōs et validōs habēbat. 5. Graecī et Trōiānī diū (inimīcōs; inimīcī) erant. 6. Ergō Graecī ē Graeciā in (Asiam; Asiā) nāvigābant.

Homēr·us -ī *m* Homer Vergili·us -ī *m* Vergil fābul·a -ae *f* story nārrant tell ōlim once Trōi·a -ae *f* Troy ubi where Trōiān·us -a -um Trojan Trōiān·ī -ōrum the Trojans habitābant lived Priam·us -ī *m* Priam tum at that time alt·us -a -um high Graecī *mpl* the Greek diū for a long time inimīc·us -ī *m* enemy ergō therefore Graeci·a -ae *f* Greece nāvigābant sailed

7. Graecī et Trōiānī extrā (mūrīs; mūrōs) pugnābant. 8. Castra Graecōrum (erat; erant) prope ōram maritimam. 9. Erat (campus; campum) inter ōram maritimam et oppidum Trōiam. 10. Graecī et Trōiānī in (campō; campum) inter castra et oppidum Trōiam pugnābant.

extrā (+ *acc*) outside pugnābant fought castr·a -ōrum *npl* camp prope (+ *acc*) near ōr·a -ae *f* maritima coastline erat there was inter (+ *acc*) between

ll. Mūrī Trōiae erant (altī et validī; altōs et validōs). 12. Ergō Graecī oppidum (Trōiam; Trōiae) nōn oppugnābant. 13. Dēnique decimō annō, Graecī equum (lignum; lignī) fabricābant. 14. Equus erat (magnum et cavum; magnus et cavus). 15. Multī Graecī intrā (equō; equum) latēbant. 16. Trōiānī equum magnum intrā (mūrōs; mūrīs) trahēbant. 17. Subitō Graecī ex (equum cavum; equō cavō) properābant.

oppugnābant attacked dēnique finally decim·us -a -um tenth ann·us -ī *m* year equ·us -ī *m* horse lign·um -ī *n* wood fabricābant made cav·us -a -um hollow intrā (+ *acc*) within latēbant hid trahēbant dragged subitō suddenly properābant rushed

18. Tum Graecī (multīs Trōiānīs; multōs Trōiānōs) necābant et oppidum Trōiam captābant. 19.

tum then necābant killed captābant captured

Battle at Troy

Graecī etiam vetulum (Priamum; Priamus) necābant. 20. Post bellum, Graecī ex Asiā in (Graeciā; Graeciam) rūrsus nāvigābant.

etiam even **vetul·us -a -um** old
post (+ *acc*) after **bell·um -ī** *n* war

rūrsus again

I. Scrambled Sentences. Remember that word endings indicate how words function in a sentence and suggest what words belong together. Unscramble the words to form sentences, placing the subject, followed by its modifier(s) at the beginning, and the verb at the end.

Example

Oppidō Rōmānus in habitat populus magnō.
Populus Rōmānus in magnō oppidō habitat.

1. multās nārrat longās Lārentia fābulās geminīs.
2. intrā Graecī mūrum multōs necābant Trōiānōs.
3. parvā in habitant Rōmulus et casā Remus.
4. ultimus Superbus erat rēx Tarquinius Rōmae.
5. multās habet Italia viās longās.
6. mūrum aedificat validum Rōmulus altum.

J. Translate the following sentences into Latin.

1. The Greeks and the Trojans were enemies.
2. The Greeks sailed to Troy.
3. The town of Troy had strong walls.
4. The Greeks built a big hollow horse.
5. Finally the Greeks captured Troy.

K. Pick out the grammatical misfit. Then give the reason for your choice.

Example

ergō mūrō forō oppidō   *ergō*
Reason: All are nouns in the ablative case; **ergō** is an adverb.

MISFIT

1. via   casa   templa   lupa
2. in   ad   ex   dē
3. īnsula   quia   fēmina   glōria
4. puerī   amīcī   ubi   geminī
5. magnus   cavus   rūrsus   validus
6. glōria   fābula   terra   extrā

L. Supply the Latin source word for the following English derivatives. If the Latin source word is a noun or adjective, use the nominative singular; if it is a verb, use the infinitive.

1. narrative ＿＿＿
2. fable ＿＿＿
3. valid ＿＿＿
4. decimal ＿＿＿
5. fabricate ＿＿＿
6. cave ＿＿＿
7. capture ＿＿＿
8. navigate ＿＿＿
9. puerile ＿＿＿

10. virile ＿＿＿
11. demonstrate ＿＿＿
12. benevolence ＿＿＿
13. glorious ＿＿＿
14. latent ＿＿＿
15. dignified ＿＿＿
16. amicable ＿＿＿
17. equine ＿＿＿
18. nominal ＿＿＿

CHAPTER 3

Nouns of the Third Declension

Masculine and Feminine

THOUGHT FOR TODAY

Vēritās vōs līberābit. The truth will set you free.

MASCULINE AND FEMININE NOUNS OF THE THIRD DECLENSION (CONSONANT STEMS)				
dux *m* leader			**soror** *f* sister	
	SINGULAR			ENDINGS
NOM.	**dux**	the leader	**soror**	—
GEN.	**duc·is**	of the leader	**sorōr·is**	*-is*
DAT.	**duc·ī**	to, for the leader	**sorōr·ī**	*-ī*
ACC.	**duc·em**	the leader	**sorōr·em**	*-em*
ABL.	**duc·e**	from, by, with the leader	**sorōr·e**	*-e*
	PLURAL			ENDINGS
NOM.	**duc·ēs**	the leaders	**sorōr·ēs**	*-ēs*
GEN.	**duc·um**	of the leaders	**sorōr·um**	*-um*
DAT.	**duc·ibus**	to, for the leaders	**sorōr·ibus**	*-ibus*
ACC.	**duc·ēs**	the leaders	**sorōr·ēs**	*-ēs*
ABL.	**duc·ibus**	from, by, with the leaders	**sorōr·ibus**	*-ibus*

MASCULINE AND FEMININE NOUNS OF THE THIRD DECLENSION
(i-STEM)

	nāvis *f* ship		**mōns** *m* hill	
		SINGULAR		**ENDINGS**
NOM.	**nāv·***is*	the ship	**mōns**	—
GEN.	**nāv·***is*	of the ship	**mont·***is*	*-is*
DAT.	**nāv·***ī*	to, for the ship	**mont·***ī*	*-ī*
ACC.	**nāv·***em*	the ship	**mont·***em*	*-em*
ABL.	**nāv·***e*	from, by, with the ship	**mont·***e*	*-e*
		PLURAL		**ENDINGS**
NOM.	**nāv·***ēs*	the ships	**mont·***ēs*	*-ēs*
GEN.	**nāv·***ium*	of the ships	**mont·***ium*	*-ium*
DAT.	**nāv·***ibus*	to, for the ships	**mont·***ibus*	*-ibus*
ACC.	**nāv·***ēs*	the ships	**mont·***ēs*	*-ēs*
ABL.	**nāv·***ibus*	from, by, with the ships	**mont·***ibus*	*-ibus*

1. **Nouns of the third declension have all sorts of endings in the nominative**. It is the genitive of a noun that gives a clue to the rest of the declension: the *genitive singular* shows the complete base of a noun, and its ending is different for each declension. Therefore the ending of the genitive singular indicates to which declension a noun belongs. That is why the dictionary always gives the nominative, the genitive, and the gender of a noun. It would be an excellent idea to memorize the nominative and genitive of each noun as it occurs.

2. **The *genitive plural* of all *i-stem* nouns of the third declension always ends in -ium.** Among the masculine and feminine -i stems of the third declension are:

   a) Nouns that end in **-is** in the nominative singular as **ign·***is* *-is m* fire; **nāv·***is* *-is f* ship,
   b) Nouns in **-ēs,** with genitive in **-is**, as **caed·***ēs* *-is f* slaughter,
   c) Most nouns in **-ns** and **-rs**, as **cliēns client·***is* *mf* client; **cohors cohort·***is* *f* cohort,

d) Nouns of one syllable in **-s** or **-x**, preceded by a consonant, as **urbs urb·is** *f* city; **arx arc·is** *f* citadel,

e) A few nouns of one syllable in **-s** or **-x** preceded by a vowel, as **mūs mūr·is** *m* mouse; **nox noct·is** *f* night; **nix niv·is** *f* snow,

f) Some nouns in **-tās**, genitive **-tātis** with a genitive plural in **-ium** such as **difficultās difficultāt·is** *f* difficulty.

3. **Gender of Third Declension Nouns.** Nouns may be either masculine, feminine, or neuter, as **arx arc·is** *f* citadel; **mōns mont·is** *m* mountain; **caput capit·is** *n* head. To be certain of the gender of a noun, you have to memorize the gender as you learn new words. However, here are a couple of hints on gender.

a) Some nouns can be masculine or feminine. These are said to be of common gender, as **host·is -is** *mf* enemy; **parēns parent·is** *mf* parent.

b) Some nouns are masculine, namely:

- nouns that refer to males or male occupations such as **pater patr·is** *m* father; **frāter frātr·is** *m* brother; **rēx rēg·is** *m* king; or **dux duc·is** *m* leader; **mīles mīlit·is** *m* soldier.
- nouns ending in **-or**, as **victor victōr·is** *m* victor.
- four nouns of one syllable ending in **-s**, with a consonant preceding the final **-s**: **dēns dent·is** *m* tooth; **mōns mont·is** *m* hill; mountain; **fōns font·is** *m* spring; **pōns pont·is** *m* bridge.

c) Some nouns are feminine, namely:

- nouns that refer to females, such as **māter mātr·is** *f* mother; **soror sorōr·is** *f* sister.
- most nouns of one syllable ending in **-x** , as **arx arc·is** *f* citadel; **lēx lēg·is** *f* law.
- most nouns of one syllable ending in **-s**, when the final **-s** is preceded by a consonant (except the four masculine nouns mentioned above), as **urbs urb·is** *f* city; **pars part·is** *f* part.
- nouns ending in **-iō** and **-ās**, as **condiciō condiciōn·is** *f* condition; **clāritās clāritāt·is** *f* clarity; fame.

PITFALL There are many exceptions to these "rules." When we speak of "rules of grammar" we are not talking about absolute laws like the laws of nature that can have no exceptions. We are really talking about "statements of general usage."

A. Change the singulars to plurals in the same case. Translate the plural phrases that you form.

Example | lēx urbis
lēgēs urbium (the laws of the cities)

VOCABULARY
alb·us -a -um white

1. bonus mīles
2. in magnā nāve
3. ad novam urbem
4. malum hostem
5. bonī ducis
6. cum bonā mātre
7. mōns altus
8. malae condiciōnis

9. in altā arce
10. bona lēx
11. dux mīlitis
12. arx urbis
13. dēns albus
14. trāns pontem parvum
15. cum duce bonō

B. Reverse the nouns in the following sentences, putting each into the proper case.

Example | **Fīlius cum mātre ambulat.** The son is walking with his mother.
Māter cum fīliō ambulat. The mother is walking with her son.

1. Dux cum mīlite pugnat.
2. Patrēs cum sorōribus ambulant.
3. Mātrēs sunt cārae sorōribus.
4. Rēx cum rēgīnā habitat.
5. Māter fābulam sorōrī meae nārrat.
6. Pater mātrī placet.
7. Ducēs mīlitibus appropinquant.
8. Victor ad ducem venit.

C. Before you read the following story, study the route of Aeneas's travels. That will help you to understand the story. Unfortunately, we don't have time to mention all the adventures that Aeneas had, such as meeting the man-eating Cyclopes and the seductive Sirens, or paying a visit to the lower world.

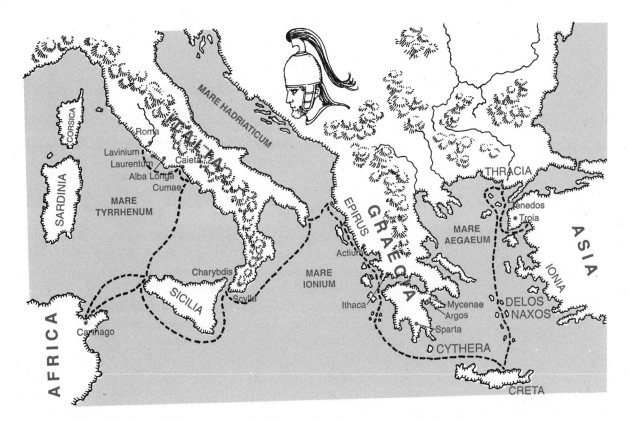

The travels of Aeneas

This passage is based on an epic poem that was written by Vergil (70-19 B.C.). He died before he could give the poem the final touches and therefore wanted it to be destroyed. Immediately after his death his book, the *Aeneid*, became a bestseller in Rome and was used in all the schools.

Supply the correct endings of the incomplete nouns of the third declension.

Aenēās Cum Amīcīs Novum Domicilium Quaerit.
Aeneas Looks for a New Home with his Friends.

I

Mīlit__ Graecī cum mīlit__ Trōiānīs decem annōs pugnant. Graecī sunt victōr__. Ūnus ex duc__ Trōiānīs est Aenēās. Pat__ Aenēae est Anchīsēs; māt__ Aenēae est Venus.

mīles mīlit·is *m* soldier **Trōiān·us -a -um** Trojan **decem** ten

ann·us -ī *m* year **ūn·us -a -um ex** (+ *abl*) one of **Aenē·ās -ae** *m* Aeneas (*For the declension, see Chapter 7*)

II

Post bellum Trōiānum, Aenēās cum patr__ et fīliō Ascaniō ex urb__ effugit. Aliī virī et fēminae etiam ex urb__ effugiunt. Aenēās novam urb__ fundāre optat. Itaque Aenēās cum amīcīs nāv__ aedificat. Deinde cum virīs fēminīsque Trōiānīs trāns mar__ nāvigat.

effugit escapes **etiam** also
ali·us -a -ud other
effugiunt escape
optat wishes **nov·us -a -um** new
itaque and so **deinde** then
trāns (+ *acc*) across **mar·e -is** *n* sea

III

Prīmum ad Thrāciam in nāv__ novīs nāvigat. Deinde ad īnsulam Crētam nāvigat. Neque autem in Thrāciā neque in īnsulā Crētā novum domicilium invenit. In Crētā, pestilentia perīculōsa magnam part__ Trōiānōrum afflictat. Etiam duc__ afflictat.

prīmum first **Thrāci·a -ae** *f* Thrace *(NW of Troy)* **neque . . . neque** neither . . . nor
autem however
domicili·um -ī *n* home
invenit finds **pestilenti·a -ae** *f* pestilence
perīculōs·us -a -um dangerous
afflictat strikes

IV

Itaque trāns mar__ ad ōram Āfricae nāvigat. Postrīdiē Trōiānī cum duc__ per ōram maritimam ambulant. Mox pulchrae part__ urb__ novae appropinquant. Urb__ est Carthāgō. Dīdō, rēgīna Carthāginis, Aenēān benignē excipit et eum ad rēgiam invītat. Rēgia est in pulchrā parte urb__. Rēgīna Aenēān adamat. Aenēās in urb__ Carthāgine in perpetuum manēre optat.

postrīdiē on the following day
per (+ *acc*) along **ambulant** walk
mox soon **pars part·is** *f (gen. pl.* **partium**)
part **appropinquant** (+ *dat*) approach
rēgīn·a -ae *f* queen **Carthāgō**
Carthāginis *f* Carthage **benignē** kindly, warmly **excipit** welcomes **eum** him
rēgi·a -ae *f* palace **invītat** invites

adamat falls in love with
in perpetuum forever **manēre** to stay

D. Based on the story that you have just read, answer the following questions in English.

    I 1. With whom did the Greek soldiers fight for a long time?
        2. Who won the war?
        3. Who were the parents of Aeneas?

II 4. After the war, with whom did Aeneas leave the city?
5. Who else escaped from the ruined city?
6. What did Aeneas want to do after the war?
7. What did Aeneas have to do before he could sail?
8. Who sailed with him?

III 9. Where did Aeneas first sail?
10. Where did Aeneas sail next?
11. What happened to many of his followers there?

IV 12. Where did Aeneas sail after that?
13. Who was the queen of Carthage?
14. What did Aeneas and his friends do the day after landing?
15. What did they approach on that walk?
16. How did Dido treat Aeneas and his followers?
17. Where did Dido invite Aeneas?
18. What was Aeneas's reason for traveling overseas in the first place?
19. What was it that caused him to change his mind?
20. Would you blame him for changing his mind?

E. Translate each English phrase into Latin; then translate the complete sentence into English.

1. (*The city of Troy*) mūrōs altōs et validōs habet.
2. Mīlitēs Trōiānī (*with the Greek soldiers*) pugnant.
3. Graecī in Asiam (*in many ships*) veniunt.
4. Mīlitēs Graecī sunt (*the victors*).
5. Trōiānī equum magnum et cavum (*into the city*) trahunt.
6. Mīlitēs Graecī (*the citadel of Troy*) oppugnant.
7. Dīdō (*the Trojan soldiers*) ad rēgiam invītat.
8. Dīdō rēgiam (*in a beautiful part of the city*) habet.
9. Trōiānī (*many parts of the city*) vīsitant.

F. In each of the following sentences, possession is shown by a form of the verb **habēre** *to have*, **habet** (*he, she, it has*) or **habent** (*they have*). Change each sentence, making the direct object the subject of the new sentence, and making the subject the dative of possession. The verb of the second sentence will be a form of the verb **esse** (*to be*), either **est** (*is*) or **sunt** (*they are*) depending on whether the new subject is singular or plural. Make the verb agree with the new subject.

Example

| Mīlitēs ducem bonum habent.
Dux bonus mīlitibus est.
The soldiers have a good general.

1. Puerī mātrem benignam habent.
2. Urbs arcem altam habet.
3. Trōiānī multōs hostēs habent.
4. Ascanius patrem bonum habet.
5. Victōrēs novum ducem habent.
6. Urbs lēgēs bonās habet.

G. SCRAMBLED SENTENCES. Rearrange the words to form sentences. Remember that the endings give you the clue to word grouping. Some general guidelines on Latin word order: the subject normally comes at the beginning of the sentence, the verb at the end; an adjective normally comes before or after the noun it modifies.

1. bonus in Aenēās bellō est mīles Trōiānō.
2. bellum urbem mīlitēs Trōiānum post captant antīquam Graecī.
3. novam Aenēās urbem fundāre pulchram optat.
4. multī multae et virī ex fēminae urbe effugiunt.
5. ad cum Crētam nāvigat Aenēās fīliō magnam Ascaniō īnsulam.

H. Pick out the grammatical misfit in each set and then give the reason for your choice.

Example

MISFIT

| virīs   urbis   mīlitis   patris   **virīs**
Reason: It is dative or ablative plural; all others are genitive singular.

1. mīlitum   nāvium   inimīcum   urbium
2. itaque   deinde   dux   mox
3. urbī   sociī   mīlitī   nāvī
4. mātrem   autem   urbem   ducem
5. agrō   amīcō   subitō   fluviō

I. Extend your Latin vocabulary. There are hundreds of Latin nouns ending in **-ās** that become English words ending in *-y*. For example, **calamitās** becomes *calamity*. If you change the **-ās** to *-y* in the following Latin nouns, which English nouns do you get? While you're at it, give the genitive of each Latin noun. And notice that they are *all* feminine and abstract, that is, they designate qualities, not physical things.

Example

| **clāritās clāritātis** *f* clarity

aequālitās	auctōritās	gravitās	necessitās
affīnitās	cūriōsitās	hūmānitās	nōbilitās
agilitās	difficultās	indignitās	quālitās
anxietās	facultās	mōbilitās	sēcūritās
atrōcitās	ferōcitās	mortālitās	vānitās

J. There are also many Latin nouns of the third declension ending in **-iō** that become English words ending in *-ion*. For example, **exceptiō -ōnis** *f* becomes *exception*. They, too, are feminine. Many of them are built on the last principal part of the verb, the past participle. The last principal part of many verbs will give you both the *doer* of the action and the *action* itself. You will easily recognize their meanings. For example, **nāvig·ō -āre -āvī -ātus** are the principal parts of the verb **nāvigāre** *to sail*. Drop off the ending **-us** of the last principal part and add **-or** for the doer of the action of sailing, **navigator**, and add the ending **-iō** for the act of sailing, **navigatio**.

Example

nāvigō nāvigāre nāvigāvī nāvigātus to sail
(doer) **nāvigātor nāvigātōr·is** *m* one who sails, navigator
(act or action) **nāvigātiō nāvigātiōn·is** *f* (act of) sailing, navigation

Now try the same with some of the verbs that have occurred thus far.

1. **aedificō aedificāre aedificāvī aedificātus** to build
2. **fabricō fabricāre fabricāvī fabricātus** to make, construct
3. **habitō habitāre habitāvī habitātus** to reside, dwell
4. **līberō līberāre līberāvī līberātus** to liberate, free
5. **oppugnō oppugnāre oppugnāvī oppugnātus** to attack

K. Supply the Latin source word for the following English derivatives. If the source word is a verb, give the infinitive; if it is a noun or adjective, give the nominative singular.

1. maternal	____		10. duke	____
2. feminine	____		11. ambulate	____
3. military	____		12. urban	____
4. afflict	____		13. sorority	____
5. annual	____		14. partial	____
6. domicile	____		15. militia	____
7. option	____		16. naval	____
8. victorious	____		17. regal	____
9. dental	____		18. conditional	____

CHAPTER 4

Nouns of the Third Declension
Neuter

THOUGHT FOR TODAY

Mēns sāna in corpore sānō. A healthy mind in a healthy body.

NEUTER NOUNS OF THE THIRD DECLENSION (CONSONANT STEMS)

	nōmen *n* name	**corpus** *n* body	**genus** *n* kind, sort	
	SINGULAR			ENDINGS
NOM.	nōmen	corpus	genus	—
GEN.	nōmin·*is*	corpor·*is*	gener·*is*	*-is*
DAT.	nōmin·*ī*	corpor·*ī*	gener·*ī*	*-ī*
ACC.	nōmen	corpus	genus	—
ABL.	nōmin·*e*	corpor·*e*	gener·*e*	*-e*
	PLURAL			ENDINGS
NOM.	nōmin·*a*	corpor·*a*	gener·*a*	*-a*
GEN.	nōmin·*um*	corpor·*um*	gener·*um*	*-um*
DAT.	nōmin·*ibus*	corpor·*ibus*	gener·*ibus*	*-ibus*
ACC.	nōmin·*a*	corpor·*a*	gener·*a*	*-a*
ABL.	nōmin·*ibus*	corpor·*ibus*	gener·*ibus*	*-ibus*

NEUTER NOUNS OF THE THIRD DECLENSION ENDING IN *-e, -al, -ar* (i-STEM)

	mare *n* sea	**animal** *n* animal	**exemplar** *n* example; copy	
	SINGULAR			ENDINGS
Nom.	mar·*e*	animal	exemplar	*-e* or —
Gen.	mar·*is*	animāl·*is*	exemplār·*is*	*-is*
Dat.	mar·*ī*	animāl·*ī*	exemplār·*ī*	*-ī*
Acc.	mar·*e*	animal	exemplar	*-e* or —
Abl.	mar·*ī*	animāl·*ī*	exemplār·*ī*	*-ī*
	PLURAL			ENDINGS
Nom.	mar·*ia*	animāl·*ia*	exemplār·*ia*	*-ia*
Gen.	mar·*ium*	animāl·*ium*	exemplār·*ium*	*-ium*
Dat.	mar·*ibus*	animāl·*ibus*	exemplār·*ibus*	*-ibus*
Acc.	mar·*ia*	animāl·*ia*	exemplār·*ia*	*-ia*
Abl.	mar·*ibus*	animāl·*ibus*	exemplār·*ibus*	*-ibus*

NOTES

1) Neuter nouns ending in **-e, -al, -ar** are called *i-stem nouns*. That is, they always have the following endings: **-ī** in the ablative singular, **-ia** in the nominative and accusative plural, and **-ium** in the genitive plural. Otherwise their forms are the same as those of the other neuter nouns of the third declension.

2) Like masculine and feminine nouns of the third declension, neuter nouns have various forms in the nominative. The genitive singular indicates the base. For example:

cor cord·*is*** *n* heart
iter itiner·*is*** *n* trip, journey
flūmen flūmin·*is*** *n* river

Don't confuse neuter nouns of the third declension ending in **-us** with masculine nouns of the second declension also ending in **-us**. The genitive singular gives the clue to the declension: its ending is **-ī** in the second declension and **-is** in the third declension Here are some common neuter nouns of the third declension ending in **-us.**

corpus corpor·is *n* body
lītus lītor·is *n* shore
opus oper·is *n* work; task, job; undertaking

pectus pector·is *n* chest, breast
tempus tempor·is *n* time
vulnus vulner·is *n* wound

NEUTER ENDINGS

| | SECOND DECLENSION | | THIRD DECLENSION | | THIRD DECLENSION I-STEMS | |
	SINGULAR	PLURAL	SINGULAR	PLURAL	SINGULAR	PLURAL
NOM.	*-um*	*-a*	(varied)	*-a*	(varied)	*-ia*
GEN.	*-ī*	*-ōrum*	*-is*	*-um*	*is*	*-ium*
DAT.	*-ō*	*-īs*	*-ī*	*-ibus*	*ī*	*-ibus*
ACC.	*-um*	*-a*	(varied)	*-a*	(varied)	*-ia*
ABL.	*-ō*	*-īs*	*-e*	*-ibus*	*ī*	*-ibus*

EXERCISES

A. Remember that neuter nouns always have identical endings in the nominative and accusative, singular as well as plural. The context of the phrase or sentence will tell you in what case the noun is. Read the following sentences and indicate whether the neuter nouns in italics are in the nominative or accusative case.

VOCABULARY

accipit receives
agit spends
Āpennīn·us -ī *m* the Apennines
caput capit·is *n* source; head
longissim·us -a -um longest

nesciō I do not know
nōn procul ab (+ *abl*) not far from
omn·is -is -e all
sita est is located
sunt there are

1. Sunt multa *flūmina* in Italiā.
2. Tiberis autem est *flūmen* longissimum.

3. Rōma est prope *flūmen* Tiberim.
4. Etiam *mare* nōn procul ab urbe Rōmā est.
5. Nesciō *nōmina* omnium flūminum Italiae.
6. Tiberis *flūmen* habet caput in Apennīnō.
7. Antīquum *nōmen* Tiberis ōlim erat Albula.
8. Rōma est sita īnfrā *flūmen* Tiberim.
9. Mīles multa *vulnera* in pectore accipit.
10. Aenēās multum *tempus* in Āfricā agit.

B. Complete the neuter nouns by supplying the proper endings. The adjectives that modify the nouns and the prepositions will let you know what case the noun is in.

VOCABULARY

bon·us -a -um good   **ill·e -a -ud** that
homō homin·is *m* man; **hominēs** people   **me·us -a -um** my

1. in illō exemplār____
2. multa gener____ hominum
3. cum illō animāl____
4. trāns mar____ perīculōsum
5. corpora multōrum animāl____
6. sine meō nōmin____
7. bonīs tempor____
8. parva corpor____
9. nōmina illōrum mar____
10. in multīs exemplār____
11. in meō cord____
12. multa vulner____ in meō pectore
13. magna oper____
14. ad illa lītor____
15. cum parvīs animāl____

C. Pick out the grammatical misfit and explain your choice.

Example

maris   animālis   amīcīs   nōminis   **amīcīs**
Reason: All are genitive singular except **amīcīs.**

MISFIT

1. corpora   casa   nōmina   exemplāria
2. pectus   corpus   mūrus   tempus
3. vulnera   tempora   capita   via
4. flūminī   cordī   amīcī   pectorī
5. corporum   animālium   capitum   equum
6. pectore   deinde   corde   flūmine

D. Rewrite the following sentences. Change all singular nouns in italics to their plural form. Change the adjectives in italics that modify these nouns so that they agree with the nouns. (The adjectives in this exercise are neuter and are declined like **oppidum**, see Chapter 2.) Change the form of the verb **est** to **sunt** in the sentences where the subject becomes plural.

Example

Caput flūminis est in montibus.
Capita flūminum sunt in montibus.
The sources of rivers are in the mountains.

Vocabulary

natat swims

perīculōs·us -a -um dangerous

pulcher pulchr·a -um beautiful

1. Rōmulus et Remus *nōmen clārum* habent.
2. Rōmulus in *flūmine* Italiae natat.
3. Aenēās trāns *mare* nāvigat.
4. *Lītus* Italiae est *pulchrum*.
5. Faustulus et Lārentia *cor bonum* habent.
6. *Mare* semper *perīculōsum* est.
7. Aenēās *iter longum* facit.
8. Aenēās in *perīculōsō marī* nāvigat.
9. Nesciō *nōmen flūminis* Graeciae.
10. Aenēās *lītus maris* vīsitat.

Read the following story, which is a continuation of the story in the previous chapter. Be sure to make the proper pauses between phrases. There will be questions to be answered on the story.

Aenēās Carthagine Nāvigat
Aeneas Sails from Carthage

I

Aenēās in urbe Carthāgine manēre dēsīderat, quia et urbem et rēgīnam amat. Iuppiter autem alia cōnsilia in animō habet prō Aenēā. Itaque Mercurium nūntium ad Aenēān mittit.

dēsīderat wishes **quia** because **et . . . et** both . . . and **Iuppiter Iov·is** *m* Jupiter **cōnsili·um -ī** *n* plan, idea **prō** (+ *abl*) for **anim·us -ī** *m* mind **Mercuri·us -ī** *m* Mercury **nūnti·us -ī** *m* messenger **mittit** sends

Dido looking out of the palace as Aeneas sails away

II

Mercurius Aenēae dīcit: "Discēde ex hāc urbe et ex hāc terrā. Nōn in hāc terrā est domicilium tuum. In Italiā trāns mare pete domicilium tuum. Ibi enim urbem novam aedificābis. Ibi Lāvīnia, fīlia rēgis, erit tua uxor."

discēde depart
terr·a -ae *f* land

pete seek
ibi there **enim** for, since **aedificābis** you will build **fīli·a -ae** *f* daughter **erit** will be **uxor uxōr·is** *f* wife

III

Aenēās, cum haec verba audit, cōnstituit ex urbe Carthāgine discēdĕre. Postrīdiē Aenēās vēla dat. Misera Dīdō autem dē rēgiā observat nāvēs Trōiānās ā lītore Āfricae discēdentēs. Misera Dīdō voluntāriam mortem petit. Prīmum nāvēs trāns mare in Siciliam nāvigant. Deinde nāvēs lītora Italiae petunt.

cum (*conj*) when **verb·um -ī** *n* word **audit** hears **cōnstituit** decides **discēdĕre** to depart **postrīdiē** on the following day **vēl·um -ī** *n* sail **vēla dat** sets sail
miser· -a -um poor **observat** watches **dē** (+ *abl*) from, down from **discēdentēs** departing **mors mort·is** *f* death **voluntāri·us -a -um** voluntary
petunt head for

E. Answer the following questions in English, based on the above passage.

    I 1. Why does Aeneas want to stay in Carthage?
       2. Who has other plans in mind?
       3. How does he make his plans known to Aeneas?

    II 4. Where is Aeneas to look for a new home?
       5. How soon does Aeneas leave Carthage?

    III 6. What does Dido watch from the palace?
       7. What is Dido's frame of mind at that time?
       8. How does Dido solve her problem?
       9. Where does Aeneas sail to first?
      10. Where does he go after that?

F. Translate into Latin.

    1. Aeneas loves Carthage.
    2. Aeneas wants to stay there.
    3. Jupiter sends Mercury to Aeneas.
    4. Mercury says: "Carthage is not your city.
    5. You will build a new city across the sea."
    6. Poor Dido watches the ships in the sea.

G. Since you will encounter analogy questions in SATs, it's a good idea for you to get some practice in perceiving relationships. The relationships can be of all kinds: similarities (synonyms), opposites (antonyms), cause and effect, container and thing contained, doer and

thing done, family relationships, etc. Throughout the book, there will be two types of analogy tests: those based on grammar and those based on culture and ideas. Analogy tests require a higher order of thinking. They test not only your knowledge of Latin but also your ability to analyze.

This analogy is based on grammar, that is, on grammatical relationships; this exercise deals with the forms of third-declension nouns.

Example

dēns : dentium :: mōns : _____

That is, **dēns** (*nom. sing.*) is to **dentium** (*gen. pl.*) as **mōns** (*nom. sing.*) is to _____ (*gen. pl.*). Therefore, the solution is:

dēns : dentium :: mōns : *montium*

1.	dux	:	ducem	::	mīles	: _____
2.	victor	:	victōrī	::	nāvis	: _____
3.	pars	:	partis	::	condiciō	: _____
4.	arcēs	:	arcibus	::	fontēs	: _____
5.	_____	:	lēgēs	::	urbs	: urbēs
6.	corpus	:	corpore	::	nōmen	: _____
7.	genere	:	generibus	::	mare	: _____
8.	exemplāris	:	exemplārium	::	animālis	: _____
9.	opus	:	opera	::	_____	: vulnera
10.	temporī	:	temporibus	::	flūminī	: _____
11.	pectoris	:	pectus	::	_____	: lītus
12.	cor	:	cordibus	::	iter	: _____
13.	vulnus	:	vulnerum	::	_____	: aequorum
14.	nōmen	:	nōminibus	::	_____	: exemplāribus

H. This analogy test is based on culture or ideas. The relationships can be of all kinds: specific name to a general name (as in the example below), parent to child, husband to wife, synonyms, antonyms, etc.

Examples

Apennīnus : mōns :: Tiberis : _____

That is, **Apennīnus** (*specific*) is to **mōns** (*general*) as **Tiberis** (*specific*) is to _____ (*general*). Therefore, the solution is:

Apennīnus : mōns :: Tiberis : *flūmen*

"Apennines" is to "mountain" as is "Tiber" to *"river"*

caput : pēs :: tēctum : _____

That is, **caput** (*item*) is to **pēs** (*its opposite*) as **tēctum** (*item*) is to _____ (*its opposite*) Therefore, the solution is:

caput : pēs :: tectum : *pavīmentum*

"Head" is to "foot" as "roof" is to *"floor"*

1. prīmus : ultimus :: inimīcus : _____
2. puella : fēmina :: _____ : māter
3. Padus : fluvius :: Ardea : _____
4. vir : fēmina :: Aenēās : _____
5. Faustulus : homō :: lupa : _____
6. vir : puer :: pater : _____
7. Italia : paeninsula :: Sicilia : _____
8. hostis : amīcus :: malus : _____
9. Carthāgō : Āfrica :: Rōma : _____
10. manēre : discēdĕre :: dare : _____

I. Give the Latin source for the following English derivatives. If the Latin source word is a noun or adjective, give the nominative singular; if it is a verb, give the infinitive.

1. nominal _____
2. exemplary _____
3. corporal _____
4. peninsula _____
5. marine _____
6. temporary _____
7. remain _____
8. voluntary _____
9. veil _____
10. miserable _____
11. observe _____
12. verbal _____
13. terrestrial _____
14. itinerary _____
15. constitution _____
16. cordial _____
17. corpuscle _____
18. vulnerable _____
19. pectoral _____
20. capital _____

CHAPTER 5

Nouns of the Fourth Declension

Masculine, Feminine, and Neuter

THOUGHT
FOR
TODAY

Manus lavat manum. One hand washes another.

FOURTH DECLENSION					
MASCULINE	FEMININE			NEUTER	
sinus *m* bay	**manus** *f* hand			**genū** *n* knee	
SINGULAR	SINGULAR	ENDINGS		SINGULAR	ENDINGS
NOM.	**sin·us**	**man·us**	*-us*	**gen·ū**	*-ū*
GEN.	**sin·ūs**	**man·ūs**	*-ūs*	**gen·ūs**	*-ūs*
DAT.	**sin·uī**	**man·uī**	*-uī*	**gen·ū**	*-ū*
ACC.	**sin·um**	**man·um**	*-um*	**gen·ū**	*-ū*
ABL.	**sin·ū**	**man·ū**	*-ū*	**gen·ū**	*-ū*
PLURAL	PLURAL	ENDINGS		PLURAL	ENDINGS
NOM.	**sin·ūs**	**man·ūs**	*-ūs*	**gen·ua**	*-ua*
GEN.	**sin·uum**	**man·uum**	*-uum*	**gen·uum**	*-uum*
DAT.	**sin·ibus**	**man·ibus**	*-ibus*	**gen·ibus**	*-ibus*
ACC.	**sin·ūs**	**man·ūs**	*-ūs*	**gen·ua**	*-ua*
ABL.	**sin·ibus**	**man·ibus**	*-ibus*	**gen·ibus**	*-ibus*

NOTES

1) The nominative and genitive singular and the nominative and accusative plural of masculine and feminine nouns of the fourth declension all end in **-us.** But notice that the **u** of the genitive singular, and the nominative and accusative plural is long (indicated by a "long" mark, called a macron), and should be pronounced long. Practice the difference in pronunciation.

2) Notice that, with the exception of the genitive singular, which ends in **-ūs,** neuter nouns of the fourth declension have the same ending, **-ū,** in every singular case. There are only four neuter nouns of the fourth declension, of which the most commonly occurring are **corn·ū -ūs** horn, and **gen·ū -ūs** knee.

3) Most of the nouns of the fourth declension are masculine. There are about a dozen that are feminine, for example, **man·us -ūs** hand; band, group; **portic·us -ūs** portico, colonnade

---

PITFALL

Nouns ending in **-us** can come from the second, third, or fourth declensions. They can be masculine, feminine, or neuter. For example:

	GENDER	DECLENSION	GENITIVE
amīc·us -ī *m* friend	masculine	II	**-ī**
māl·us -ī *f* apple tree	feminine	II	**-ī**
vulg·us -ī *n* general public	neuter *(rare)*	II	**-ī**
virtus, virtūt·is *f* valor	feminine	III	**-is**
lepus lepor·is *m* hare	masculine	III	**-is**
corpus, corpor·is *n* body	neuter	III	**-is**
exercit·us -ūs *m* army	masculine	IV	**-ūs**
man·us -ūs *f* hand, band	feminine	IV	**-ūs**
cas·us -us *m* adventure	masculine	IV	**-ūs**

In addition, there are Latin adverbs that end in **-us,** for example, **intus** *inside,* **dīvīnitus** *by divine agency,* **rūrsus** *again.* So be careful!

---

4) **Domus** *f* house, home, shows forms of both the fourth and second declensions, all of which are feminine. In the following paradigm, the less common form is given in parentheses:

	SINGULAR		PLURAL	
NOM.	**dom·us**		**dom·ūs**	
GEN.	**dom·ūs**		**dom·ōrum**	**(dom·uum)**
DAT.	**dom·ō**	**(dom·uī)**	**dom·ibus**	
ACC.	**dom·um**		**dom·ōs**	**(dom·ūs)**
ABL.	**dom·ō**		**dom·ibus**	
LOC.	**dom·ī**			

Prepositions are used with **domum** (acc. of motion) when modified by an adjective, e.g., **ad domum meam** *to my home* or **in domum meam** *into my house.* The locative **domī** *at home* takes the possessive adjective in the genitive case, e.g., **domī suae** *at his own home*, **meae domī** *at my home.*

EXERCISES

A. Supply the correct form of **domus** as suggested by these sentences. In cases where two forms are possible, use the preferred form, that is, the form listed first.

1. Ascanius is going *home.*
2. Faustulus is not *at home.*
3. The roofs *of the homes* were of straw.
4. Larentia is coming *from home.*
5. Aeneas could see *the homes* of Carthage.
6. Latinus stayed *at his own home.*
7. The Rutulians came *into my home.*
8. *The homes* of the Trojans were destroyed.

B. Change the following phrases from the plural to the singular.

VOCABULARY
palm·a -ae *f* palm

1. in sinibus
2. per manūs
3. palmae manuum
4. porticūs domōrum
5. in genibus
6. ducēs exercituum
7. ante exercitūs
8. sine exercitibus
9. lītora marium
10. capita et corpora
11. vulnera in corporibus

C. Complete the Latin sentences by translating the English words into Latin.

1. Aenēās (*many adventures*) habet.
2. Aenēās Dīdōnī nārrat (*about the great adventures*).
3. Latīnus Aenēae prōmīsit (*the hand of Lavinia*).
4. Turnus (*a large band of Rutilians*) dūcit.
5. Rēx Latīnus (*a beautiful home*) habet.
6. (*The home*) rēgis Latīnī (*a large colonnade*) habet.
7. Latīnus et Amāta (*in the colonnade*) erant.
8. Nōn omnēs (*homes*) habent (*colonnades*).

D. Give the nominative and accusative plural of the following nouns.

Example | **sinus**   NOMINATIVE PLURAL: **sinūs**   ACCUSATIVE PLURAL: **sinūs**

1. amīcus
2. mālus
3. vulgus
4. virtus

5. lepus
6. corpus
7. exercitus
8. manus

E. **Pick** out the grammatical misfit, and then give the reason for your choice.

Example | domus   porticus   manus   virtus   **virtus**
Reason: All are nouns of the fourth declension except **virtus,** which is a noun of the third declension.

MISFIT

1. exercitus   sinus   intus   porticus
2. domus   manus   porticus   sinus
3. sinus   exercitus   corpus   manus
4. rūrsus   porticus   exercitus   manus
5. exercitus   amīcus   sinus   porticus

F. Extend your Latin Vocabulary. Most nouns of the fourth declension are formed from the past participle of verbs, which is also called the fourth principal part. For example, the noun **exercit·us -ūs** *m* comes from the fourth principal part or past participle of **exerc·eō -ēre -uī exercitus** *to exercise, train,* and therefore means "trained unit" and therefore "army." So, if you know a lot of principal parts of verbs, you know a lot of nouns of the fourth declension.

Well, to prove how easy it is, here are the principal parts of some common verbs. You give the fourth-declension noun, its genitive, and its meaning.

Example

gem·ō -ĕre gemuī gemitus *to sigh*   **gemitus -ūs** *m* a sigh

1. **son·ō -āre sonuī sonitus** to sound
2. **mon·eō -ēre monuī monitus** to warn
3. **fl·eō -ēre flēvī flētus** to cry
4. **rīd·eō -ēre rīsī rīsus** to laugh
5. **succēd·ō -ĕre successī successus** to succeed
6. **adven·iō -īre advēnī adventus** to arrive
7. **accēd·ō -ĕre accessī accessus** to approach
8. **ex·eō -īre exiī exitus** to go out, exit
9. **iub·eō -ēre iussī iussus** to order

G. Complete the Latin sentences by translating the English words into Latin.

1. Faustulus audit (*the cries*) geminōrum.
2. Ego audiō (*the laughter*) puerōrum.
3. Faustulus ambulat ad (*the exit*) casae.
4. Aenēās audit (*the warnings*) Mercuriī.
5. Latīnus observat (*the arrival*) Aenēae.
6. Priamus observat (*the approach*) exercitūs Graecī.
7. Dux nōn videt (*the warnings*) mīlitum.
8. Faustulus audit (*the sounds*) geminōrum.
9. (*The successes*) exercitūs Graecī sunt magnī.
10. Dīdō benignē excipit (*the arrival*) Aenēae.
11. Exercitus Turnī appropinquat (*the army*) Aenēae.
12. Mercurius ad Aenēān cum a (*warning*) vēnit.
13. Verba Mercuriī sunt plēna (*of warnings.*)
14. Iuppiter successum (*to the army*) Aenēae dat.
15. Exercitus Aenēae sine (*a sound*) vēnit.
16. Mīlitēs nōn audiunt (*the orders*) ducis.

Trojans and Rutulians
in combat

Read this story of the continued adventures of Aeneas.

Aenēās in Latium Pervenit.
Aeneas Arrives in Latium.

I

Post multōs casūs, nāvēs Trōiānae ad lītus Italiae perveniunt. Prīmum Aenēās castra pōnit in lītore prope ōstium Tiberis flūminis. Deinde Aenēās nūntiōs et multa dōna pretiōsa ad Latīnum rēgem mittit.

cas·us -ūs *m* adventure
perveniunt arrive **castr·a -ōrum** *npl* camp
pōnit places, sets up **ōsti·um -ī** *n* mouth
dōn·um -ī *n* gift
pretiōs·us -a -um precious
Latīn·us -ī *m* Latinus (*a local king*)

II

Nam Latīnus est rēx illīus regiōnis. Nōmen regiōnī est Latium. Latīnus rēx dīcit: "Dux Trōiānus erit marītus fīliae meae Lāvīniae. Domus mea erit domus eius. Aliēnī nunc sunt Trōiānī. Sed abhinc erunt Latīnī. Generābunt novam et clāram gentem."

regiō regiōn·is *f* region **Lati·um -ī** *n* Latium (*district in which Rome lies*)
erit will be
marīt·us -ī *m* husband **Lāvīni·a -ae** *f* Lavinia **aliēn·us -ī** *m* alien, foreigner
abhinc from now on **erunt** they will be
generābunt they will produce
gēns gent·is *f* a people, nation **clār·us -a -um** famous

III

Sed māter Lāvīniae, rēgīna Amāta, dīcit: " O mea cāra fīlia, Turnus erit marītus tuus." Rēgīna enim Lāvīniam Turnō iam dūdum prōmīsit. Turnus est rēx Rutulōrum. Caput Rutulōrum est Ardea. Turnus Lāvīniam in mātrimōnium dūcĕre optat. Turnus Latīnum in genibus supplicat, sed Latīnus mentem nōn mūtat. Exercitus Turnī igitur cum exercitū Trōiānō pugnāre parat.

Amāt·a -ae *f* Amata **cār·us -a -um** dear
Turn·us -ī *m* Turnus
enim indeed
iam dūdum long ago
prōmīsit promised
Rutul·ī -ōrum *mpl* Rutulians (*a native tribe*) **caput capit·is** *n* capital
mātrimōni·um -ī *m* marriage
in mātrimōnium dūcĕre to marry
supplicat begs **mēns ment·is** *f* mind
mūtat changes **eius** his **exercit·us -ūs** *m* army **parat** prepares

H. Answer the following questions in English, based on the story that you have just read.

I   1. What was the first thing that Aeneas did after arriving in Italy?
2. Where did he do this?
3. What did Aeneas send to King Latinus?
4. Why do you think Aeneas did this?

II   5. What was the name of the realm of King Latinus?
6. What was King Latinus willing to offer to Aeneas?
7. What change was in store for the Trojans?

III   8. What plans did Queen Amata have for Lavinia?
9. What were Turnus's hopes and desires?
10. How did King Latinus react to Turnus's pleas?
11. What action did Turnus finally take?
12. Who in your opinion had the better claim on Lavinia?
13. Why?

I. SCRAMBLED SENTENCES. Rearrange the words to form sentences.

1. cum Aenēās nāvibus in pervenit Trōiānīs Italiam
2. ad rēgem multa mittit Aenēās dōna Latīnum
3. fīliam prōmīsit Lāvīniam Turnō Rēgīna Amāta

J. Translate the following sentences into Latin.

1. After many adventures Aeneas arrives in Latium.
2. The ships are in a small bay.
3. The Trojans set up their camp near the shore.
4. Turnus wants to marry Lavinia.
5. King Latinus prefers (**praefert**) Aeneas, but Queen Amata prefers Turnus.
6. Vergil tells (**nārrat**) the adventures of Aeneas.

WORD POWER

K. Supply the Latin source for the following English derivatives. If the source is an adjective, give the masculine only; if it is a verb, give the infinitive.

1. manual _____
2. domicile _____
3. marital _____
4. regional _____
5. precious _____
6. filial _____
7. promise _____
8. alienate _____
9. sinuses _____
10. supplicate _____
11. donation _____
12. domesticate _____
13. virtuous _____
14. mental _____
15. ridicule _____
16. matrimony _____
17. commute _____
18. generate _____

CHAPTER 6

Nouns of the Fifth Declension

Feminine and Masculine

THOUGHT FOR TODAY

Dum vīta est, spēs est.   As long as there is life, there is hope.

FIFTH DECLENSION			
FEMININE		MASCULINE	ENDINGS
rēs *f* thing; affair		**diēs** *m* day	
SINGULAR			
NOM.	r·*ēs* — the thing	di·*ēs*	-*ēs*
GEN.	r·*eī* — of the thing	di·*eī*	-*eī*
DAT.	r·*eī* — to, for the thing	di·*eī*	-*eī*
ACC.	r·*em* — the thing	di·*em*	-*em*
ABL.	r·*ē* — from, by, with the thing	di·*ē*	-*ē*
PLURAL			
NOM.	r·*ēs* — the things	di·*ēs*	-*ēs*
GEN.	r·*ērum* — of the things	di·*ērum*	-*ērum*
DAT.	r·*ēbus* — to, for the things	di·*ēbus*	-*ēbus*
ACC.	r·*ēs* — the things	di·*ēs*	-*ēs*
ABL.	r·*ēbus* — from, by, with the things	di·*ēbus*	-*ēbus*

1) Nouns of the fifth declension are regularly feminine, except **diēs** *day* and **merīdiēs** *midday*. But even **diēs** is sometimes feminine in the singular, especially when it means an *appointed day*, for example, **cōnstitūtā diē** *on the appointed day*; also when it is used for time in general, for example, **longa diēs** *a long time*.

One more point about the use of **diēs**. The Romans did not use prepositions with expressions of time such as: **proximō diē** *on the next day*; **decem diēs** *for ten days*; **decem diēbus** *within ten days*. However, they might say **per tōtum diem** *throughout the entire day*.

2) After struggling with what seems to be a huge Latin vocabulary, you won't believe it, but Cicero said that the vocabulary (**cōpia verbōrum**) of the Latin language was rather small. As a result, most Latin words carry many meanings. Notice that only two meanings were given above for the word **rēs**, namely, *thing* and *affair*. Well, that's an oversimplification. Here are some additional meanings: *fact, reality; matter, topic; property, wealth; act, deed; business; purpose, object; situation; event; factor*. In addition, the word **rēs** has specialized meanings in certain phrases. You need not remember all these meanings right now. But you should be aware of the fact that most Latin words have a wide range of meanings.

ENDINGS OF NOUNS OF ALL FIVE DECLENSIONS							
FIRST	**SECOND**		**THIRD**		**FOURTH**		**FIFTH**
SINGULAR							
f	*m*	*n*	*m/f*	*n*	*m/f*	*n*	*f*
NOM. -*a*	-*us* (-*er*, -*ir*)	-*um*	varied	varied	-*us*	-*ū*	-*ēs*
GEN. -*ae*	-*ī*	-*ī*	-*is*	-*is*	-*ūs*	-*ūs*	-*eī*
DAT. -*ae*	-*ō*	-*ō*	-*ī*	-*ī*	-*uī*	-*ū*	-*eī*
ACC. -*am*	-*um*	-*um*	-*em*	varied	-*um*	-*ū*	-*em*
ABL. -*ā*	-*ō*	-*ō*	-*e*	-*e* (-*ī*)	-*ū*	-*ū*	-*ē*
PLURAL							
NOM. -*ae*	-*ī*	-*a*	-*ēs*	-*a* (-*ia*)	-*ūs*	-*ua*	-*ēs*
GEN. -*ārum*	-*ōrum*	-*ōrum*	-*um* (*ium*)	-*um* (-*ium*)	-*uum*	-*uum*	-*ērum*
DAT. -*īs*	-*īs*	-*īs*	-*ibus*	-*ibus*	-*ibus*	-*ibus*	-*ēbus*
ACC. -*ās*	-*ōs*	-*a*	-*ēs*	-*a* (-*ia*)	-*ūs*	-*ua*	-*ēs*
ABL. -*īs*	-*īs*	-*īs*	-*ibus*	-*ibus*	-*ibus*	-*ibus*	-*ēbus*

NOTE

Remember that the genitive singular will give you the clue to the base of a noun and its declension.

A. Complete the following sentences by translating the English words into Latin.

VOCABULARY

faciēs faciēī *f* face   **posteā** *adv* after that, later   **spēs speī** *f* hope
laet·us -a -um happy   **proxim·us -a -um** next

1. Trōiānī multōs *(days)* nāvigant.
2. Nāvēs ūnō *(day)* ad Thrāciam vēniunt.
3. Proximō *(day)* Trōiānī iterum nāvigant.
4. Tribus *(days)* ad īnsulam Dēlum veniunt.
5. Ibi deus Apollō novam *(hope)* Trōiānīs dat.
6. *(The faces)* Trōiānōrum sunt laetae.
7. Proximō *(day)* ab īnsulā Crētā nāvigant.
8. Multōs *(days)* posteā Trōiānī Carthāginem veniunt.
9. Trōiānī multōs *(days)* cum Dīdōne manent.
10. Nunc Aenēās est plēnus *(of hope)*.
11. Et Trōiānī sunt plēnī *(of hopes)*.
12. Nunc Trōiānī nōn sunt sine *(hope)*.
13. *(Hope)* in *(the faces)* omnium est.
14. Dīdō quoque magnās *(hopes)* habet.
15. Poēta Vergilius hās *(things)* nōbīs nārrat.

B. Translate into Latin.

VOCABULARY
aci·ēs -ēī *f* troops (in battle formation)   **merīdi·ēs -ēī** *m* noon
ante *prep* (+ *acc*) in front of   **r·ēs -eī** *f* matter
fid·ēs -eī *f* trust, faith; word of honor

1. without hope
2. before noon
3. after noon

4. to have trust
5. to give (one's) word of honor
6. about many matters
7. throughout the days and nights
8. the end of hope
9. with the Trojan troops
10. in front of the Trojan troops

Aeneas and Turnus in duel

Now read about the events that take place after Aeneas arrives in Italy.

Bellum inter Trōiānōs et Rutulōs
The War between the Trojans and the Rutulians

I

Aenēās pōnit omnēs spēs in pāce. Turnus autem omnēs spēs in bellō pōnit; nam magnam spem victōriae habet.

pōnit places **pāx pāc·is** *f* peace
autem however
nam for, since

II

Posterō diē nūntius ad Aenēān properat et nūntiat: "Dēfende castra tua! Turnus nōn pācem sed bellum dēsīderat. Iam iter facit hūc cum Rutulīs sociīsque suīs."

nūnti·us -ī *m* messenger
properat rushes **nūntiat** announces
iam already **iter itiner·is** *n* trip, way; *(mil)* march **iter facit** is marching **hūc** here
su·us -a -um his (her, their) **soci·us -ī** *m* ally

III

Aenēās respondet: "Ego neque Turnum neque Rutulōs timeō; nam ego fidem meam in deīs et in meīs Trōiānīs pōnō. Turnus equidem spēs falsās victōriae habet."

timeō I fear **neque. . . neque** neither . . . nor **equidem** indeed
fals·us -a -um false

IV

Posterō diē Turnus aciem suam ante castra Trōiāna īnstruit. Aenēās deinde Trōiānōs ē castrīs ēdūcit. Aciēs Turnī multōs diēs cum aciē Trōiānā ācriter pugnat. Caedēs utrimque magna est.

poster·us -a -um following, next
īnstruit deploys
ēdūcīt leads out

ācriter hard **caed·ēs -is** *f* bloodshed
utrimque on both sides

V

Rēx Latīnus et Rēgīna Amāta duās aciēs ex arce spectant. Animus

duo duae duo two
arx arc·is *f* citadel **spectant** watch **anim·us**

Latīnī est plēnus speī victōriae Trōiānae. Amāta spērat victōriam Turnī et aciēī Rutulōrum.

-ī *m* heart **plēn·us -a -um** (+ *gen* or *abl*) full of **spērat** hopes for

VI

Dēnique post multōs diēs et multa proelia, Turnus dīcit: "Haec hāctenus! Ego sōlus cum Aenēā pugnābō. Victor Lāvīniam et rēgnum habēbit"

dēnique finally
proeli·um -ī *n* battle **haec hāctenus** enough of this **sōl·us -a -um** alone **pugnābō** I shall fight **habēbit** shall have **rēgn·um -ī** *n* realm, kingdom

VII

Aenēās avidē prōvocātiōnem accipit. Aciēs Trōiāna et aciēs Rutuliāna in herbā cōnsīdunt et certāmen anxiē spectant. Ducēs fortiter pugnant. Dēnique Aenēās Turnum graviter vulnerat. Turnus, moriēns, dīcit: "Victōria est tua; et Lāvīnia nunc erit tua uxor." Haec locūtus, Turnus mortuus est.

avidē eagerly **prōvocātiō prōvocātiōn·is** *f* challenge
herb·a -ae *f* grass **cōnsīdunt** sit down **certāmen certāmin·is** *n* (single) combat, duel **anxiē** anxiously **fortiter** bravely **vulnerat** wounds **graviter** seriously **moriēns** dying
erit will be **haec locūtus** having said this **mortuus est** died

C. Answer these questions in English, based on the story above.

I 1. What did Aeneas hope for?
   2. What did Turnus put his trust in?
   3. Why did Turnus want war?

II 4. Who came rushing to Aeneas?
   5. What was Aeneas told to defend?
   6. What did he say Turnus wanted?
   7. Where was Turnus marching?
   8. With whom was Turnus marching?

III 9. Whom did Aeneas not fear?
    10. In whom did Aeneas put his trust?
    11. What did Turnus falsely hope for?

IV 12. Where did Turnus deploy his troops?
    13. When did Turnus deploy his troops?

14. What did Aeneas do in turn?
15. How long did the troops of Turnus fight the Trojans?
16. What happened on both sides?

V 17. From where did Latinus and Amata watch the battle?
18. For which side did Latinus root?
19. Which side did Amata favor?

VI 20. Who challenged whom to a duel?
21. When did this challenge take place?
22. What, according to Turnus, would the winner get?

VII 23. Did Aeneas fear or welcome the challenge?
24. What did the troops on both sides do during the duel?
25. What caused Turnus to end the duel?
26. What was Aeneas' reward for winning the duel?
27. Did Turnus prove himself a decent character?
28. Would Lavinia be flattered to have two warriors fight over her?
29. Did Lavinia have any real choice of a husband?
30. Was it Latinus or Amata who had most say in the choice?
31. Do you think Lavinia should have had some say in the matter?

D. Translate each English word or phrase into Latin to complete the sentence. Then translate the sentence.

VOCABULARY

anim·us -ī *m* heart	**gaudi·um -ī** *n* joy	**servāre** to keep
estne is?	**nūll·us -a -um** no	**timor timōr·is** *m* fear

1. Nūlla (*hope*) mihi est.
2. Turnus nūllam (*faith*) in deīs pōnit.
3. Aenēās omnem (*hope*) in pāce pōnit.
4. Rutulī falsās (*hopes*) habent.
5. Turnus (*hope*) victōriae habet.
6. Multōs (*days*) Trōiānī cum Rutulīs pugnant.
7. (*The faces*) Rutulōrum sunt plēnae timōris.
8. Nūlla (*hope*) victōriae Rutulīs est.
9. Aenēās dat Trōiānīs (*great hope of victory*).
10. Post certāmen, Rutulī erat sine (*hope*).
11. Dēnique animī Trōiānōrum sunt plēnī (*of hope*).
12. Posterō (*day*) Latīnus (*word of honor*) servat.

13. *(The face)* Rēgis Latīnī est plēna gaudiī.
14. Sed nūllum gaudium est in *(the face)* Amātae.
15. Gaudium autem est in *(the faces)* Trōiānōrum.
16. Estne autem gaudium in *(the face)* Lāvīniae?

E. Similarity of endings can be misleading. How good is your memory?

1. In what three cases can the form **rēs** be?
2. In what case is **rērum?**
3. In what two cases can **aciēbus** be?
4. In what two cases can **faciēī** be?
5. In what case is **rē?**

F. Again, similarity of endings can be misleading. Pick out the grammatical misfit in each set, and give the reason of your choice.

1. victōriam   casam   iam   herbam
2. rēbus   faciēbus   spēbus   spērāmus
3. spem   autem   nāvem   fidem
4. casa   proelia   domicilia   oppida
5. pater   puer   ācriter   amīcus
6. fidēs   nāvēs   speciēs   faciēs

G. The following analogy exercise is based on culture. See Chapter 4, Exercises **F** and **G**, for an explanation and example of analogy exercises.

1. Aenēās   :   _____   ::   Turnus   :   Rutulī
2. māter   :   Amāta   ::   _____   :   Lāvīnia
3. Latīnus   :   rēx   ::   Amāta   :   _____
4. rēx   :   populus   ::   dux   :   _____
5. Diāna   :   Apollō   ::   soror   :   _____
6. sōl   :   Apollō   ::   lūna   :   _____
7. Sāturnus   :   Iuppiter   ::   pater   :   _____
8. diēs   :   nox   ::   pāx   :   _____

H. Give the Latin source for the following English derivatives. If it is a noun or adjective, give the nominative singular; if it is a verb, give the infinitive.

Example   bellicose   **bellum**

1. vulnerable ____
2. itinerary ____
3. pugnacious ____
4. victorious ____
5. solo ____
6. fidelity ____
7. plenary ____
8. provocation ____
9. avidly ____

10. herb ____
11. nocturnal ____
12. instruction ____
13. pacify ____
14. multiply ____
15. associate ____
16. animated ____
17. nullify ____
18. timorous ____

WORD POWER

CHAPTER 7

Greek Nouns

THOUGHT
FOR
TODAY

Prō Deō et Patriā. For God and Country.

You will be running into Greek proper names in both Roman history and mythology, and in several chapters in this book. Many Greek names have been Latinized and are declined like the nouns of the first declension; for example, **Athēn·a -ae** *f* Athena. But others retain traces of their Greek case-forms. Since different Roman authors used various forms in certain cases, alternate forms will be indicated here.

FIRST DECLENSION			
	Aenēās *m* Aeneas	**Anchīsēs** *m* Anchises	**Daphnē** *f* Daphne
Nom.	**Aenē·ās**	**Anchīs·ēs**	**Daphn·ē**
Gen.	**Aenē·ae**	**Anchīs·ae**	**Daphn·ēs**
Dat.	**Aenē·ae**	**Anchīs·ae**	**Daphn·ae**
Acc.	**Aenē·ān**	**Anchīs·ēn**	**Daphn·ēn**
Abl.	**Aenē·ā**	**Anchīs·ē**	**Daphn·ē**
Voc.	**Aenē·ā**	**Anchīs·ē**	**Daphn·ē**

NOTES

1) Greek nouns of the first declension that end in **-ās** and **-ēs** are masculine; those that end in **ē** are feminine.

Other nouns declined like **Anchīsēs:**

Achātēs -ae *m* Achates (Aeneas's right-hand man)
Androclēs -ae *m* Androcles (famous for his experience with a lion*)*

Other nouns declined like **Daphnē**:

Arachn·ē -ēs *f* Arachne (girl changed into a spider by Minerva)
Ariadn·ē -ēs *f* Ariadne (daughter of Minos, king of Crete)
Daphn·ē -ēs *f* Daphne (woodland nymph, loved by Apollo)
Hecub·ē -ēs *or* **Hecub·a -ae** *f* Hecuba (wife of King Priam)
Helen·ē -ēs *f* Helen (wife of Menelaus, king of Sparta)

2) You can see that we, too, Anglicize some names such as "Helen" and prefer the Latinized version of some as "Hecuba", or keep the Greek version, as in " Daphne."

	SECOND DECLENSION	THIRD DECLENSION	
	Tenedos *f* Tenedos	**Īlion** *n* Ilium (Troy)	**Dīdō** *f* Dido
NOM.	**Tened·os** *or* **-us**	**Īli·on** *or* **-um**	**Dīdō**
GEN.	**Tened·ī**	**Īli·ī**	**Dīdōn·is**
DAT.	**Tened·ō**	**Īli·ō**	**Dīdōn·ī**
ACC.	**Tened·on** *or* **-um**	**Īli·on** *or* **-um**	**Dīdōn·em**
ABL.	**Tened·ō**	**Īli·ō**	**Dīdōn·e**
VOC.	**Tened·ō**	**Īli·on** *or* **-um**	**Dīdō**

NOTES

1) Greek nouns of the second declension end in **-os** or **-ōs** and are masculine or feminine. Those ending in **-on** are neuter. In the plural, when they occur, they follow the regular plural second declension. Some Roman writers used the Greek form, others preferred the names with Latinized endings. **Īlion** (or **Īlium**) is another name for **Trōia**.

2) There are other Greek nouns of the third declension with Greek forms of inflection; they are not presented here because they do not occur in the stories of this book.

A. Complete the following sentences by translating the English word into Latin. Use the first form given in the declension of these nouns.

Example

Nāvēs Graecae post īnsulam *(of Tenedos)* latēbant.
Nāvēs Graecae post īnsulam Tenedon latēbant.
The Greek ships were hiding behind the island of Tenedos.

VOCABULARY

dōn·um -ī *n* gift   **fugit** flees
excipit welcomes   **nepōs nepōt·is** *m* grandson

1. Exercitus Graecus cum exercitū Trōiānō ante *(Ilium)* pugnat.
2. Aenēās *(with Anchises)* et Ascaniō ex urbe *(Ilium)* fugit.
3. Anchīsēs est pater *(of Aeneas)*.
4. Ascanius est nepōs *(of Anchises)*.
5. Dīdō *(Aeneas and Achates)* benignē excipit.
6. Aenēās *(with Dido)* diū manet.
7. Aenēās multa dōna *(to Dido)* dat.
8. Turnus *(with Aeneas)* pugnat.
9. Aenēās est amīcus *(of Achates)*.
10. Aenēās *(Dido)* amat.
11. Et Dīdō *(Aeneas)* amat.
12. Aenēās nōn est marītus *(of Dido)*.
13. Apollō amat *(Daphne)*.
14. Māter *(of Daphne)* est fēmina Graeca.
15. Ego *(Tenedos)* saepe vīsitō.
16. Aenēās cum *(Achates)* Carthāginem venit.

RELIGION ROMAN STYLE

The Romans would have found the idea of "separation of Church and State" unrealistic and offensive. Their religious beliefs and practices were an essential part of public and political life. Their priests were politicians, initially chosen only from the patrician class. They held some priesthoods for a limited period, others for life. Roman priests didn't go around preaching sermons, teaching morality, or administering sacraments. Their job was to find out what the gods wanted, and to win their favor or appease their anger by offering sacrifices and holding festivals in their honor.

There were various priestly boards called *colleges* (**collēgi·um -ī** *n).* For instance, there was a college of augurs who took the auspices, that is, they interpreted the will of the gods and predicted the future by observing the flight, cries, and eating habits of birds, as well as by noting thunder and lightning and other unusual natural phenomena, and by examining the vital organs of sacrificial animals. No important political or military action was taken without consulting the auspices. The first meaning of **Auspicium** is "bird-watching"! Cicero, who had been a member of the college of augurs, didn't believe in it but considered it politically necessary for keeping the common people under control.

There was a board of six unmarried priestesses called Vestal Virgins (**virgō virgin·***is* *f* **Vestālis**), devoted to the goddess Vesta. One of their important duties was to keep the eternal flame burning in the little round shrine in the Roman forum. They spent thirty years of their lives as virgins in the service of Vesta in the "convent" next to the shrine of Vesta, called the Atrium of Vesta. They appeared regularly at public events and commanded great respect. For instance, if a criminal were being led out to execution and met a Vestal Virgin on the way, she could set him free instantly. After their thirty years of service, the Vestal Virgins could marry, but few of them did.

The Romans didn't "attend church." They gathered outdoors before the temple **(profānum** means "before the temple", and the usage of "profane" in expressions like "religious and profane music" refers to secular as opposed to liturgical music.) The priest made burnt offerings on an altar in front of the temple after his attendant had killed the steer, sheep, or pig at the altar. The altar had to be kept outside the temple since the smoke from the burnt offerings would have blackened the temple interior. After the sacrifice, the priest went inside the temple and stood in front of the statue of the god to consult with him. He then came out to announce the will of the god to the people gathered outside. Then the priests and other officials had a nice meal prepared for them from the meat of the sacrificial animals.

Roman religion, like most religions of the world, involved the worship of many gods and goddesses. The Romans did not have weekends in their calendar, but feasts in honor of various gods and goddesses were liberally sprinkled over the year. The five-day feast in honor of Minerva, goddess of wisdom, marked the beginning of the school year for Roman children who were wealthy enough to attend school. One of the feasts that provided most fun was the **Saturnalia** in honor of Saturn, the god of agriculture, who gave us "Saturday" (Saturn's Day). This favorite holiday began on December 17 and lasted seven days. The philosopher Seneca tells us that all Rome

APOLLO

URANUS

JUNO

JUPITER

PLUTO

SATURN

DIANA

Uranus, Juno, Jupiter, Apollo, Diana, Saturn, and Pluto

seemed to have gone mad on that holiday. Families gathered to celebrate and exchange gifts. Slaves were waited on by their masters and treated as if they were equals. The Romans had a saying: "**Nōn semper Sāturnālia erunt,**" which sounded to the Roman ear like: "It's not Christmas every day!"

Most the stories about gods and goddesses come from the poets. They depict them as having all of our human faults. They bicker, they cheat, they try to trip each other up; they can be generous, but they can also be jealous and vengeful. Jupiter was at times unfaithful to his wife Juno, who is sometimes depicted as nagging him. In fact, many of the incidents in the lives of the gods and goddesses sound like the stuff of which soap operas are made. They were an interesting group as depicted by the poets. The gods and goddesses differed from us poor human beings only in that they were immortal. Their home was not in the sky, as we imagine heaven, but on Mount Olympus in Thessaly, a district of Northern Greece.

Now let's learn a little more about some of the gods and goddesses.

Deī Deaque in Olympō
Gods and Goddesses on Olympus

I

Domus deōrum deārumque est in Monte Olympō, ubi in rēgiā splendidā habitant. Via aurea ad rēgiam dūcit. Deī deaeque vītam bonam et laetam in Monte Olympō dūcunt.

de·us -ī *m* god **de·a -ae** *f* goddess **-que** and *(joins the word to which it is attached to the previous word)* **rēgi·a -ae** *f* palace **aure·us -a -um** golden, of gold **dūcit** leads **laet·us -a -um** happy **dūcunt** lead

II

Iuppiter est rēx deōrum deārumque. In thronō aureō sedet. Aquila ad pedēs Iovis semper stat. Fulmina manū tenet. Iuppiter pluviam in terram dēmittit. Ā rēgiā, Iuppiter tōtam terram spectāre potest. Omnēs deī et hominēs Iovem timent. Templum Iovis stat in monte Capitōlīnō.

Iuppiter Iov·is *m* Jupiter **thron·us -ī** *m* throne **sedet** sits **aquil·a -ae** *f* eagle **pēs ped·is** *m* foot **semper** always **tenet** holds **fulmen fulmin·is** *n* lightning bolt **pluvi·a -ae** *f* rain **dēmittit** sends down **tōt·us -a -um** whole **spectāre** to look at **potest** can **omn·is -is -e** all **timent** fear **Capitōlīn·us -a -um** Capitoline

III

Pater Iovis est Sāturnus, deus agricultūrae; avus Iovis est Ūranus, deus caelī. Plūtō, frāter Iovis, est rēx mortuōrum in regiōne subterrāneā, ubi Proserpina est rēgīna regiōnis subterrāneae.

Sāturn·us -ī *m* Saturn **agricultūr·a -ae** *f* agriculture **av·us -ī** *m* grandfather
Ūran·us -ī *m* Uranus **cael·um -ī** *n* sky
Plūtō Plūtōn·is *m* Pluto **mortu·ī -ōrum** *mpl* the dead **subterrāne·us -a -um** below the earth **Proserpin·a -ae** *f* Persephone

IV

Iūnō est rēgīna deōrum deārumque. Fēminae Rōmānae Iūnōnem amant et adōrant. Mēnsis Iūnius est sacer Iūnōnī. Avis Iūnōnis est pāvō. Templum Iūnōnis stat in arce Rōmānā.

Iūnō Iūnōn·is Juno

adōrant adore
mēns·is -is *m* month Iūni·us -a -um of June av·is -is *f* bird pāvō pavōn·is *m* peacock arx arc·is *f* citadel, hill

V

Diāna est dea lūnae et silvārum et bēstiārum. Diāna noctū in caelō habitat, sed interdiū in terrā habitat. Per silvās obscūrās ambulāre amat. Arcum et sagittās manū semper tenet. Diāna bēstiīs benigna semper est. Itaque bēstiae Diānam nōn timent, et bēstiae sunt cārae Diānae.

lūn·a -ae *f* moon
bēsti·a -ae *f* wild beast noctū at night
interdiū during the day
obscūr·us -a -um dark
arc·us -ūs *m* bow
sagitt·a -ae *f* arrow
benign·us -a -um (+ *dat*) kind (to)
cār·us -a -um (+ *dat*) dear (to)

VI

Frāter Diānae est Apollō, deus sōlis et mūsicae. Ut Diāna est dea lūnae, sīc Apollō est deus sōlis. Ut sōl omnia videt, sīc Apollo omnia videt. Quia omnia videt, Apollō est deus prophēticus. Apollō futūra praedīcĕre potest. Ōrāculum Apollinis est Delphīs. Īnsula Delos est sacra Apollinī et Diānae.

Apollō Apollin·is *m* Apollo
sōl sōl·is *m* sun mūsic·a -ae *f* music
ut . . . sīc as . . . so
videt sees

prophētic·us -a -um prophetic
futūr·a -ōrum *npl* the future
praedīcĕre to predict Delph·ī -ōrum *mpl* Delphi, town and shrine on Mount Parnassus in central Greece

B. Nunc Latīnē respondē ad quaestiōnēs.

   I 1. Ubi est domus deōrum deārumque?
        2. Qualis (*what kind of*) via ad rēgiam dūcit?

  II 3. Quis est rēx deōrum deārumque?
        4. Quid Iuppiter manū tenet?
        5. Quid ad pedēs Iovis stat?
        6. Quid Iuppiter in terram dēmittit?
        7. Quid Iuppiter ā rēgiā spectāre potest?
        8. Quis Iovem timet?
        9. Ubi est templum Iovis?

 III 10. Quis est pater Iovis?
      11. Quis est avus Iovis?
      12. Quis est frāter Iovis?
      13. Ubi est Plūtō rēx?
      14. Quis est uxor Plūtōnis?

  IV 15. Quis est rēgīna deōrum deārumque?
      16. Quis Iūnōnem adōrant?
      17. Quis (*which*) mēnsis est sacer Iūnōnī?
      18. Quae (*what*) avis est cāra Iūnōnī?
      19. Ubi templum Iūnōnis stat?

   V 20. Quis est dea lūnae?
      21. Ubi Diāna noctū habitat?
      22. Ubi Diāna interdiū habitat?
      23. Ubi Diāna ambulāre amat?
      24. Cūr bēstiae Diānam nōn timent?
      25. Quid Diāna manū semper tenet?

  VI 26. Quis est frāter Diānae?
      27. Cūr est Apollō prophēticus?
      28. Ubi est ōrāculum Apollinis?

C. Expand your Latin vocabulary through word groups. Words that belong to such a group are called "cognates." **(Cognātus** means "related by blood"; as a masculine noun it means "relative.") These cognates are related to the same root. Seeing them all together at a "family reunion" will help you to understand and easily remember their meanings. Here's a group of fourteen verbal sisters, brothers, cousins, uncles, and aunts; this entire verbal family tree is derived from their common root **rēg-,** which has the sense of "rule." You have already met some of them.

rēgāl·is -is -e regal, royal, kingly
rēgi·a -ae *f* palace (a shortened form for **domus rēgia** *royal home.* **Domus** is sometimes used alone for *palace.*)
rēgiē *adv* royally, like a king
rēgīn·a -ae *f* queen
rēgi·us -a -um kingly, royal
rēgnātor rēgnātōr·is *m* one who rules as king, ruler
rēgnāre to reign, be king
rēgn·um -ī *n* realm, kingdom
rēgĕre to rule
rēgul·a -ae *f* rule, principle; ruler (used in school)
rēgulār·is -is -e according to the rule, regular
rēgulāriter *adv* as a general rule, regularly
rēgulāre to regulate, direct
rēgul·us -ī *m* petty king, king of a small realm; prince (this is a diminutive form)

We can try another group of cognates.

dom·us -ūs *f* house or home.

A **domin·us -ī** *m* is the homeowner, master of a household. And the diminutive form **dominul·us -ī** *m* means "young owner." And a **domin·a -ae** *f* is a female head of a household, the lady of the house, the owner. A **domuncul·a -ae** *f* is a diminutive form, meaning *a little house* or *cottage.*

Domestic·ī -ōrum *mpl* are members of a household, servants, domestics. The adjective **domestic·us -a -um**, as you can guess, means *of a home* or *belonging to a home.* So it sometimes means domestic, home-grown, native, as opposed to foreign. We, too, speak of domestic and foreign products.

The verb **domāre** means *to tame* or *to domesticate* animals so that they can be used around the home. The verb **dominor dominārī dominātus sum** means *to be a master of a household* and so to be in control like an owner.

We saw in the chapter on nouns of the fourth declension that those nouns come from the last principal part of a verb. In this case, **dominātus** gives us the noun **domināt·us -ūs** *m* and means *ownership* and then *absolute rule, dominion.*

From the last principal part **dominātus** we drop off the ending **-us** and add the ending **-iō** and we get **dominātiō dominātiōn·is** *f,* which means first of all *the position of authority of the owner;* then it means *absolute control* in general, *domination.*

The noun **domini·um -ī** *n* means *ownership,* and then *rule, dominion.* You should therefore know that a "condominium" means "ownership with someone else."

D. Reinforce your mastery of Latin words through antonyms. A good way to help remember a Latin word is through antonyms (opposites). Here you have a list of such antonyms. They may be nouns, adjectives, adverbs, or prepositions. Find the number of the word in the second column that is the opposite of the word in the first column. If you get them all correct, give yourself a pat on the back.

magnus ____	1. prope	antiquus ____	11. parvus
diēs ____	2. urbs	bellum ____	12. mors
pēs ____	3. marītus	rūs ____	13. sine
amīcus ____	4. pāx	suprā ____	14. novus
procul ____	5. prīmus	semper ____	15. multī
cum ____	6. post	sōl ____	16. nox
miser ____	7. lūna	ultimus ____	17. bonus
paucī ____	8. falsus	malus ____	18. inimīcus
ante ____	9. caput	vērus ____	19. īnfrā
uxor ____	10. numquam	vīta ____	20. laetus

ANALOGIES

E. This analogy exercise is based on culture. For directions and examples, see Chapter 4, Exercises **G** and **H.**

1. pater	:	fīlius	::	Sāturnus	:	____
2. Proserpina	:	Plūtō	::	____	:	Iuppiter
3. Apollō	:	mūsica	::	____	:	arcus et sagitta
4. rēx	:	rēgīna	::	____	:	Iūnō
5. frāter	:	soror	::	Apollō	:	____
6. pāvō	:	Iūnō	::	____	:	Iuppiter
7. Apollō	:	sōl	::	Diāna	:	____
8. avus	:	nepōs	::	Ūranus	:	____

WORD
POWER

F. Supply the Latin source word for the following English derivatives. If the Latin source word is a noun or adjective, give the nominative singular; if it is a verb, give the infinitive.

1. prediction	____		6. lunacy	____
2. deity	____		7. archery	____
3. mortuary	____		8. benign	____
4. subterranean	____		9. oracular	____
5. adoration	____		10. obscure	____

CHAPTER 8

Prepositions and Locative Case

THOUGHT
FOR
TODAY

Per aspera ad astra. Through the rough to the stars.

I. PREPOSITIONS IN ENGLISH AND LATIN

Various prepositions were introduced when you studied the accusative and ablative cases. Now you'll see a few new prepositions as well as additional meanings for those earlier ones. Remember, English prepositions are those little words like *on, in, after, to, from,* etc. The noun or pronoun which follows a preposition is called the *object* of a preposition. A preposition and its object(s) form a *prepositional phrase*, for example, "on a snowy day". Here the preposition is *on* and its object is *day.* But be careful. There are differences in the English and Latin usage of prepositions.

1. Sometimes we use a preposition in English where **Latin uses no preposition**.

Examples

bellō	*in* war
decimō diē	*on* the tenth day
decem diēs	*for* ten days
decem diēbus	*within* or *in* ten days
in īnsulā Siciliā	*on* the island *of* Sicily

1) You learned earlier that Latin does not use a preposition **to indicate possession**; Latin simply uses the genitive case. But we often use the preposition "of" when translating the genitive case.

Examples

tēctum cas*ae*	the roof *of* the cottage
plēnus spe*ī*	full *of* hope

2) **Locative Case**. Latin does not use prepositions with names of cities and small islands. With the names of cities and small islands, the accusative case without a preposition indicates the place *to which* one goes. The ablative case without a preposition indicates the place *from which* one comes. A special case, called the locative case, also without a preposition, indicates the place *in which* one is. For example:

Examples

	City: **Rōm·a -ae** *f*	Rome	Island: **Cythēr·a -ōrum** *n*	Cythera
Acc.	**Rōmam**	*to* Rome	**Cythēra**	*to* Cythera
Abl.	**Rōmā**	*from* Rome	**Cythērīs**	*from* Cythera
Loc.	**Rōmae**	*in* Rome	**Cythērīs**	*on* Cythera

	City: **Delph·ī** Delphi **Delph·ōrum** *mpl*		City: **Carthāgō** Carthage **Carthāgin·is** *f*	
Acc.	**Delphōs**	*to* Delphi	**Carthāginem**	*to* Carthage
Abl.	**Delphīs**	*from* Delphi	**Carthāgine**	*from* Carthage
Loc.	**Delphīs** ·	*at* Delphi	**Carthāginī**	*in* Carthage

NOTE

There are two common words that take no prepositions in Latin: **dom·us -ūs** *f* home, and **rūs rūr**is *n* country.

Examples

Acc.	**domum**	home, homeward	**rūs**	*to* the country
Abl.	**domō**	*from* home	**rūre**	*from* the country
Loc.	**domī**	*at* home	**rūrī**	*in* the country

2. Sometimes Latin uses a preposition but not the one we would expect.

Examples **Lāvīnia *ā* dextrā stābat.** Lavinia was standing *on* the right (side).
Aenēās *in* Āfricam vēnit. Aeneas came *to* Africa.

In the second example, using the preposition **ad** with the name of a country **(ad Āfricam)** would convey the sense that Aeneas sailed *toward* Africa but did not enter Africa.

Normally the object of a preposition comes right after the preposition. However, quite often a noun in the genitive case can come between the preposition and its object.

in Minervae templō   in Minerva's temple (in the temple of Minerva)

propter patris dolōrem   because of the father's grief

In the first example, **templō** is the object of the preposition; in the second, **dolōrem** is the object of the preposition. Did you notice that in the translation "in Minerva's temple" we do the same thing in English that the Latin does? "Temple" is the object of the preposition, but the possessive form "Minerva's" is sandwiched between the preposition and its object.

II. PREPOSITIONS TAKING THE ACCUSATIVE

ad (+ *acc*)	to; at; on; to the house of	**intrā** (+ *acc*)	within, inside
		ob (+ *acc*)	because of; for
ante (+ *acc*)	in front of; before; off the coast of	**per** (+ *acc*)	through; throughout; along; during; through the agency of
apud (+ *acc*)	near; in the writings of; at the house of; before, in the presence of (*a judge, magistrate*)		
		post (+ *acc*)	after; behind
		prope (+ *acc*)	near
		propter (+ *acc*)	because of, for the sake of
circum (+*acc*)	around		
contrā (+ *acc*)	against	**sub** (+ *acc*)	under; toward, just before; at about
extrā (+ *acc*)	outside; beyond		
in (+ *acc*)	into; to; against		
īnfrā (+ *acc*)	below; south of	**suprā** (+ *acc*)	over, above; north of; beyond
inter (+ *acc*)	between, among; during		

(The examples are given in the order of the prepositions above. Furthermore, the examples for the various meanings of each preposition follow the order of the meanings given under each preposition above.)

ad

Magistrātus abit *ad* forum.   The magistrate goes off *to* the forum.

Faustulus *ad* ōstium stat.   Faustulus is standing *at* the door.

Ad dexteram et *ad* sinistram sunt templa.	Temples are *on* the right and *on* the left.
Aenēās *ad* Latīnum rēgem vēnit.	Aeneas came *to the house of* King Latinus.

ante

Dīdō *ante* templum stat.	Dido is standing *in front of* the temple.
Nāvēs *ante* hiemem nāvigant.	The ships sail *before* winter.
Proelium *ante* Dēlon fiēbat.	The battle took place *off the coast of* Delos.

apud

Proelium *apud* Ardeam fiēbat.	The battle took place *near* Ardea.
Ego haec *apud* Vergilium lēgī.	I read this *in the writings of* Vergil.
Achātēs *apud* mē manet.	Achates stayed *with* me (i.e., *at my house*).
Nūntiī *apud* rēgem Latīnum stant.	The messengers stand *before* (or *in the presence of*) King Latinus.

circum

Trōiānī *circum* Dēlon nāvigant.	The Trojans sail *around* Delos.
Amīcī *circum* Aenēan stant.	(His) friends stand *around* Aeneas.

contrā

Rutulī *contrā* Trōiānōs pugnant.	The Rutulians fight *against* the Trojans.

extrā

Carthāgō erat prīma colōnia *extrā* Italiam.	Carthage was the first colony *outside* Italy.
Germānia est *extrā* fīnēs Italiae.	Germany lies *beyond* the boundaries of Italy.

in

Aenēās *in* arcem Carthāginis ambulat.

Aeneas walks *into* the citadel of Carthage.

Trōiānī iter *in* Italiam faciunt.

The Trojans travel *to* Italy.

Catō ōrātiōnem *in* Caesarem habet.

Cato is delivering a speech *against* Caesar.

īnfrā

Turnus stat *īnfrā* arcem Ardeae.

Turnus is standing *below* the citadel of Ardea.

Italia est *īnfrā* Alpēs.

Italy is *south of* the Alps.

inter

Erat rīvālitās *inter* Aenēān et Turnum.

There was a rivalry *between* Aeneas and Turnus.

Inter diēs fēstōs iter facimus.

We take a trip *during* the holidays.

intrā

Domūs *intrā* mūrōs sēcūrae erant.

The homes *within* the walls were safe.

ob

Ob tempestātēs Aenēās multās nāvēs perdit.

Because of the storms, Aeneas loses many ships.

Ob hās causās Trōiānī Neptūnum timent.

For these reasons the Trojans fear Neptune.

per

Manūs Graecōrum *per* viās Trōiae properant.

Bands of Greeks rush *through* the streets of Troy.

Per tōtam noctem Dīdō vigilat.

Dido is awake *throughout* the entire night.

Nāvēs *per* lītus nāvigant.

The ships sail *along* the shore.

Per cēnam Aenēās bellum Trōiae recordat.	*During* dinner Aeneas recalls the war at Troy.
Nāvēs *per* magnum Iovem salvae sunt.	The ships are safe *through the agency* of mighty Jupiter.

post

Post aliquot diēs tempestās redit.	*After* some days the storm returns.
Nāvēs Graecae *post* īnsulam Tenedon latent.	The Greek ships hide *behind* the island of Tenedos.

prope

Ascānius semper stat *prope* patrem.	Ascanius always stands *near* his father.

propter

Turnus *propter* honōrem pugnat.	Turnus fights *for the sake of* (his) honor.

sub

Parvus Ascanius *sub* lectulum rēpit.	Little Ascanius crawls *under* the bed.
Sub noctem ad urbis portās pervenīmus.	We arrive at the city gates *toward* night (*at* nightfall).
Sub idem tempus Aenēās advenit.	*At about* the same time Aeneas arrives.

suprā

Pictūra in Iovis templō *suprā* ōstium est.	There is a painting *above* the doorway in the temple of Jupiter.
Etrūria est *suprā* Latium.	Etruria is *north of* Latium.
Opus erat *suprā* vīrēs meās.	The task was *beyond* my strength.

III. PREPOSITIONS TAKING THE ABLATIVE

ā, ab (+ *abl*)	from, away from; by; after; on	**prō** (+ *abl*)	in front of; for (the sake of); on behalf of; instead of
cum (+ *abl*)	with; against		
dē (+ *abl*)	down from; about, concerning	**sine** (+ *abl*)	without
ē, ex (+ *abl*)	out of; of; from ... on; by; from	**sub** (+ *abl*)	under; at the foot of
in (+ *abl*)	in; on; among	**super** (+ *abl*)	about, concerning

ā, ab

Mōns Palātīnus nōn procul *ā* flūmine est.	The Palatine Hill is not far (*away*) *from* the river.
Haec verba *ab* Aeneā dīcuntur.	These words are spoken *by* Aeneas.
Lāvīnium *ā* Latīnī fīliā nōminātur.	Lavinium is named *after* the daughter of Latinus.
Amīcī *ā* dext(e)rā et *ā* sinistrā stant.	Friends are standing *on* (or *to*) the right and *on* (or *to*) the left.

cum

Turnus *cum* multīs Rutulīs venit.	Turnus comes *with* many Rutulians.
Turnus *cum* Trōiānīs pugnat.	Turnus fights *against* the Trojans.

dē

Lupa *dē* Aventīnō dēscendit.	A she-wolf comes *down from* the Aventine Hill.
Homērus *dē* bellō Trōiānō nārrat.	Homer tells *about* the Trojan War.

ē, ex

Trōiānī *ex* urbe nōn veniunt.	The Trojans are not coming *out of* the city.
Ūnus *ē* rēgibus Rōmānīs erat Numa Pompilius.	One *of* the Roman kings was Numa Pompilius.
***Ex* tē requīrō ubi nāvēs sint.**	I ask (*of*) you where the ships are.

Statua *ex* aurō in fōrō stat.	A statue *of* gold stands in the forum.
Ex eō tempore Rōma flōrēre incēpit.	*From* that time *on* Rome began to flourish.
Mārs geminōs *ex* Rhēā Silviā generat.	Mars has twins *by* Rhea Silvia.
Ego haec saepe *ex* tē audiō.	I often hear this *from* you.

in

Templum Minervae *in* urbe Trōiā ōlim stābat.	A temple to Minerva once stood *in* the city of Troy.
Templum Iovis *in* Capitōliō stat.	The temple of Jupiter stands *on* the Capitoline Hill.
Achātēs *in* decem legātīs erat.	Achates was *among* the ten ambassadors.

prō

Ascānius *prō* patre Aenēā sedet.	Ascanius is sitting *in front of* his father Aeneas.
Turnus *prō* patriā mortuus est.	Turnus died *for* his country.
Nunc duōs rēgēs habēmus *prō* ūnō.	Now we have two kings *instead of* one.

sine

Aenēās *sine* timōre mortis pugnat.	Aeneas fights *without* fear of death.

sub

Nunc Turnus *sub* terrā iacet.	Now Turnus lies *under* ground.
Rōma *sub* rēgibus urbs valida erat.	Rome was a powerful city *under* the kings.
Est oppidum *sub* monte.	There is a town *at the foot of* the hill.

super

Dīdō multa *super* Priamō rogitat.

Dido keeps asking many questions *about* Priam.

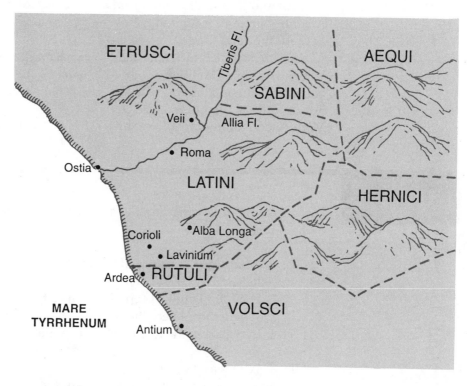

Map of Early Italy

Now read over this passage.

Aenēās et Ascanius in Italiā Cōnsīdunt
Aeneas and Ascanius Settle in Italy

I

Post bellum, pāx est inter Trōiānōs et Italōs. Latīnus fīliam suam Lāvīniam Aenēae in mātrimōnium dat. Aenēās novum oppidum fundat nōn procul ā lītore. Aenēās oppidum ab nōmine uxōris Lāvīnium nōminat.

Ital·ī -ōrum *mpl* Italians
in mātrimōnium dat gives in marriage

nōminat calls, names

II

Post Aenēae mortem, Ascanius fīlius rēgnat. Post fermē trīgintā annōs, Ascanius oppidum novum sub Albānō Monte fundat et id Albam Longam nōminat. Post Ascaniī mortem, decem rēgēs in Albānōs rēgnant. Ultimus rēx Albae Longae est Numitor. Fīlium nōn habet sed ūnam fīliam, Rhēam Silviam. Rhēa geminōs fīliōs ex Mārte habet, Rōmulum et Remum.

mors mort·is *f* death
rēgnat reigns, is king **fermē** about
trīgintā *(indecl.)* thirty
Albānus Mōns Alban Mount (some 15 miles south of Rome) **id** it *(the town)*

rēgnant in (+ *acc*) rule over **Albān·ī -ōrum** *mpl* the Albans **ultim·us -a -um** last **ūn·us -a -um** one

EXERCISES

A. Answer the following questions in English, based on the passage you have just read.

I 1. What was the nature of the relations between Trojans and Italians?
2. How did Latinus keep his promise to Aeneas?
3. Where did Aeneas build his town?
4. In regard to the town, how did Aeneas honor his wife?

II 5. Who was Ascanius?
6. Approximately how many years had Ascanius ruled before he founded Alba Longa?
7. How many kings ruled the Albans after the death of Ascanius?
8. Who was the last of the Alban kings?
9. How many children did Numitor have?
10. How many grandchildren did Numitor have?
11. By whom did Rhea have twins?

B. Choose the best translation of the following phrases according to the story.

1. **inter Trōiānōs et Italōs**
   a) between the Trojans and Italians
   b) against the Trojans and Italians
   c) for the Trojans and Italians

2. **Lāvīniam in mātrimōnium dat**
   a) he marries Lavinia
   b) he gave Lavinia into marriage
   c) he gives Lavinia in marriage

3. **nōn procul ā lītore**
   a) not far to the shore
   b) not far from the shore
   c) not far on the shore

4. **ab nōmine uxōris**
   a) after his wife's name
   b) from his wife's name
   c) by his wife's name

5. **sub Albānō Monte**
   a) beneath the Alban Mount
   b) at the foot of the Alban Mount
   c) under the Alban Mount

C. Look at the pictures below. Then choose the completion of the sentence that best describes each picture.

1. **Dīdō et Aenēās stant**
   a) in templō.
   b) ante templum.
   c) suprā templum.

2. **Rutulī et Trōiānī sedent**
   a) circum Turnum et Aenēān.
   b) post Turnum et Aenēān.
   c) prope Turnum et Aenēān.

3. **Aquila volat**
   a) in capite Aenēae.
   b) suprā caput Aenēae.
   c) ā capite Aenēae.

4. **Nāvēs Trōiānae sunt**
   a) cum portū
   b) in portū.
   c) extrā portum.

5. **Dīdō ambulat**
   a) ante Aenēān.
   b) post Aenēān.
   c) ad Aenēān.

6. **Aenēās pugnat**
   a) propter Turnum.
   b) sine Turnō.
   c) cum Turnō.

7. **Ascanius currit**
   a) inter parentēs.
   b) ad parentēs.
   c) ā parentibus.

8. **Nāvēs Trōiānae nāvigant**
   a) inter mare.
   b) trāns mare.
   c) sub marī.

D. Extend your English vocabulary. Now that you have learned the meanings of a good number of prepositions, you can easily build on that knowledge. Here's how to do it. When a preposition is joined to the beginning of a noun, adjective, adverb, or verb, it is called a *prefix* .(The word prefix comes from the Latin and means "attached before.")

To make pronunciation easier, the Romans made the final consonant of the prefix the same as the first consonant of the word to which it was attached. Let's see how that works with the verb **cēdō cēdĕre cessī cessum** to go, to come.

Examples   **ad + cēdĕre = ac + cēdĕre = accēdĕre** to go to (accede)
sub + cēdĕre = suc + cēdĕre = succēdĕre to come after (succeed)

The preposition **cum** changes to **con-** as a prefix.

Example   **cum + cēdĕre = con + cēdĕre = concēdĕre** to go with (concede)

The preposition **ē, ex** uses either form as a prefix.

Example   **ex + cēdĕre = excēdĕre** to go out (exceed)

The prepositions **prō** and **inter** do not change as prefixes.

Examples   **prō + cēdĕre = prōcēdĕre** to go forward (proceed)
inter + cēdĕre = intercēdĕre to go between (intercede)

There are two commonly used prefixes that do not occur as separate prepositions: **re-** which means "back" or "again" and **sē-** that means "away, apart."

Examples   **recēdĕre** to go back (recede)
sēcēdĕre to go away *or* apart (secede)

Now try your hand at it, using the prefixes below with the verb **dūcō dūcĕre dūxī ductus** *to lead, take* and following the same procedure as above.

1. **ad-**   3. **dē-**   5. **intrō-**   7. **re-**
2. **cum-**   4. **in-**   6. **prō-**   8. **sē-**

E. Reinforce your Latin mastery of words through antonyms. Here are prepositions with opposite meanings. Match up the antonyms, each preposition in the second column with its opposite in the first column.

1. ad _____   a. sine   5. īnfrā _____   e. post
2. ante _____   b. contrā   6. prō _____   f. suprā
3. cum _____   c procul ab   7. prope _____   g. ab
4. in _____   d. ex

F. Supply the Latin source word for the following English derivatives. If the Latin source word is a noun or adjective, give the nominative singular; if it is a verb, give the infinitive.

1. generate _____   5. rural _____
2. nominate _____   6. domestic _____
3. submarine _____   7. mortal _____
4. intramural _____   8. ultimatum _____

Part II
Adjectives
and
Adverbs

CHAPTER 9

Adjectives, First and Second Declensions

Semper parātus. Always prepared.
(Motto of the U.S. Coast Guard)

An adjective is a word that describes a noun (rarely a pronoun). Adjectives must be clearly distinguished from adverbs, which modify verbs, adjectives, or other adverbs. This is another way of saying that we distinguish between adjectives and adverbs by observing how they function in a sentence. Note the distinction in the following sentence:

Example   The *good* general fought *bravely*.

In this sentence, *good* describes the general (a noun) and therefore it is an adjective. The word *bravely* describes how he fought (a verb), and therefore it is an adverb. In the next sentence the only way of distinguishing between adjective and adverb is by observing how they function.

Example   The *fast* runner ran *fast* again today.

Here the first *fast* describes the runner and therefore is an adjective; the second *fast* describes how he ran and therefore is an adverb.

In Latin there are two groups of adjectives: those of the first and second declensions, like those below; and those of the third declension. In this chapter we will deal only with the first group.

ADJECTIVES: FIRST AND SECOND DECLENSIONS

	MASCULINE	FEMININE	NEUTER	MASCULINE	FEMININE	NEUTER

bon·us -a -um good

	SINGULAR			PLURAL		
NOM.	bon·us	bon·a	bon·um	bon·ī	bon·ae	bon·ā
GEN.	bon·ī	bon·ae	bon·ī	bon·ōrum	bon·ārum	bon·ōrum
DAT.	bon·ō	bon·ae	bon·ō	bon·īs	bon·īs	bon·īs
ACC.	bon·um	bon·am	bon·um	bon·ōs	bon·ās	bon·a
ABL.	bon·ō	bon·ā	bon·ō	bon·īs	bon·īs	bon·īs

miser· -a -um poor, pitiful

	SINGULAR			PLURAL		
NOM.	miser	miser·a	miser·um	miser·ī	miser·ae	miser·a
GEN.	miser·ī	miser·ae	miser·ī	miser·ōrum	miser·ārum	miser·ōrum
DAT.	miser·ō	miser·ae	miser·ō	miser·īs	miser·īs	miser·īs
ACC.	miser·um	miser·am	miser·um	miser·ōs	miser·ās	miser·a
ABL.	miser·ō	miser·ā	miser·ō	miser·īs	miser·īs	miser·īs

āter ātr·a -um black

	SINGULAR			PLURAL		
NOM.	āter	ātr·a	ātr·um	ātr·ī	ātr·ae	ātr·a
GEN.	ātr·ī	ātr·ae	ātr·ī	ātr·ōrum	ātr·ōrum	ātr·ōrum
DAT.	ātr·ō	ātr·ae	ātr·ō	ātr·īs	ātr·īs	ātr·īs
ACC.	ātr·um	ātr·am	ātr·um	ātr·ōs	ātr·ās	ātr·a
ABL.	ātr·ō	ātr·ā	ātr·ō	ātr·īs	ātr·īs	ātr·īs

NOTE

In the adjectives of the first and second declensions listed in the table above, notice that the only difference between the adjective **miser** and the adjective **āter** is that the **e** of **āter** drops out in all cases after the masculine nominative singular.

<h2>I. AGREEMENT OF ADJECTIVES</h2>

1. A Latin adjective agrees **with the noun it modifies in gender, number, and case.**

Examples

bon*us* amīc*us*	a good friend
miser*a* patri*a*	a miserable country
nov*um* oppid*um*	a new town

2. When one adjective modifies two nouns of different gender or number, the adjective agrees **with the nearest noun.**

Examples
or

Ascānius *bonum patrem et mātrem* habēbat.
Ascānius *patrem et mātrem bonam* habēbat.
Ascanius had a good father and mother.

NOTES

1) An adjective modifying a noun does not need to have the same ending as the noun. This is especially the case when the adjective and the noun it modifies are of different declensions.

Examples

bon*us* puer	a good boy
nost*er* amīc*us*	our friend
bon*us* dux	a good general

2) Be especially careful with masculine nouns of the first declension.

Examples

bon*us* āthlēt*a*	a good athlete
bon*us* accol*a*	a good neighbor

1. In Latin, adjectives occur as frequently before a noun as after a noun. Demonstrative adjectives, like **hic, haec, hoc,** generally come before the noun. So also adjectives indicating number or size.

multī magistrātūs	many officials
hic puer	this boy
magnus error	a big mistake

2. Possessive adjectives, like **meus, tuus, vester, noster,** occur a little more frequently before the noun than after the noun.

Examples

in meā causā	in my case
noster Pompēius	our (friend) Pompey

3. When two adjectives modify the same noun, they are sometimes connected with **et,** or one may come before the noun and one after it.

Examples

or

Sicilia est īnsula magna et pulchra.
Sicilia est magna īnsula pulchra. } Sicily is a big, beautiful island.

You must realize that at times Roman authors, especially the poets, will have other words coming between the adjective and the noun that it modifies. Just keep an eye on the endings; they will give you a clue as to what words belong together. You have perhaps heard of someone graduating **summā cum laude** (with highest honors). Here the preposition **cum** comes between the adjective **summā** and the noun that it modifies.

II. USE AS SUBSTANTIVES

An adjective can be used alone when the noun it would modify is understood from the context. Such an adjective is then called a substantive. "Substantive" in Latin means "the quality of existing by itself."

Examples

Multī **negābunt;** *paucī* **assentient.**	Many will say no; few will agree.
Bonī **assentient;** *malī* **negābunt.**	The good will agree; the bad will say no.

NOTE

The Romans were especially fond of using neuter plural substantives.

Examples

Dīdō *multa* **super Priamō rogitābat.**

Dido asked many (questions) about Priam.

Amor vincit *omnia.*

Love conquers all (things).

Haec **dīxit Paulus.**

Paul spoke these words.

Haec **recordāvit Aenēās.**

Aeneas recalled these (*or* the following) events.

III. COMMON ADJECTIVES OF THE FIRST AND SECOND DECLENSIONS

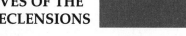

aetern·us -a -um eternal
alb·us -a -um white
alt·us -a -um high, deep
āter ātr·a -um black
aure·us -a -um golden
bellicōs·us -a -um warlike
bon·us -a -um good
cār·us -a -um dear
callid·us -a -um clever
cav·us -a -um hollow
clār·us -a -um famous
claud·us -a -um lame
decim·us -a -um tenth
dexter dextr·a -um right
dign·us -a -um worthy, deserving
fer·us -a -um fierce
fīd·us -a -um trusty, faithful
indign·us -a -um unworthy, undeserving
inimīc·us -a -um unfriendly
laet·us -a -um happy
lāt·us -a -um wide
long·us -a -um long
magn·us -a -um great, big, large

mal·us -a -um bad
me·us -a -um my
miser· -a -um poor, pitiful
mult·ī -ae -a many
mult·us -a -um much
nov·us -a -um new
nūll·us -a -um no
parv·us -a -um small
perīculōs·us -a -um dangerous
plēn·us -a -um full
poster·us -a -um following, next
pretiōs·us -a -um precious
prīm·us -a -um first
proxim·us -a -um next
pūr·us -a -um pure
rotund·us -a -um round
sēcūr·us -a -um safe
sinister sinistr·a -um left
subterrāne·us -a -um below the earth
tu·us -a -um your
ultim·us -a -um last
valid·us -a -um strong
vetul·us -a -um old

A. Look at the following lines from the poet Catullus who was away on a journey when his brother died. Now he has come back to his brother's graveside. Notice how the poet sometimes separates the adjective from the noun it modifies.

VOCABULARY

adveniō I come	**hās** these *(fem. pl. acc.)*
aequor aequor·is *n* ocean , sea	**īnferi·ae -ārum** *fpl* funeral rites
gēns gent·is *f* nation, people *(here:* country)	**vectus** having traveled

Multās **per gentēs et** *multa* **per aequora vectus**
adveniō *hās miserās*, **frater, ad īnferiās.**

Indicate the nouns that these adjectives modify. Note whether they precede or follow the noun that they modify.

1. multās
2. multa

3. hās
4. miserās

B. Give the correct form of the adjective in parentheses that modifies the noun. This will be a good opportunity to review some of the nouns that you have met in previous chapters.

1. (validus) virī____
2. (sacer) ōrāculum____
3. (miser) Dīdō____
4. (validus) fundāmentum____
5. (bonus) cibus____
6. (ultimus) rēx____
7. (bonus) mātrum____
8. (malus) dē inimīcīs____
9. (novus) domicilium____
10. (perīculōsus) per viās____
11. (benignus) verbōrum____
12. (altus) in flūmine____

13. (multī) cum honōribus____
14. (falsus) cum spēbus____
15. (pulcher) domuum____
16. (perīculōsus) inter tempestātem____
17. (magnus) propter īram____
18. (clārus) in urbe____
19. (laetus) faciēbus____
20. (magnus) rēgum____
21. (parvus) urbium____
22. (albus) dentēs____
23. (longus) pāx____

C. Complete the Latin sentences by filling in the proper endings of the adjectives.

Vocabulary

appropinquābant approached
deinde then
fabricābant built
fīn·is -is (*gen pl* **-ium**) *m* end
īnfirm·us -a -um weak
latēbant hid

necābant killed
oppugnābant attacked, assaulted
properābant rushed
subitō suddenly
trahēbant dragged
tum at that time

1. Bellum Trōiānum erat long____.
2. Caedēs erat magn____.
3. Tum rēx Priamus erat vetul____ et īnfirm____.
4. Etiam miser____ uxor eius, rēgīna Hecuba, erat vetul____ et īnfirm____.
5. Mīlitēs Graec____ mūrōs alt____ saepe oppugnābant.
6. Sed mūrī urbis erant alt____ et valid____.
7. Graecī dēnique magn____ equum alt____ fabricābant.
8. Mult____ mīlitēs Graecī in equō cav____ latēbant.
9. Deinde virī Trōiānī equum alt____ trahēbant per portās urbis.
10. Subitō mīlitēs Graec____ ex equō cav____ properābant.
11. Erat fīnis urbis antiqu____ et pulchr____.
12. Graecī deinde rēgī vetul____ et rēgīnae īnfirm____ appropinquābant.
13. Fēminae miser____ cum līberīs parv____ in domibus obscūr____ latēbant.
14. Graec____ mīlitēs deinde mult____ Trōiānōs miser____ necābant.
15. Viae urbis erant plēn____ corporum Trōiānōrum mortu____.

Now let's get acquainted with the rest of the Twelve Olympians.

Deī Olympicī
Olympic Gods

I

Neptūnus erat deus marīnus. Erat vērō rēx maris flūminumque. Erat frāter Iovis. Tridentem manū tenēbat. Nautae Rōmānī Neptūnum adōrābant. In aquīs ōceanī domum habēbat. Neptūnus erat benignus nautīs.

marīn·us -a -um -sea, of the sea
vērō *adv* in fact
tridēns trident·is *m* trident

ōcean·us -ī *m* ocean

MARS

VULCAN

CUPID

VENUS

NEPTUNE

MINERVA

MERCURY

VESTA

Neptune, Mars, Venus and Cupid,
Vulcan, Minerva, Mercury, and Vesta

II

Mārs, fīlius Iovis et Iūnōnis, erat rōbustus deus bellī. Mīlitēs Mārtem praecipuē adōrābant. Mēnsis Mārtius erat sacer Mārtī. Mārs erat deus ferus et bellicōsus. Sed Mārs erat bonus pater Rōmulī et Remī ex Rhēā Silviā.

rōbust·us -a -um robust, muscular
praecipuē especially mēns·is -is
(*gen pl* -ium) *m* month
fer·us -a -um fierce bellicōs·us -a -um
warlike ex (+ *abl*) by

III

Venus, fīlia Iovis, erat dea pulchra et benigna. Erat dea amōris. Avis Veneris erat tenera columba. Fīlius parvus, Cupīdō, erat Venerī. Puellae Rōmānae Venerem et Cupīdinem praecipuē adōrābant. Cupīdō manibus arcum et sagittās tenēbat. Ālās in dorsō habēbat.

Venus Vener·is *f* Venus
pulcher pulchr·a -um beautiful amor
amōr·is *m* love av·is -is (*gen pl* -ium) *f*
bird tener -a -um tender columb·a -ae *f*
dove Cupīdō Cupīdin·is *m* Cupid

arc·us -ūs *m* bow sagitt·a -ae *f* arrow
āl·a -ae *f* wing dors·um -ī *n* back

IV

Vulcānus erat dūrus fīlius Iovis et Iūnōnis. Erat deus ignis. Vulcānus erat faber ferrārius. Officīna Vulcānī sub monte erat, ubi fulmina Iovis fabricābat. Vulcānus erat claudus.

Vulcān·us -ī *m* Vulcan dūr·us -a -um
tough, hardy ign·is -is (*gen pl* -ium) *m*
fire faber fabr·ī ferrāri·us -ī *m*
blacksmith officīn·a -ae *f* workshop ubi
where fabricābat made
claud·us -a -um lame

V

Minerva erat dea sapientiae et bellī. Ut Mārs, sīc etiam Minerva galeam in capite gerēbat et scūtum magnum manū sinistrā tenēbat. Būbō erat avis sacra Minervae. Minerva erat patrōna discipulōrum.

sapienti·a -ae *f* wisdom
ut . . . sīc etiam as . . . so also gale·a -ae *f*
helmet gerēbat wore scūt·um -ī *n* shield
sinister sinistr·a -um left būbō bubōn·is
m owl patrōn·a -ae *f* patroness
discipul·us -ī *m* student

VI

Mercurius erat fīdus nūntius deōrum deārumque. In pedibus

fīd·us -a -um trusty, faithful
pēs ped·is *m* foot

sandalia cum ālīs gerēbat. In capite
petasum cum ālīs gerēbat. Inter
caelum et terram saepe volābat.
Mercurius erat callidus et astūtus.

sandali·um -ī *n* sandal
petas·us -ī *m* hat
volābat flew
callid·us -a -um clever **astūt·us -a -um**
shrewd

VII

Vesta, soror Iovis, erat virgō pūra.
Parvum templum Vestae in forō
Rōmānō antīquō erat. Templum
erat rotundum. In templō erat flam-
ma aeterna. Sex virginēs Vestālēs
flammam aeternam cūrābant.

soror sorōr·is *f* sister **virgō virgin·is** *f*
virgin **pūr·us -a -um** pure
antīqu·us -a -um ancient
rotund·us -a -um round **flamm·a -ae** *f*
flame **aetern·us -a -um** eternal **sex**
(*indeclinable*) six **Vestāl·is -is -e** Vestal, of
Vesta **cūrābant** took care of, looked after

D. Latīnē responde ad quaestiōnēs.

I 1. Quis erat rēx maris flūminumque?
   2. Quid manū tenēbat?
   3. Quis Neptūnum adōrābat?
   4. Ubi erat domus Neptūnī?

II 5. Quis erat deus bellī?
   6. Quis (*which*) mēnsis erat sacer Mārtī?
   7. Dā (*give*) nōmina eius fīliōrum.
   8. Dā nōmen mātris geminōrum.

III 9. Quae (*what*) erat avis Veneris?
   10. Quis erat parvus fīlius Veneris?
   11. Quid Cupīdō manibus tenēbat?
   12. Quid in dorsō habēbat Cupīdō?

IV 13. Quis erat deus ignis?
   14. Dā nōmen mātris Vulcānī.
   15. Ubi erat officīna Vulcānī?
   16. Quid Vulcānus ibi fabricābat?

V 17. Quis erat dea sapientiae?
   18. Quid Minerva in capite gerēbat?
   19. Quid manū sinistrā tenēbat?
   20. Quae (*what*) avis erat sacra Minervae?

VI 21. Quis erat nūntius deōrum deārumque?

22. Quid in pedibus gerēbat?

23. Ubi saepe volābat?

VII 24. Ubi erat templum Vestae?

25. Quis flammam aeternam Vestae cūrābat?

E. Give one Latin adjective (with the correct ending) that describes the following deities.

1. Mārs   3. Vesta   5. Venus

2. Mercurius   4. Vulcānus

WORD
POWER

F. Give the Latin source word for each of the following derivatives. If the Latin source word is a verb, give the infinitive; if it is a noun or an adjective, give the nominative singular.

1. astute   ____   7. eternity   ____

2. rotunda   ____   8. purity   ____

3. amorous   ____   9. patronize   ____

4. venereal   ____   10. benign   ____

5. arch   ____   11. dorsal   ____

6. bellicose   ____   12. office   ____

CHAPTER 10

Adjectives, Third Declension

THOUGHT FOR TODAY

Ubi voluntās, ibi via est. Where there is a will, there is a way.

THIRD DECLENSION: TWO ENDINGS		THIRD DECLENSION: THREE ENDINGS		
MASC. & FEM.	NEUTER	MASCULINE	FEMININE	NEUTER
facilis easy		**ācer** sharp, shrill		
SINGULAR				
NOM. facil·*is*	facil·*e*	**ācer**	ācr·*is*	ācr·*e*
GEN. facil·*is*	facil·*is*	ācr·*is*	ācr·*is*	ācr·*is*
DAT. facil·*ī*	facil·*ī*	ācr·*ī*	ācr·*ī*	ācr·*ī*
ACC. facil·*em*	facil·*e*	ācr·*em*	ācr·*em*	ācr·*e*
ABL. facil·*ī*	facil·*ī*	ācr·*ī*	ācr·*ī*	ācr·*ī*
PLURAL				
NOM. facil·*ēs*	facil·*ia*	ācr·*ēs*	ācr·*ēs*	ācr·*ia*
GEN. facil·*ium*	facil·*ium*	ācr·*ium*	ācr·*ium*	ācr·*ium*
DAT. facil·*ibus*	facil·*ibus*	ācr·*ibus*	ācr·*ibus*	ācr·*ibus*
ACC. facil·*ēs*	facil·*ia*	ācr·*ēs*	ācr·*ēs*	ācr·*ia*
ABL. facil·*ibus*	facil·*ibus*	ācr·*ibus*	ācr·*ibus*	ācr·*ibus*

THIRD DECLENSION: ONE ENDING

	MASC. & FEM.	NEUTER	MASC. & FEM.	NEUTER	MASC. & FEM.	NEUTER
	fēlīx lucky; happy		**prūdēns** prudent, wise		**vetus** old	

SINGULAR

	MASC. & FEM.	NEUTER	MASC. & FEM.	NEUTER	MASC. & FEM.	NEUTER
NOM.	fēlīx	fēlīx	prūdēns	prūdēns	vetus	vetus
GEN.	fēlīc·*is*	fēlīc·*is*	prūdent·*is*	prūdent·*is*	veter·*is*	veter·*is*
DAT.	fēlīc·*ī*	fēlīc·*ī*	prūdent·*ī*	prūdent·*ī*	veter·*ī*	veter·*ī*
ACC.	fēlīc·*em*	fēlīx	prūdent·*em*	prūdēns	veter·*em*	vetus
ABL.	fēlīc·*ī*	fēlīc·*ī*	prūdent·*ī*	prūdent·*ī*	veter·*e*	veter·*e*

PLURAL

	MASC. & FEM.	NEUTER	MASC. & FEM.	NEUTER	MASC. & FEM.	NEUTER
NOM.	fēlīc·*ēs*	fēlīc·*ia*	prūdent·*ēs*	prūdent·*ia*	veter·*ēs*	veter·*a*
GEN.	fēlīc·*ium*	fēlīc·*ium*	prūdent·*ium*	prūdent·*ium*	veter·*um*	veter·*um*
DAT.	fēlīc·*ibus*	fēlīc·*ibus*	prūdent·*ibus*	prūdent·*ibus*	veter·*ibus*	veter·*ibus*
ACC.	fēlīc·*ēs*	fēlīc·*ia*	prūdent·*ēs*	prūdent·*ia*	veter·*ēs*	veter·*a*
ABL.	fēlīc·*ibus*	fēlīc·*ibus*	prūdent·*ibus*	prūdent·*ibus*	veter·*ibus*	veter·*ibus*

NOTES

1) As we saw in the previous chapter, adjectives ending in **-us -a -um** belong to the first and second declensions.

Examples **cār·*us*** *m*   **cār·*a*** *f*   **cār·*um*** *n*   dear

Some adjectives of the first and second declension end in **-er, -era, -erum** and some adjectives end in **-er** in the masculine nominative singular, but drop the **e** in all other forms.

Examples **mis*er*** *m*   **miser·*a*** *f*   **miser·*um*** *n*   poor, pitiful, miserable

pulch*er* *m*   **pulchr·*a*** *f*   **pulchr·*um*** *f*   beautiful; handsome

2) On the other hand, adjectives of the third declension typically end in **-is -is -e** in the nominative masculine, feminine, and neuter. Adjectives of this type with two endings are the most common of the third-declension adjectives.

Examples **facil·*is*** *m*   **facil·*is*** *f*   **facil·*e*** *n*   easy

omn·*is* *m*   **omn·*is*** *f*   **omn·*e*** *n*   every, all

Some adjectives of the third declension have three endings and end in **-er, -eris, -ere** and some adjectives end in **-er** in the masculine nominative singular, but drop the **e** in all other forms.

Examples	**celer** *m*	**celer·is** *f*	**celer·e** *n*	swift
	ācer *m*	**ācr·is** *f*	**ācr·e** *n*	sharp, bitter

3) Other adjectives of the third declension, ending in **-āns, -ēns** or **-x,** have the same ending for the nominative masculine, feminine, and neuter. There is one adjective that ends in **-us.** These adjectives are called single-ending adjectives.

Examples	**amāns** *m*	**amāns** *f*	**amāns** *n*	loving
	innocēns *m*	**innocēns** *f*	**innocēns** *n*	innocent
	fēlīx *m*	**fēlīx** *f*	**fēlīx** *n*	happy; lucky
	vetus *m*	**vetus** *f*	**vetus** *n*	old

Exercises

A. Expand your Latin vocabulary. The meanings of adjectives like **prūdēns** should be obvious. Take the full stem from the genitive form **prūdent*is*,** drop off the ending, and you have your English meaning. Do the same for the following adjectives.

Example	*Nominative*	**prūdēns**	*Genitive*	**prūdentis**
	Base	**prūdent-**	*Translation*	*prudent*

1. innocēns	5. intelligēns	9. excellēns	13. silēns
2. benevolēns	6. ēminēns	10. cōnfīdēns	14. urgēns
3. clēmēns	7. indulgēns	11. neglegēns	15. vehemēns
4. currēns	8. imminēns	12. prōminēns	

B. In the following exercise, the meanings of adjectives of the first and second declension should be familiar to you since they occurred in earlier chapters. The meanings of adjectives of the third declension can easily be guessed from their English derivatives, as we just saw. And the endings will indicate that they belong to the third declension. In case of doubt, consult the vocabulary at the end of the book. Supply the feminine and neuter forms and meanings.

	masculine	feminine	neuter	translation
Examples	benignus	**benigna**	**benignum**	*benign*
	patiēns	**patiēns**	**patiēns**	*patient*
	līberālis	**līberālis**	**līberāle**	*liberal, generous*

1. prīmus
2. nōbilis
3. ultimus
4. prūdēns
5. parvus
6. difficilis
7. antīquus
8. dīligēns
9. obēdiēns
10. magnus
11. violēns
12. patiēns
13. plēnus
14. rūrālis
15. novus
16. pulcher
17. sinister
18. immortālis
19. altus
20. recēns
21. omnipotēns
22. clārus
23. praesēns
24. perīculōsus

C. Make the adjective **fēlīx fēlīc·is** (*happy; lucky*) agree with the nouns in the following expressions. The nouns that the adjectives modify come before the adjectives.

1. Amīci meī sunt ____.
2. Cum amīcīs ____ lūdō.
4. Deī vītās ____ dūcunt.
5. Quis parentēs ____ nōn habet?
6. Faciem puellae ____ vīdi.
7. Faciēs magistrārum ____ vidī.
8. Verba ____ audīvimus.

D. Make the adjective **vetus veter·is** agree with the nouns in italics in the following sentences.

1. Sunt multa *templa* ____ in forō.
2. Statuae deōrum in *templīs* ____ sunt.
3. Mūrī *templōrum* ____ pictūrās pulchrās habent.
4. *Rōmānī* ____ in templīs deum adōrant.
5. *Viae* prope templa sunt ____.
6. Ego cum *amīcīs* ____ templa vīsitō.

E. Make the adjective **prūdēns prūdēnt·is** agree with the nouns in italics in the following sentences.
1. Rōmānī *cōnsulēs* ____ habēbant.
2. ____ *līberī* parentēs suōs amant.

3. *Frāter et soror* mea sunt ____.
4. *Mēns* ____ rārō errat.
5. Ego cum *virīs* ____ habitō.
6. Omnēs verba *virōrum* ____ auscultant.

F. Convert the following expressions from the singular to the plural. Keep the verb in the infinitive.

1. esse fortis mīles
2. habitāre in oppidō vetere
3. dare respōnsum difficile
4. stāre prope flūmen celere
5. vocāre nōmen discipulī dīligentis
6. dare dōnum deō immortālī

The Greeks and Romans enjoyed romantic tales, but instead of writing novels about people in everyday life, they preferred to use myths for their tales of romance. For instance, Venus is said to have married Anchises and to have become the mother of Aeneas and the grandmother of Ascanius, also called Julus, and as such became the founder of the Julian family tree, to which Julius Caesar and Augustus belonged.

Ovid, a Roman poet (43 B.C.-A.D. 18) collected a large number of love stories that involved transformations. In fact, he called his book "Transformations," or, in Latin, **Metamorphōsēs**. Many of these love affairs involved gods and human beings. In many instances, the consequences proved tragic for the human beings who became involved with the gods. The following story of Daphne, daughter of a river god, and Apollo is typical of such romances.

Apollō Daphnēn Petit.
Apollo Chases After Daphne.

I

Daphnē, nympha innocēns, est fīlia ēlegāns Pēnēī flūminis celeris in Thessaliā. In obscūrīs silvīs Thessaliae errāre amat. Omnēs iuvenēs Daphnēn amant et eam in mātrimōnium dūcěre dēsīderant; timida Daphnē autem omnēs amantēs recūsat.

nymph·a -ae *f* nymph
Pēnē·us -ī *m* river god **celer celer·is -e** fast **Thessali·a -ae** *f* Thessaly (district north of Greece) **errāre** to roam
iuven·is -is *m* young man
eam her **timid·us -a -um** shy, timid
amāns amant·is *m* lover **recūsat** turns down

Daphne becomes a laurel tree.

II

Etiam trīstis pater saepe fīliam interrogat: "Daphnē, mea dulcis fīlia, quandō mihi nepōs erit? Iam vetus sum et nōndum nepōtem dulcem habeō." Daphnē autem respondet: "Optō, Ō pater, esse virgō in perpetuum, perinde ac Diāna. Vēnātiō in silvīs est mea dēlectātiō."

trīst·is -is -e sad **interrogat** asks, questions **dulc·is -is- -e** sweet, delightful **quandō?** when? **nepōs nepōt·is** *m* grandson **erit** will be **iam** already **nōndum** not yet **respondet** replies **optō** desire **virgō virgin·is** *f* unmarried girl, virgin **in perpetuum** forever **perinde ac** just like **vēnātiō vēnātiōn·is** *f* hunting **dēlectātiō dēlectātiōn·is** *f* (source of) delight

III

Quōdam diē Apollō Daphnēn ēlegantem videt. Statim Apollō nympham adamat et eam in mātrimōnium dūcĕre dēsīderat. Per silvās nympham celerem petit et acclāmat: "Ego nōn sum amāns hūmānus; nōn sum pauper rūsticus; sum omnipotēns deus. Sī mea uxor eris, nōmen tuum erit illūstre in perpetuum."

quōdam diē one day **Apollō Apollin·is** *m* Apollo **statim** immediately **adamat** falls in love with **petit** chases (after) **acclāmat** yells to **hūmān·us -a -um** human **pauper pauper·is** *(single ending adj)* poor **rūstic·us -ī** *m* hick **omnipotēns omnipōtent·is** powerful **eris, erit** will be **illūstr·is -is -e** famous

IV

Daphnē autem per silvās properat. Apollō audāx nympham timidam petit. Dēnique Daphnē est dēfessa. Ut nympha ad patris flūmen appropinquat, ōrat: "Pater, servā mē! Servā fīliam tuam. Mūtā formam meam. Deinceps ego Apollinī nōn diūtius grāta erō."

properat rushes **audāx audāc·is** *(single ending adj)* bold **dēnique** finally **dēfess·us -a -um** exhausted **ut** as **appropinquat ad** (+ *acc*) approaches **servā** save **mūtā** change **deinceps** then, after that **nōn diūtius** no longer **grāt·us -a -um** attractive **erō** will be

V

Pater vōcem ācrem fīliae trīstis audit et statim nympham mūtat in arborem. Nōn diūtius comam habet

vōx vōc·is *f* voice **ācer ācr·is -e** shrill

com·a -ae *f* hair **foli·um -i** *n* leaf

sed folia; nōn diūtius bracchia lēvia habet sed rāmōs. Nunc Daphnē nōn iam trīstis est; est laurus fēlīx.

bracchi·um -ī *n* arm **rām·us -ī** *m* branch **lēv·is -is -e** smooth **laur·us -ī** *f* laurel tree

VI

Trīstis Apollō laurum spectat et dīcit: "Numquam uxor mea eris. Sed utique mea laurus semper eris. Tua folia ēlegantia corōnābunt fēlīcēs victōrēs in omnibus certāminibus.

spectat looks at
numquam never
utique at least
corōnābunt will crown
certāmen certāmin·is *n* contest

G. Answer the following questions based on the story you have just read in English or in Latin.

I   1. Where does Daphne live?
    2. What is unusual about her father?
    3. Where does Daphne love to roam?
    4. Who wants to marry Daphne?
    5. Why does she turn down all lovers?

II   6. Why does her father want her to marry?
    7. Why does he feel that his request is urgent?
    8. In what way does Daphne want to be like Diana?
    9. What is Daphne's source of delight?

III 10. Which god sees Daphne?
    11. What are his intentions?
    12. What does he say he is not?
    13. What does he boast of being?
    14. What does he promise her if she marries him?

IV 15. What is Daphne's reaction?
    16. Why does she finally stop running?
    17. When or where does she address her father?
    18. What does she beg her father to do?
    19. Why does she want her father to do that?

V 20. Into what does her father change Daphne?
    21. What happens to her hair?
    22. What happens to her arms?

VI 23. What does Apollo say about the transformation?
    24. How will laurel leaves be used in the future?

H. Some words are missing in the following Latin passage. First read the entire story to get its meaning. Then complete each of the blanks with one Latin word, taken from the pool of words below. Look for contextual clues to help you supply the missing words.

Example

Trōia est oppidum in Asiā. Trōiānī oppidum occupant. Sed Graecī in mille __1__ nāvigant in Asiam et cum __2__ pugnant. Mūrī Trōiae erant altī et __3__. Intrā mūrōs domūs erant __4__.
Answers: 1. nāvibus 2. Trōiānīs 3. crassī 4. sēcūrae

WORD POOL

Apollō	diē	laurum	serva
audīvit	flūmen	montibus	silvīs
dēlectātiō	folia	nepōtem	Thessaliā
dūcĕre	formam	rāmōs	virgō

Daphnē, nympha ēlegāns et fēlīx, in __1__ habitābat. Pater nōn erat homō mortālis sed __2__. Daphnē nōn in urbe sed rūrī habitat. .In obscūrīs __3__ errāre amat. Nōn amātōrēs sed vēnātiō erat Daphnēs __4__. Omnēs iuvenēs Daphnēn amant et eam in mātrimōnium __5__ dēsīderant. Trīstis pater Daphnēn interrogat: "Quandō ego __6__ habēbō?" Daphnē respondet : "Ego marītum nōn dēsīderō. Ego in perpetuum erō __7__. Ego fēlix sum quandō in __8__ errō."

Quōdam __9__ Daphnē in silvīs errat. Deus __10__ nympham videt et eam adamat et eam petit. Daphnē autem aufugit (*runs away*) et ōrat patrem: "O pater, ego magnō in perīculō sum. Sī mē amās, __11__ mē! Mūtā __12__ meam!" Pater ācrem vōcem fīliae trīstis __13__. Statim pater mūtat formam ēlegantem fīliae in __14__. Mūtat comam in __15__. Mūtat bracchia lēvia fīliae in __16__.

I. Expand your Latin vocabulary. Many adjectives of the third declension ending in the suffix **-ālis** are derived from nouns. The suffix **-ālis** is added to the base, or stem, of the noun. Remember that you find the complete stem of a noun by dropping the ending of the genitive form. Observing the examples, you will easily be able to derive adjectives from their related nouns.

Examples

NOUN	MEANING	GENITIVE	STEM	ADJECTIVE	MEANING
rēx	*king*	**rēgis**	rēg-	**rēgālis**	*regal*
fīnis	*end*	**fīnis**	fīn-	**fīnālis**	*final*

VOCABULARY

1. mūrus   wall   ____
2. tempus   time   ____
3. dorsum   back   ____
4. mors   death   ____
5. vīta   life   ____
6. caput   head   ____
7. nōmen   name   ____
8. mēns   mind   ____

9. corpus   body   ____
10. pēs   foot   ____
11. virgō   girl   ____
12. nāvigātiō   navigation   ____
13. fundāmentum   foundation   ____
14. regiō   region   ____
15. agricultūra   agriculture   ____

WORD POWER

J. Give the Latin source word for each of the following English derivatives. If the Latin source word is a verb, give the infinitive. If it is a noun or adjective, give the nominative singular.

1. coronation   ____
2. juvenile   ____
3. nepotism   ____
4. response   ____
5. pauper   ____
6. rustic   ____

7. illustrious   ____
8. err   ____
9. human   ____
10. omnipotent   ____
11. audacious   ____
12. acclamation ____

CHAPTER 11

Comparison of Adjectives

THOUGHT
FOR
TODAY

Ad māiōrem glōriam Deī. To the greater glory of God.

In Latin, as in English, there are three degrees of comparison: the *positive*, the *comparative*, and the *superlative*. In English we regularly form the comparative of an adjective by adding *-er* to its positive form, e.g. *higher*, and we form the superlative by adding *-est* to the positive degree, e.g., *highest*.

I. FORMS

1. In Latin **the comparative degree** is regularly formed by adding **-ior** for masculine and feminine and **-ius** for neuter to the base of the positive. An adjective of the first and second declension, e.g., **alt·us -a -um** *(high, deep)* becomes an adjective of the third declension in the comparative degree, that is, **alt***ior* alt*ius*. **The superlative** is regularly formed by adding *-issim·us -a -um* to the base of the positive. Remember that with adjectives of the third declension it is the genitive case that gives you the clue to the base.

POSITIVE	COMPARATIVE	SUPERLATIVE
MASC. FEM. NEUTER	MASC. & FEM. NEUTER	MASC. FEM. NEUTER
alt·us -a -um high	**alt***ior* alt*ius* higher	**alt***issim·us -a -um* highest
prūdēns wise	**prūdent***ior* prūdent*ius* wiser	**prūdent***issim·us -a -um* wisest
fēlīx happy	**fēlīc***ior* fēlīc*ius* happier	**fēlīc***issim·us -a -um* happiest

You remember that **prūdēns** and **fēlīx** are single-ending adjectives.

2. **Adjectives ending in -er** of the first and second declension as well as those of the third declension form the superlative by adding **-rim·*us* -*a* -*um*** instead of **-issim·*us* -*a* -*um*** to the base of the nominative.

POSITIVE	COMPARATIVE	SUPERLATIVE
MASC. FEM. NEUTER	MASC. & FEM. NEUTER	MASC. FEM. NEUTER
miser miser·*a* -*um* sad	miser*ior* miser*ius*	miser*rim·us* -*a* -*um*
sacer sacr·*a* -*um* sacred	sacr*ior* sacr*ius*	sacer*rim·us* -*a* -*um*
celer celer·*is* -*e* fast	celer*ior* celer*ius*	celer*rim·us* -*a* -*um*
ācer ācr·*is* -*e* sharp, bitter	ācr*ior* ācr*ius*	ācer*rim·us* -*a* -*um*

NOTES

1) Adjectives like **miser** or **celer**, which retain the **e** as they are being declined in the positive degree, retain the e in the comparative degree.

2) Adjectives like **sacer** or **ācer**, which drop the e as they are being declined in the positive degree, drop the e in the comparative degree.

3. **Five adjectives ending in -lis** (**facilis** easy, **difficilis** difficult, **similis** similar, like, **dissimilis** dissimilar, unlike, **humilis** low, humble) form the superlative by adding **-lim·*us* -*a* -*um*** to the base.

POSITIVE	COMPARATIVE	SUPERLATIVE
MASC. FEM. NEUTER	MASC. & FEM. NEUTER	MASC. FEM. NEUTER
facil·*is* facil·*e* easy	facil*ior* facil*ius*	facil*lim·us* -*a* -*um*

DECLENSION OF THE COMPARATIVE

alt·*us* -*a* -*um* high; deep

	SINGULAR		PLURAL	
	MASC. & FEM.	NEUTER	MASC. & FEM.	NEUTER
NOM.	altior	altius	altiōr·*ēs*	altiōr·*a*
GEN.	altiōr·*is*	altiōr·*is*	altiōr·*um*	altiōr·*um*
DAT.	altiōr·*ī*	altiōr·*ī*	altiōr·*ibus*	altiōr·*ibus*
ACC.	altiōr·*em*	altius	altiōr·*ēs*	altiōr·*ēs*
ABL.	altiōr·*e*	altiōr·*e*	altiōr·*ibus*	altiōr·*ibus*

A. Change the adjective in italics from the positive to the comparative.

Example

domus *cārī* **amīcī**   the home of a *dear* friend
domus *cāriōris* **amīcī**   the home of a *dearer* friend

VOCABULARY

certāre to compete   **cognōscĕre** to find out, learn
vīvĕre to live

1. audīre verba *prūdentis* virī
2. esse fīnis *longī* itineris
3. aedificāre *pulchrum* templum
4. vīvĕre cum *sincērīs* amīcīs
5. vīvĕre in rēgnō *potentis* rēgis
6. habēre *longam* ōrātiōnem
7. dare nōmen *novae* urbī
8. esse dux *fortium* mīlitum
9. certāre cum *validō* āthlētā
10. cognōscĕre nōmina *clārōrum* virōrum

B. Read over each sentence. Then complete it by supplying the correct form of the adjective in italics in the comparative degree.

Example

Nōmen Remī est *clārum;* **nōmen Rōmulī est** *clārius.*
The name of Remus is famous; the name of Romulus is more famous.

1. Mūrus Trōiae erat *altus;* mūrus Rōmae erat ____.
2. Aquae Tiberis sunt *altae;* aquae Padī sunt ____.
3. Nāvēs Graecae erant *celerēs;* nāvēs Rōmānae erant ____.
4. Turnus erat *nōbilis;* Aenēās erat ____.
5. Iūnō est *potēns,* sed Iuppiter est ____.
6. Nōmen Priamī est *clārum,* sed nōmen Aenēae est ____.
7. Via ad Campāniam est *longa;* via ad Umbriam est ____.
8. Faustulus in *humilī* casā habitābat; Numitor in ____ casā habitābat.
9. Faustulus erat *fēlīx;* Lārentia erat ____.
10. Rēgia Priamī erat *splendida;* rēgia Dīdōnis erat ____.

C. Read over each sentence. Then complete it by supplying the correct form of the comparative and the superlative of the adjective in italics.

Mea vīta est *difficilis;* tua vīta est ____; vīta meī amīcī est ____.

Mea vīta est difficilis; tua vīta est *difficilior;* vīta meī amīcī est difficillima.

My life is difficult; your life is more difficult; the life of my friend is most difficult.

VOCABULARY

av·us -ī *m* grandfather   **humil·is -is -e** low   **sedēbat** sat`

1. Mea soror est *prūdēns;* meus frāter est ____; mea māter est ____.
2. Diāna est dea *potēns;* Iūnō est dea ____; Iuppiter est deus ____.
3. Ego sum *celer;* amīcus meus est ____; āthlēta est ____.
4. Iūnō est *pulchra;* Diāna est ____; Venus est ____.
5. Mōns Palātīnus est *altus;* Mōns Capitōlīnus est ____; Mōns Albānus est ____.
6. Fīlius est *similis* frātrī; est ____ patrī; est ____ avō.
7. Via Latīna est *longa;* Via Flāminia est ____; Via Appia est ____.
8. Meus pater est *ācer;* tuus pater est ____; pater meī amīcī est ____.
9. Nōmen Diānae est *sacrum;* nōmen Apollinis est ____; nōmen Iovis est ____.
10. Montēs Siciliae sunt *altī;* montēs Italiae sunt ____; montēs Graeciae sunt ____.
11. Ego vītam *difficilem* dūcō; parentēs meī vītam ____ dūcunt; magistrae vītam ____ dūcunt.
12. Pater sub arbore *humilī* sedēbat; frāter meus sub arbore ____ sedēbat; soror mea sub arbore ____ sedēbat.

II. USES AND MEANINGS

1. The comparative can have several meanings.

Example   **Hoc iter erat longius.**   This trip was longer. This trip was rather long. This trip was too long.

If the word **quam** *than* occurs in the sentence, **longius** will mean *longer.* If there is no other term of comparison, that is, if **hoc iter** is not compared with anything else, then **longius** will mean *rather long* or *too long.*

NOTE

Where there is ambiguity, the adverb **nimis** (*too*) can be used with the positive form.

Example   **Hoc iter est nimis longum.**   This trip is too long.

2. The superlative, too, can have several meanings.

Examples

Rōmulus erat prūdentissimus.	Romulus was very wise.
Rōmulus erat prūdentissimus omnium.	Romulus was the wisest of all.
Rōmulus est prūdentissimus.	Romulus is most wise.

NOTE

The Romans at times expressed the superlative by adding the prefix **per-** to the positive degree.

Example

perlong·us -a -um very long   **peracūt·us -a -um** very sharp

3. When we compare two items in English, we generally use the word **than.** The Romans expressed this idea in two ways:

Example

or

Alba Longa est vetustior *quam* **Rōma.**
Alba Longa est vetustior **Rōmā.**

} Alba Longa is older *than* Rome.

Both sentences mean exactly the same thing. In the first sentence, the two items that are being compared (**Alba Longa** and **Rōma**) are in the same case (the nominative). In the second sentence, instead of using **quam** followed by the nominative, the Romans put the second term of comparison (**Rōmā**) into the ablative case. This use of the ablative is called the *ablative of comparison.*

4. Sometimes a word such as **paulō** (*a little*, literally *by a little*) or **multō** (*much*, literally *by much*) is used with comparatives to indicate the degree of difference. This usage is called the *ablative of degree of difference.*

Example

or

Via Appia est *multō* **longior quam Via Latīna.**
Via Appia est *multō* **longior Viā Latīnā.**

} The Appian Way is *much* longer than the Via Latina.

Example

or

Mōns Capitōlīnus est *paulō* **altior quam Mōns Palātīnus.**
Mōns Capitōlīnus est *paulō* **altior Monte Palātīnō.**

} The Capitoline Hill is *a little* higher than the Palatine Hill.

III. IRREGULAR FORMS

There are irregular forms of the comparative and superlative in English. For example, *good, better,* best; bad, worse, worst. So also there are irregular comparatives and superlatives in Latin. There are some Latin adjectives that lack a positive, comparative, or a superlative form. So also in English; there is no positive or superlative form, for example, of *former.*

IRREGULAR COMPARATIVE FORMS

POSITIVE	COMPARATIVE	SUPERLATIVE
MASC. FEM. NEUTER	MASC. FEM. NEUTER	MASC. FEM. NEUTER
bon·*us -a -um* good	mel*ior* mel*ius* better	optim·*us -a -um* best
mal·*us -a um* bad	pē*ior* pē*ius* worse	pessim·*us -a -um* worst
parv·*us -a -um* small	min*or* min*us* smaller	minim·*us -a -um* smallest
magn·*us -a -um* big	mā*ior* mā*ius* bigger	maxim·*us -a -um* biggest
mult·*us -a -um* much	plūs *(neut. noun)* more	plūrim·*us -a -um* most
mult·*ī -ae -a* many	plūr·*ēs -a* more	plūrim·*ī -ae -a* most
īnfer·*us -a -um* below	īnfer*ior* īnfer*ius* lower	īnfim·*us -a - um* lowest
		īm·*us -a -um* lowest
super·*us -a -um* above	super*ior* super*ius* higher	suprēm·*us -a -um* highest
		summ·*us -a -um* highest
vetus, veter·*is* old	vetust*ior* vetust*ius* older	veterrim·*us -a -um* oldest
	pr*ior* pr*ius* former	prīm·*us -a -um* first
	prop*ior* prop*ius* nearer	proxim·*us -a -um* nearest, next
	ulter*ior* ulter*ius* farther	ultim·*us -a -um* farthest

NOTES

1) The declension of **melior melius** and the other irregular comparatives is the same as that of **altior altius.**

2) **Parvus** can mean *young* or *small.* **Minor** or **minor nātū** means *younger* (literally: *less by birth*); **minimus** or **minimus nātū** means *youngest.* **Māior** or **māior nātū** means *older;* **maximus** or **maximus nātū** means *oldest.*

3) The comparative form **plūs** is a neuter noun rather than an adjective. Therefore, if a noun follows it, that noun is put into the genitive case.

Example   **Rōmulus plūs cibī dēsīderat.**   Romulus wants more food (lit: more *of* food).

D. In the following sentences, use the ablative of comparison in place of **quam** and the nominative. Look at the example given above (in II-3).

1. Numitor erat paulō māior nātū quam Aemūlius.
2. Rōmulus nōn erat māior nātū quam Remus.
3. Mōns Aventīnus est propior Tiberī quam Mōns Palātīnus.
4. Ardea est minor quam Rōma.
5. Pāx est multō melior quam bellum.
6. Tarquinius Superbus erat pēior quam Tarquinius Prīscus.
7. Caesar erat multō potentior quam Pompēius Magnus.
8. Vergilius est clārior poēta quam Catullus.

E. In the following sentences, supply the correct forms of the comparative and superlative of the adjective in the positive degree.

Example

> Mārcus est parvus. Sextus est ____. Cornēlius est ____.
> **Mārcus est parvus. Sextus est *minor*. Cornēlius est *minimus*.**
> Marcus is small (young). Sextus is smaller (younger). Cornelius is the smallest (youngest).

1. Ascanius erat clārus. Aenēās erat ____. Anchīsēs erat ____.
2. Diāna est dea bona. Iūnō est dea ____. Venus est dea ____.
3. Achātēs erat fortis. Turnus erat ____. Aenēās erat ____.
4. Priamus erat vetus. Eius pater erat ____. Eius avus erat ____.
5. Mūrus Ardeae erat validus. Mūrus Albae Longae erat ____. Mūrus Rōmae erat ____.
6. Neptūnus est deus potēns. Mārs est deus ____. Iuppiter est deus ____.
7. Templum Apollinis erat sacrum. Templum Vestae erat ____. Templum Iovis erat ____.
8. Casa mea erat humilis. Casa tua erat ____. Casa Faustulī erat ____.
9. Diāna erat celeris. Mārs erat ____. Mercurius erat ____.
10. Ego sum laetus. Frāter meus est ____. Soror mea est ____.
11. Ego amīcōs bonōs habeō. Marcus amīcōs ____ habet. Claudia amīcās ____ habet.
12. Rōmulus in rēgiā magnā habitābat. Ancus Mārcius in rēgiā ____ habitābat. Tarquinius Superbus in rēgiā ____ habitābat.
13. Ardea multās viās habet. Alba Longa ____ viās habet. Rōma autem ____ viās habet.
14. Familia mea in domō vetere habitat. Cōnsōbrīnus meus in domō ____ habitat. Amīcī meī in domibus ____ habitant.

15. Dīdō fortūnam *(luck)* malam habēbat. Daphnē fortūnam ___ habēbat. Thisbē autem fortūnam ___ habēbat.

16. Multī hominēs Athēnās vīsitant. ___ Rōmam vīsitant. Sed ___ domī manent.

17. Crassus erat dux bonus. Pompēius erat dux ___. Caesar erat dux ___.

18. Mīsēnum erat oppidum magnum. Vēiī erant oppidum ___. Capua erat oppidum ___.

LOVE AND MARRIAGE
ROMAN STYLE

If you could have visited Rome in ancient days, you would have been surprised to learn how young boys and girls were when they became engaged. Cicero, the greatest Roman lawyer, politician, and caring father, arranged for his daughter Tullia's engagement when she was only ten years old and for her marriage when she was only thirteen. This arrangement probably was not unusual at that time; and it shows that these matters were controlled entirely by the parents, as is still the case in some countries in modern times. It was an arrangement designed to make sure that property stayed in the right hands. If, however, there was a strong dislike beween the boy and the girl, the engagement could be broken off.

In the early days of Rome, until 445 B.C., marriage between members of the wealthy patrician class and the poor plebeian class was forbidden by law. Marriages between Roman citizens and foreigners were legal, but the children of such marriages were not Roman citizens unless the father was a Roman citizen. If a Roman girl married a non-Roman, the children were not considered Romans unless Rome had a special treaty conferring the right of intermarriage on the husband's city.

When the day of the wedding arrived, the girl dedicated her dolls to the household gods to symbolize that the carefree days of her childhood were over. The bride **(nova nūpt·a -ae** *f)* wore an orange-colored veil and a long white dress. Her hair was divided by a spear-shaped comb into six strands, and for the first time she wore ribbons in her hair. On her head, she wore a crown of flowers.

The Latin verb for getting married was not the same for the boy and the girl. For the girl, the verb was **nūbĕre** (+ *dat).* **Nūbĕre** means "to wear a veil." The expression for the boy was **in mātrimōnium dūcĕre** or **uxōrem dūcĕre** "to lead into matrimony" or "to lead the bride home", since this

Roman wedding

"taking home of the bride" was one of the official acts of a marriage. **Mātrimōnium** means "motherhood."

The bride waited at her father's home for the bridegroom **(novus marīt·us -ī** *m)* to come to take her to his home. Before he took her home, the omens were consulted. May was a particularly ill-omened month. The most favorable time for marriage was the second half of June. If the omens were good, the bridal pair declared their consent by joining right hands at the direction of the matron of honor, who acted as the representative of the goddess Juno, the patroness of marriage. The words spoken were not "I do" but

"Ubi Gāius, ego Gāia" (*Where Gaius is, there I, Gaia, will be.*) This formula remained unchanged over the centuries, no matter what the names of the bride or groom.

The wedding reception was then held at the home of the bride, ending with a banquet. Toward evening, the bridegroom conducted his bride to his home, accompanied by a procession of relatives and friends. At the head of the procession were three boys. One of the boys carried the lighted wedding torch with which the bride would light the fireplace in the home of the groom. The other two boys led the bride by the hand. The rest of the procession, including flute players, followed behind, singing wedding songs. On arriving at the home of the groom, the bride anointed the doorposts with fat and olive oil and wrapped strands of wool around the doorposts. She was then carried across the threshold to make sure that she wouldn't stumble as she entered, since that would have been regarded as a bad omen.

Once inside the home, the bride lighted the fire in the hearth with the torch. When the torch was put out, she threw it to the guests for good luck, just as a bride today throws her bouquet to the young ladies in her bridal group. The bridegroom then gave her fire and water as a sign of their future life together. The bride then gave her husband a dowry from her father, which would have to be returned to him in case of death or divorce. The dowry consisted of money or land.

Well, that was love and marriage Roman style. Do you prefer it or our modern style?

Now read this love story of a boy named Pyramus and a girl named Thisbe, which was first told by the poet Publius Ovidius Naso (43 B.C.–A.D. 18), whom we call Ovid.

> ### Pȳramus et Thisbē Erant Amātōrēs.
> Pyramus and Thisbe Were Lovers.

I

Pȳramus et Thisbē domōs adiacentēs occupābant. Pȳramus erat pulcherrimus iuvenis in urbe; nūlla virgō in urbe erat pulchrior aut venustior quam Thisbē. Tempore

adiacēns adiacent·is adjacent **occupābant** occupied **iuven·is -is** *m* young man **pulcher pulchr·a -um** handsome; beautiful **nūll·us -a -um** no **venust·us -a -um** charming **tempore** in

Thisbe finding dying
Pyramus

amor inter iuvenem et virginem
magis magisque crēvit.

time **amor amōr·is** *m* love **magis magisque** more and more **crēvit** grew

II

Pȳramus vērō Thisbēn in
mātrimōnium dūcĕre dēsīderābat.
Parentēs autem mātrimōnium prohibuērunt. Sed quod parentēs
prohibēre nōn poterant, erat amor
inter amantēs.

vērō in fact

parēns parent·is *m/f* parent
prohibuērunt prohibited, prevented
quod what
poterant were able
amāns amant·is *m/f* lover

III

Quōdam diē duo amantēs cōnsilium sēcrētum cēpērunt: fūrtim
rēpĕre ē domō posterā nocte et con-

cōnsili·um -ī *n* plan
cēpērunt formed *(a plan)* **fūrtim** secretly
rēpĕre to sneak **poster·us -a -um**

venīre extrā urbem sub quādam mōrō. Illa mōrus erat prope frīgidissimum fontem.

following **convenīre** to meet **quīdam quaedam quoddam** a certain **mōr·us -ī** *f* mulberry tree **frīgid·us -a -um** cold **fōns font·is** *m* spring

IV

Thisbē prīma ad mōrum pervēnit et sub arbore cōnsēdit. Ecce leō, ōre cruentō ā recente caede, ad fontem vēnit. Thisbē territa in proximam spēluncam fūgit. Ut fūgit, vēlāmen dēmīsit. Leō vēlāmen ōre cruentō laniāvit. Postquam leō aquam ex fonte pōtāvit, in silvam rediit.

pervēnit arrived **cōnsēdit** sat down **ecce** look! **leō leōn·is** *m* lion **ōs ōr·is** *n* mouth **cruent·us -a -um** bloody **recēns recent·is** recent **caed·ēs -is** *f* kill **territ·us -a -um** terrified **spēlunc·a -ae** *f* cave **fūgit** fled **ut** as **vēlāmen vēlāmin·is** *n* wrap **dēmīsit** dropped **laniāvit** tore up **postquam** after **pōtāvit** drank **rediit** returned

V

Paulō post, Pȳramus ad mōrum pervēnit. Vēstīgia leōnis et vēlāmen cruentum vīdit. "Tū, mea Thisbē" inquit Pȳramus "fuistī dignissima longā vītā. Nēmō erat amābilior quam tū. Ego sum causa mortis tuae. Ego enim iussī tē noctū hūc venīre. Sine tē, vīta erit ācerrima." Deinde pectus sīcā fodicāvit.

vēstīgi·um -ī *n* track, footstep

inquit says **dign·us -a - um** (+ *abl*) deserving of **fuistī** were **amābil·is -e** lovable, loving **iussī** told, bid **noctū** at night **hūc** here **erit** will be **sīc·a -ae** *f* dagger **fodicāvit** stabbed **pectus pector·is** *n* chest

VI

Thisbē ē spēluncā vēnit et corpus cruentum Pȳramī vīdit. "Pȳrame!" Thisbē susurrāvit, "cūr hōc fēcistī? Pȳrame, tua cārissima Thisbē tē nōminat." Ut autem vēlāmen cruentum suum vīdit, tandem causam vēram mortis intellēxit.

susurrāvit whispered **cūr** why **fēcistī** did **nōminat** calls (*by name*) **ut** when, as **tandem** at last **vēr·us -a -um** true, real **caus·a -ae** *f* cause **intellēxit** understood

Ad nōmen Thisbēs, Pȳramus oculōs aperuit, sed nihil dīcĕre poterat. "Ō parentēs miserrimī" clāmāvit Thisbē, "vōs nōs vīventēs sēgregāvistis; nunc ultima hōra vītae nōs iunget." Haec verba dīcēns, pectus sīcā fodicāvit.

ocul·us -ī *m* eye **aperuīt** opened
nihil nothing
vīventēs living, while alive
sēgregāvistis kept apart **ultim·us -a -um** last, final **iunget** will join
dīcēns dīcent·is saying

F. Latīnē respondē ad quaestiōnēs.

I   1. Quis erat virgō bellissima in urbe?
    2. Quis iuvenis virginem amāvit?

II   3. Quid puer dēsīderābat?
    4. Quis mātrimōnium amantium prohibuit?
    5. Quid parentēs prohibēre nōn poterant?

III   6. Quis cōnsilium sēcrētum cēpit?
    7. Ubi erat mōrus?
    8. Quid erat prope mōrum?

IV   9. Quis prīmus ad arborem extrā urbem pervēnit?
    10. Quae bēstia ad fontem vēnit?
    11. Quō (*whereto*) fūgit Thisbē?
    12. Quid Thisbē casū (*accidentally*) dēmīsit?
    13. Quō (*whereto*) leō rediit, postquam aquam potāvit?

V   14. Quandō Pȳramus ad mōrum vēnit?
    15. Quid Pȳramus ibi vīdit?
    16. Quem (*whom*) Pȳramus accūsāvit ob (*for*) mortem Thisbēs?
    17. Quid Pȳramus deinde fēcit?

VI   18. Unde (*from where*) Thisbē ad mōrum vēnit?
    19. Quid Thisbē ibi vīdit?
    20. Quid Thisbē rogat?

VII   21. Ad nōmen Thisbēs, quid Pȳramus fēcit?
    22. Quid Pȳramus nōn poterat?
    23. Quem Thisbē accūsāvit ob mortem Pȳramī?
    24. Quem tū accūsās ob mortem amantium?

G. The following analogies are based on *grammar*. For explanations and examples, see Chapter 4, Exercises **F** and **G**.

1. melior	: bonus	::	pēior	:	____
2. parvus	: minor	::	magnus	:	____
3. melius	: optimum	::	pēius	:	____
4. superior	: suprēmus	::	____	:	īnfimus
5. prius	: prīmum	::	proprius	:	____

H. Supply the Latin source for the following English derivatives. If it is a noun or adjective, give the nominative singular. If it is a verb, give the infinitive.

1. veteran	____	13. speluncist	____
2. ameliorate	____	14. supreme	____
3. invent	____	15. pessimist	____
4. accelerate	____	16. optimist	____
5. inferiority	____	17. approximate	____
6. acrid	____	18. minority	____
7. oculist	____	19. priority	____
8. segregate	____	20. fugitive	____
9. prohibition	____	21. reptile	____
10. frigid	____	22. juvenile	____
11. prime	____	23. parental	____
12. ultimate	____	24. convention	____

I. Now that you have given the source word for various English derivatives, complete the following sentences. At times all you need is a synonym.

Example | An *altimeter* is an instrument that measures how ____ an airplane is.
An *altimeter* is an instrument that measures how **high** an airplane is.

1. An *optimist* always looks at the ____ side of things.
2. A *speluncist* is a person who investigates ____.
3. A *veteran* is an ____ soldier.
4. A *pessimist* always looks at the ____ side of things.
5. The United States *Supreme* Court is the ____ court of the land.
6. The *pectoral* bone is to be found in the ____.

7. A *fugitive* from justice is a person who ___ from the law.
8. The *prime* goal in life is the ___ goal in life.
9. If you go to see an *oculist,* he/she will examine your ___.
10. When people settle an disagreement *amicably,* they settle it in a ___ manner.
11. A situation is said to *ameliorate* when it gets ___.
12. When you *approximate* a number, you don't know the exact number but give the ___ number.
13. When young people announce their *nuptials,* you know that they are getting ___.
14. The *summit* of a mountain is the ___ point of the mountain.
15. My *superior* is a person who is ___ in rank than I am.
16. When you set your *priorities,* you decide what are the things that must be done ___ other things.
17. When people have *marital* problems, they have trouble with their ___.

CHAPTER 12

Formation and Comparison of Adverbs

THOUGHT
FOR
TODAY

Bis dat quī dat cito. He gives twice who is quick to give.
[lit: who gives quickly]

I. FORMATION OF ADVERBS

Adverbs are for the most part derived from adjectives. In English, the typical ending of an adverb derived from an adjective is *-ly*, for example, *dearly, sadly*. But there are a good number of English adverbs that are not derived from adjectives and therefore do not end in *-ly*; for example, *soon, so, now*. The same holds true for Latin. The typical endings of adverbs derived from adjectives are **-ē** and **-iter**. And then there are Latin adverbs not derived from adjectives, like **mox** *soon*, **ita** *so*, **nunc** *now*.

1. **Adverbs derived from adjectives of the first and second declensions** are formed by adding **-e** to the base. Remember that the base is found by dropping the ending from the genitive singular.

ADJECTIVE	BASE	ADVERB	MEANING
avid*us*	avid·	avid*ē*	eagerly
cārus	cār·	cārē	dearly

1) Some adverbs derived from adjectives of the first and second declensions are formed by adding **-ō** to the base. One adverb, **cito** ends with a short **-o.**

ADJECTIVE	BASE	ADVERB	MEANING
continu*us*	continu·	continuō	immediately
fals*us*	fals·	falsō	falsely
rār*us*	rār·	rārō	rarely
subit*us*	subit·	subitō	suddenly

2) There are two adverbial forms derived from **prīmus,** one ending in **-ō** and another in **-um,** with a slight difference in meaning and function. **Prīmō** means *at first* or *in the beginning*. **Prīmum,** on the other hand, means *first* and begins a series, usually followed by **dein(de)** *then,* or **mox** *then,* or **tum** *then,* and **postrēmō** *finally.*

2. Adverbs derived from adjectives of the third declension are formed by adding **-iter** to the base. Again, the base is found by dropping the ending from the genitive singular.

ADJECTIVE	BASE	ADVERB	MEANING
ācer	ācr·	ācr*iter*	sharply, bitterly
celer	celer·	celer*iter*	fast, speedily
ferōx	ferōc·	ferōc*iter*	fiercely
fort*is*	fort·	fort*iter*	bravely

NOTE

However, adjectives ending in **-ns** add **-er** rather than **-iter** to the base.

ADJECTIVE	BASE	ADVERB	MEANING
ēlegāns	ēlegant·	ēlegant*er*	elegantly
innocēns	innocent·	innocent*er*	innocently

3. Other adverbs. There are many adverbs that are not derived from adjectives and have all sorts of forms.

iam already	**nunc** now	**sīc** thus, so
mox soon	**saepe** often	

A very recognizable ending of a good number of adverbs is **-im.**

fūrtim stealthily	**paulātim** little by little	**prīvātim** privately
interim meanwhile	**praesertim** especially	**statim** immediately

---

PITFALL

Not all adverbs obediently follow the rules or fall neatly into the above groupings. You will run into exceptions to these "rules." For example, according to the rule, the adjective **hūmān·us -a -um** *human, humane, kind,* should form its adverb by adding **-ē** to the base, that is, **hūmānē.** Actually, the adverbial form is **hūmāniter** *kindly, humanely.* Then look at what happens to **facil·is -is -e** *(easy),* obviously an adjective of the third declension. The adverb should therefore be **faciliter,** shouldn't it? Well, it shamelessly breaks our nice rule and turns out to be **facile.** The great Roman educator Quintilian tells us that some pedants, trying to be super-correct, say **faciliter,** but all other people say **facile.** We therefore have the following results:

ADJECTIVE	**hūmān·us -a -um**	ADVERB	**hūmāniter**
	facil·is -is -e		**facile**

II. USES OF ADVERBS

Adverbs answer the questions: how? when? where?

1. When an adverb answers the question "*how?*" we call it an adverb of manner.

Example **Dīdō Aenēan *benignē* excēpit.**   Dido welcomed Aeneas *warmly.*

2. When an adverb answers the question "*when*", we call it an adverb of time.

Example **Post multōs casūs Aenēās in Italiam *tandem* pervēnit.**   After many adventures, Aeneas *finally* arrived in Italy.

3. When an adverb answers the question "*where*?" we call it an adverb of place.

Example **Deī *ubīque* sunt.** The gods are *everywhere.*

A. Test your memory. Adverbs are much harder to remember than nouns, adjectives, and verbs. All the adverbs below have occurred in the previous chapters. See whether you can match the adverbs with their meanings.

deinde	1. for a long time	avidē	7. indeed
semper	2. once (upon a time)	dēnique	8. again
mox	3. finally, at last	rūrsus	9. always
ibi	4. soon	equidem	10. eagerly
ōlim	5. then, next	igitur	11. there
tum	6. then, at that time	diū	12. therefore

B. Form the adverb from the following adjectives. Then give the English meaning of the adverb.

Example | *adjective* **avidus** *adverb* **avidē** *meaning* eagerly

1. dignus	4. astūtus	7. falsus	10. rārus
2. fortis	5. dīligēns	8. nōbilis	11. timidus
3. celer	6. cārus	9. ēlegāns	12. amābilis

III. COMPARISON OF ADVERBS

Now that we have formed the positive degree of adverbs, the comparative and superlative are easy. The comparative of all regular adverbs is the same as the nominative neuter singular form of the comparative of the adjective (**-*ius*** form). The superlative of adverbs is formed by changing the **-us** of the superlative of the adjective to **-ē.**

REGULAR FORMS

Adjective	Positive Adverb	Comparative Adverb	Superlative Adverb
cārus	cārē dearly	cārius	cārissimē
dignus	dignē worthily	dignius	dignissimē
ācer	ācriter bitterly	ācrius	ācerrimē
celer	celeriter swiftly	celerius	celerrimē
fortis	fortiter bravely	fortius	fortissimē
prūdēns	prūdenter wisely	prūdentius	prūdentissimē
ferōx	ferōciter fiercely	ferōcius	ferōcissimē

IRREGULAR FORMS

Adjective	Positive Adverb	Comparative Adverb	Superlative Adverb
bonus	benĕ well	melius better	optimē best
malus	malĕ badly	pēius worse	pessimē worst
magnus	magnopere greatly	magis more, rather	maximē most, especially
multus	multum much, a lot	plūs more, rather	plūrimum most; mostly
parvus	parum little	minus less	minimē least
—	saepĕ often	saepius oftener	saepissimē very often
—	diū long	diūtius longer	diūtissimē a very long time
—	nūper recently	—	nūperrimē most recently
—	—	potius rather	potissimum especially
—	—	prius sooner	prīmum (at) first

NOTES

1) Just as in English we use the adverb *more* with the positive of certain adjectives and adverbs to express the comparative, especially those of three or more syllables, so Latin uses **magis** with the positive of certain adjectives and adverbs. In the same way, **maximē** is used to express the superlative.

Example	**idōneus** suitable	**assiduē** constantly
	magis idōneus more suitable	**magis assiduē** more constantly
	maximē idōneus most suitable	**maximē assiduē** most constantly

2) A common idiom is the combination of the adverb **quam** plus a superlative adverb or adjective with the sense of *as . . . as possible*.

Example

quam celerrimē	as fast as possible
quam saepissimē	as often as possible
quam plūrimī	as many as possible
quam prīmum	as soon as possible
quam diūtissimē	as long as possible

EXERCISES

C. Change the adverb from the positive to the comparative. Then give the meaning of the phrase with the comparative.

Example | *diū* rēgnāre   ***diūtius* rēgnāre** to rule *longer*

1. *miserē* vīvĕre
2. *ācriter* pugnāre
3. *multum* amāre
4. *cito* ambulāre
5. *saepĕ* vīsitāre
6. *benignē* excipĕre
7. *assiduē* rogitāre
8. *fēlīciter* rīdēre

D. In the following sentences, supply the correct forms of the comparative and superlative of the adverb in italics.

Example | Mārcus *dīligenter* labōrat. Gāius ____ labōrat. Sextus ____ labōrat.
Mārcus *dīligenter* labōrat. Gāius *dīligentius* labōrat. Sextus *dīligentissimē* labōrat.
Marcus works *hard*. Gaius works *harder*. Sextus works *hardest*.

VOCABULARY

currit runs	**legit** reads	**rēgnāvit** reigned

1. Rōmulus *diū* rēgnāvit. Numa Pompilius ____ rēgnāvit. Tarquinius Prīscus ____ rēgnāvit.
2. Thisbē *celeriter* currit. Pȳramus ____ currit. Leō autem ____ currit.
3. Lātīnus Aenēān *avidē* exspectat. Amāta eum ____ exspectat. Lārentia eum ____ exspectat.
4. Ego frātrem *cārē* amō. Sorōrem ____ amō. Mātrem autem ____ amō.
5. Ego *bene* lēgō. Frāter ____ legit. Pater autem ____ legit.

E. Use **quam** with the superlative form of the following adverbs and adjectives and then translate.

Example | dīligenter: quam _____
| dīligenter: **quam *dīligentissimē*** as carefully as possible

1. magnoperĕ:	quam ___		4. altus:	quam ___
2. paucī:	quam ___		5. saepĕ:	quam ___
3. breviter:	quam ___		6. facilis:	quam ___

The following is one of the most touching legends from early Roman history, told by Rome's greatest historian, Livy (59 B.C.-A.D. 17). It demonstrates the strong bond between a mother and her son. It took place at the time when Rome was breathing the first air of liberty in the years after cruel King Tarquinius the Proud had been driven out of the City. It is a story about the unusual career of Coriolanus. His original name was Gnaeus Marcius, and he received the honorary name **(cognōmen)** "Coriolanus" for the heroism that he displayed as a young soldier at the capture of the Volscan town of Corioli, near Alba Longa, some 20 miles south of Rome. The Volsci at that time were Rome's greatest enemy. Coriolanus was acclaimed a war hero.

Returning to civilian life, he became a radical in championing the cause of the aristocratic patricians against the poor plebeians. During a famine that had broken out because the fields has not been tilled during the war with the Volsci, Coriolanus wanted to starve the plebeians into giving up the civil rights they had won during a sit-down strike, or secession, on the **Mōns Sacer** on the outskirts of Rome. He particularly resented the fact that the plebeians had wrung permission from the Senate to elect their own officials, the tribunes of the commoners **(tribūnī plēbis),** who had the power to veto any measure by any patrician magistrate. He was determined to eliminate that office.

Because of his extreme position, he lost the support even of the Senate. He was impeached and condemned to exile in 491 B.C. Of all things, he took refuge with Rome's mortal enemy, the Volsci, and promised to assist them in their war against Rome. Having been commissioned a general in the Volscan army, Coriolanus captured many towns until he encamped within sight of Rome itself. Crowds gathered on top of the walls of the city to peer

Coriolanus, his mother, and wife

at the strange sight of the Volscan camp. The Roman Senate sent embassy after embassy consisting of the most distinguished citizens to Coriolanus at his camp near Rome.

Now read the story in Latin and see how it all turned out. Note the adverbs, which are in italics.

I

Tum exercitus Rōmānus Coriolōs obsidēbat. *Subitō* Volsca legiō ab Antiō invādit exercitum Rōmānum. *Simul* hostēs ex oppidō ērumpunt et impetum contrā Rōmānōs faciunt. *Forte* in statiōne Mārcius est.

Coriol·ī -ōrum *mpl* small town in Latium **obsidēbat** besieged **Volsc·us -a -um** Volscan **legiō legiōn·is** *f* legion, division *(about 5000 men)* **Anti·um -ī** *n* Volscan town on the seacoast **invādit** attacks **simul** at the same time **ērumpunt** rush out **impet·us -ūs** *m* attack, **impetum faciunt** mount an attack **forte** by chance; **forte est** happens to be **statiō statiōn·is** *f* guard; **in statiōne est** is on guard

II

Statim Mārcius manum mīlitum dūcit contrā oppidānōs. *Prīmum* Mārcius oppidānōrum impetum retundit. *Deinde* per patentem portam *quam celerrimē* inruit. *Mox* multōs in eā parte urbis occīdit. *Tandem* aedificia intrā moenia incendit. *Itaque* exercitus Rōmānus oppidum Coriolōs *facile* et *impūnē* capit. *Deinceps* cognōmen Coriolānus est Mārciō.

man·us -ūs *f* group **oppidān·ī -ōrum** *mpl* townspeople

retundit blunts **patens patent·is** open **inruit** rushes in **mox** next **is ea id** that **occīdit** kills **moen·ia -ium** *npl* walls **incendit** sets on fire **itaque** and so **impūnē** safely **capit** captures **deinceps** from then on **cognōmen cognōmin·is** *n* surname, nickname

III

Post bellum *autem* hic clārus patricius erat ācerrimus in plēbem. *Paulātim etiam* sēnātus crūdēlem rātiōnem eius condemnat. Ex urbe *igitur* expulsus, ad Volscōs, ācerrimōs Rōmānōrum hostēs, trānsit. Volscī *utpote* Mārcium ducem exercitūs *libenter* creant. Cōpiās Rōmānās *saepe* vincit. Aliud oppidum ex aliō capit. *Etiam* Coriolōs prō Volscīs recipit.

patrici·us -ī *m* patrician **ācer in** (+ *acc*) harsh toward **plēbs plēb·is** *f* the common people, plebeians **paulātim** little by little **crūdēl·is -is -e** cruel **rātiō rātiōn·is** *f* policy **igitur** therefore **expulsus** having been expelled **trānsit** crosses over **utpote** as you might expect **libenter** gladly **creant** appoint, make **cōpi·ae -ārum** *fpl* troops **vincit** conquers **alius ... ex aliō** one ... after another **recipit** recaptures, regains

IV

Dēnique Mārcius cum Volscōrum cōpiīs venit in cōnspectum Rōmae. *Frūstrā* lēgātī ex urbe veniunt, pacemque implōrant. In lēgātīs sunt patriciī prīmōrēs. *Etiam* sacerdōtēs sunt in lēgātīs. Sed *frustrā* rogant. *Postrēmō*, Vetūria, māter, et Volumnia, uxor *ūnā* cum duōbus parvulīs, ex urbe ad castra Volscōrum veniunt. Lacrimīs precibusque commōtus, Coriolānus castra *retrō* ab urbe movit. *Quāpropter* Volscī Coriolānum ut prōditōrem ad mortem dant.

in cōnspectum within sight (of)
frūstrā in vain **lēgāt·us -ī** *m* ambassador
implōrant beg for **in** (+ *abl*) among
prīmōr·ēs -um *mpl* leading men, leaders
sacerdōs sacerdōt·is *m* priest
rogant beg
ūnā cum (+ *abl*) together with
parvul·us -ī *m* little one, baby
prex prec·is *m* prayer, entreaty
commōt·us -a -um touched, moved
retrō back **quāpropter** for that reason **ut** as **prōditor prōditōr·is** betrayer
ad mortem dant put to death

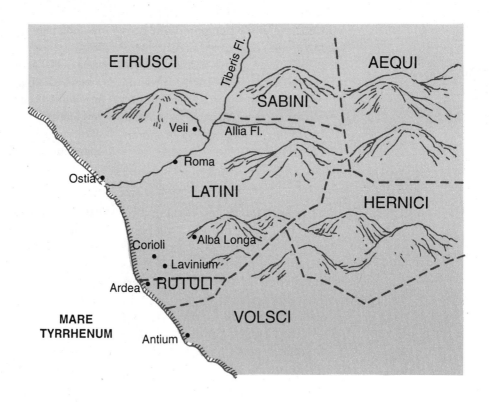

Map of early Latium and environs

F. Now choose the best answer, A, B, C, or D, based on the story you have just read.

I   1. Volscan troops came from Antium to Corioli A) to help the Romans; B) to see which side would be the victor; C) to help the townspeople; D) to share in the booty.

II   2. The soldiers in Corioli rushed out of the town A) because they were starving; B) to attack the Roman camp; C) to greet the troops from Antium; D) to surrender to the Romans.

3. When the soldiers in Corioli rushed out of the town, young Marcius A) seemed stunned for a long while; B) tried to hide initially; C) quickly assumed a role of leadership; D) let his fellow soldiers do the fighting.

4. The first thing Marcius did was A) to rush into the city through the open gates; B) to set fire to the buildings outside the walls; C) to blunt the attack of the soldiers as they rushed out of Corioli; D) to show mercy toward the civilians inside the town.

5. The Roman army A) lifted the blockade of Corioli because of high casualties; B) did not have time to capture the city; C) found it easy going to take the city; D) ended the war with a treaty.

III   6. After the war Coriolanus A) was not interested in politics; B) initially sided with the common people; C) initially had the support of the Senate; D) initially was hated and feared by all patricians and plebeians alike.

7. Coriolanus A) left Rome in disgust; B) left Rome as a hero; C) was banished in disgrace; D) was appointed general of the Roman army.

8. While head of the Volscan army Coriolanus A) avoided the town of Corioli; B) liberated the town from the Romans; C) gave the town to the Romans as a sign of good will; D) set the town on fire.

IV   9. The Romans sent embassies to the camp of Coriolanus A) to beg him to stop the war against Rome; B) to warn him of a trap; C) to lure him to Rome; D) to arrest him.

10. Of the various people in these embassies, the persons who were most influential with Coriolanus were A) the priests; B) the leading patricians; C) the Senators; D) his own family.

G. Supply the Latin source for the following English derivatives. If it is a verb, give the infinitive. If it is a noun or an adjective, give the nominative singular.

1. obsessed ____
2. invasion ____
3. eruption ____
4. incensed ____
5. Patricia ____

6. incendiary ____
7. creation ____
8. invincible ____
9. frustration ____
10. expulsion ____

Part III

Pronouns;
Roman
Numerals

CHAPTER 13

Personal, Reflexive, Intensive Pronouns, and Possessive Adjectives

THOUGHT
FOR
TODAY

Cuique suum. To each his own.

I. PERSONAL PRONOUNS

Latin personal pronouns correspond to the English *I, you, he, she, it,* etc. Strictly speaking, Latin lacks pronouns of the third person and substitutes in their place the demonstrative pronouns **is** *he*, **ea** *she*, **id** *it*. A pronoun must agree with its antecedent (the word to which it refers) in gender, person, and number. However, the case of the pronoun is determined by its use in the sentence or clause in which it stands; in other words, the pronoun is independent of its antecedent in the matter of case.

Example   This is my *brother*. I think you know *him*.

Here the antecedent is "brother"; it is in the subjective case. The pronoun is "him"; it is masculine in gender, singular in number, third person, just as its antecedent. But "him" is in the objective case because, within its own sentence, it functions as the direct object of the verb "know." These same rules hold true for Latin pronouns.

DECLENSION OF PERSONAL PRONOUNS

	FIRST PERSON	SECOND PERSON	THIRD PERSON		
SINGULAR					
NOM.	**ego** I	**tū** you	**is** he	**ea** she	**id** it
GEN.	**meī**	**tuī**	**eius**	**eius**	**eius**
DAT.	**mihi**	**tibi**	**eī**	**eī**	**eī**
ACC.	**mē**	**tē**	**eum**	**eam**	**id**
ABL.	**mē**	**tē**	**eō**	**eā**	**eō**
PLURAL					
NOM.	**nōs** we	**vōs** you	**eī** they	**eae** they	**ea** they
GEN.	**nostrum**	**vestrum**	**eōrum**	**eārum**	**eōrum**
	nostrī	**vestrī**			
DAT.	**nōbīs**	**vōbīs**	**eīs**	**eīs**	**eīs**
ACC.	**nōs**	**vōs**	**eōs**	**eās**	**ea**
ABL.	**nōbīs**	**vōbīs**	**eīs**	**eīs**	**eīs**

1. Latin omits the personal pronoun as the subject of a sentence if it can be understood from the context, that is, from the preceding sentence(s). However, the personal pronoun is used as the subject of a sentence or clause if there is a **shift of subject**. For example, if someone has been talking for a while about a friend and then shifts to oneself, **ego** or **nōs** will be used. The pronoun will also be used **for emphasis**, especially in contrasts.

Example   **Quis mē audit?** *Ego* **tē audiō**   Who hears me? *I* hear you.

2. The personal pronouns of the first and second persons , **nōs** and **vōs,** have two forms of the genitive plural, namely **nostrum / nostrī** and **vestrum / vestrī**. The forms **nostrī** and **vestrī** are used with the few verbs and adjectives which require the genitive case. In all other instances, the forms **nostrum** and **vestrum** are used.

Examples   **Ego sum semper memor** *vestrī*.   I am always mindful *of you.*

   Quis *vestrum* **Rōmam vidisti?**   Who *among you* has ever seen Rome?

3. In **cum**-phrases, the preposition is joined to the pronoun of the first and second persons.

mēcum	with me	**nōbīscum**	with us
tēcum	with you	**vōbīscum**	with you

4. Although *it* is neuter in English, remember that in Latin the thing to which *it* refers may be masculine, feminine, or neuter.

Examples

Leō ad fontem vēnit. Thisbē *eum* **statim vīdit.**

A lion came to the spring. Thisbe saw *it* immediately.

Lupa geminōs clārōs servāvit. Geminī *eam* **nōn timēbant.**

A wolf saved the famous twins. The twins were not afraid of *it*.

NOTE

The pronouns **is, ea, id** also serve as demonstrative adjectives.

Example

Numa in *eā* **parte urbis templum dēdicāvit.**

Numa dedicated a temple in *that* quarter of the city.

EXERCISES

A. In the following sentences, supply the personal pronoun in place of the noun in italics that acts as its antecedent.

Example

Patriciī *Coriolānum* laudant. Patriciī ＿＿ etiam timent.
Patriciī Coriolānum laudant. Patriciī *eum* **etiam timent.**
The patricians praise Coriolanus. The patricians also fear *him*.

1. *Priamus* erat rēx Trōiae. ＿＿ erat rēx bonus.
2. Aenēās cum *sociīs* in Āfricam nāvigāvit. Aenēās cum ＿＿ in Āfricam nāvigāvit.
3. Dīdō erat *rēgīna* Carthāginis. Aenēās ＿＿ adamābat.
4. Aenēās cum *Dīdōne* vīvěre optābat. Aenēās cum ＿＿ vīvěre optābat.
5. Aenēās cum *Turnō* pugnābat. Aenēās cum ＿＿ pugnābat.
6. Aenēās *Lāvīnium* fundāvit. Aenēās ＿＿ fundāvit.
7. Aenēās oppidum ab *Lāvīniā* nōmināvit. Aenēās oppidum ab ＿＿ nōmināvit.
8. *Rēgēs* Rōmānī diū rēgnābant. ＿＿ diū rēgnābant.
9. *Rōmulus* erat prīmus rēx Rōmae. ＿＿ urbem Rōmam fundāvit.
10. Faustulus *geminōs* cum lupā invēnit. Faustulus ＿＿ cum lupā invēnit.
11. Faustulus in humilī *casā* habitāvit. Faustulus in ＿＿ habitāvit.

B. Here is a speech that Coriolanus is preparing to give before the senate which no longer wants to support his cause. You need to have read about Coriolanus' heroism in the previous chapter to understand this speech. The speech is complete except for the pronouns to be inserted. Read the speech carefully so that you can convert the English pronouns into Latin.

VOCABULARY

cēpit captured
commīles commīlit·is *m* fellow soldier
corōn·a -ae *f* **mūrālis** "mural crown" a decoration received by a soldier for being the first to penetrate the enemy's walls.
damus we give
dedit gave

inruī, inruistis rushed in
laus laud·is *f* praise
placēre (+ *dat*) to please
pugnāvī, pugnāvistī fought
umquam ever
tam . . . quam as . . . as
timeō I fear
vulnerāvērunt wounded

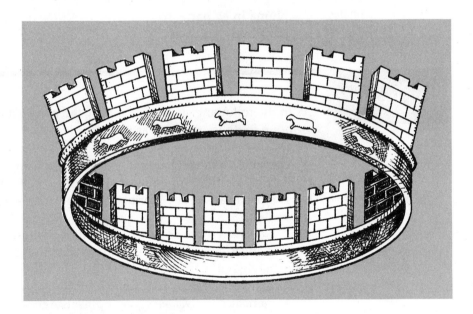

Mural crown

Senātōrēs, (*I*) ____ prō patriā saepe pugnāvī. Quis (*of you*) ____ tam fortiter pugnāvistī quam (*I*) ____? (*I*) ____ per portam Coriolōrum inruī. Quandō (*you*) ____ per hostium portam inruistis? Hostēs (*me*) ____ vulnerāvērunt. Quandō hostēs (*you*) ____ umquam vulnerāvērunt? Imperātor (*to me*) ____ corōnam mūrālem dedit. Quandō autem imperātor (*to you*) ____ corōnam mūrālem dedit? (*To me*) ____ est cognōmen

Coriolānus. Estne simile cognōmen (*to you*) ___? Propter (*me*) ___, nōn propter (*you*) ___, exercitus Rōmānus Coriolōs facile cēpit. Deī sunt (*with me*) ___, nōn (*with you*) ___. (*I*) ___ optō placēre (*them*) ___, nōn (*you*) ___. (*I*) ___ timeō (*them*) ___, sed nōn (*you*) ___. (*I*) ___ et commīlitēs laudem (*to them*) ___ damus, nōn (*to you*) ___.

C. For each of the nouns in italics substitute the proper pronoun in the correct case. Each sentence is given twice, with the noun the first time and with a blank for the pronoun the second time. Reading over the story of Coriolanus in the preceding chapter will make it easier to understand this exercise.

Example

Mārcius est mīles fortis. ***Is* est mīles fortis.**
Marcius is a brave soldier. *He* is a brave soldier.

VOCABULARY

dat gives
impetum faciunt mount an attack

inimīcus -a -um hostile
mandāt·a -ōrum *n* instructions

1. *Volscī* impetum faciunt. ___ impetum faciunt.
2. Mārcius forte est in *statiōne*. Mārcius forte est in ___.
3. Exercitus Rōmānus *Coriolōs* obsidet. Exercitus Rōmānus ___ obsidet.
4. Mārcius *mīlitēs* per patentem portam dūcit. Mārcius ___ per patentem portam dūcit.
5. Tandem *aedificia* in eā parte urbis incendit. Tandem ___ in eā parte urbis incendit.
6. Itaque Rōmānī *oppidum* facile capiunt. Itaque Rōmānī ___ facile capiunt.
7. Populus multam laudem *Mārciō* dat. Populus multam laudem ___ dat.
8. Post bellum Coriolānus est inimīcissimus in *plēbem*. Post bellum Coriolānus est inimīcissimus in ___.
9. Posteā senātus *Coriolānum* condemnat. Posteā senātus ___ condemnat.
10. Coriolānus ad *Volscōs* trānsit. Coriolānus ad ___ trānsit.
11. Volscī *Coriolānum* ducem libenter creant. Volscī ___ dūcem libenter creant.
12. Coriolānus deinde *cōpiās Rōmānās* vincit. Coriolānus deinde ___ vincit.
13. Etiam Coriolōs prō *Volscīs* recipit. Etiam Coriolōs prō ___ recipit.
14. Dēnique *Coriolānus* venit in cōnspectum Rōmae. Dēnique ___ venit in cōnspectum Rōmae.
15. Senātus mittit *lēgātōs* ad Coriolānum. Senātus mittit ___ ad Coriolānum.
16. In *lēgātis* sunt etiam sacerdōtēs. In ___ sunt etiam sacerdōtēs.

17. Lēgātī mandāta *Coriolānō* dant. Lēgātī mandāta ____ dant.
18. Vetūria, māter *Coriolānī*, ad castra venit. Vetūria, māter ____, ad castra venit.
19. Vetūria *fīlium* cum lacrimīs supplicat. Vetūria ____ cum lacrimīs supplicat.
20. Tum Coriolānus castra ab *urbe* retrō movet. Tum Coriolānus castra ab ____ retrō movet.

II. REFLEXIVE PRONOUNS

Pronouns, such as *myself, yourself, themselves,* are called "reflexive" when the action of the verb, instead of being directed at someone else, is directed at the subject, that is, when the subject and the direct or indirect object are identical. "Reflexive" in Latin means "bent, turned back."

Example **Coriolānus *sē* dēfendit.**   Coriolanus defended *himself.*

1. FORMS

DECLENSION OF REFLEXIVE PRONOUNS					
FIRST PERSON		SECOND PERSON		THIRD PERSON	
SINGULAR	PLURAL	SINGULAR	PLURAL	SINGULAR AND PLURAL	
NOM.					
meī	**nostrum/nostrī**	**tuī**	**vestrum/vestrī**	**suī**	GEN.
mihi	**nōbīs**	**tibi**	**vōbīs**	**sibi**	DAT.
mē	**nōs**	**tē**	**vōs**	**sē**	ACC.
mē	**nōbīs**	**tē**	**vōbīs**	**sē**	ABL.

NOTES

1) The forms of the reflexive pronouns of the first and second persons, singular and plural, are the same as the forms of the personal pronouns, except that there is no nominative.

Examples **Ego *mē* lavō.**   I am washing *myself.*

Ego *mihi* nocuī.   I hurt *myself.* (**nocēre** always takes the dative.)

Cūr tū *tē* lavās?   Why are you washing *yourself?*
Ego et frāter *nōs* lavāmus.   My brother and I are washing *ourselves.*

2) The reflexive pronoun of the third person serves for all genders and for both singular and plural. Thus it may mean *himself, herself, itself,* or *themselves* according to the subject. The form **suī** is rarely found.

Examples

Frāter meus *sibi* **nocuit.**   My brother hurt *himself.*

Soror mea *sibi* **nocuit.**   My sister hurt *herself.*

Mīlitēs *sibi* **nocuērunt.**   The soldiers hurt *themselves.*

3) The form **sē** serves for both the accusative and the ablative of the third person.

Examples

accusative:
Gāius *sē* **lavat.**   Gaius is washing *himself.*

Gaīa *sē* **lavat.**   Gaia is washing *herself.*

Vulgus sē lavat.   The crowd is washing *itself.*

Geminī *sē* **lavant.**   The twins are washing *themselves.*

ablative:
Senātor dē *sē* **semper dīcit.**   The senator always talks *about himself.*

Soror mea dē *sē* **semper dīcit.**   My sister always talks *about herself.*

Senātus dē *sē* **semper dīcit.**   The senate always talks *about itself.*

Senātōrēs dē *sē* **semper dīcunt.**   The senators always talk *about themselves.*

2. REFLEXIVE VERBS

When the reflexive pronoun is the object of the verb, we call the verb itself a *reflexive verb.* The reflexive pronoun is often used to make a transitive verb function intransitively.

Examples

Lārentia geminōs lavat.   Larentia is washing the twins.

Geminī sē lavant.   The twins are washing (themselves).

In translating the second sentence, it is not necessary to say "themselves," since in English the verb "wash" can be transitive or intransitive (that is, take a direct object or not). But if the Romans heard the sentence **Geminī lavant** *(The twins are washing)*, they would ask "whom or what are they washing?" because they felt that the transitive verb **lavāre** should have a direct object. Here are other examples of the reflexive pronoun employed to make a normally transitive verb intransitive.

Examples

Faustulus *sē* **ad lupam** *vertit.*	Faustulus *turned* toward the wolf.
Lupa *sē* **ex locō nōn** *mōvit.*	The wolf *did* not *move* from the spot.
Faustulus geminōs *ad sē* *vocāvit.*	Faustulus *called* the twins.
Āthlētae *sē* **cotīdiē** *exercent.*	Athletes *train* every day.

Consider the verb **vocāre**. Standing by itself, it is ambiguous because it can mean "to call" in the sense of "to name" or "to summon." The English verb "to call" happens to cover both senses. If the Romans heard the words **Faustulus geminōs vocāvit,** they would say, "Well, did he *name* them or *summon* them?" However, in the sentence **Faustulus geminōs ad sē vocāvit,** the sense would be clear. It could only mean "Faustulus called the twins" (in the sense that he summoned them).

Exercēre is a transitive verb and means "to train (someone)." When it is reflexive, it means "to train oneself" or simply "to train." Thus, **āthlētae sē nunc exercent** means "the athletes are now training".

So you can see that the reflexive pronoun is used more frequently in Latin than in English. It is also used frequently in indirect statements.

NOTES

1) All Latin reflexive pronouns have at times a *reciprocal* force. The reciprocal pronouns in English are *each other* (when two are involved) and *one another* (when more than two are involved). Latin didn't have reciprocal pronouns, and so the Romans used reflexive pronouns with the preposition **inter.**

Examples

Pȳramus et Thisbē *inter sē* **amant.**	Pyramus and Thisbe love *each other*.
Patriciī *inter sē* **rārō pugnant.**	The patricians rarely fight *with one another.*

2) Of course, a reflexive pronoun can be used in a sentence without being the object of the verb.

Coriolānus *per sē* **in urbem inruit.**   Coriolanus rushes into town *by himself.*

III. POSSESSIVE ADJECTIVES

The possessive adjectives corresponding to the personal and reflexive pronouns are adjectives of the first and second declensions. They indicate possession or ownership.

	SINGULAR		PLURAL	
FIRST PERSON	**me·us -a -um**	my	**noster nostr·a -um**	our
SECOND PERSON	**tu·us -a -um**	your	**vester vestr·a -um**	your
THIRD PERSON	**su·us -a -um**	his, her, its	**su·us -a -um**	their

NOTES

1) **Su**us *-a -um* is used only as a reflexive, referring to the subject. It is used when the possessive adjective refers to the subject of the sentence.

Examples   **Brūtus Caesarem** *manū suā* **interfēcit.**   Brutus killed Caesar with *his own hand*

Puer *frātrem suum* **necāvit.**   The boy killed *his (own) brother.*

2) Since the possessive adjective of the third person did not exist in Latin, to express possession the Romans used the genitive of the pronouns **is, ea, id,** namely **eius,** which means *his, her, its* and their plural forms **eōrum, eārum, eōrum,** which mean *their.* (See the full declension at the beginning of this chapter.)

Examples   **Puer** *frātrem suum* **necāvit.**   The boy killed *his (own) brother.*

Puer *frātrem eius* **necāvit.**   The boy killed *his (someone else's) brother.*

3) The gender of the possessive adjective is determined by the noun that it modifies, not by the gender of the person to whom it refers.

Examples   *mea* **māter** *my mother*   *tuum* **oppidum** *your town.*

D. Translate the following sentences into English. Pay particular attention to the pronouns.

VOCABULARY

caput capit·is *n* capital	**fundat** founds	**per sē** by himself
culpat blames	**multa** many things	**servat** saves
ēducat raises	**nocet** (+ *dat*) hurts, harms	

1. Rōmānī urbem *suam* amant; saepe prō *eā* pugnant.
2. Rōmānī *sē* contrā Volscōs dēfendunt.
3. Faustulus geminōs servat et *eōs* ēducat.
4. Turnus est rēx Rutulōrum; caput *eōrum* est Ardea.
5. Aenēās *sē* contrā Turnum dēfendit.
6. Horātius per *sē* pontem dēfendit.
7. Pȳramus *sibi* sīcā nocet.
8. Dīdō multa dē *sē* Aenēae nārrat.
9. Rōmulus urbem fundat; mūrī *ejus* sunt altī et crassī.
10. Coriolānus numquam *se* culpat.

E. Having seen the reflexive pronouns in action in the previous exercise, complete the following Latin sentences by supplying the correct form of the reflexive pronouns.

VOCABULARY

cōnfīdimus (+ *dat*) trust	**nocuistīne** (+ *dat*) did you hurt . . .?
dēcipitis you deceive	**proeli·um -ī** *n* battle

1. Rōmānī ____ contrā hostēs dēfendunt.
2. Nocuistīne ____ in proeliō?
3. Rōmulus et Remus ____ nōn servant.
4. Ego ____ cotīdiē lavō.
5. Patriciī omnia prō ____ faciunt.
6. Quid tū dē ____ dīcis?
7. Ego et soror mea ____ nōn cōnfīdimus.
8. Amīcī meī, ____ dēcipitis.
9. Pȳrame, cūr ____ culpās?
10. Thisbē ____ sīcā fodicat.
11. Pȳramus et Thisbē ____ nocent.
12. Iuvenis et puella ____ servāre nōn possunt.
13. Mīlitēs ante proelium ____ exercent.

14. Sacerdōs ____ ad Iovis statuam vertit.
15. Senātōrēs, nihil adhūc dē ____ dīcitis.

F. Translate the following sentences into Latin. Pay particular attention to the pronouns.

1. Turnus loves his city; he often fights for it.
2. The Rutuli defend themselves against the Trojans.
3. Coriolanus always speaks about himself.
4. King Latinus summoned Aeneas (called Aeneas to himself).
5. Thisbe hurts herself with a sword.

IV. INTENSIVE PRONOUNS

Intensive pronouns add emphasis to the nouns or pronouns with which they are associated. The meaning of a sentence would not change if the intensive pronoun were dropped. However, the sentence would be incomplete if the reflexive pronoun were dropped.

DECLENSION OF INTENSIVE PRONOUNS					
MASCULINE		**FEMININE**		**NEUTER**	
SINGULAR					
NOM.	**ipse**	himself	**ipsa**	herself	**ipsum**	itself
GEN.	**ipsīus**		**ipsīus**		**ipsīus**	
DAT.	**ipsī**		**ipsī**		**ipsī**	
ACC.	**ipsum**		**ipsam**		**ipsum**	
ABL.	**ipsō**		**ipsā**		**ipsō**	
PLURAL					
NOM.	**ipsī**	themselves	**ipsae**	themselves	**ipsa**	themselves
GEN.	**ipsōrum**		**ipsārum**		**ipsōrum**	
DAT.	**ipsīs**		**ipsīs**		**ipsīs**	
ACC.	**ipsōs**		**ipsās**		**ipsa**	
ABL.	**ipsīs**		**ipsīs**		**ipsīs**	

The forms of **ipse** are translated "myself," "yourself," "himself," "herself," "itself," or "ourselves,", yourselves," "themselves" according to the person, number, and gender of the word with which they are associated.

Examples	**Vetūria *ipsa* in castra Coriolānī vēnit.**	Veturia *herself* came to the camp of Coriolanus.
	Coriolānus *ipse* ex castrīs vēnit.	Coriolanus *himself* came out of the camp.
	Ego ipse cum Coriolānō mīlitāvī.	I *myself* was in the army with Coriolanus.

NOTE

We must clearly distinguish between reflexive and intensive pronouns. They can easily be confused in English because both end in *-self,* but in Latin they are completely different in form.

| *Examples* | *(intensive)* **Imperātor *ipse* in culpā erat.** | The general *himself* was to blame. |
| | *(reflexive)* **Imperātor *sē* culpāvit.** | The general blamed *himself*. |

WORD ORDER

The intensive pronoun follows the noun or pronoun with which it is associated. However, when it means "very", it precedes the noun.

| **Gāius cōnsul creātus est *ipsō diē* quō pater mortuus est.** | Gaius was elected consul on the *very* day on which his father died. |

EXERCISES

G. Indicate whether the pronouns in the following sentences are intensive or reflexive.

1. I *myself* admire Coriolanus for his heroism at Corioli.
2. After a while, the Romans *themselves* feared the Volsci.
3. Naturally, Coriolanus couldn't do everything *himself*.
4. The plebeians complained that the patricians were out for *themselves*.

5. The patricians caused all the trouble *themselves*.
6. Coriolanus convinced *himself* that he was doing the right thing.
7. I can't believe that Pyramus and Thisbe killed *themselves*.
8. You are only fooling *yourself* if you don't practice.
9. Now it's going to be every man for *himself*.
10. In *itself*, losing a game is not a disgrace.
11. Dido convinced *herself* that Aeneas would settle down in Carthage.
12. In the end Coriolanus did it all *himself*.

H. Supply the correct form of **ipse** for each blank. The blank always occurs after the word that the pronouns modifies.

1. Rōmānī ____ oppidum Coriolōs obsident.
2. Oppidānī in oppidō ____ in perīculō sunt.
3. Parentēs Mārciī ____ timent prō fīliō suō.
4. Mārcius ____ nōn sōlus per portas patentēs inruit.
5. Tandem Mārcius aedificia oppidī ____ incendit.
6. Post bellum, senātus ____ Coriolānum ex urbe expellit.
7. Volscī ____ Mārcium ducem libenter creant.
8. Deinde Mārcius contrā Rōmānōs ____ pugnat.

I. In the following sentences, supply the correct form of the reflexive or intensive pronoun for each blank.

1. Mūcius Scaevola ____ est fortis mīles Rōmānus.
2. Senātōrēs ____ Mūcium in hostium castra mittunt.
3. Mūcius numquam dē ____ timet.
4. Mūcius prō patriā, nōn prō ____ pugnat.
5. Mūcius in castra hostium — venit.
6. Hōc modō Mūcius nōn sōlum ____ sed etiam exercitum Rōmānum servat.

THE SAGA OF HORATIUS COCLES

When Tarquinius the Proud, the last king of Rome, was expelled from the city in 509 B.C., the 250-year period of the monarchy came to an end, and 500 years of Republican rule began. From then on, the Romans elected two magistrates every year, called consuls. (Can you imagine our country electing two presidents every year, each with veto power over the other?) The two consuls, together with other officials and the senate, took over the reigns of government. It was not a democracy; the senate and the patricians decided "what was good for the country."

But the Tarquinian clan didn't take their expulsion from the city lying down. They appealed for help to Lars Porsenna, king of the Etruscan town of Clusium, about 90 miles north of Rome. He marched on Rome with a mighty army in order to restore Tarquinius the Proud to the throne. He took possession of the Janiculum Hill, just north of the Tiber. From that hill he could look down on the whole of Rome.

There was only one wooden bridge across the Tiber in those early days, the **Pōns Sublicius,** connecting the Janiculum Hill with Rome. ("Sublician" means "supported on wooden trusses.) The year was 508 B.C. That's where our hero Horatius Cocles comes in. Of course, he, like all early heroes of Rome, was a young patrician. His family name meant "one-eyed." Many Roman family names referred to bodily characteristics. Although we don't know the first name of Horatius Cocles, he surely had one, since all Roman citizens had three names:

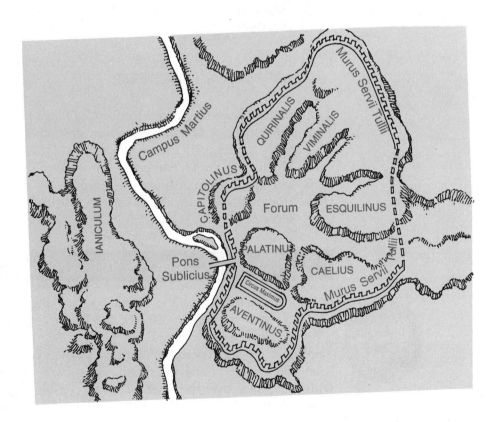

Map of Rome

praenōmen first name, e.g., **Gāius**
nōmen clan name, e.g., **Jūlius**
cognōmen family name, e.g., **Caesar**

A person could also acquire a nickname, or honorary name, for some famous exploit. Publius Cornelius Scipio was given the honorary name **Āfricānus** for having defeated the Carthaginians in northern Africa and bringing an end to the Second Punic War (218-201 B.C.). That **cognōmen** was sometimes called **agnōmen**.

Now read of the saga of "Horatio at the Bridge," and then answer some questions on the passage.

Horātius apud Pontem
Horatio at the Bridge

I

Postquam populus Rōmānus Tarquinium Superbum ex urbe expellit, Tarquinius ipse ad Lartem Porsennam perfugit. Porsenna enim est rēx Clūsiī, oppidī Etrūscī. Tarquinius auxilium ab eō petit.

postquam after

expellit expels **Lar·s -tis Porsenn·a -ae** *m* king of Clusium **perfugit** takes refuge **enim** for, since **Clūsi·um -ī** *n* Clusium **auxili·um -ī** *n* help **petit** asks for

II

Porsenna ipse igitur maximum exercitum comparat et eum contrā Rōmam addūcit. Mox Etrūscī occupant Iāniculum ipsum. Ūnus pōns sōlus trāns Tiberim sēparat Iāniculum ab urbe. Etrūscī hōc ponte flūmen trānsīre cōnstituunt.

comparat gets together
addūcit leads
Iānicul·um -ī *n* Janiculum Hill north of the Tiber **ūn·us -a -um** one **pōn·s -tis** *m* bridge **sōl·us -a -um** only, alone **hic haec hoc** this **trānsīre** to cross **cōnstituunt** decide

III

Sed ūnus iuvenis, nōmine Horātius, forte in statiōne pontis pōnitur. Eī cognōmen est Cocles. Horātius clāmat: "Pontem, Rōmānī, quam celerrimē dēstruite! Vōs servāte! Ego ipse et meī duo commīlitēs in

forte by chance **stati·ō -ōnis** *f* guard post **pōnitur** is stationed **cognōm·en -inis** family name **clāmat** shouts
quam celerrimē as quickly as possible
dēstruite destroy, tear down
commīl·es -itis *m* fellow soldier

Horatio at the bridge

ponte remanēbimus ac contrā Etrūscōs pugnābimus.

remanēbimus we will stay behind
pugnābimus will fight

IV

Diū et ācriter Horātius ac duo commīlitēs contrā Etrūscōs pugnant. Tandem, iussū Horātiī, commīlitēs eius ad rīpam tūtam recēdunt. Nunc Horātius sōlus in ponte contrā Etrūscōs pugnat. Deinde Horātius magnam fragōrem ruptī pontis audit.

diū et ācriter long and hard

iussū at the order
tūt·us -a -um safe
recēdunt withdraw **rīp·a -ae** *f* river bank

magn·us -a -um loud **frag·or -ōris** *m*
crash **rupt·us -a -um** broken **audit** hears

V

Horātius Cocles, armātus, in Tiberim dēsilit et statim pōns ruptus in aquam dēcidit. Horātius incolumis ad suōs trānsnat. Sīc Horātius sē servat.

dēsilit jumps down **statim** immediately
dēcidit falls down
incolum·is -is -e unharmed **trānsnat**
swims across

J. Test your reading comprehension. Choose the best answer from A, B, C, or D, based on the story.

I 1. Tarquinius Superbus was: A) a proud Roman senator; B) a Roman ambassador; C) the first king of Rome; D) the last king of Rome.

2. The phrase **ex urbe** refers to: A) any city; B) Clusium; C) Rome; D) Ardea.

3. The form **oppidī Etrūscī** indicates that: A) it is nominative plural masculine; B) it is in apposition with "Clūsiī"; C) it is neuter plural; D) it is in the locative case.

4. The **eō** in **ab eō** refers to: A) Porsenna; B) Tarquinius Superbus; C) Clusium; D) the Roman people.

II 5. Porsenna got together a large army to: A) fight Tarquinius's troops; B) protect his city of Clusium; C) show his strength; D) help Tarquinius Superbus.

6. **Eum** (second line) refers to: A) the army; B) Porsenna; C) Tarquinius Superbus; D) a prisoner of war.

7. The Etruscans occupied the Janiculum Hill because A) they mistook it for Rome; B) they were afraid to advance farther; C) they didn't trust Tarquinius Superbus; D) it would give them a good view of the area around the bridge.

8. The bridge was important because: A) it was the only approach to the city; B) it was hidden from view; C) it was near the Janiculum Hill; D) the Romans weren't guarding it.

III 9. Horatius A) chose to be at the bridge; B) just happened to be stationed there; C) wasn't near the bridge at the time; D) initially avoided guard duty there.

10. **Eī** (line 2) is A) nominative plural; B) genitive singular; C) singular dative of possession; D) ablative of means.

11. Horatius called upon the Romans A) to protect the bridge; B) lock the far side of the bridge; C) save the bridge for themselves; D) demolish the bridge.

12. Horatius said that A) he would fight the enemy alone; B) he and his two fellow soldiers would destroy the bridge; C) he would kill two enemy soldiers; D) he and two fellow soldiers would fight the enemy.

13. Horatius decided on this action A) to show his strength; B) to give a good example to others; C) to give the Romans time to demolish the bridge; D) to gain the Roman medal of honor.

IV 14. The two fellow soldiers withdrew to the Roman shore because: A) they were exhausted; B) they saw that the situation was hopeless; C) Horatius ordered it; D) they were cowards.

15. Horatius left the bridge when A) he was wounded; B) he heard the bridge crash behind him; C) the Etruscans pushed him back; D) he had proved himself a hero.

V 16. Just as Horatius jumped into the river A) the Etruscans reached the bridge; B) Father Tiber spoke to Horatius; C) the bridge collapsed; D) his armor sank to the bottom of the Tiber.

K. Answer the following questions in English, based on the above story.

1. Quis Tarquinium Superbum ex urbe expellit?
2. Ad quem Tarquinius perfugit?
3. Ubi est Lars Porsenna rēx?
4. Quem collem (*hill*) exercitus Etrūscus occupat?

5. Quid sēparat Iāniculum ab urbe?
6. Ubi tum Horātius Cocles pōnitur?
7. Quōmodo *(how)* Horātius Cocles sē servat?

L. Translate the following sentences into Latin.

1. Tarquinius defends himself.
2. The Romans themselves expel him from the city.
3. Tarquinius himself asks for help from Porsenna.
4. Porsenna gets together a large army.
5. Porsenna leads his army against Rome itself.
6. His army occupies the Janiculum itself.
7. Etruscans decide to cross the bridge.
8. Horatius Cocles saves himself.

WORD POWER

M. Give the Latin source for each of the following English derivatives. If the Latin source word is a noun or adjective, give the nominative singular. If it is a verb, give the infinitive.

1. coronation	____	6. recess	____
2. unique	____	7. transit	____
3. expulsion	____	8. station	____
4. auxiliary	____	9. destruction	____
5. occupy	____	10. remain	____

Demonstratives

Ūsus est optimus magister. Experience is the best teacher.

A demonstrative points out a person or object as *here* or *there*. The demonstratives are:

hic this (one)   **is, ille, iste** that (one)   **īdem** the same (one)

(See Chapter 13 for the declension of **is ea id. Iste** is declined like **ille**.)

	DECLENSION OF DEMONSTRATIVES					
	hic this					
	SINGULAR			PLURAL		
	MASCULINE	FEMININE	NEUTER	MASCULINE	FEMININE	NEUTER
NOM.	**hic**	**haec**	**hoc**	**hī**	**hae**	**haec**
GEN.	**huius**	**huius**	**huius**	**hōrum**	**hārum**	**hōrum**
DAT.	**huic**	**huic**	**huic**	**hīs**	**hīs**	**hīs**
ACC.	**hunc**	**hanc**	**hoc**	**hōs**	**hās**	**haec**
ABL.	**hōc**	**hāc**	**hōc**	**hīs**	**hīs**	**hīs**

ille that					
SINGULAR			**PLURAL**		
MASCULINE	FEMININE	NEUTER	MASCULINE	FEMININE	NEUTER
NOM. ille	illa	illud	illī	illae	illa
GEN. illīus	illīus	illīus	illōrum	illārum	illōrum
DAT. illī	illī	illī	illīs	illīs	illīs
ACC. illum	illam	illud	illōs	illās	illa
ABL. illō	illā	illō	illīs	illīs	illīs

īdem the same					
SINGULAR			**PLURAL**		
MASCULINE	FEMININE	NEUTER	MASCULINE	FEMININE	NEUTER
NOM. īdem	eadem	idem	eīdem	eaedem	eadem
GEN. eiusdem	eiusdem	eiusdem	eōrundem	eārundem	eōrundem
DAT. eīdem	eīdem	eīdem	eīsdem	eīsdem	eīsdem
ACC. eundem	eandem	idem	eōsdem	eāsdem	eadem
ABL. eōdem	eādem	eōdem	eīsdem	eīsdem	eīsdem

NOTE

Note that in the declension of **īdem eadem idem,** an **m** before **-dem** changes to **n**. For instance, the accusative form **eum** becomes **eundem.** The masculine nominative plural can be either **eīdem** or **iīdem,** and the dative and ablative plural can be **eīsdem** or **iīsdem.**

1. If demonstratives **stand alone,** they function as pronouns. However, much more frequently they **stand with nouns,** and then they function as adjectives. They then can be called **demonstrative adjectives.**

Examples

hic this (one)	**hic puer** this boy
ille that (one)	**ille puer** that boy
iste that (one)	**iste puer** that (bad) boy
is that *or* this (one)	**is puer** that *or* this boy
īdem the same one	**īdem puer** the same boy

2. As you saw in the previous chapter, **is, ea, id** also serve frequently as personal pronouns in the third person *he, she, it*. When they are demonstratives, they are **weak demonstratives,** that is, they can mean *this* or *that* and refer to a person or a thing previously mentioned or implied without a strong demonstrative sense. For instance **eō annō** *in that year* is demonstrative, but not in a local sense.

3. **ille** and **hic** have a definite local sense. **hic** refers to a person or thing **near the speaker** and **ille** to a person or thing **further away. ille . . . hic** mean *the former* (i.e., the one mentioned earlier) . . . *the latter* (i.e., the last mentioned).

<table>
<tr><td>*Example*</td><td>**Caesar et Bibulus eōdem annō cōnsulēs erant.** *Illum* **omnēs timēbant;** *hunc* **neglegēbant.**</td><td>Caesar et Bibulus were consuls in the same year. All feared *the former;* they ignored *the latter.*</td></tr>
</table>

4. The demonstrative **iste, ista, istud** differs from **ille, illa, illud** in that the former often conveys a **negative tone,** or a sense of dislike and sometimes means *that . . . of yours;* **ille**, on the other hand, conveys a **positive tone** and sometimes means *that famous . . . .* The declension of **iste** is exactly the same as that of **ille.**

<table>
<tr><td>*Examples*</td><td>**Corinthiōrum amātor iste verbōrum, iste, iste rhētor!** (Cicero)</td><td>That admirer of Corinthian words, that, that (miserable) rhetorician!</td></tr>
<tr><td></td><td>**Ego sum ille rēx Philippus!**</td><td>I am the (famous) king Philip!</td></tr>
</table>

5. The **neuter plural haec** as a pronoun can have **various meanings,** depending on the context. Latin is very fond of this construction.

<table>
<tr><td>*Examples*</td><td>**Lēgātus** *haec* **senātuī nūntiāvit.**</td><td>The ambassador announced *this news* to the senate.</td></tr>
<tr><td></td><td>**Lēgātus** *haec* **senātuī dīxit.**</td><td>The ambassador said *these words* *or* The ambassdador said *the following (words)* to the senate.</td></tr>
<tr><td></td><td>*Haec* **senātum perturbāvērunt.**</td><td>*These matters* upset the senate.</td></tr>
<tr><td></td><td>**Itaque senātus** *haec* **inquisīvit.**</td><td>And so the senate asked *these questions.*</td></tr>
<tr><td></td><td>**Lēgātus deinde** *haec* **respondit.**</td><td>The ambassador then gave *this response.*</td></tr>
</table>

A. In the following sentences, supply the correct forms of **hic, haec, hoc**, which in this exercise always precede the nouns that they modify.

VOCABULARY

cīv·is -is (*gen pl* **cīvium**) *mf* citizen   **dīxērunt** said   **timuērunt** feared

1. Rōmānī nōminant ____ urbem Rōmam.
2. Omnēs cīvēs in ____ urbe sunt sēcūrī.
3. Nam moenia ____ urbis sunt alta et crassa.
4. Rōmulus nōmen suum ____ oppidō dedit.
5. Rōmulus in ____ oppidō diū rēgnāvit.
6. Vītae ____ cīvium sunt fēlīcēs.
7. Cīvēs Rōmānī Tarquinium Superbum ex ____ urbe expulērunt.
8. ____ rēx erat arrogāns. Itaque omnēs cīvēs ____ rēgem timuērunt.
9. Horātius Cocles ____ urbem servāvit.
10. Itaque senātus corōnam auream ____ fortī mīlitī dedit.
11. Senātōrēs ____ verba in cūriā dīxērunt.
12. Populus verba ____ senātōrum laudāvit.

B. You saw above, in note **5**, how the neuter plural pronoun **haec** can have various meanings, depending on the context. Using the examples given there of the use of **haec** as your model, complete the following sentences by providing the Latin translation for the English words.

1. Vetūria, māter Coriolānī, (*said the following*).
2. (*These matters*) Coriolānum perturbāvērunt.
3. Deinde Vetūria dē Volscīs (*asked these questions*).
4. Coriolānus deinde (*gave this response*).

C. In the following sentences, supply the correct form of **hic, haec, hoc** in the first slot, and the correct form of **ille, illa, illud** in the second slot. The demonstratives in this exercise always precede the nouns they modify.

1. ____ oppidum est novum, sed ____ oppidum est vetus.
2. Moenia alta ____ oppidīs sunt, sed nōn ____.
3. Cīvēs ____ oppidī sunt sēcūrī, sed cīvēs ____ oppidī sunt in perīculō.
4. Vītae ____ patriciōrum sunt fēlīcēs, sed vītae ____ plēbēiōrum sunt miserae.

5. Viae ___ oppidōrum sunt perīculōsae, sed viae ___ oppidī nōn sunt periculōsae.
6. Aquae ___ flūminis sunt altae, sed aquae ___ flūminis sunt tenuēs *(shallow)*.
7. Nōmen ___ flūminī est Tiberis, sed nōmen ___ flūminī est Padus.
8. Rōma nōn procul est ab ___ flūmine, sed Alba Longa est procul ab ___ flūmine.
9. Rutulī in ___ castrīs sunt, sed Trōiānī in ___ castrīs sunt.
10. ___ sunt nāvēs Graecae, sed ___ sunt nāvēs Trōiānae.

D. Supply the correct form of **īdem, eadem, idem**, which in the following sentences always precede the nouns they modify.

VOCABULARY

convēnērunt met   **fodicāvērunt** stabbed   **potābant** drank

1. Omnēs frātrēs meī in ___ domō habitant.
2. ___ tempore avunculus meus Ardeae habitat.
3. Omnēs cīvēs ___ oppidum amant.
4. Avus meus ___ fabulam dē Rōmulō et Remō nārrat.
5. Faustulus et Lārentia in ___ casā habitant.
6. Cūr tū ___ verba semper dīcis?
7. Nōs omnēs habēmus ___ spēs et ___ timōrēs.
8. Pȳramus et Thisbē ad ___ arborem convēnērunt.
9. Pȳramus et Thisbē _____ sīcā sē fodicāvērunt.
10. Rōmānī et Etrūscī aquam dē ___ flūmine potābant.

E. Translate the English phrases into Latin to complete the sentences.

1. Horātius Cocles natat *(in the same river)*.
2. Etrūscī ambulant *(across the same bridge)*.
3. Horātius accēpit *(the same golden crown)*.
4. Thisbē sē fodicāvit *(with the same dagger)*.
5. *(The same towns)* in rīpā Tiberis sunt.

The war between Lars Porsenna of Clusium and the Romans produced three outstanding heroes. You saw how Horatius Cocles *(One-eyed)* distinguished himself at the Sublician Bridge. Now read the account, again recorded by the great historian Livy (59 B.C.-17 A.D.), about the heroism of a young patrician named Gaius Mucius Scaevola *(Lefty)*.

Historia dē Mūciō Scaevolā
The Story of Mucius Scaevola

I

Lars Porsenna et eius exercitus Tiberim Ponte Sublicio trānsīre temptābant. Sed Horātius cum eius commīlitibus eōs prohibuit. Porsenna autem urbem diū obsidēbat; mox Rōmānī erant dēspērātī quod eīs cibus nōn erat.

temptābant tried
prohibuit prevented
diū a long time **obsidēbat** blockaded
dēspērāt·us -a -um desperate **quod** because **cib·us -ī** *m* food

II

Tandem Gāius Mūcius, mīles fortis et iuvenis nōbilis, hoc cōnsilium cēpit: ad senātum properāvit et "ego ipse" inquit "in castra hostium fūrtim rēpĕre volō et istum dūcem Etrūscōrum necāre. Hōc modō istī hostēs hanc urbem nōn iam obsidēre poterunt." Senātus utpote hoc cōnsilium libenter approbāvit.

cōnsilium cēpīt formed a plan
properāvit rushed
inquit he says
volō I want **fūrtim rēpĕre** to sneak

mod·us -ī *m* way **nōn iam** no longer
poterunt will be able
utpote *adv* as you might expect, of course
approbāvit approved of **libenter** gladly

III

Itaque Gāius Mūcius sīcam suam cēpit et in castra hostium fūrtim irrēpsit. Ubi eō pervēnit, Mūcius in turbā prope suggestum latēbat. Forte scrība prope rēgem in suggestū sedēbat et simillimum ōrnātum gerēbat. Porrō scrība illō tempore stīpendium mīlitibus dābat. Itaque Mūcius eum prō rēge necāvit.

sīc·a -ae *f* dagger
cēpīt took
irrēpsit sneaked in **ubi** when **eō** there
pervēnit arrived **turb·a -ae** *f* crowd
suggest·us -ūs *m* platform **latēbat** hid
forte by chance **scrīb·a -ae** *m* secretary
ōrnāt·us -ūs *m* outfit, uniform **gerēbat** wore **porrō** besides **stīpendi·um -ī** *n* pay
dābat was giving **prō** (+ *abl*) instead of

IV

Dum ille viam per turbam sibi cito facit, rēgiī satellitēs Mūcium appre-

dum while **cito** quickly
apprehendērunt arrested **rēgi·us -a -um**

Mucius before King Porsenna

hendērunt et ad Porsennam rēgem ipsum trāxērunt. "Quis es tū," rogāvit rēx, "et cūr meum scrībam necāvistī?"

royal, king's **satelles satellit·is** *m* body-guard, attendant **trāxērunt** dragged

V

"Ego," inquit Mūcius, "cīvis Rōmānus sum. Tē, Ō rēx, tē hostem patriae meae, necāre temptābam. Sed vīta tua semper in perīculō erit. Nam trēcentī aliī iuvenēs sunt

erit will be
trecent·ī -ae -a three hundred **ali·us -a**

parātī tē necāre. Ego neque mortem neque dolōrem timeō." Eōdem tempore iniēcit manum dextram in ignem, quī prope rēgem erat.

-ud other **parāt·us -a -um** ready
dolor dolōr·is *m* pain
iniēcīt thrust
ign·is -is *m* fire

VI

Hīs verbīs Mūcius rēgem perterruit et admīrātiōnem eius mōvit. Rēx Mūcium dīmīsit et deinde lēgātōs ad senātum Rōmānum dē pace mīsit. Deinde exercitum suum ā Iāniculō remōvit. Ob hōc factum virtūtis, Rōmānī huic fortī mīlitī cognōmen Scaevolam dedērunt.

perterruit terrified
admīrātiō admīrātiōn·is *f* admiration
mōvit stirred **dīmīsit** dismissed, let go

mīsit sent
ob (+ *acc.*) because of **fact·um -ī** *n* deed
virtūs virtūt·is *f* courage

F. Answer the following questions in English, based on the above story.

I 1. What did Lars Porsenna and his army attempt to do?
   2. Why didn't he succeed?
   3. What was the next measure that Porsenna took?
   4. What effect did that measure have on the Roman people?

II 5. Did Mucius belong to the patrician or plebeian class?
   6. What plan did Gaius Mucius form?
   7. Whose approval did Gaius seek for his plan?
   8. What did the senate think of his idea?

III 9. Why did Gaius Mucius take a dagger rather than a sword?
   10. Since the one and only bridge was down, how did he cross the river?
   11. Once he arrived in the enemy's camp, how did he escape notice?
   12. Why couldn't he tell the difference between the king and his secretary?
   13. What was the result of this misidentification?

IV 14. What did Gaius Mucius try to do after killing the secretary?
   15. What did the bodyguards do with Gaius Mucius after they caught him?
   16. How would you describe the attitude of Gaius under questioning?

V 17. What reason did Gaius give for trying to kill King Porsenna?

18. Why would it have done little good for Porsenna to kill Gaius?

19. How did Gaius demonstrate that he feared neither death nor pain?

VI 20. What effect did this act by Gaius have on Porsenna?

21. What action did Porsenna take toward Rome as the result of this incident?

22. What military action did Porsenna take?

23. How did the senate honor Gaius Mucius?

24. Whom do you consider a greater wartime hero, Coriolanus or Gaius Mucius?

G. Translate into Latin.

1. Mucius and his fellow soldiers were on the same bridge.
2. These brave young men defended that bridge.
3. Porsenna and his army tried to cross this bridge.
4. Mucius himself showed no fear of King Porsenna.
5. Mucius sneaked into the camp of these same enemies.
6. He killed the secretary of that king.

 There were also Roman women who were heroes. One such was the Roman virgin **Cloelia.** She had been one of the hostages given to Porsenna. She managed to escape from the Etruscan camp and swam across the Tiber to Rome. She was sent back by the Romans to Porsenna, who was so struck by her gallantry that he not only set her free, but allowed her to take with her a number of hostages. Porsenna also rewarded her with a horse adorned with splendid trappings, and the Romans rewarded her with a statue of a female on horseback.

H. Now read the exploits of Cloelia in Latin and complete the demonstratives. All of the demonstrative adjectives in this exercise except **ipse,** precede the nouns that they modify. **Ips·e -a -um,** as we learned, follows the noun it emphasizes. The adjective **hic, haec, hoc** is suggested by **h,** and the adjective **īdem, eadem, idem** is suggested by ____ **dem.**

VOCABULARY

dedērunt gave, dedicated

effūgit escaped

porrō furthermore

remīsērunt sent back

fortitūdō fortitūdin·is *f* gallantry
nōn sōlum . . . sed etiam not only . . . but also . . .
obses obsid·is *mf* hostage

trānsnatāvit swam across
virgō virgin·is *f* (unmarried) girl, virgin

Erat ____dem tempore in (*among*) ill__ obsidibus virgō Rōmāna. Nōmen h____ virginī erat Cloelia. H____ virgō autem ex castrīs Etrūscīs effūgit et trāns Tiberim trānsnatāvit. Ist__ Rōmānī autem h____ virginem ad ist__ rēgem Porsennam remīsērunt. Porsenna ips____ fortitūdinem h____ virginis laudāvit. Itaque rēx nōn sōlum lībertātem h____ virginī dedit, sed etiam decem ex ill____ obsidibus. Rēx etiam equum splendidum h____ virginī dedit. Deinde Cloelia cum ill__ obsidibus Rōmam rediit. Nunc Rōmānī ips__ fortitūdinem h____ ____dem virginis laudāvērunt. Porrō, Rōmānī nunc statuam pulchram h____ ____dem virginī dedērunt.

I. Complete the Latin sentences by translating the English words. Use **is, ea, id** for the personal pronouns (he, she, they, etc.). Remember that if *they* refers to both a male and female, the masculine form of the pronoun is used.

VOCABULARY
stābant stood

1. Scaevola et Cloelia erant (*in the same*) castrīs, sed nōn (*at the same*) tempore.
2. Stābant apud (*the same*) rēgem.
3. (*They*) dēmonstrāvērunt (*the same*) fortitūdinem.
4. Rēx (*himself*) laudāvit (*their*) fortitūdinem.
5. Stābant in (*the same*) tribūnālī cum rēgē (*himself.*)
6. Scaevola et Cloelia nōn timēbant rēgem (*himself.*)
7. Virgō et iuvenis trānsnatāvērunt (*the same*)flūmen, sed nōn (*at the same*) tempore.
8. Quis (*this*) fortem puerum et (*that*) fortem puellam nōn laudābit?

WORD POWER

J. Give the Latin source for each of the English derivatives. If it is a noun or adjective, give the nominative form; if it is a verb, give the infinitive.

1. tempt ____
2. civic ____
3. mode ____
4. approbation ____
5. scribe ____
6. satellite ____
7. dolorous ____
8. inject ____
9. fact ____
10. fortitude ____
11. latent ____
12. ignition ____
13. tractor ____
14. motion ____
15. obsession ____
16. stipend ____
17. traction ____
18. apprehension ____
19. igneous ____
20. remission ____

WORD SEARCH

K. First find the answer to each clue. Note that in some cases the Latin form is called for, in others the English form. Then circle that word in the puzzle below. The words may run from right to left, from left to right, up or down, or diagonally.

1. King of the Rutuli.
2. King of Clusium.
3. River near Rome. *(Latin)*
4. Capital of the Rutuli.
5. Wife of King Latinus.
6. Grandfather of Romulus and Remus.
7. Port city of Rome.
8. Nickname of Gaius Mucius for losing his right hand.
9. Queen of Carthage.
10. Nickname of Marcius for storming the enemy's gate.
11. God of war.
12. Shepherd who discovered Romulus and Remus.
13. Rome's enemy during the battle for the town of Corioli. *(Latin)*
14. Queen of Troy.
15. Hill from which Porsenna launched his attack against Rome. *(English)*
16. God who pursued the nymph that was changed into a tree.
17. Type of tree into which the nymph was changed.
18. Son of Aeneas.

19. King of Troy. *(Latin)*
20. Wife of Jupiter.
21. Nymph who was changed into a tree.
22. Wife of the shepherd who saved Romulus and Remus.

```
D  S  U  L  U  T  S  U  A  F  Q  A
A  Q  N  U  M  I  T  O  R  K  N  S
P  Y  S  H  O  N  U  J  D  N  X  C
H  L  U  E  S  D  T  X  E  S  M  A
N  A  N  C  T  I  U  S  A  C  U  N
E  R  A  U  I  D  R  S  S  A  L  I
L  E  L  B  A  O  N  I  U  E  U  U
E  N  O  A  P  A  U  R  M  V  C  S
R  T  I  S  O  T  S  E  A  O  I  S
U  I  R  X  L  A  Y  B  I  L  N  R
A  A  O  Y  L  M  U  I  R  A  A  A
L  K  C  Z  O  A  K  T  P  K  J  M
K  M  U  R  V  O  L  S  C  I  A  T
```

CHAPTER 15

Relative and Interrogative Pronouns

Frustrā labōrat quī omnibus placēre studet.	You can't please everybody. [*lit:* one strives in vain who is eager to please all.]

I. RELATIVE PRONOUNS

DECLENSION OF RELATIVE PRONOUNS					
	SINGULAR			PLURAL	
	MASCULINE	FEMININE	NEUTER	MASCULINE	FEMININE	NEUTER
NOM.	quī	quae	quod	quī	quae	quae
GEN.	cuius	cuius	cuius	quōrum	quārum	quōrum
DAT.	cui	cui	cui	quibus	quibus	quibus
ACC.	quem	quam	quod	quōs	quās	quae
ABL.	quō	quā	quō	quibus	quibus	quibus

1. The relative pronouns **qui, quae, quod,** (in English, *who, which,* or *that*) refer to a previously mentioned noun in the same sentence; the noun to which the relative pronoun refers is called **its antecedent.** In English this antecedent must occur in the same sentence as the relative pronoun. In Latin the antecedent can be in the previous sentence. In English there must be a specific word to which the pronoun refers. In Latin a whole clause can be the antecedent. For example, in formal English it would be incorrect to say "He broke his leg, which caused him to miss school." In that case the whole clause "he broke his leg" would be the antecedent. That sentence needs to be revised: "He missed school because he had broken his leg."

2. The relative pronoun **agrees with its antecedent in number and gender,** but its case depends on its function in its own clause.

Example **Casa *in quā Faustulus habitābat* in Monte Palātīnō erat.** The cottage *in which Faustulus lived* stood on the Palatine Hill.

In this sentence, **casa** is the antecedent and is in the nominative case because it is the subject of **erat** in the main clause. The relative pronoun **quā** is in the ablative case because it is the object of the preposition **in** within the relative clause (which is in italics).

3. In English we may sometimes omit the relative pronoun. For example, in the sentence "Here is the candy I really love," the relative pronoun "which" or "that" is omitted. Latin never omits the relative pronoun. However, Latin sometimes omits the antecedent in a sentence.

Example **Sunt *quī* pilā lūdĕre amant.** There are *those* who love to play ball.

In this sentence, because the antecedent is omitted, we have to supply it, namely "those."

Incidentally, when **sunt** or **est** comes at the beginning of a sentence, it should be translated "there are" or "there is."

4. We saw that the preposition **cum** is attached to personal and reflexive pronouns: **mēcum, tēcum, nōbīscum, vōbīscum, sēcum.** However, **cum** can, but needn't, be attached to relative pronouns: **quōcum** or **cum quō, quibuscum** or **cum quibus.**

PITFALL Unless you read a Latin sentence with comprehension, there is a danger that you will choose the verb of the subordinate clause (that is, of the relative clause) as the main verb. Therefore, know where the relative clause begins and ends. The Romans did not use commas as we do to set off the subordinate clause. What did they do? They *began* the relative clause with the relative pronoun and *ended* the relative clause with the verb. Of course, if the relative pronoun were the object of a preposition, the Romans would put the preposition before the pronoun, as **in quā** in the sentence in note **2.**

A. According to the ending, some forms of the relative pronoun can indicate only one case, while others can indicate several different cases. Unless you are aware of this fact, you can run into problems when reading Latin. List the cases that each form of the relative pronoun can take.

Example | **quī :**   nom. masc. sing. / nom. masc. pl.

1. quae __ __ __ __
2. quibus __ __ __
3. quod __ __
4. cui __ __ __

5. quōrum __ __
6. cuius __ __ __
7. quō __ __

B. The following partial sentences contain a noun as antecedent and a short relative clause. Complete the sentences with the correct relative pronouns. Remember that the pronoun must agree with its antecedent in gender and number, but that its case is determined by its use within its own clause.

Example | Ager in ___ Clūsium situm est
Ager *in quō* Clūsium situm est
The district *in which* Clusium lies

VOCABULARY

cogitō I think   **dōn·um -ī** *n* gift   **lūdēbam** I played

1. Urbs in ____ ego habitō
2. Verba ____ Turnus dīcit
3. Mīlitēs ____ diū et ācriter pugnant
4. Aenēās ____ Dīdō benignē excēpit
5. Flūmen in ____ līberī natant
6. Moenia ____ hostēs appropinquābant
7. Rēx ____ Aenēās dōna pretiōsa dābat
8. Templa ____ in Capitōliō sunt
9. Portae urbis per ____ Coriolānus inruit
10. Arx īnfrā ____ Turnus stābat
11. Nāvēs in ____ Graecī ad Asiam nāvigābant
12. Fīlia dē ____ ego saepe cogitō
13. Amīcī sine ____ vīta mea est misera
14. Parentēs ____ amōrem meum ego dō

15. Statua ex aurō ____ in Iovis templō stābat
16. Pater ____ līberī in scholā sunt
17. Puer ____ Thisbē amābat
18. Patria prō ____ Turnus pugnābat
19. Puellae cum ____ ego saepe lūdēbam
20. Urbēs ____ Coriolānus superāvit
21. In cūriā in ____ senātōrēs sedent
22. In templīs in ____ statuae sacrae sunt
23. Viae in ____ puerī lūdunt
24. Parentēs ____ amōrem ego dēsīderō

C. Combine each set of two sentences into one by using a relative pronoun. The word that is to become the pronoun is in italics.

Example

Rōmulus erat rēx. Omnēs *rēgem* amābant.
Romulus was king. All loved the *king*.
Rōmulus erat rēx *quem* omnēs amābant.
Romulus was a king *whom* all loved.

VOCABULARY

bāsi·um -ī *n* kiss   **causās agēbat** pleaded cases

1. Rōma erat urbs. Multī in *urbe* habitābant.
2. Faustulus in casā habitābat. *Casa* erat parva.
3. Templum Sāturnī est in forō. *Templum* est proximum rōstrīs.
4. Cūria est in forō. *Cūria* est proxima rōstrīs.
5. Cicerō erat clārus ōrātor. *Eius* ōrātiōnēs etiam hodiē legimus.
6. Cūria est prope basilicam. Cicerō causās saepe agēbat in *eā*.
7. Capitōlium est mōns. Templum Iovis in *eō* ōlim stābat.
8. Thisbē erat bella puella. Pȳramus *puellam* amābat.
9. Thisbē erat puella. Pȳramus bāsia *puellae* dedit.
10. Dīdō erat rēgīna. Tōta Carthāgō *rēgīnam* amābat.
11. Horātius erat fortis puer. Senātus corōnam auream *Horātiō* dedit.
12. Clūsium erat oppidum Etrūscum. Lars Porsenna erat rēx in *eō*.

D. First read over each sentence carefully for comprehension. Next, identify the entire relative clause. Don't forget that in Latin the relative clause begins with the relative pronoun and ends with the verb. Then supply the correct form of the relative pronoun required in each relative clause.

Example | Venus ____ māter Aenēae est dea pulchritūdinis est.
Venus *quae māter Aenēae est* **dea pulchritūdinis est.**
Venus, who is the mother of Aeneas, is the goddess of beauty.

VOCABULARY

adhūc *adv* still

av·us -ī *m* grandfather

dūr·us -a -um hard, tough

lign·um -ī *n* wood

multō posteā long after

pāstor pāstōr·is *m* shepherd

reddidērunt gave back, returned

1. Rōma est urbs ____ Rōmulus nōmen suum dedit.
2. Lupa ____ geminōs in flūminis rīpā invēnit eīs benigna erat.
3. Pāstor ____ geminōs domum dūxit eōs ēducāvit.
4. Flūmen in ____ geminī expositī erant praeter Rōmam fluit.
5. Pōns per ____ Rōmānī ad Iāniculum trānsībant ex lignō factus est.
6. Prīmō, oppidum ____ Rōmulus fundāvit paucās casās habēbat.
7. Casae in ____ pāstōrēs habitābant parvae et humilēs erant.
8. Numitor ____ Albae Longae rēgnābat avus geminōrum erat.
9. Numitōris frāter ____ nōmen Amūlius erat ipse rēgnāre dēsīderābat.
10. Itaque Amūlius ____ perīculōsus vir erat frātrem ex urbe expulit.
11. Deinde Amūlius geminōs ____ māter Rhēa Silvia erat in flūmine exposuit.
12. Multō posteā, geminī ____ nunc iuvenēs erant, Numitōrem regnō reddidērunt.
13. Pāstōrēs ____ casae in Palātīnō erant vītam dūram dūcēbant.
14. Faustulus ____ casa prope Tiberim erat Rōmulum et Remum servāvit.
15. Eī ____ parentēs adhūc vīvunt fēlīcēs sunt.

II. INTERROGATIVE PRONOUNS

DECLENSION OF INTERROGATIVE PRONOUNS

	SINGULAR		PLURAL		
	MASC. & FEM.	NEUTER	MASCULINE	FEMININE	NEUTER
NOM.	quis	quid	quī	quae	quae
GEN.	cuius	cuius	quōrum	quārum	quōrum
DAT.	cui	cui	quibus	quibus	quibus
ACC.	quem	quid	quōs	quās	quae
ABL.	quō	quō	quibus	quibus	quibus

1. The interrogative pronoun asks a question.

Examples

RELATIVE
Mīles, *quī* magnam virtūtem praebuit, corōnam mūrālem accēpit.
The soldier *who* displayed great valor received a mural crown.

INTERROGATIVE
***Quis* plūs virtūtis praebuit quam Mūcius Scaevola?**
Who displayed more courage than Mucius Scaevola?

2. As shown in the table above, the plural of interrogative pronouns follows the declension of the relative pronoun. The plural form of the interrogative pronoun is used when the person asking the question knows that more than one person is involved, as the following examples from Cicero show.

Examples

Quī, malum, quī istī sunt?	Who the heck, who are those people?
Quōs Catilīna nōn offendit?	Whom has Catilina not offended?

3. The interrogative adjective, **quī** *what?, which?* is declined exactly like the relative pronoun, namely, **quī quae quod,** etc.

Examples

Quī homō patriam suam nōn amat?	What man does not love his country?
Quod templum est proximum rōstrīs in forō?	Which temple is next to the rostrum in the forum?

EXERCISES

E. Supply the correct form of the Latin interrogative pronoun whose English counterpart is given in parentheses. When you have finished that task, answer the questions in Latin.

Example

(Against whom) Contrā ____ Graecī decem annōs pugnābant?
Contrā *quem* Graecī decem annōs pugnābant? *Trōiānōs.*
Against *whom* did the Greeks fight for ten years? *The Trojans.*

1. (Who) ____ erat ultimus rēx Rōmae?
2. (Whose) ____ pater erat Anchīsēs?
3. (Whom) ____ Aenēās in urbe Carthāgine adamāvit?
4. (To whom) ____ senātus cognōmen Coriolānum dedit?

5. (To whom) Ad ____ Aenēās dōna pretiōsa mīsit?
6. (With whom) Cum ____ Faustulus in Monte Palātīnō habitābat?
7. (Whom) ____ Aenēās nōn placēbat?
8. (Before whom) Apud ____ Mūcius dexteram manum in ignem iniēcit?
9. (What) ____ Trōiānī in urbem suam trahēbant?
10. (Who) ____ erat mīles fortissimus in Ponte Subliciō?
11. (Whose) ____ urbs erant Coriolī?
12. (For whom) Prō ____ Lars Porsenna contrā Rōmānōs pugnāvit?

F. Supply the correct form of the interrogative adjective. Remember that it is inflected like the relative pronoun. Then translate the sentence.

Example

| ____ deus erat rēx deōrum hominumque?
| ***Quī* deus erat rēx deōrum hominumque?**
| *What* god was the king of gods and men?

1. ____ oppidum Ascanius fundāvit?
2. Dē ____ rēbus Rēx Latīnus cum Aeneā dīxit?
3. Ex ____ urbe Lars Porsenna vēnit?
4. ____ manum Mūcius Scaevola in ignem iniēcit?
5. ____ lēgātī Rōmānī ad Coriolānum in castra vēnērunt?
6. In ____ templīs erant statuae aureae?
7. ____ iuvenis Thisbēn amāvit?
8. ____ urbem exercitus Rōmānus obsidēbat?
9. ____ magistrātūs populus Rōmānus post rēgēs creāvit?
10. Post ____ bellum erat pāx inter Trōiānōs et Graecōs?
11. In ____ agrō iacet Rōma?
12. Prope ____ flūmen est Mōns Aventīnus?

ANDROCLES AND THE LION

Here is a fantastic story. The ancient writer said that he himself would find it hard to believe, except for the fact that he was in the great arena in Rome, the Circus Maximus, and witnessed the incredible scene. It must have been the talk of the town for months thereafter. (The **Circus Maximus**, meaning "Biggest Race Course" and lying between the Palatine and Aventine Hills, was used for chariot racing as well as gladiatorial events and wild-animal shows until the Colosseum was built in A.D. 80. The emperor lived in a palace on the Palatine Hill and had a box seat overlooking the Circus Maximus.) After the incident between Androcles and the lion, the emperor asked Androcles for an explanation. Here's what Androcles told the emperor as people eagerly leaned forward to overhear what he was saying.

"My master was governor of the Roman province in North Africa. Because of the constant flogging he gave me, I ran away into the desert. To escape the scorching sun, I took shelter in a cave and hid myself in its cool, dark interior. Soon thereafter, a huge lion with one paw lame and bleeding came into the same cave, which happened to be his lair. When he spotted me, he approached me gently and held up his bleeding paw. I got out a splinter and cleaned out the badly infected wound. Then the lion, putting his paw into my hand, lay down and went to sleep. For three years we shared the same cave as well as the choicest bits of venison that the lion brought me in the cave. I had no fire, and so I roasted it in the noonday sun."

"But getting bored with life in the wild, I left the cave and after three days was caught by some Roman soldiers and taken from Africa to my master in Rome. He at once condemned me to be thrown to the wild beasts as punishment." **(ad bēstiās dare** or **condemnāre** was the regular term for the punishment of being thrown to the wild beasts.) Below is the account that the ancient author gives of the incredible scene in the Circus Maximus.

Androcles in the cave

Androcles and the Lion
in the Circus Maximus

Androclēs et Leō
Androcles and the Lion

I

In Circō Maximō saepe sunt vēnātiōnēs, quae populum dēlectant. Eō diē forte ego spectātor ibi fuī. Multae ibi bēstiae erant, quae magnitūdine et ferōciā excellēbant, sed praetereā leōnēs. Erat autem ūnus leō quī animōs omnium in sē convertit, propter eius magnitūdinem et terrificum fremitum.

vēnātiō vēnātiōn·is *f* wild-animal show
dēlectant entertain
bēsti·a -ae *f* wild animal
excellēbant (+ *abl*) excelled (*or* outdid) in
magnitūdō magnitūdin·is *f* size ferōci·a
-ae *f* ferocity praetereā especially erat
there was convertit drew anim·ī -ōrum
mpl attention terrific·us -a -um
frightening fremit·us -ūs *m* roar

II

Erat servus inter multōs aliōs quem mīlites in arēnam intrōdūxerant. Eī servō Androclēs nōmen fuit. Ubi ille leō illum servum procul vīdit, repentē īlicō cōnstitit; et deinde gradātim atque placidē Androclae appropinquāvit, tamquam nōscitāns servum. Nam erat īdem leō, quōcum Androclēs ōlim in spēluncā habitāverat.

serv·us -ī *m* slave
intrōdūxerant had brought in
ubi when
procul from far off
repentē suddenly īlicō on the spot, in his tracks cōnstitit stopped gradātim gradually placidē calmly, peacefully tamquam nōscitāns as if recognizing

III

Tum caudam mōvit, more canis, et iuxtā servum cōnsēdit. Servus iam prope exanimātus erat timōre. Sed leō manūs hominis lambit.

caud·a -ae *f* tail mōvit wags more (+ *gen*) in the manner of, like can·is -is *m* dog iuxtā (+ *acc*) next to cōnsēdit sat down prope almost exanimāt·us -a -um fainting timor timōr·is *m* fear lambit licked

IV

Androclēs, inter illa blandīmenta tam ferōcis bēstiae, animum recuperat et oculōs gradātim aperit et leōnem spectat. Tum quasī mūtuā recognitiōne dēlectātī, homō et leō laetissimī sunt.

inter (+ *acc*) during blandīment·um -ī *n* act of endearment tam such, so anim·us -ī *m* courage recuperat regains quasi as if mūtu·us -a -um mutual dēlectāt·us -a -um delighted laet·us -a -um happy

V

Populus, quem ea rēs tam admīrābilīs excitāvit, maximē clāmat et applaudit. Caesar ipse, quī tōtam rem vīdit, Androclēn ad sē vocat et rogat: "Cūr ille ferōcissimus leō tibi sōlī pepercit?" Tum Androclēs tōtam rem mīrificam nārrāvit.

rēs rĕī *f* thing, affair, sight admīrābil·is -is -e astonishing excitāvit excited maximē very loudly clāmat cheers applaudit applauds

sōl·us -a -um alone pepercit (+ *dat*) spared mīrific·us -a -um surprising

Epilogue

The ancient author says (remember, he was there) that, as the story which was told to the emperor spread throughout the Circus Maximus, the people demanded that Androcles be freed, acquitted, and presented with the lion. The emperor acceded to their wishes. "Afterwards," says the ancient author, "we used to see Androcles with the lion, attached to a thin leash, making the rounds of the shops throughout the city; Androcles was given money, the lion was sprinkled with flowers. Everywhere they went, people pointed to them and said: " This is the lion that befriended that man; this is the man who was the lion's doctor."

EXERCISES

G. Answer the following questions in English which are based on the story that you have just read.

I 1. What was the purpose of the wild-animal shows?
2. Who was one of the spectators?
3. In what regard did the wild animals excel?
4. Which ones stood out especially?
5. Why did the one lion attract the attention of all?

II 6. How was it that Androcles was in the arena?
7. What did that lion do when it first saw Androcles?
8. In what manner did the lion approach Androcles?
9. Why did the lion seem to act in this manner?

III 10. What did the lion do when it first reached Androcles?
11. What did the lion do next?
12. What was the reaction of Androcles?
13. What did the lion do next to show goodwill?

IV 14. What caused Androcles to gradually open his eyes?
15. What did Androcles expect to see?
16. What was the mood of the lion and Androcles?

V 17. How did the spectators react to the scene?
18. Why might they have been disappointed at first?
19. What did Caesar do?

H. Complete the following sentences by supplying the appropriate relative pronoun for each blank.

VOCABULARY

loc·us -ī *n* place (*pl* **loc·a -ōrum** *npl* places)   **mīr·us -a -um** strange

1. Circus Maximus est locus, in ____ ego bēstiās spectō.
2. Ego ipse eram in spectātoribus, ____ illum leōnem spectābant.
3. Bēstiae, ____ in arēnam vēnērunt, erant ferōcissimae.
4. Erat ūnus leō, ____ animōs omnium in sē convertit.
5. Androclēs, ____ *(dative)* ille leō appropinquābat, erat perterritus.
6. Leō autem, ____ Androclēs timuit, erat vetus amīcus.
7. Spectātōrēs ____ hanc mīram rem spectābant, clāmāvērunt et applaudērunt.
8. Spectātōrēs, ____ admīrātiōnem Androclēs excitāvit, diū applausērunt.

WORD POWER

I. Give the Latin source word for each of the following English derivatives. If the source word is a noun or adjective, give the nominative singular; if it is a verb, give the infinitive.

1. applause   ____
2. delectable   ____
3. convert   ____
4. admirable   ____
5. caudal   ____
6. terrific   ____
7. bestial   ____
8. magnitude   ____
9. ferocity   ____
10. placid   ____
11. introduction   ____
12. leonine   ____
13. locate   ____
14. clamor   ____
15. parsimonious   ____

CHAPTER 16

Roman Numerals

THOUGHT FOR TODAY

Ubi thēsaurus est, ibi est cor tuum. Where your treasure is, there is your heart.

DECLENSION OF NUMERALS

ūnus one   **duo** two

	SINGULAR			PLURAL ONLY		
	MASCULINE	FEMININE	NEUTER	MASCULINE	FEMININE	NEUTER
NOM.	ūnus	ūna	ūnum	duo	duae	duo
GEN.	ūnīus	ūnīus	ūnīus	duōrum	duārum	duōrum
DAT.	ūnī	ūnī	ūnī	duōbus	duābus	duōbus
ACC.	ūnum	ūnam	ūnum	duōs	duās	duo
ABL.	ūnō	ūnā	ūnō	duōbus	duābus	duōbus

trēs three   **mīlle** thousand   **mīlia** thousand(s)

	PLURAL ONLY		INDECLINABLE	PLURAL ONLY
	MASC. & FEM.	NEUTER	MASC., FEM., NEUTER	NEUTER
NOM.	trēs	tria	mīlle	mīlia
GEN.	trium	trium	mīlle	mīlium
DAT.	tribus	tribus	mīlle	mīlibus
ACC.	trēs	tria	mīlle	mīlia
ABL.	tribus	tribus	mīlle	mīlibus

	ROMAN NUMERALS	CARDINALS	ORDINALS
1	I	ūn·us -a, -um	prīm·us -a -um
2	II	duo, duae, duo	secundus
3	III	trēs, tria	tertius
4	IV	quattuor	quārtus
5	V	quīnque	quīntus
6	VI	sex	sextus
7	VII	septem	septimus
8	VIII	octō	octāvus
9	IX	novem	nōnus
10	X	decem	decimus
11	XI	ūndecim	ūndecimus
12	XII	duodecim	duodecimus
13	XIII	tredecim	tertius decimus
14	XIV	quattuordecim	quārtus decimus
15	XV	quīndecim	quīntus decimus
16	XVI	sēdecim	sextus decimus
17	XVII	septendecim	septimus decimus
18	XVIII	duodēvīgintī	duodēvīcēsimus
19	XIX	ūndēvīgintī	ūndēvīcēsimus
20	XX	vīgintī	vīcēsimus
21	XXI	vīgintī ūnus *or* ūnus et vīgintī	vīcēsimus prīmus
22	XXII	vīgintī duo *or* duo et vīgintī	vīcēsimus secundus
30	XXX	trīgintā	trīcēsimus
40	XL	quadrāgintā	quadrāgēsimus
50	L	quīnquāgintā	quīnquāgēsimus
60	LX	sexāgintā	sexāgēsimus
70	LXX	septuāgintā	septuāgēsimus
80	LXXX	octōgintā	octōgēsimus
90	XC	nōnāgintā	nōnāgēsimus
100	C	centum	centēsimus
101	CI	centum ūnus *or* centum et ūnus	centēsimus prīmus
200	CC	ducent·ī -ae -a	ducentēsimus
300	CCC	trecent·ī -ae -a	trecentēsimus
400	CCCC	quadringent·ī -ae -a	quadringentēsimus
500	D	quīngent·ī -ae -a	quīngentēsimus
600	DC	sescent·ī -ae -a	sescentēsimus

700	DCC	septingent·ī -ae -a	septingentēsimus
800	DCCC	octingent·ī -ae -a	octingentēsimus
900	DCCCC	nōngent·ī -ae -a	nōngentēsimus
1,000	M	mīlle	mīllēsimus
2,000	MM	duo mīlia	bis mīllēsimus

NOTES

1) Ordinal numbers like **prīm·us -a -um** are declined like **bon·us -a -um**.

2) The following adjectives are declined like **ūnus,** that is, they end in **-īus** in the genitive singular and in **-ī** in the dative singular:

nūll·us -a -um no(ne)　　　　　　**tōt·us -a -um** whole, entire
sōl·us -a -um alone　　　　　　　**ūll·us -a -um** any

3) The plural of **ūn·us -a -um** is regular and is used with nouns that are plural in form but singular in meaning. For example, **scōp·ae -ārum** *fpl* means "broom"; it is plural in form but singular in meaning; therefore **ūnae scōpae** means "one broom." The word **littera** means "letter" in the sense of a single letter of the alphabet; the plural form **litterae** can mean letters of the alphabet or an epistle. Therefore the Romans said **ūnae litterae** when they meant "one letter" in the mail.

4) The numerals from **quattuor** (four) through **vīgintī** and the tens, e.g., **trīgintā, quadrāgintā**, etc., through **centum** are indeclinable.

Examples　　**septem montēs Rōmae**　　　　the seven hills of Rome

　　　　　　　sex Virginēs Vestālēs　　　　six Vestal Virgins

　　　　　　　novem Mūsae　　　　　　　the nine Muses

5) **Mīlle** is an indeclinable adjective, but **mīlia** is a neuter plural noun and is followed by the genitive.

Examples　　**mīlle nāvēs**　　　　　　　a thousand ships

　　　　　　　duo mīlia nāvium　　　　two thousand ships (*lit:* two thousands of ships)

　　　　　　　duo mīlia passuum　　　two miles (two thousand paces; *lit:* two thousands of paces)

6) The numerals that we use today (Arabic numerals) were not introduced into Europe until about a thousand years after the time of Julius Caesar. In the Roman system, the placement of vertical lines (for one) *after* a numeral indicates *addition;* for example, VII means 5 + 2, XIII means 10 + 3. The placement of vertical lines *before* a numeral indicates *subtraction;* for example, IV means 5-1, IX means 10-1.

7) The Romans for some strange reason sometimes named their children by ordinal numbers, for example, **Secundus, Quīntus, Sextus, Septimus, Decimus.** The name **Quīntus** did not indicate that that son was the fifth son or child in the family; it was simply a name. **Octāvius** was the name of a Roman clan, or extended family. The person who became the emperor **Augustus** belonged to that clan; his name, before he became **Augustus,** was **Gāius Octāvius.**

EXERCISES

A. Read the following numbers aloud and write the corresponding Roman numerals.

Example | **ūndēvīgintī**   XIX

1. quīndecim
2. octō
3. vīgintī quattuor
4. trīgintā
5. novem
6. trēs
7. centum
8. sēdecim
9. duodēvīgintī
10. vīgintī quīnque
11. quattuor
12. sex
13. octōgintā
14. trecentī
15. duo mīlia

B. Write out these numerals in Latin.

Example | **XXXIV**   *trīgintā quattuor*

1. VI
2. XV
3. IX
4. XI
5. XVII
6. XXV
7. XXX
8. XLVII
9. XVIII
10. XIX
11. M
12. CCC
13. XCIII
14. CCXXII
15. XXIX

C. Imagine yourself in a math class in ancient Rome. You arrive just in time to do some fast additions. See whether you can compete with the Roman boys and girls.

Example | **Quot sunt ūnus et duo? — Ūnus et duo sunt trēs.**
How much (*lit:* how many) are one and two? — One and two are three.

1. Quot sunt trēs et quattuor?
2. Quot sunt decem et decem?
3. Quot sunt novem et quattuor?
4. Quot sunt decem et quīnque?
5. Quot sunt septem et septem?
6. Quot sunt sex et quattuor?
7. Quot sunt decem et octō?
8. Quot sunt ūndecim et duodecim?
9. Quot sunt octō et quīnque?
10. Quot sunt quattuordecim et sex?

D. Now test your skill at problems of substraction.

Example | **Quot sunt duo dē quīnque? — Duo dē quīnque sunt trēs.**
How much are two from five (*or* five minus two)? — Five minus two are three.

1. Quot sunt sex dē novem?
2. Quot sunt quattuor dē duodecim?
3. Quot sunt quattuor dē decem?
4. Quot sunt octō dē sēdecim?
5. Quot sunt sex dē trīgintā?
6. Quot sunt ūndecim dē vīgintī duōbus?
7. Quot sunt duo dē vigīntī?
8. Quot sunt quīndecim dē trīgintā?

E. Write the ordinal numbers corresponding to the following cardinal numbers.

Example | **duodecim** *duodecimus*

1. decem	5. sex	8. ūnus
2. duo	6. trēs	9. octō
3. quattuor	7. vīgintī	10. quīnque
4. septem		

F. Here is a list of the seven kings of Rome in the order in which they ruled. Indicate the order by using the ordinal numbers **prīmus,** etc.

1. Rōmulus ____ rēx Rōmae fuit.
2. Numa Pompilius ____ rēx Rōmae fuit.
3. Tullus Hostilius ____ rēx Rōmae fuit.
4. Ancus Marcius ____ rēx Rōmae fuit.
5. Tarquinius Prīscus ____ rēx Rōmae fuit.
6. Servius Tullius ____ rēx Rōmae fuit.
7. Tarquinius Superbus ____ rēx Rōmae fuit.

G. Indicate the order of the months by using the ordinal numbers **prīmus, secundus,** etc.

1. Augustus est ____ mēnsis annī. Februārius est ____ mēnsis annī.
2. Mārtius est ____ mēnsis annī. December est ____ mēnsis annī.
3. September est ____ mēnsis annī. Māius est ____ mēnsis annī.
4. Iānuārius est ____ mēnsis annī. November est ____ mēnsis annī.
5. Iūnius est ____ mēnsis annī. Aprīlis est ____ mēnsis annī.
6. Octōber est ____ mēnsis annī. Iūlius est ____ mēnsis annī.

H. Choose the correct form in parentheses; then translate.

1. tria mīlia (hominēs; hominum)
2. mīlle (mīlitēs; mīlitum)
3. sex mīlia (passūs; passuum)
4. mīlle (spectātōrēs; spectātōrum)
5. sēdecim mīlia (passūs; passuum)
6. duo mīlia (templa; templōrum)

I. In Chapter 1, in **III. 4.,** you were reminded that the accusative case is used to indicate length of time. The ablative of degree of difference is used with **ante/a** *earlier* and **poste/a** *later.* Translate the following expressions of time into Latin. Notice the position of **abhinc** *ago.*

Examples	**abhinc trēs diēs**	three days ago
	tribus diēbus anteā	three days earlier
	tribus diēbus posteā	three days later
	duōs annōs ex hōc tempore	two years from now
	Quīnque annōs mīlitāvit.	He served (for) five years.

1. ten years ago
2. five days earlier
3. twenty years from now
4. fifteen years later
5. eight days ago
6. six years earlier
7. thirty-five years from now
8. eighteen years later
9. Romulus reigned thirty-seven years.
10. Numa Pompilius reigned thirty-nine years.

J. In Chapter 2, in **III. 6.**, you were reminded that the ablative case is used to express time *at which* or time *within which*. Translate the following expressions into Latin.

Examples

trībus diēbus	in *or* within three days
tertiō diē	on the third day
tertiō annō	in the third year

1. in the tenth year
2. on the first day
3. within twelve days
4. in the fifth year
5. in ten days
6. within ten years

K. You will see dates on buildings and in books given in Roman numerals. Give the Roman numerals for the following dates.

Examples

1942	**MCMXLII**
1893	**MDCCCXCIII**
1475	**MCCCCLXXV**

1. 753 (Founding of Rome)
2. 509 (Roman Republic)
3. 476 (Fall of Roman Empire)
4. 1492 (Discovery of America)
5. 1939 (beginning of World War II)

THE LIFE AND CAREER OF CICERO

Knowing the life of Cicero will help you to understand the nature and the fall of the Roman Republic. The life and career of Marcus Tullius Cicero spans the last half-century of the Republic, which had lasted almost 500 years from after the expulsion of the kings in 509 B.C. Born in 106 B.C., in Arpinum, a small town in the Volscian mountains, he did so well in the local school that his father decided to move the family to Rome so that his sons, Marcus and Quintus, could attend a better school. After completing his studies in Rome, he traveled to Greece and Asia Minor (Turkey) "to see the world" and also to continue his education at Athens (the great university town) and Rhodes. Upon his return to Rome, he soon gained fame as a brilliant lawyer. His family belonged to the Roman middle class, or

Bust of Cicero

business class, called knights (**equit·ēs -um** *mpl),* a big step below the senatorial aristocracy.

Politically, these were stormy years. When he was sixteen, the Social War (also called Italic War) broke out as many cities of Italy that were associates of Rome tried to gain their independence from Rome. Cicero served briefly in that war. Rome won the war. There was also a bloody civil war in which Cicero's hometown hero Marius, the favorite of the lower classes, led his troops against Sulla, the champion of the senatorial aristocracy. Many aristocrats were put to death and their estates confiscated. When Sulla regained power, he in turn slaughtered some 6000 and confiscated their property. Even Cicero had to leave the country for a while to escape a similar fate. There was also a slave rebellion under the leadership of the gladiator Spartacus. Some 70,000 runaway slaves joined Spartacus and defeated two Roman armies and almost conquered Rome itself. In addition, Rome was fighting a foreign war almost every year.

In the year 76, at age 30, Cicero began his political career, called **cursus honōrum**, by being elected quaestor (**quaestor quaestōr·is** *m* minister of finance). (A high office was called **honor** because the magistrate served without pay, just for the honor it brought.) The following year he served as quaestor in Sicily. By holding this office, he automatically became a member of the senate for life. Because no one in his family had ever been a magistrate, Cicero was regarded as a newcomer (**novus homō**).

In the year 70, at age 36, he was elected aedile (**aedīl·is -is** *m* commissioner of public works). In this capacity he and the other aediles were reponsible for law and order in the city, for the construction and upkeep of public buildings, and for organizing public games such as chariot races, gladiatorial shows, and wild-animal shows, as well as theatrical performances. Admission was free! And Cicero, like every other politician, knew that he could advance his career by putting on spectacular shows.

In the year 67, at age 39, he was elected praetor (**praetor praetōr·is** *m* minister of justice.) His long experience in the law courts made him well qualified for the position. Then, in 63 B.C., at age 43, he was elected consul (**cōnsul cōnsul·is** *m)* at the earliest age allowed by law. He was extremely proud of this achievement.

Because he had made it to the top of the senatorial order through the republican system that was dominated by the senate, you can understand why he became a vigorous champion of that system. Naturally, he wanted to perpetuate a system in which he had done so well. Then Julius Caesar came along and threatened to change that form of government for a one-man rule. Caesar relied on the loyal support of his veterans who had fought under his command for the previous decade in Europe and on the support of the common people.

When Caesar was stabbed to death on the senate floor by Brutus, Cassius, and twenty-three other senators on March 15, 44 B.C., the senate and Cicero rejoiced because they thought that the Republic could be saved after all. But neither Cicero nor the 600 other senators could hold back the tide of change. After a bloody civil war, in which both Cicero and his brother were executed, together with 300 senators and 2000 equestrians, Gaius Octavius, the grandnephew and adoptive son of Julius Caesar, was given the title "Augustus" (meaning "venerable") and established the Empire in 27 B.C. It lasted some 500 years.

Now read a short "autobiography" of Cicero and see whether you can discover the secret of his success. Note that **nātus sum** is a verb meaning "I was born"; but **vīgintī annōs nāt·us (-a)** means "at the age of twenty."

You'll be glad you learned your numbers, since this autobiography is loaded with them. For your convenience, the years B.C. are placed in square brackets.

Vīta Cicerōnis
The Life of Cicero

I

[106] Ego sum Mārcus Tullius Cicerō. Ego nātus sum Arpīnī, oppidī in Volscīs montibus, circiter sexāgintā mīlia passuum īnfrā Rōmam. Ego ūnum frātrem habeō, sed sorōrem nūllam. [97] Novem annōs nātus, ego cum patre et mātre et frātre Rōmam per Viam Appiam migrāvī.

Cicerō Cicerōn·is *m* Cicero **Arpīn·um -ī** *n* Arpinum **Volsc·us -a -um** Volscan **circiter** approximately **mīlia passuum** miles

migrāvī moved

II

Scholam excellentem ibi frequentābam. [90] Sēdecim annōs nātus, albam togam virīlem assūmpsī. [89] Septendecim annōs nātus, Bellō Ītalicō inter Rōmam et sociōs mīlitāvī. Post bellum ego iūrī et philosophiae studēbam.

frequentābam attended

tog·a -ae *f* **virīlis** toga of manhood **assūmpsī** assumed, began to wear

mīlitāvi served in the army **iūs iūr·is** *n* law **studēbam** (+ *dat*) studied

III

[86] Vīgintī annōs nātus, prīmum librum meum composuī. Deinde advocātus factus sum, et multās causās in forō ēgī. [79] Vīgintī septem annōs nātus, ego ūnā cum Quīntō frātre et cōnsōbrīnō per Graeciam et Asiam iter iūcundum fēcī. Ibi multās urbēs clārās vīsitāvimus, praecipuē Athēnās. In illā urbe clārissimī professōrēs Graecī mē docuērunt.

composuī wrote **advocāt·us -ī** *m* lawyer **factus sum** I became **caus·a -ae** *f* case; **causās ēgī** pleaded cases, served at the bar **ūnā cum** (+ *abl*) together with **cōnsōbrīn·us -ī** *m* cousin **iter fēcī** took a trip **iūcund·us -a -um** pleasant **praecipuē** especially

IV

[77] Postquam Rōmam rediī, ego, iam ūndētrīgintā annōs nātus, Terentiam in mātrimōnium dūxī. [76] Proximō annō, trīgintā annōs nātus, quaestor creātus sum. Eōdem annō Terentia fīliolam Tulliam peperit. [75] Proximum annum in Siciliā ut quaestor cōnsūmpsī. [74] Deinde Rōmam rediī, ubi iterum causās agēbam.

rediī returned
iam now

proxim·us -a -um following
creātus sum was elected
fīliol·a -ae *f* little daughter, baby girl
peperit gave birth to, produce
ut as
cōnsūmpsī spent
ubi where **iterum** again

V

[73-71] Per proximum triennium, Spartacus ille gladiātor et multa mīlia servōrum contrā Rōmam rebellāvērunt. Profectō Spartacus duōs exercitūs Rōmānōs superāvit et paene Rōmam ipsam expugnāvit.

trienni·um -ī *n* three years

rebellāvērunt rebelled **profectō** as a matter of fact **superāvit** conquered
paene nearly **expugnāvit** captured

VI

[70] Trīgintā sex annōs nātus, aedīlis creātus sum, et proximō annō illum magistrātum gerēbam. Simul causās agēbam. Eō annō multa munera gladiātōria et lūdōs scaenicōs ēdidī. Eōdem annō pater mortuus est.

magistrāt·us -ūs *m* office, magistracy
gerēbam held *(office)* **simul** at the same time **mūnus mūner·is** *n* show
lūd·us scaenic·us -ī *m* stage play
ēdidī produced, put on

VII

[67] Ūndēquadrāgintā annōs nātus, praetor creātus sum. [65] Duōbus annīs post, Terentia fīliolum Mārcum peperit. [63] Dēnique, quadrāgintā trēs annōs nātus, cōnsul creātus sum. Ad summum honōrem in rē pūblicā pervēnī. Eōdem annō istam cōnspīrātiōnem Catilīnae dētēxī et compressī.

rēs reī *f* **pūblica** government **hon·or -ōris** *m* office **pervēnī ad** (+ *acc*) reached
cōnspīrātiō conspiration·is *f* conspiracy

Quamobrem senātus populusque Rōmānus mē "patrem patriae" nōmināvērunt.	**Catilīn·a -ae** *m* Catiline *(notorious politician)* **dētēxī** uncovered **compressī** crushed **quamobrem** for that reason

L. Answer the following questions based on the "autobiography" of Cicero in English.

I 1. What is the name of the special case of **Arpīnī**?
2. In what direction from Rome is Arpinum?
3. What word suggests that Arpinum does not lie in a plain?
4. How many brothers and sisters did Cicero have?
5. At what age did Cicero move to Rome?
6. By what famous highway did Cicero travel?

II 7. What did Cicero think of his new school in Rome?
8. At what age did Cicero assume a toga worn by adults?
9. How long after that did Cicero enter the service?
10. Who fought whom in that civil war?
11. What two subjects did he take up after the war?

III 12. What unusual achievement marked his twentieth year?
13. Why did Cicero travel to Greece and Asia (Minor)?
14. How did he show his studiousness in Athens?

IV 15. How old was Cicero when he got married?
16. Whom did Cicero marry?
17. How long after his marriage did he become quaestor?
18. When was his daughter born?
19. Where did he serve his term as quaestor?
20. What was his job as quaestor? *(See introduction above)*
21. What was his occupation when he returned to Rome?

V 22. How long did Spartacus' rebellion last?
23. How many slaves did Spartacus attract to his army?
24. What indicates that Spartacus' army was a serious threat?

VI 25. At what age was Cicero elected aedile?
26. What was his job as aedile? *(See introduction above)*
27. What did he do as aedile that would make him popular?
28. What sad event marked the year of his aedileship?
29. How old was Cicero at that time?

VII 30. How old was Cicero when he was elected praetor?
31. What was his job as praetor? *(See introduction above)*
32. How many children did Cicero and Terentia have?
33. How old was Cicero when he was elected consul?
34. What was his outstanding deed as consul?
35. What title did he receive as the result of this action?

WORD
POWER

M. Provide the Latin origin of the following English derivatives. If the source word is a noun or adjective, give the nominative; if it is a verb, give the infinitive.

1. nullify	____	11. detector	____
2. migration	____	12. assume	____
3. virility	____	13. to frequent	____
4. simultaneous	____	14. consume	____
5. detective	____	15. detect	____
6. scenic	____	16. to rebel	____
7. edit	____	17. republic	____
8. advocate	____	18. compression	____
9. composition	____	19. compose	____
10. consumption	____	20. create	____

N. Now try to think of all the English words that come from the Latin word **ūnus**, such as unicorn (having one horn, from **ūnus** and **cornū**), unify (to make one, from **ūnus** and **facĕre**). Then look up the words beginning with *uni-* in your dictionary. You should easily find another fifteen there. The other Roman numbers will provide you with additional derivations. Answer these questions.

VOCABULARY

1. How many fight in a *duel?*
2. How many sing a *duet?*
3. What are *dual* controls in an automobile?
4. How many notes are there in an *octave?*
5. How often do *quinquennial* games occur? (Notice the *-enni* comes from **annī** *years.*)
6. How many feet does a *quadruped* have?
7. What is the Latin source word for *cent?*
8. Why do we call it a *cent?*
9. What does a *centennial* celebration commemorate?
10. To *decimate* means to kill off every tenth person. What is its further meaning?

11. On what number is the *decimal* system based?
12. On what number is the *duodecimal* system based?
13. Give an example of the use of the *duodecimal* system.
14. What is a *duplex* apartment?
15. What is a *millennium?*
16. How many paces were there in a Roman *mile?*
17. What part of a meter is a *centimeter?*
18. How many musicians are there in a string *quartet?*
19. And what sort of animal is a *millipede?*
20. Which is bigger, a gram or a *milligram?*
21. How many tentacles does an *octopus* have?
22. What part of a gallon is a *quart?*
23. How many legs is a *centipede* said to have?
24. How often does a *quarterly* magazine come out?
25. How many sides and angles does an *octagon* have?
26. Before the year 153 B.C., when the year used to begin on March 1, what months were *September, October, November, December?*
27. How many candles should a *centennarian* have on his or her birthday cake?
28. How many angles does a *quadrangle* have?
29. How many days of prayer constitute a *novena?*
30. Why are horses, dogs, cows, sheep called *quadrupeds?*
31. Why is it difficult to ride a *unicycle?*
32. How many prongs does Neptune's *trident* have?
33. If a mother gives birth to *quintuplets,* how many children has she produced?
34. How many *decimeters* make one meter?

Part IV
Verbs

Preamble

Before you begin the sytematic study of Latin verbs, you'll need to know some basic facts about verbs. Verbs are sometimes called action words because they tell what action the subject of a sentence is either taking or undergoing. The term *action words* does not cover all situations. In the sentence "Dinosaurs *were* huge," the subject isn't doing anything and nothing is being done to the subject. We will discuss that problem a little later.

A Latin verb consists of three parts:

1) the *stem*, which is the part of the verb that does not change as it is conjugated and that gives the basic meaning of the verb. (We *conjugate* verbs when we change the endings to match the subject, for instance, I sing, he sings.) For example, in the verb **cantāmus,** *we sing,* **cant-** is the stem and has the basic meaning of *sing.*

2) the *connecting vowel,* which connects the stem with the personal endings. In the case of **cantāmus,** the connecting vowel is *-a-* . The connecting vowels tells you to which verb group (or conjugation) a verb belongs. It might also be called the *typical vowel* of each conjugation.

3) the *personal endings,* which tell you whether the subject is first, second, or third person, singular or plural. The personal endings for the present tense are the following:

-ō	I	**-mus**	we
-s	you	**-tis**	you
-t	he, she, it	**-nt**	they

In the case of **cantāmus,** the personal ending *-mus* shows that "we" are doing the singing.

There are four verb groups in Latin (usually called *conjugations*), each with its typical connecting vowel. As you just saw, the typical connecting vowel of the first conjugation is **-a-**. To form the present infinitive, you add **-āre** to the stem, for example, **cantāre** = to sing. Thus, the first conjugation can be called the **-āre** verb group.

The *principal parts* of a verb are those forms that we need to know in order to form the different tenses. In English, verbs have three principal parts, for example: *sing, sang, sung*. If we know the infinitive of any verb (e.g., *sing*), the past tense (e. g., *sang*), and the past participle (e. g., *sung*), we can apply the regular rules to form all the other tenses of that verb. In Latin, a verb normally has four principal parts. For instance,

1) **amō**	I love (present tense, first person singular)
2) **amāre**	to love (present infinitive)
3) **amāvī**	I loved, have loved (perfect tense, first person singular)
4) **amātus**	loved, having been loved (perfect passive participle)

A verb is said to be in the *active voice* if the subject is doing the action; it is said to be in the *passive voice* if the subject receives or undergoes the action.

Examples   *active voice:*   **amō**   I love

passive voice: **amor**   I am loved

Verbs can be *transitive* or *intransitive*. "Transitive" in Latin means "going across," that is, the action crosses over directly from the subject of a sentence (the doer of the action) to the direct object (the direct receiver of the action). A verb is said to be *intransitive* if the action does not cross over directly from the subject to the direct object.

Examples   *transitive:*   **Puella librum legit.**   The girl is reading a book.

intransitive: **Puella legit.**   The girl is reading.

Some verbs can be transitive in one instance and intransitive in another, as **legĕre** in the preceding examples. Some verbs are always intransitive; for example **stāre** to stand, **sedēre** to sit, **esse** to be.

Some verbs that are only intransitive in Latin can be transitive or intransitive in English. For example, **stāre** (to stand) is always intransitive. But the English verb *to stand* can be intransitive (e.g., *they stand alone*) or transitive (e.g., *I can't stand the cold.*)

On the other hand, some verbs that are transitive in English (i.e., they take a direct object) may be intransitive in Latin (i.e., they don't take a direct object in the accusative case but rather an indirect object in the dative case.) Here are some frequently occurring intransitive verbs.

PITFALL

crēd·ō -ĕre crēdidī crēditūrus (+ *dat*) to believe, trust
fav·eō -ēre fāvī fautūrus (+ *dat*) to favor
ignōsc·ō -ĕre ignōvī ignōtūrum (+ *dat*) to pardon, forgive
imper·ō -āre -āvī imperātum (+ *dat*) to command
noc·eō -ēre -uī nocitūrus (+ *dat*) to harm, hurt
pār·eō -ēre -uī pāritum (+ *dat*) to obey
persuād·eō -ēre persuāsī persuasūrus (+ *dat*) to persuade
plac·eō -ēre -uī -itūrus (+ *dat*) to please
serv·iō -īre -iī -ītūrus (+ *dat*) to serve (as a slave), be a slave to

Your dictionary will indicate whether a Latin verb is intransitive and therefore takes the dative.

English frequently uses *auxiliary* or *helping* verbs to express verb tenses and progressive forms of verbs. Notice in the following examples that Latin does not use an auxiliary verb to express these ideas.

Examples	*verb tense:*	**Rōmam semel vīdī.**	I *have* seen Rome one time.
	verb tense:	**Rōmam aliquandō vīsam.**	I *shall* go to see Rome someday.
	progressive form:	**Avēs cantant.**	The birds *are* singing.
	progressive form:	**Avēs cantābant.**	The birds *were* singing.

Sometimes a Latin verb is equivalent to an English verb plus a preposition. This must be kept in mind especially when translating from English to Latin.

| *Examples* | **Līberī nōn semper parentēs** *auscultant.* | Children do not always *listen to* their parents. |
| | **Puer calceōs** *dētrāxit.* | The boy *took off* his shoes. |

Latin verbs have six tenses: present, imperfect, future, perfect, pluperfect, future perfect. These tenses will be explained in separate lessons. Now we will explain the present tense of the indicative and imperative, active voice, of the first, second, and third conjugations, the **-āre, -ēre**, and **-ĕre** verb families.

CHAPTER 17

Present Tense Active, Indicative and Imperative
First, Second, and Third Conjugation Verbs

Semper avārus eget. A greedy person always feels need.

I. PRESENT INDICATIVE

PRESENT TENSE INDICATIVE		
FIRST CONJUGATION **-āre**	SECOND CONJUGATION **-ēre**	THIRD CONJUGATION **-ĕre**
amō amāre amāvī amātus to love	**doceō docēre docuī doctus** to teach	**scrībō scrībĕre scrīpsī scrīptus** to write
amō I love	**doc**eō I teach	**scrīb**ō I write
amās you love	**doc**ēs you teach	**scrīb**is you write
amat he, she, it loves	**doc**et he, she, it teaches	**scrīb**it he, she, it writes
amāmus we love	**doc**ēmus we teach	**scrīb**imus we write
amātis you love	**doc**ētis you teach	**scrīb**itis you write
amant they love	**doc**ent they teach	**scrīb**unt they write

1. The present tense is formed by adding the personal ending **-ō, -s, -t, -mus, -tis, -nt** to the stem by means of the **connecting vowel**. Note that in the first person singular in the first and third conjugations the connecting vowel is dropped, and in the third person plural in the third conjugation it becomes *u.*

   The typical connecting vowel (connecting the stem and the personal endings) of the first conjugation is *a.* The typical connecting vowel of the second conjugation is *e.* The typical connecting vowel of the third conjugation is *i.*

2. The present tense may be translated as a general present or as a progressive or emphatic present.

Example	*present general:*	**Latīnē doceō**	I teach Latin.
		Latīnē discō.	I learn Latin.
	present progressive:	**Latīnē doceō.**	I am teaching Latin.
		Latīnē discō.	I am learning Latin
	present emphatic:	**Latīnē doceō.**	I do teach Latin.
		Latīnē discō.	I do learn Latin.

NOTE

When the adverb **iam** occurs with a present tense, the verb is translated as a present perfect.

Example	**Iam diū Latīnē studeō.**	I have been studying Latin a long time.

PITFALL English uses the helping verbs *am, is, are* to form the present progressive; Latin does not use a helping verb. Therefore, do not use the forms of **sum** to form the Latin present progressive. Notice the example of the present progressive sense of **doceō** and **discō** above.

3. The personal pronouns **(ego, tū,** etc.) are not generally used as subject if they can be understood from the context, that is, from the previous sentence(s). In such cases where the context is clear, the personal endings of the verb indicate the person. However, when Latin uses a personal pronoun, it does so for emphasis or clarity.

-ō = I	**-mus** = we
-s = you *(sing)*	**-tis** = you *(pl)*
-t = he, she, it	**-nt** = they

Examples

Puella legi*t*. Novum librum habe*t*.

The girl is reading. *She* has a new book.

Puellae stude*nt*. Quid stude*nt*?

The girls are studying. What are *they* studying?

Magistra tē vocā*t*. Cūr nōn respondē*s*?

The teacher is calling on you. Why don't *you* answer?

Ego **librōs** legō; *tū* **nōn** legis.

I read books; *you* don't.

WORD ORDER

The verb often comes at the end of a sentence, but not always.

II. NEGATIVE AND INTERROGATIVE FORMS

1. A verb may be made negative by placing **nōn** before it.

Example

Latīnē intellegō.
Latīnē *nōn intellegō*.

I understand Latin.
I do not understand Latin.

Of course, **nōn** can modify other elements of a sentence.

Example

Līberī *nōn semper* parentēs auscultant.

Children do *not always* listen to their parents.

2. Asking questions in Latin. Strangely enough, the Romans did not use a question mark. Nor, for that matter, did they use quotation marks or commas or semicolons. In fact, to save space and money, they wrote all words together, separating them with a centered period. (See the section of the manuscript.)

Therefore, if they wanted to ask a question, they would attach the particle **-ne to the first word** of the sentence, very often the verb. Why to the first word? So that the hearer or reader would know immediately that a question was coming up. The **-ne** is also often attached to the pronouns **ego** or **tū** (less often to other words), which is then placed first in the sentence. The particle **-ne** is called an *enclitic*, from the Greek, mean-

CARMINATVMMELIVSCUMVENERITIPSECANEMVS·
CONQVAESITIO·DEAGRIS·CVM·GALLO·CORNELIO·
IOI EXTREMVMHVNCARETHVSAMIHICONCEDELABOREM·
RAVCAMEOGALLOSETQVAELEGATIPSALYCORIS
CARMINASVNTDICENDANEETQVISCARMINAGALLO
SICTIBICVMFLVCTVSSVBTERLABRESICANOS
DORISAMARASVAMNONINTERMISCEATVNDAM
INCIPESOLLICITOSGALLIDICAMVSAMORES·
DVMTENERAATTONDENTSIMAVIRGVLTACAPELLAE·
NONCANIMVSSVRDISRESPONDENTOMNIASILVAE·
QVAENEMORAAVTQVIOSSALTVSHABVEREPVELLAE
NAIDESINDIGNOCVMGALLVSAMOREPERIBAT·
NAMNEQVEPARNASIIVOBISIVGA·NAMNEQVEPINDI
VLLAMORAMFECERENEQVEAONIAEAGANIPPE
ILIVMETIAMLAVRI·ETIAMFLEVEREMYRICAE·
PINIFERILIVMETIAMSOLASVBRVPELACENTEM
MAENALVSETGELIDIFLEVERVNTSAXALYCAEI·
STANTETOVISCIRCVMNOSTRINECPAENITAETILLAS·
NECTAEPENITAEATPECORISDIVINEPOETA
ETFORMONSVSOVISADFLVMINALAVITADONIS
VENITETPASTORTARDEVENERESVBVLCI·
TVVIDVSHIBERNAVENITDEGLANDEMENALCAS·
OMNESVNDEAMORISTEROGANTIBVENITAPOLLO·

Section of Latin
manuscript

ing "to lean on," since it "leans on" or is always attached to the previous word.

Examples

Habentne discipulae librōs? Do the students have books?

Subrīdetne magistra tua saepe? Does your teacher smile often?

Tūne eam culpās? Do you blame her?

NOTES

1) The sign of the question, **-ne,** however, is unnecessary if a sentence contains an interrogative word.

Examples	*Cūr dē mē fūrtim exscrībis?*	*Why* are you secretly copying from me?
	Ubi est tuum praescrīptum domesticum?	*Where* is your homework?

2) If a positive answer to a question is expected, the question is introduced by the interrogative adverb **nonne**.

Examples	*Nonne* tū es in dēliciīs magistrae?	You're the teacher's pet, *aren't you?*
	Nonne probātiō est difficilis?	The test is hard, *isn't it?*

3) If a negative answer to a question is expected, the question is introduced by **num**.

Examples	*Num* interrogātum intellegis?	You don't understand the question, *do you?*
	Num mendum in exercitiō numquam habēs?	You never make a mistake in your exercise, *do you?*

III. PRESENT IMPERATIVE

The imperative is used to give a command. The imperative in Latin has two forms: the singular and the plural. Notice that the imperative shows the typical vowel of each conjugation: first conjugation: *a*; second conjugation: *e*; third conjugation: *i* in the plural. The singular is usually the same as the present stem; the plural is formed by adding *-te* to the singular.

PRESENT IMPERATIVE					
FIRST CONJUGATION -āre		SECOND CONJUGATION -ēre		THIRD CONJUGATION -ĕre	
SINGULAR	PLURAL	SINGULAR	PLURAL	SINGULAR	PLURAL
amā! love!	**amāte!** love!	**docē** teach!	**docēte** teach!	**scrībe** write!	**scrībite** write!

NOTE

For negative commands, **nōlī** plus infinitive is used for the singular, and **nōlīte** plus infinitive for the plural.

Examples	*singular*	**lege!**	Read!	**Nōlī legĕre!**	Don't read!
	plural:	**legite!**	Read!	**Nōlīte legĕre!**	Don't read!

Roman schools were quite different from modern schools. Since the Romans lived in an agricultural society, the boys were taught farming by their fathers. In the earlier period, before there were schools, the father also taught his sons reading, writing, and arithmetic. Girls learned homemaking from their mothers at home. According to tradition, the Romans did without schools until about 250 B.C., that is, for about the first 500 years of their history. For Americans, that would be equal to the period from 1492 to 1992!

The first schooling took place in private homes, often under Greek slaves. When schools were finally introduced, the teachers were often Greeks. Elementary school was called **lūdus;** the teacher in an elementary school was called **litterātor,** who taught the three R's: reading, 'riting, 'rithmetic, or **lūdī magister** *school teacher.* This elementary education continued until the boy was about twelve years old, when he went to the more advanced school, called **schola,** and where the teacher was called **grammāticus.** He taught more than just grammar; he also taught literature and basic Roman law, as well as the Greek language and Greek literature, especially the works of Homer, of which students memorized hundreds of lines. In the same way, we speak of a *grammar* school, although more than grammar is taught there.

Roman schools were something like our old one-room schoolhouses, in that all grades were taught by a single teacher. The schoolroom was regularly an open porch **(pergul·a -ae** *f),* to take advantage of fresh air and sunlight at a time when there was no electricity to light up an enclosed room. Girls did not go to school at all in the early centuries. When they did, it is not certain whether boys and girls were taught together or separately. The length of the school day is not exactly known, but school often began at dawn. There were long summer vacations during the intense summer heat of Italy, and holidays during the school year seem to have been numerous.

Listen to an ancient writer recount how Marcus Porcius [Porky!] Cato (234-149 B.C.), a rugged farmer, soldier, and statesman, looked after the education of his son. The writer, Plutarch, says:

> "As soon as his son began to learn with understanding, he [Cato] decided to give his personal attention to his education. For, he tells us, if his son's progress happened to be slow, he had no intention of having him scolded or his ear pulled by a

A Roman school

slave; nor did he wish so important a thing as education to be left to a slave. So he taught him literature and law himself; and also the necessary sports, javelin-throwing, hand-to-hand fighting, riding, boxing, and swimming, even in rapid rivers, and how to endure heat and cold. He also tells us that he wrote out stories for him, to acquaint him with the romance and the traditions of his country."

It should be noted that Roman schools had no fancy frills. The teacher did not sit behind a desk but simply in a chair (**cathedr•a -ae** *f)*. Students sat on a bench (**subselli•um -ī** *n*). They had no desk to write on. They held their wax tablets in their laps and wrote on them. Since books were rare and expensive, most written exercises (**exerciti•um -ī** *n*) were done on wax tablets (**tabul•a -ae** *f* **cērāta**) that could be smoothed out and used again and again, just as school children in early America used a "slate" and chalk.

Instead of a ballpoint pen or lead pencil, a sharp instrument (**stil·us -ī** *m)* was used, made of bone, or metal. (Our word "style" comes from **stilus.)** Books were in the form of rolls, often made from the inner bark of trees (**liber libr·ī** *m)* and this then became the regular word for "book." The reader held his "book" in both hands, rolling up with his left and unrolling with his right as he read. The plant from which books were made was the papyrus plant, which gives us our word "paper." The common Latin word for paper made of papyrus was **chart·a -ae** *f.* The Romans had a number of terms for paper, according to its size and cost. Since paper was very expensive, it was rarely used in regular school work. When it was used, students wrote with a pen made of reed (**calam·us -ī** *m)* and ink (**ātrāment·um -ī** *n)*, which means "black stuff" made from lamp soot.

A rich boy would continue his education under a professor of public speaking (**rhētor rhētor·is** *m)*, sometimes in Athens, the great university town of its day. (This is what Cicero did, as you saw in the previous chapter.) He would also accompany his father to the forum to hear speeches delivered from the rostrum there, to the great law court (**basilic·a -ae** *f)* to learn about Roman law, and to the Senate building (**cūri·a -ae** *f)* to learn about politics.

Here's a chance for you to look in on a Roman school and see what's going on there. Read carefully, since there will be some questions for you to answer at the end of the reading.

Schola Rōmāna
A Roman School

I

Cum prīmum magister scholam intrat, silentium postulat et nōmina recitat. Deinde dīcit: "Cōnsīdite in subsellīs vestrīs et prōmite praescrīpta domestica vestra. Nunc tempus est compositiōnēs vestrās ēmendāre, quās ego assignāvī."

cum prīmum as soon as **intr·ō -āre -āvī -ātus** to enter **silenti·um -ī** *n* silence **postul·ō -āre -āvī -ātus** to call for **nōmina recitāre** to call roll **cōnsīd·ō -ĕre cōnsēdī** to sit down **prōm·ō -ĕre -psī -ptus** to get out **praescrīpt·um -ī** *n* **domesticum** (written) homework **compositiō compositiōnis** *f* composition **ēmendāre** to correct **assignāvī** assigned

II

Ego statim compositiōnem meam prōmō, quae rem pūblicam Rōmānam tractat. In eā ego dēscrībō partēs magistrātuum et senātūs populīque Rōmānī. Compositiōnem meam identidem legō sed mendum nūllum video.

rēs re·ī *f* pūblica government
tract·āre to deal with
dēscrīb·ō -ĕre dēscrīpsī dēscrīptus to describe part·ēs -ium *fpl* role
identidem again and again
leg·ō -ĕre lēgī lēctus to read mend·um -ī *n* error (*esp. in writing*) vid·eō -ēre vīdī vīsus to see

III

Deinde magister rogat: "Quot menda in tuō exercitiō sunt?" Ego respondeō; "Ego meam compositiōnem identidem legō, sed mendum nūllum video." Magister ex cathedrā surgit et ad subsellium meum ambulat. Deinde meam compositiōnem cito legit.

rog·ō -āre -āvi -ātus to ask quot (*indecl*) how many exerciti·um -ī *n* exercise

surg·ō -ĕre surrēxī surrēctum to get up

IV

"Vērum dīcis," inquit magister. "Ego ipse mendum nūllum video. Compositiō tua est perfecta. Surge et clārē lege tuam compositiōnem tōtī classī."

vērum dīcis you're right (*lit: you say the truth*) inquit says
perfect·us -a -um perfect
clārē aloud tōt·us -a -um whole
class·is -is *f* class

EXERCISES

A. Indicate whether the following statements based on the story you have just read are true or false. If false, correct the statement.

I 1. As soon as the teacher enters the room, he sits down.
2. The teacher checks to see who is absent.
3. The teachers tells the students to sit around him.
4. The teacher tells the students to get out their homework.

II 5. The teacher reads each one's homework.
6. The student wrote a composition dealing with Roman government.
7. The student, on rereading the composition, found several errors.

III 8. The teacher asked the student to look once more for additional errors.

9. The student is asked to bring the homework to the teacher.

IV 10. The teacher, after reading the composition himself, finds no errors.

11. As a reward for the fine work, the teacher give the student a gift.

12. The teacher reads the composition aloud to the class.

B. It is important to note that the verb must agree with the subject in number. Choose the verb form that agrees with the subject. Most of the words occur in the reading passage in this chapter.

Example

Omnēs amīcī meī Latīnē ____   (discit; discunt)
Omnēs amīcī meī Latīnē *discunt*.
All (of) my friends are learning Latin.

1. Magistra silentium ____ .   (postulant; postulat)
2. Ego et aliae discipulae clārē ____ .   (legō; legimus)
3. Discipulae librōs suōs ____ .   (prōmunt; prōmimus)
4. Magistra et Claudia eundem librum ____ .   (legit; legunt)
5. Quem vōs prō hīs mendīs ____ ?   (culpās; culpātis)
6. Tōta classis compositiōnem nunc ____ .   (scrībunt; scrībit)
7. Ego et tū menda nostra ____ .   (ēmendāmus; ēmendō)
8. Magistra ex cathedrā subitō ____ .   (surgunt; surgit)
9. Ego et amīca compositiōnem identidem   (legō; legimus)

    ____ .
10. Ego ipse nūllum mendum ____ .   (videō; vidēmus)
11. Quot menda in tuā compositiōne ____ ?   (habētis; habēs)
12. Cūr magistra praescrīptum domesticum   (assignat; assignant)

    ____ .
13. Tōta classis ____ .   (surgit; surgunt)
14. Cūr tū et frāter tuus nōn cotīdiē scholam   (frequentās;
    ____ ?   frequentātis)

C. Now try a few sentences in which the verb is supplied and you are to choose the subject that agrees with it.

1. ____ scholam nōn amant.   (hic puer; hī puerī)
2. Quot menda ____ in hāc compositiōne vidēs?   (tū; vōs)
3. Videntne ____ tabulam ātram?   (discipulī; discipula)

4. Scrībitisne ____ praescrīptum domesticum? (tū et amīcus;
   amīcī tuī)

5. ____ omnēs compositiōnēs meās legit. (magistra mea;
   magistrae nostrae)

6. ____ in subsellīs nostrīs cōnsīdimus. (amīcae meae; ego et
   amīcae meae)

7. Nōn ____ scholam amant. (omnis discipulus;
   omnēs discipulī)

8. Nunc ____ praescrīptum domesticum (magistrae;
   ēmendant. magistra)

D. Test your comprehension. Choose the verb that fits the sense of the sentence.

Example | Discipulus ante tabulam ātram ____. (stat; habet)
           | **Discipulus ante tabulam ātram *stat*.**
           | The student is standing in front of the blackboard.

VOCABULARY

coniugātiō coniugātiōn·is *f* conjugation **hab·eō -ēre -uī -itus** to have
dēclīnātiō dēclīnātiōn·is *f* declension **man·eō -ēre -sī -sūrus** to stay, remain
exerc·eō -ēre -uī -itus to practice **sed·eō -ēre sēdī sessūrus** to sit
grammatic·a -ae *f* grammar **sil·eō -ēre -uī** to be silent

1. Magistra menda nostra ____. (ēmendat; manet)
2. Cūr vōs in subselliīs nōn ____? (habētis; sedētis)
3. Magister silentium ____. (videt; postulat)
4. Discipulī dēclīnātiōnēs ____. (spectant; exercent)
5. Sī magistra mē rogat, ego ____. (sedeō; respondeō)
6. ____ novum magistrum? (Timēsne; Docēsne)
7. Cūr, Claudia, mē semper ____? (culpās; manēs)
8. Nōs grammaticam Latīnam ____. (sedēmus; exercēmus)
9. Sī magistra silentium postulat, nōs ____. (silēmus; surgimus)
10. Ego et Glōria stilō ____. (studēmus; scrībimus)
11. ____ coniugātiōnem prīmam? (Exercēsne; Manēsne)
12. Ego coniugātiōnem secundam nunc ____. (sedeō; exerceō)

E. Supply the correct form of the present tense of the suggested verbs.

Example | Cūr discipulae _____? (subrīdēre)
           | **Cūr discipulae *subrīdent*?**
           | Why are the students smiling?

aegrē with difficulty   respōns·um -ī *n* answer

disc·ō -ĕre didicī to learn   stō stāre stetī statūrus to stand

1. Discipulī in subselliīs ____.   (sedēre)
2. Ego magistram nōn ____.   (timēre)
3. Nōs magistram semper ____.   (auscultāre)
4. Cūr tū ante classem ____?   (stāre)
5. Magistra respōnsum ____.   (postulāre)
6. Vōs librōs novōs ____.   (habēre)
7. Magister nōs Latīnē ____.   (docēre)
8. Classis grammaticam Latīnam ____.   (discĕre)
9. Magistra menda nostra ____.   (ēmendāre)
10. Puerī grammaticam aegrē ____.   (discĕre)
11. Nōs discipulī in scholā Latīnē ____.   (legĕre)
12. Ego et amīca mea cotīdiē domī ____.   (studēre)

F. In the following sentences, change the subject and verb to the plural.

Example | *Ego* istam scholam nōn cūrō.   I don't care for that school.
Nōs **istam scholam nōn cūrā*mus*.**   We don't care for that school.

1. Puella exercitium suum scrībit.
2. Discipulus chartam nōn habet.
3. Ego menda tua ēmendō.
4. Discipula magistram auscultat.
5. Magister historiam Rōmānam docet.
6. Cūr tū hunc librum iterum legis?
7. Discipulus coniugātiōnem exercet.
8. Magistra menda nostra corrigit.
9. Ego dēclīnātiōnēs et coniugātiōnēs discō.
10. Discipula nōn respondet.
11. Tū numquam respōnsum auscultās.
12. Ego grammaticam Latīnam discō.

G. Make each sentence interrogative.

Example | Discipulī magistram auscultant.
The students listen to the teacher.
Auscultantne **discipulī magistram?**
Do the students listen to the teacher?

1. Magister Latīnē docet.
2. Tū ante tabulam ātram stās.
3. Discipula stilum manū tenet.
4. Magistra silentium postulat.
5. Vōs exercitium scrībitis.
6. Nōs praescrīptum domesticum ēmendāmus.
7. Tū verba in tabulā ātrā nōn vidēs.
8. Magistra nōmina nunc recitat.
9. Dēclīnātiō tertia difficilior est quam prīma.
10. Tū omnia verba prīmae coniugātiōnis discis.

H. Give first the imperative singular and plural of the following verbs, then the negative commands.

Example	legĕre	**lege!**	read!	**nōlī legĕre!**	do not read!
		legite!	read!	**nōlīte legĕre!**	do not read!

1. surgĕre
2. subrīdēre
3. stāre
4. respondēre
5. scrībĕre
6. manēre
7. cōnsīdĕre
8. studēre
9. currĕre
10. ambulāre

I. Complete the following analogies. These analogies are based on ideas, not grammar. They may be based on synonyms, antonyms (i.e., opposite), or related ideas. See Chapter 4, Exercises **G** and **H** for further explanations and examples.

1. docēre : magistra :: discĕre : _____
2. stāre : sedēre :: rogāre : _____
3. cathedrae : magistrī :: subsellia : _____
4. dīcĕre : silēre :: surgĕre : _____
5. compositiō : scrībĕre :: liber : _____

J. Complete the following analogies, based on grammar.

1. discō : discimus :: sedeō : _____
2. vidē : vidēte :: surge : _____
3. exercētis : exercēs :: postulātis : _____
4. spectāte : spectā :: respondēte : _____
5. sedent : sedet :: _____ : scrībit
6. manēmus : maneō :: _____ : sileō
7. amā : amāte :: intellege : _____
8. surgō : surgimus :: culpō : _____

K. Pick out the cultural misfit; then give the reason for your choice.

exercitium   praescrīptum   templum   mendum   **templum**
(exercise, written assignment, temple, mistake (in writing)
Reason: All nouns deal with school work except **templum** *(temple)*

1. grammāticus   magistra   magister   dexter
2. discipulus   calamus   stilus   ātrāmentum
3. classis   discipulī   mīlitēs   discipulae
4. dēclīnātiō   grammātica   coniugātiō   admīrātiō
5. cathedra   subsellium   mendum   tabula ātra

L. Pick out the grammatical misfit; then give the reason for your choice.

1. magistra   menda   respōnsa   nōmina
2. librī   ubi   puerī   discipulī
3. discĕre   studēre   legĕre   surgĕre
4. deinde   et   saepe   numquam
5. dō   postulō   surgō   culpō
6. vocās   amās   casās   rogās
7. iterum   silentium   mendum   ātrāmentum
8. discipulum   aedificium   exercitium   respōnsum
9. crēdō   imperō   discō   amīcō
10. montēs   respondēs   timēs   habēs
11. amīcīs   legis   curris   applaudis
12. crēdō   auscultō   discō   legō
13. currite   sedēte   mīlite   legite
14. legitis   scrībitis   intellegitis   docētis
15. rogāmus   studēmus   exercēmus   manēmus

M. For each of the English derivatives, supply the Latin source. If the Latin word is a noun or adjective, give the nominative form; if it is a verb, give the infinitive.

1. prescription	____	11. sedentary	____
2. emendation	____	12. silent	____
3. description	____	13. status	____
4. legible	____	14. responsible	____
5. resurgent	____	15. session	____
6. culpable	____	16. recitation	____
7. studious	____	17. response	____
8. scribe	____	18. scholar	____
9. style	____	19. tablet	____
10. chart	____	20. surge	____

CHAPTER 18

Present Tense Active, Indicative and Imperative
Third -iō and Fourth ConjugationVerbs

THOUGHT FOR TODAY	Quī māiōra cupit, saepe minōra capit.	Don't bite off more than you can chew. [*lit:* Who desires bigger things often gets the smaller (ones)]

I. PRESENT INDICATIVE

PRESENT TENSE INDICATIVE	
THIRD CONJUGATION **-iō (ĕre)**	FOURTH CONJUGATION **-īre**
capiō capĕre cēpī captus to take	**audiō audīre audīvī audītus** to hear
capi**ō** I take **cap**i**s** you take **cap**i**t** he, she, it takes	**aud**i**ō** I hear **aud**ī**s** you hear **aud**i**t** he, she, it hears
capi**mus** we take **cap**i**tis** you take **cap**i**unt** they take	**aud**ī**mus** we hear **aud**ī**tis** you hear **aud**i**unt** they hear

NOTES

1) The present tense is formed by adding the personal endings **-ō, -s, -t, -mus, -tis, -nt** to the stem by means of the connecting vowel **i**. Note that in these two conjugations, the personal ending of the third person plural is **-unt** instead of **-nt**.

2) The verbs of the third conjugation "**-iō**" and the verbs of the fourth conjugation resemble each other closely, but note that the connecting vowel **i** in three places (in the second person singular, the first person plural, and the second person plural) is long in the fourth conjugation. These three forms are italicized in the table above.

II. PRESENT IMPERATIVE

Notice that the imperative plural shows the typical vowel of each conjugation: the third **-iō** conjugation has a short **i** in the plural, and the fourth conjugation has a long **ī** in the singular and plural.

PRESENT IMPERATIVE			
THIRD CONJUGATION **-iō (ĕre)**		FOURTH CONJUGATION **-īre**	
SINGULAR	PLURAL	SINGULAR	PLURAL
cape take!	**capite** take!	**audī** hear!	**audīte** hear!

NOTE

For negative commands, **nōlī** plus infinitive is used for the singular, and **nōlīte** plus infinitive for the plural.

Example	*singular:*	**venī!**	Come!	**Nōlī venīre!**	Don't come!
	plural:	**venīte!**	Come!	**Nōlīte venīre!**	Don't come!

EXERCISES

A. Change the following positive commands to negative commands.

1. scrībe, scrībite
2. cape, capite

3. audī, audīte
4. revenī, revenīte
5. īnspice, īnspicite

B. Give the present tense of the following verbs.

faciō facĕre to do, make
veniō venīre to come

ego	____	nōs	____
tū	____	vōs	____
is, ea, id	____	eī, eae, ea	____

III. COMPOUND VERBS

1. When a prefix such as **ad-** is attached to a verb like **capiō capĕre,** that is, verbs of the third **-iō** conjugation, the **a** of the stem changes to **i** and the meaning also changes.

Examples　　**capĕre** to take
　　　accipĕre to accept　　　　**incipĕre** to begin
　　　dēcipĕre to deceive　　　**percipĕre** to perceive, notice
　　　excipĕre to except; to welcome　**recipĕre** to get back; to receive

　　　facĕre to do, make
　　　conficĕre to accomplish　　**perficĕre** to finish
　　　reficĕre to redo, repair　　　**sufficĕre** to suffice

2. When a prefix such as **ad-** is attached to a verb like **veniō venīre,** that is, verbs of the fourth conjugation, the **e** of the stem does not change; however, the prefix changes the meaning of the basic verb.

Examples　　**venīre** to come
　　　advenīre to come to, arrive
　　　convenīre *intr* to come together; *tr* to come together with, meet
　　　dēvenīre to come down
　　　ēvenīre to come out, emerge; to turn out
　　　intervenīre to come between, intervene
　　　invenīre to come upon, find
　　　pervenīre to arrive
　　　revenīre to come back; to come again

Houses in Rome, with a population of about one million at the time of Augustus, who ruled from 27 B.C. to A.D. 14., came in all shapes and sizes, just as houses do today. Most people in Rome lived in small one- or two-room apartments (**cēnācul·um -ī** *n*) in large tenement buildings (**īnsul·a -ae** *f*) that were real firetraps. The floor at street level contained larger apartments as well as shops open to the street. The narrow, crooked streets of Augustan Rome were poorly lighted at night, if at all. Those who dared to walk the streets at night lighted their way with torches. For the first 750 years of Rome's history, there was no police force or fire brigade until Augustus organized a department of 7000 men, who doubled as firemen and policemen (**vigil -is** *m*). People living in these dingy apartments had no running water and no bathrooms. Chamber pots had to do. They drew their water from a well in the central courtyard or from a fountain at the street corner.

Only the fairly well-to-do had houses of their own (**dom·us -ūs** *f*). The early type had one chief room (**ātri·um -ī** *n*), around which were grouped a few small rooms. The atrium was so called because its ceiling was black (**āter**) with smoke from the fire that was lighted there. It was the living room, where guests were received, where work such as spinning and weaving was done, and where the family ate their meals in the early days. Here, too, was the shrine to the household gods (**larāri·um -ī** *n*), as well as wax busts of family ancestors, which were carried in family funeral processions.

The most striking feature of the atrium was the big square opening, an open skylight (**compluvi·um -ī** *n*) in the middle of the roof (**tēct·um -ī** *n*) which was sloped inward so that rain (**pluvi·a -ae** *f*) drained into a rain basin (**impluvi·um -ī** *n*) built into the floor below. The rain water was stored in cisterns (**cistern·a -ae** *f*) below the floor (**pavīment·um -ī** *n*) of the atrium to supply the family with water. If the water supply ran out, they, or rather their servants, had to fetch water from the fountain at the street corner.

Bedrooms (**cubicul·um -ī** *n*) surrounding the atrium, even in the homes of the wealthy, were very small. There was room for a bed or two (**lect·us -ī** *m*) and maybe a chest (**armāri·um -ī** *n*) for clothes. There were no built-in closets and apparently no dressers. The bedrooms had no windows; all light came from the doorway to the atrium. The thick stone walls were almost sound-proof against the noise of the streets.

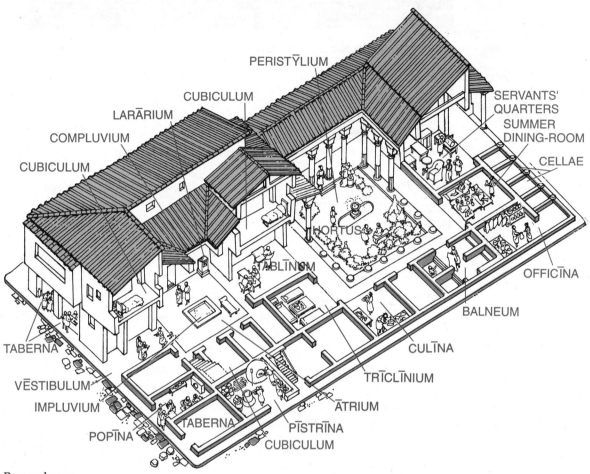

PERISTYLIUM

CUBICULUM

LARARIUM

COMPLUVIUM

CUBICULUM

SERVANTS'
QUARTERS
SUMMER
DINING-ROOM

CELLAE

HORTUS

TABLINUM

OFFICINA

BALNEUM

TABERNA

VESTIBULUM

IMPLUVIUM

POPINA

TABERNA

PISTRINA

CUBICULUM

ATRIUM

TRICLINIUM

CULINA

Roman house

In the course of time, houses became more elaborate. Even then the Roman house did not have a front yard or a back yard, and the walls of the house generally had no windows looking to the outside. Stepping from a very narrow sidewalk, one passed through the entrance way (vēstibul·um -ī *n*) into the **ātrium.** Passing beyond the **ātrium,** one reached the study (tablīn·um -ī *n*) and the dining room (trīclīni·um -ī *n*) where adult members of the family and guests reclined on couches around the table. Near the dining room was the kitchen (culīn·a -ae *f*). A corridor led to a courtyard with covered colonnade (peristȳli·um -ī *n*) around a garden (hort·us -ī *m*) of flowers (flōs flōr·is *m*), with perhaps a fountain and some statues. The rooms leading off the garden were the kitchen (culīn·a -ae *f*), bath (balne·um -ī *n*, balneol·um -ī *n*), toilet (latrīn·a -ae *f*), storerooms (cell·a -ae *f*), servants' quarters, and stable.

Atrium

Shops (**tabern·a -ae** *f*) that opened to the street usually had no doorway leading into the house. The reason was that the owner of the house who rented out these shops didn't want the shopkeepers to disturb the privacy of his home. The shop might be a bakery (**pīstrīn·a -ae** *f*), where grain was ground and bread was baked and sold; it might be a fast-food restaurant (**popīn·a -ae** *f*), a shoemaker's shop (**sūtrīn·a -ae** *f*), or some other workshop (**officīn·a -ae** *f*).

Now read a description that Publius Claudius Pulcher (*the Handsome*) gives of his plush home on the Palatine Hill and the activities there. You will have to forgive him if he sounds boastful. After all, he belongs to one of the most distinguished families of the Roman Republic, the Claudii. One

Peristyle

of his ancestors was a member of the Board of Ten who wrote the "Twelve Tables" in 450 B.C., the foundation of all Roman law. Another, Appius Claudius Caecus *(the Blind)* built the first aqueduct and the first highway, the Via Appia, in 312 B.C.

He changed his name from Claudius to Clodius (to show his sympathy with the plebeian class) and was the notorious enemy of aristocratic Cicero, who was his next-door neighbor on the Palatine Hill. It was Clodius who helped the Triumvirs Pompey, Crassus, and Caesar drive Cicero into a year-long exile in 58 B.C. Not only did Clodius drive Cicero into exile; he demolished his house while Cicero was in exile. Clodius' sister Clodia was famous for her striking beauty and notorious for her political intrigues. The famous poet Catullus was just one of her many lovers. Considering the wild life that he led, it's not surprising that our narrator, Clodius, was murdered in 52 B.C. amid the monuments of his ancestors on the Appian Way by Milo, a political opponent. Can you guess who defended Milo and got him acquitted of the murder of Clodius? None other than the great lawyer Cicero.

Look over the description of the typical Roman house for the name and function of the various rooms.

Domus Rōmāna
A Roman Home

I

Cupisne īnspicĕre meam domum in Viā Novā in Monte Palātīnō? Mea domus multa conclāvia habet. Maximum conclāve est ātrium. Cum hospitēs ad mē adveniunt, in ātriō conveniunt. Crassus et Pompēius et Caesar ipse saepe veniunt. Sed Cicerō, meus vicīnus, numquam venit. Neque eum vocō. In ātriō sunt larārium et imāginēs māiōrum meōrum.

cup·iō -ĕre -īvī *or* **-iī -ītus** to wish
īnspic·ĕre to look at, inspect
conclāv·e -is *n* room

cum when **hospēs hospit·is** *mf* guest **ad mē** at my house
Pompēi·us -ī *m* Pompey
vicīn·us -ī *m* neighbor
vocāre to invite
imāgō imāgin·is *f* bust
māiōr·ēs -um *mpl* ancestors

II

Ab ātriō, hospitēs, quī omnēs patriciī sunt, in meum tablīnum magnificum veniunt. Ibi ego bibliothēcam admīrābilem habeō. Hospitēs librōs meōs mīrōs īnspicĕre saepe cupiunt. Ibi ego etiam meum negōtium omne faciō.

magnific·us -a -um magnificent
bibliothēc·a -ae *f* library **admīrābil·is -is -e** admirable
mīr·us -a -um wonderful
etiam also **negōti·um -ī** *n* business
fac·iō -ĕre fēcī factus to do, carry on

III

Deinde, sī hospitēs meī ēsuriunt, eōs ad cēnam in trīclīnium vocō. Meae coquae cibōs sapidissimōs in culīnā coquunt. Servī cibum et vīnum ex culīnā in trīclīnium portant.

ēsur·iō -īre to be hungry
cēn·a -ae *f* dinner **vocāre** to invite
coqu·a -ae *f* cook **sapid·us -a -um** delicious **cib·us -ī** *m* food; meal **coqu·ō -ĕre coxī coctus** to cook, bake **vīn·um -ī** *n* wine

IV

Post cēnam hospitēs in peristȳlium veniunt, ubi hortus amoenus est. In hortō sunt multī flōrēs pulchrī. Ego et hospitēs in peristȳlium ambulāmus et flōrēs īnspicimus.

peristȳli·um -ī *n* courtyard *(surrounded by a colonnaded walk)* **amoen·us -a -um** pleasant

flōs flōr·is *m* flower

V

Sī hospitēs cupiunt, in cubiculīs nostrīs dormīre possunt. Hospitēs apud mē interdum pernoctant. Quīnque cubicula habēmus. In ūnō cubiculō ego ipse dormiō. Clōdia soror in alterō dormit. Parentēs in tertiō cubiculō dormiunt. Sunt etiam duo hospitia. Haec duo cubicula sunt prō hospitibus nostrīs.

apud mē at my house **interdum** sometimes **pernoctāre** to spend the night

alter alter·a -um a second (one)

hospiti·um -ī *n* guest room

C. Select the best answer from the choices given based on the story.

I   1. The home of Clodius is located: A) in a wealthy suburb; B) in a small town; C) on one of the Seven Hills of Rome; D) in a valley between two hills of Rome.
     2. The biggest room in the house is: A) the vestibule; B) the study; C) the dining room; D) the atrium.
     3. Clodius says that the atrium is the place where A) meals are eaten; B) guests are received; C) parties are held; D) the family gathers.
     4. Clodius indicates that A) all guests are welcome; B) few guests are welcome; C) one particular person is not invited; D) guests may come without invitation.

II   5. The tablīnum is used for: A) eating; B) reading and writing; C) entertaining; D) relaxing.
     6. Clodius says that the tablīnum is also used for A) storing busts of ancestors; B) business; C) campaigning; D) dining.

III   7. Clodius says that A) his guests rarely dine with him; B) the cooks often serve poor meals; C) the cooks prepare the meals in the dining room; D) if they are hungry, the guests are served delicious meals.

IV 8. After dinner, the guests: A) listen to poetry; B) go to bed; C) go to the courtyard to enjoy the garden; D) go into the garden to pick flowers.

V 9. Clodius says that: A) there aren't enough rooms for overnight guests; B) there are five guest rooms; C) guests sometimes spend the night; D) guests never stay overnight.

10. Clodius gives the overall impression that 1) he is embarrassed by the small size of his house; B) he is bragging about his house; C) he is simply being factual; D) takes his house for granted.

D. Here is a restatement of the description that Clodius gave of his home. Some Latin words are missing in the following passage. First read the entire description to get its meaning. Then complete each of the blanks with one Latin word each, selected from the word pool. The context should give you clues to help you find the missing word.

Examples

Nōmen mihi est __1__. In urbe __2__ habitō, ubi domum magnificam habeō.
Answers: 1. **Clōdius** 2. **Rōmā**.

WORD POOL

a. flōrēs	d. bibliothēca	g. culīnā	j. cubicula
b. ātrium	e. imāginēs	h. Cicerō	k. trīclīniō
c. flōrēs	f. hortus	i. cubiculō	l. Palātīnō

Ego sum Pūblius Claudius Pulcher. Amīcī mē Clōdium vocant. Mea domus est in Monte __1__. Maximum conclāve in meā domō est __2__. In ātriō sunt __3__ maiōrum meōrum. Multī hospitēs mē vīsitant, sed numquam meus vicīnus __4__. In tablīnō est mīra __5__. Saepe ego hospitēs ad cēnam in __6__ vocō. Meae coquae sapidissimōs cibōs in __7__ coquunt. Post cēnam, ego et hospitēs in peristȳlium ambulāmus, ubi amoenus __8__ est. In hortō sunt multī pulchrī __9__. Ego et hospitēs __10__ īnspicimus. Sī hospitēs pernoctāre cupiunt, in __11__ dormiunt. Sunt duo __12__ prō hospitibus in domō meā.

E. Add the correct ending of the present tense active.

1. Hospitēs ad vēstibulum adven____.
2. Pater meus hospitēs in vēstibulō excip____.
3. Amīcī meī in ātriō saepe conven____.
4. Tū et amīcī in cubiculīs dorm____.

5. Cupisne in domō meā dorm____?
6. Māter in culīnā coqu____.
7. Māter deinde ex culīnā ēven____.
8. Soror mea in balneō sē lav____.
9. Ego et amīcus meus librōs in tablīnō īnspic____.
10. Servae cibum in trīclīnium port____.
11. Pluvia per compluvium in impluvium dēven____.
12. Hospitēs in hortō flōrēs īnspicĕre cup____.

F. Translate the sentences in Exercise **E** into English.

G. Read the following questions carefully so that you understand them completely. Then complete the answers using the verb in the question in its correct form.

VOCABULARY
haur·iō -īre hausī haustus to draw

1. Quis ēsurit?
   Ego et tōta familia ____.
2. Quis cibōs in culīnā coquit?
   Māter et soror ____.
3. Quis aquam ex cisternā haurit?
   Tū et frāter tuus aquam ____.
4. Quis flōrēs in peristȳliō īnspicit?
   Hospitēs flōrēs in peristȳliō ____.
5. Quis ad vēstibulum advenit?
   Amīci meī ____.
6. Quis in ātriō convenit?
   Vōs in ātriō ____.
7. Quid tū in officīnā reficis?
   Ego tunicās in officīnā ____.
8. Quid vōs in cellā invenītis?
   Cibum et vīnum in cellā ____.
9. Quid in hortō audīs?
   Ego līberōs in hortō ____.
10. Quis vestīmenta mea semper capit?
    Sorōrēs tuae vestīmenta tua semper ____.

H. Complete the sentences with the correct forms of the verbs of the fourth conjugation.

234   *Verbs*

aper·iō -īre -uī -tus to open   **sciō scīre scīvī scītus** to know

1. (dormīre) Frāter meus in cubiculō ____.
2. (venīre) Amīcī meī in meum ātrium ____.
3. (audīre) Ego puerōs in hortō ____.
4. (aperīre) Servus iānuam cubiculī ____.
5. (scīre) Omnēs respōnsum ____.
6. (invenīre) Quid vōs in trīclīniō ____.
7. (pervenīre) Hospitēs ad vēstibulum domūs ____.
8. (ēvenīre) Amīcī meī ex istā īnsulā altā ____.
9. (convenīre) Cūr omnēs hospitēs in tablīnō ____.
10. (haurīre) Quis aquam ex cisternā ____?

I. Complete the sentences with the correct forms of the verbs of the **-iō** third conjugation.

1. (facĕre) Quid pater in officīnā ____?
2. (facĕre) Quid servae in culīnā ____?
3. (dēcipĕre) Cūr Clōdius Cicerōnem ____?
4. (recipĕre) Ubi tuī parentēs hospitēs ____?
5. (facĕre) Quid vōs in peristȳliō ____?
6. (reficĕre) Quid pater in officīnā ____?
7. (cupĕre) Quid tū in trīclīniō facĕre ____?
8. (incipĕre) Quandō servī labōrāre ____?
9. (perficĕre) Quandō coquae cēnam ____?
10. (dīcipĕre) Cūr tū parentēs ____?

J. Change each verb to the singular. If the **i** of the ending is long, mark it.

Example	Scītisne respōnsum?	Do you *(pl.)* know the answer?
	Scīsne respōnsum?	Do you *(sing.)* know the answer?

praeter (+ *acc*) besides

1. Venītisne ab ātriō?
2. Quid praeter librōs in tablīnō inveniunt?
3. Cūr in peristȳliō semper convenīmus?
4. Audītisne līberōs in cubiculō?
5. Quandō aquam ex cisternā haurītis?
6. Cūr ex ātriō nōn ēvenītis?

K. Complete the Latin translations.

1. Mother is welcoming her son.
   Māter fīlium ____.
2. Father is completing his business.
   Pater negōtium ____.
3. I wish to hear his answer.
   Ego respōnsum ____.
4. Who is coming out of the toilet?
   Quis ex latrīnā ____?
5. Are you finally repairing the roof?
   ____ne tandem tēctum?
6. Mark, what are you accomplishing at home?
   Mārce, quid domī ____?
7. I hear the cook in the kitchen.
   Coquam in culīnā ____.
8. Girls, are you finally coming out of the bathroom?
   ____ne, puellae, tandem ē balneō?
9. Boys, come into the garden!
   Puerī, ____ in hortum.
10. Senator, do you wish to look at my study?
    ____ne, senātor, īnspicĕre meum tablīnum?
11. Baker, are you baking bread in the bakery?
    ____ne, pīstor, pānem in pīstrīnā?
12. Father is repairing the bench in the shop.
    Pater subsellium in officīnā ____.

L. Complete the following sentences by supplying the imperative of the verb in parentheses.

Example	**(dormīre)** Puerī, ____ in vestrō cubiculō.
	Puerī, *dormīte* in vestrō cubiculō.
	Boys, *sleep* in your bedroom!

1. (audīre) Servī, ____ verba mea.
2. (reficĕre) Serve, ____ nostrum larārium.
3. (accipĕre) Mī amīcī, ____ haec dōna.
4. (revenīre) Hospitēs, ____ mox.
5. (īnspicĕre) Cicerō, ____ meum librum novum.
6. (nōn coquĕre) Pīstor, ____ ____ pānem hodiē.
7. (haurīre) Servae, ____ aquam ex cisternā

8. (convenīre) Hospitēs, ____ in ātriō.
9. (nōn venīre) Hospitēs, ____ ____ in peristӯlium.
10. (excipĕre) Pater, ____ hospitēs in vēstibulō.

M. The following analogies are based on culture. For examples and directions, see Chapter 4, Exercises **G** and **H**.

1. coquĕre : culīna :: dormīre : ____
2. cibus : trīclīnium :: ____ : impluvium
3. flōrēs : hortō :: lectus : ____
4. legĕre : tablīnum :: sē lavāre : ____
5. reficĕre : officīna :: pānem coquĕre : ____
6. larārium : ātrium :: bibliothēca : ____

N. The following analogies are based on grammatical relationships.

1. dormītis : dormīs :: capitis : ____
2. audīte : audī :: capite : ____
3. īnspiciō : īnspicĕre :: conveniō : ____
4. ēsurīmus : ēsuriō :: ____ : coquō
5. imāgō : imāginēs :: hospes : ____
6. flōs : flōribus :: negōtium : ____
7. coquite : coque :: ____ : venī
8. facit : faciunt :: ēsurit : ____
9. conclāvis : conclāvium :: cibī : ____
10. invenīre : ēvenīre :: dare : ____
11. vocās : vocātis :: ____ : īnspicitis
12. vocā : vocāte :: ____ : īnspicite

O. Give the Latin source for the following English derivatives. If the source word is a noun or adjective, give the nominative singular. If the source word is a verb, give the infinitive.

1. advent ____
2. convene ____
3. dormitory ____
4. audible ____
5. incipient ____
6. audition ____
7. dormant ____
8. culinary ____
9. cubicle ____
10. floral ____
11. vicinity ____
12. image ____
13. negotiate ____
14. horticulture ____
15. inspection ____

Imperfect Tense Active

Vestēs hominem faciunt. Clothes make the man.

IMPERFECT TENSE				
I	II	III	III-iō	IV
amō amāre	doceō docēre	scrībō scrībĕre	capiō capĕre	audiō audīre
amāvī amātus	docuī doctus	scrīpsī scrīptus	cēpī captus	audīvī audītus
to love	to teach	to write	to take	to hear
am ā bam	doc ē bam	scrīb ē bam	cap iē bam	aud iē bam
am ā bās	doc ē bās	scrīb ē bās	cap iē bās	aud iē bās
am ā bat	doc ē bat	scrīb ē bat	cap iē bat	aud iē bat
am ā bāmus	doc ē bāmus	scrīb ē bāmus	cap iē bāmus	aud iē bāmus
am ā bātis	doc ē bātis	scrīb ē bātis	cap iē bātis	aud iē bātis
am ā bant	doc ē bant	scrīb ē bant	cap iē bant	aud iē bant

1. The imperfect tense is formed by adding the endings **-bam, -bās, -bat, -bāmus, -bātis, -bant** to the stem plus connecting vowels. That is easily remembered, since the endings are the same for all conjugations. In the first conjugation the connecting vowel is ā; in the second and in the third the vowel is ē; in the third **-iō** and in the fourth the vowels are **iē**.

2. The term "imperfect" might sound strange to you, implying that there is something wrong with that tense. But the fact is that when English teachers of Latin first began to teach Latin centuries ago, they simply took over the terms of Latin grammarians and translated them too literally. "Imperfect" in Latin simply means **"uncompleted,"** in contrast to the "perfect" tense, which means "completed" tense. The imperfect tense is like a motion picture, whereas the perfect tense is like a snapshot.

3. The imperfect tense indicates an **action or state that is** *continued* **or** *repeated* **in the past**.

Example	**docēbam**	*progressive:*	I was teaching
		simple:	I taught
		habitual:	I used to teach
		emphatic:	I did teach

How do you know which meaning to use? All you can do is try to make the most reasonable choice according to the context. For instance, **legēbat** can be translated "he was reading" (as he was doing something else or over an extended time) or "he used to read" (as a repeated or habitual act).

EXERCISES

A. Change the verb from the present to the imperfect tense.

| *Example* | **Māter mea mē manū** *capit.* | My mother *takes* me by the hand. |
| | **Māter mea mē manū** *capiēbat.* | My mother *took* me by the hand. |

1. Ego animālia amō.
2. Amātisne animālia?
3. Ita, animālia amāmus.

4. Quid scrībis?
5. Praescrīptum domesticum scrībō.
6. Scrībuntne etiam amīcī tuī?
7. Ita, scrībunt.
8. Magistra, quid docēs?
9. Ego Latīnē doceō.
10. Hī magistrī mē Latīnē docent.
11. Ego magistram audiō.
12. Audītisne magistram?
13. Nōs magistram semper audīmus.
14. Quis mē manū capit?
15. Parentēs mē ēducant.

Roman Clothes

Much of our knowledge of Roman clothes is derived from statues, reliefs, and some wall paintings. But Roman authors also tell us about the fabrics, their dyeing, and the styles. Clothes were made of wool for the first seven centuries of Roman history. Cotton, ideal for the warm climate of Italy, did not come into use until the first century A.D. At about the same time, silk became popular among the wealthy. In general, the Romans did not wear hats or stockings. Men and boys never wore pants. In Romans' eyes, only "barbarians" wore pants **(brāc•ae -ārum** *fpl).*

All Romans—men, women, boys, and girls—wore a loose-fitting, knee-length garment with short sleeves or, less commonly, without sleeves, called a tunic **(tunic•a -ae** *f).* Adults sometimes wore the tunic below the knees or even full-length; young people wore it just above the knees. A man of senatorial rank wore a broad purple stripe running down each side from the shoulder to the hem in the front and back; the tunic of a senator's son had narrower stripes. On official occasions, a man wore a pure-white toga **(tog•a pūr•a -ae** *f),* the proud emblem of Roman citizenship. Candidates for political office wore a bright white toga **(tog•a candid•a -ae** *f).* Boys, on the other hand, until about the age of sixteen, wore a toga with a purple border **(toga praetexta)** just like high-ranking officials. Around his neck a boy wore a locket **(bull•a -ae** *f)* containing a charm to ward off evil. At sixteen the boy would begin to wear the toga of manhood **(toga virīlis)**, a plain white toga, and would dedicate his locket to the household gods. Naturally, the occasion was marked with festivities.

TUNICA

STOLA
AND
PALLA

BULLA

LACERNA

TOGA

PAENULA

CALCEUS

SOLEA

FĪBULA

INAURĒS

MONĪLE

ARMILLA

ĀNULUS

TUNICA

Clothes and jewelry

The typical footwear was sandals (**sole·a -ae** *f).* The proper footwear to be worn with the toga was the shoe called **calce·us -ī** *m.* Senators wore special red shoes.

For more formal occasions, women would wear an ankle-length, half-sleeved gown (**stol·a -ae** *f)* and over it a colorful wrap (**pall·a -ae** *f),* the counterpart to a man's toga. They would wear low shoes (**socc·us -ī** *m)* of different colors and decorated with pearls.

For jewelry, a woman might wear a ring (**ānul·us -ī** *m),* a necklace (**monīl·e -is** *n),* earrings (**inaur·ēs -ium** *fpl),* or a bracelet (**armill·a -ae** *f),* which was not worn over the wrist where it would get in the way but on the upper arm. She would also wear a decorative pin (**fībul·a -ae** *f)* on her dress. (The Romans never used buttons!) Her hair might be tied with a ribbon (**taeni·a -ae** *f)* decorated with jewels (**gemm·ae -ārum** *fpl).* Pearls (**margarīt·a -ae** *f)* were very popular, and a pearl necklace (**monīl·e -is** *n* **bacātum)** could be quite expensive.

It wasn't always warm and sunny in Italy. If the weather became chilly, the Romans would wear several tunics, one on top of the other. In rainy weather, they might wear a hooded raincoat (**paenul·a -ae** *f).* On cold days they might choose to wear a cape (**lacern·a -ae** *f)* that was tied at the neck and could be slipped over the head in case of rain. One thing is sure: shoppers kept the clothing store (**tabern·a -ae** *f* **vestiāria)** and the jeweler (**gemmāri·us -ī** *m)* busy.

 Imagine yourself waiting on a street corner in the Subura, Rome's business district near the Senate Building just outside the Roman forum. Two young ladies run into each other and stop to chat. You listen in on their conversation. Many of the words they use are to be found in the description of Roman clothing.

Taberna Vestiāria
A Clothing Store

DIĀNA: Salvē, Lȳdia. Quid agis?

LȲDIA: Salvē et tū, Lȳdia. Quid tū in Subūrā hodiē māne faciēbās?

salvē hello **quid agis?** how are you?
salvē et tū hello yourself
hodiē māne this morning

DIĀNA: In Subūrā dēambulābam, quia vestīmenta emĕre cupiēbam.

dēambul·āre to walk around
quia because **vestīment·a -ōrum** *npl*
clothes **em·ō -ĕre ēmī emptus** to buy

LȲDIA: Quid ibi inveniēbās?

 inven·iō -īre invēnī inventus to find

DIĀNA: Īnspiciēbāsne illam novam tabernam vestiāriam prope veterem librāriam?

LȲDIA: Etiam. Est taberna admīrābilis. Tabernārius est commodissimus.

 librāri·a -ae *f* bookstore
 etiam yes **tabern·a -ae** *f* shop
 admīrābil·is -is -e wonderful
 tabernāri·us -ī *m* shopkeeper
 commod·us -a -um nice, obliging

DIĀNA: Prīmum omnium, novōs soccōs et stolam flāvam emĕre cupiēbam.

LȲDIA: Quantī cōnstābant illī soccī?

 flāv·us -a -um yellow

 quantī? how much? (*gen of indefinite price*) **cōnst·ō -āre cōnstitī** to cost (*with abl of definite price*)

DIĀNA: Soccī vīgintī dēnāriīs cōnstābant.

LȲDIA: Quantī stola flāva cōnstābat?

 dēnāri·us -ī *m* denarius (*silver coin worth about a dollar*)

DIĀNA: Stola tantummodo trīgintā dēnāriīs cōnstābat.

LȲDIA: At tū "prīmum omnium" dīcēbās. Quid aliud emēbās?

 tantummodo only

 quid aliud? what else?

DIĀNA: Quid aliud? Inaurēs et armillam auream.

LȲDIA: Quantī cōnstābant inaurēs?

DIĀNA: Cārae erant. Cōnstābant decem dēnāriīs.

LȲDIA: Et quantī cōnstābat armilla?

DIĀNA: Armilla tantummodo octō dēnāriīs cōnstābat.

LȲDIA: Dīc mihi, Diāna, cūr illa omnia emēbās? Habēsne novum amantem?

 illa omnia all those things

 amāns amant·is *m* boyfriend

DIĀNA: Minimē vērō. Frāter meus togam virīlem hodiē sūmit.

 minimē vērō not at all
 sūm·ō -ĕre -psī -ptus to put on

Multī amīcī ad eius
convīvium veniunt. Et ego
quoque convīviō intererō.

LĪDIA: Nunc teneō. Bene valē!

DIĀNA: Nunc valē.

convīvi·um -ī *n* party
quoque too **intererō** (+ *dat*) I will
attend
teneō I get it **bene valē** goodbye
nunc valē goodbye for now

EXERCISES

B. Answer the following questions on the dialogue you just read.

1. Why is Diana in the Subura?
2. Where is the dress shop located in the Subura?
3. What does Lydia like about the dress shop?
4. What did Diana want to buy?
5. What cost more, the dress shoes, or the yellow gown?
6. What else did Diana want to buy besides shoes and a gown?
7. What was more expensive, the earrings or the bracelet?
8. Why did Diana want to buy new clothes and jewelry?

C. Read the following sentences. Then give the infinitives of the verbs used.

VOCABULARY

forīs outside, out of doors   **gerēbant** wore   **strepit·us -ūs** *m* noise

1. Strepitum forīs audiēbāmus.
2. Stābātisne diū in vēstibulō?
3. Omnēs gerēbant soleās in ātriō.
4. Quid tū ex meō armāriō capiēbās?
5. Quis hospitēs in ātriō recipiēbat?
6. Cūr tot vestēs herī emēbātis?
7. Illī puerī togās praetextās gerēbant.
8. Gemmārius in tabernā sōlus sedēbat.
9. Tū et soror eāsdem stolās habēbātis.
10. Māter illam novam pallam amābat.

D. Test your knowledge of grammar. Choose the verb that has the correct form.

VOCABULARY

dētrahō -ĕre dētrāxī dētractus to take off (*clothes, shoes, ring*)
mūtō -āre to change

1. Diāna fībulam auream in stolā (gerēbam; gerēbat).
2. Tū et māter inaurēs semper (gerēbās; gerēbātis).
3. Vōs multās vestēs (emēbant; emēbātis).
4. Ego et tū in tabernā vestiāriā diū (manēbam; manēbāmus).
5. Clōdius novōs calceōs (dētrahēbat; dētrahēbant).
6. Ego et amīca mea soleās (mūtābam; mūtābāmus).
7. Diāna et Lȳdia ōrnāmenta (īnspiciēbat; īnspiciēbant).
8. Aedīlis et cōnsul in Subūrā hodiē (dēambulābat; dēambulābant).
9. Nōs omnēs strepitum ante tabernam vestiāriam (audiēbant; audiēbāmus)
10. Ego cum pātre meō ad convīvium (veniēbam; veniēbāmus).

E. First read the sentences for comprehension. Many of the words occurring here appeared in the conversation above. Then change the present to the imperfect.

1. Māter stolam et soccōs gerit.
2. Puerī tunicās et lacernās gerunt.
3. Nōs calceōs in vēstibulō dētrahimus.
4. Cūr tū armillum meum īnspicis?
5. Quid soror dē meīs inauribus dīcit?
6. Cūr meum monīle iterum geris?
7. Cūr vōs togās in peristȳliō mūtātis?
8. Puerī vestēs in balneō dētrahunt.
9. Ego ānulum dē gemmāriō emō.
10. Quid vōs in tabernā vestiāriā emitis?
11. Cūr puerī Rōmānī numquam brācās gerunt?
12. Quantī illī calceī cōnstant?
13. Ego nihil dē novīs tabernīs audiō.
14. Quandō tū et soror in Subūrā dēambulātis?
15. Quō diē hospitēs ad tuam domum perveniunt?

F. Answer the following questions by completing the Latin sentences.

Vocabulary

etiam yes   **modo** just now

1. Quis brācās gerēbat?   Puerī in Germāniā brācās ____.
2. Ubi modo stābās?   Ego in ātriō ____.
3. Vōsne in cubiculō dormiēbātis?   Etiam, in cubiculō ____.
4. Quis monīle bacātum gerēbat?   Omnēs monīle bacātum ____.
5. Quid tū in tabernā vestiāriā   Ego pallam ____.
   emēbās?

6. Quis monīle tuum capiēbat?   Sorōrēs meae monīle ____

7. Ubi illōs dēnāriōs inveniēbātis?   Nōs hōs dēnāriōs ante basilicam

                                                ____

8. Quis in familiā tuā togam praetextam gerēbat?   Frāter meus togam praetextam ____

9. Audiēbāsne dē gemmīs in tabernā novā?   Etiam, omnēs dē illīs gemmīs ____

10. Quis bullās aureās gerēbat?   Puerī, decem annōs nātī, illās bullās ____

G. Complete the following analogies. They are based on grammar. For examples and directions, see Chapter 4, Exercises **G** and **H**.

1. audiēbam : audiēbāmus :: audiō : ____
2. habēbant : habēbat :: audiēbant : ____
3. dīcis : dīcitis :: culpās : ____
4. amātis : amās :: emitis : ____
5. gerēbam : gerēbāmus :: īnspiciēbam : ____
6. habeō : habēbāmus :: stō : ____
7. scrībēbātis : scrībēbās :: ____ : audiēbās
8. capiō : ____ :: sciō : sciēbam

H. Pretend you are the teacher correcting papers. Read the sentences carefully. If the form of the verb is correct, write **C** next to the number of the sentence; if the form of the verb is incorrect, put a check mark and write the correct form after it.

Vocabulary

cēnāre to eat dinner

1. Omnēs in tabernā vestiāriā iam diū stābat.
2. Ego et soror vestēs novās rārō emō.
3. Tū et amīca tua similēs ānulōs habēs.
4. Vōsne calceōs novōs emĕre cupitis?
5. Pater et hospitēs nostrī in trīclīniō cēnat.
6. Cēnābātisne tū et amīcus in hortō?
7. Quis omnia respōnsa sciēbat?
8. Ego et māter vestīmenta nova emēbam.

CHAPTER 20

Future Tense Active

Nōn vīvēs aliter in sōlitūdine, aliter in forō.	Don't live one way in private, another in public.

FUTURE TENSE				
I	**II**	**III**	**III-iō**	**IV**
amō amāre	**doceō docēre**	**scrībō scrībĕre**	**capiō capĕre**	**audiō audīre**
amāvī amātus	**docuī doctus**	**scrīpsī scrīptus**	**cēpī captus**	**audīvī audītus**
to love	to teach	to write	to take	to hear
am ā bō	**doc ē bō**	**scrīb am**	**cap i am**	**aud i am**
am ā bis	**doc ē bis**	**scrīb ēs**	**cap i ēs**	**aud i ēs**
am ā bit	**doc ē bit**	**scrīb et**	**cap i et**	**aud i et**
am ā bimus	**doc ē bimus**	**scrīb ēmus**	**cap i ēmus**	**aud i ēmus**
am ā bitis	**doc ē bitis**	**scrīb ētis**	**cap i ētis**	**aud i ētis**
am ā bunt	**doc ē bunt**	**scrīb ent**	**cap i ent**	**aud i ent**

1. The future tense of the first and second conjugation is formed by adding the endings **-bō, -bis, -bit, -bimus, -bitis, -bunt** to the stem plus connecting vowel. In the first conjugation the connecting vowel is **a;** in the second the vowel is **e.**

2. The future tense of the third and fourth conjugations is formed by adding the endings **-am, -ēs, -et, -ēmus, -ētis, -ent** to the stem, plus connecting vowel for the third **-iō** and the fourth conjugations. In the third **-iō** and the fourth conjugations, the connecting vowel is **i.** Note that there is no vowel between the stem and the ending in the third conjugation.

Examples   **scrīb am** I shall write   **em am** I shall buy   **dīc am** I shall say

NOTES
1) The **-e-** of the ending in the third and fourth conjugations is short before final **-t** and **-nt.**

2) The future tense in Latin does not take a helping verb; in English we use the helping verbs *shall* and *will.*

ENDINGS OF THE FUTURE TENSE			
FIRST AND SECOND		**THIRD AND FOURTH**	
CONJUGATIONS		**CONJUGATIONS**	
-bō	*-bimus*	*-am*	*-ēmus*
-bis	*-bitis*	*-ēs*	*-ētis*
-bit	*-bunt*	*-et*	*-ent*

PITFALL

Present or future? Because the endings **-ēs, -et, -ēmus, -ētis, -ent** are exactly the same for the present tense of verbs of the second conjugation and the future tense of verbs of the third conjugation, you can easily confuse the two.

These is also a danger that the present and future of verbs of the third conjugation may be confused, e.g., **dīcis** *you say* and **dīcēs** *you will say.* You simply have to know the principal parts of verbs in order to avoid confusing those forms. You have some help with verbs of the third **-iō** and fourth conjugation, since the ending is preceded by an **-i.**

A. Let's start by making sure that we can tell the difference between the present and future of verbs with the endings **-ēs, -et, -ēmus, -ētis, -ent.**

Examples

Verb	Conjugation	Tense	Meaning
videt	II	present	he, she, it sees
faciet	III-iō	future	he, she, it will do, make
movent	II	present	they move, are moving
audient	IV	future	they will hear

1. docent
2. emet
3. dīcēs
4. habētis
5. īnspicient
6. legēmus
7. surget
8. cōnsīdent
9. timēs
10. discēmus

B. Write out the forms of the imperfect and future tenses of **vidēre** *to see.*

ego	___ ___	nōs	___ ___
tū	___ ___	vōs	___ ___
is, ea, id	___ ___	eī, eae, ea	___ ___

C. Write out the forms of the imperfect and future tenses of **discĕre** *to learn.* You will note that the endings of the future of **discĕre** are different from the endings of the future of **vidēre.**

ego	___ ___	nōs	___ ___
tū	___ ___	vōs	___ ___
is, ea, id	___ ___	eī, eae, ea	___ ___

Roman Religion

The earliest Romans were simple farmers and shepherds. Their religion was also simple. They worshipped various spirits and sacrificed to them in the hope that these spirits would not harm their crops and herds. They did not at that time represent their gods in human form. There were many things that they had to endure but could not understand, such as floods and drought, untimely frost and excessive heat, and disease that could attack crops, livestock, as well as human beings. It seemed that behind all these happenings was the work of spirits that at times were kind and at other times harmful. The Romans figured that they could win the blessings of these spirits by sacrifices and ceremonies. In fact, the Roman calendar had forty-one days set aside as festivals in honor of their gods. These festivals were connected with the important seasons of the farmer's year.

Religion was purely local; each household, clan, or tribe had its own gods and rites. The family shrine (larāri·um -ī *n)* stood in the atrium and was the center of family religion in which the father of the family served as priest.

It was from the religion of the farm and household that the Roman State religion developed. For example, as the women of the household looked after the fire in the hearth, so the Vestal Virgins kept the eternal flame going in their shrine in the forum. (Remember that in a time when there were no matches, it was a great inconvenience to allow the fire in the hearth to go out.) As Janus guarded the door of the home, so he guarded the gates of the town. Romans were elected to the priesthoods of the state religion just as to any political office. The priests did not preach or administer any sacraments. They were concerned with ritual and sacrifice to win the favor of the gods.

Centuries later, the Romans came into contact with the Greeks, whose gods had a definite form, usually human. They found that many Greek deities had qualities similar to their spirits, and so they adopted them. Let's now look at some of these Romanized Greek deities. Here is a list of the Roman deities and their Greek equivalents.

ROMAN		GREEK
Apollo	god of the sun, prophecy, and music	**Apollo**
Bacchus	god of wine	**Dionysus**
Ceres	goddess of grain	**Demeter**
Cupid	god of love	**Eros**
Diana	goddess of the hunt and of the moon	**Artemis**
Janus	two-headed god of doorways and of beginnings	—
Juno	queen of the gods	**Hera**

Lararium in an atrium

Jupiter	king of the gods, god of rain, thunder, and lightning	**Zeus**
Lares	gods of the household, often associated with the Penates	—
Mars	god of war	**Ares**
Mercury	messenger of the gods and god of diplomacy	**Hermes**
Minerva	goddess of wisdom, of war, and of arts and trades	**Athena**
Neptune	god of the sea	**Poseidon**
Penates	gods of the household, often associated with the Lares	—
Pluto	king of the lower world, god of wealth	**Hades**

Proserpina	goddess of the lower world	**Persephone**
Saturn	god of the harvest	**Cronos**
Venus	goddess of beauty	**Aphrodite**
Vesta	goddess of the hearth	**Hestia**
Vulcan	god of fire	**Hephaistus**

Now read this account of some of the major gods and goddesses.

Deī et Deae
Gods and Goddesses

I

Initiō, deī in Monte Olympō habitābant, et Titānī in terrā habitābant. Titānī autem diū et ācriter cum deīs Olympiīs pugnābant, et Montem Olympum ipsum occupāre temptābant. Dēnique deī Olympiī Titānōs superāvērunt.

initiō in the beginning, initially
Olymp·us -ī *m* Mount Olympus *(in northern Greece)*
Olympi·us -a -um Olympian

Titān·us -ī *m* Titan *(one of a race of gods who preceded the Olympians)*
superō -āre -āvī -ātus to vanquish

II

Post victōriam, Iuppiter novum ōrdinem prōclāmāvit: "Nōn iam Titānī terram occupābunt. Sub terrā in obscūrō Tartarō vīvent. Ego ipse in caelō et in terrā rēgnābō, sed praecipuē in caelō. Pluviam dē caelō dēmittam. Voluntātem meam tonitrū et fulguribus indicābō.

ōrdō ōrdin·is *m* order **prōclāmāre** to proclaim **nōn iam** no longer
Tartar·us -ī *m* Tartarus, lower world
obscūr·us -a -um dark **vīvō vīvĕre vīxī victūrus** to live **praecipuē** especially
pluvi·a -ae *f* rain **dēmittō -ĕre dēmīsī dēmissus** to send down **voluntās voluntāt·is** *f* will, wishes **tonitr·us -ūs** *m* thunder **fulgur fulgur·is** *n* flash of lightning

III

"Sed nōn sōlus in caelō rēgnābō. Diāna, dea lūnae, terram noctū illūminābit et Phoebus Apollō, deus

illūmināre to illuminate **noctū** at night
Phoeb·us -ī *m* Phoebus *(epithet of Apollo as*

sōlis, terram interdiū illūminābit.
Radiīs eius terram calefaciet.

sun god) **interdiū** during the day **radi·us
-ī** *m* ray **calefaciō -ěre calefēcī calefactus**
to warm

IV

"Plūtō frāter in Tartarō obscūrō
rēgnābit. Ibi mānēs habitābunt.
Canis trīceps, Cerberus, iānuam
Tartarī semper custōdiet. Circum
Tartarum flūmen Styx fluet.
Mercurius mortuōs ad rīpam istīus
flūminis dūcet. Inde portitor
Charōn mānēs trāns aquās Stygis
nāviculā trānsportābit.

Plūtō Plūtōn·is *m* Pluto
mān·ēs -ium *mpl* ghosts
trīceps trīcipit·is three-headed **Cerber·us
-ī** *m* Cerberus **custōd·iō -īre -īvī** *or* **-iī
-ītus** to guard **Styx Styg·is** *m* Styx **flu·ō
-ěre flūxī flūxum** to flow
dūc·ō -ěre dūxī ductus to take, guide
inde from there **portitor portitōr·is** *m*
ferryman **Charōn Charon·is** *m* Charon
nāvicul·a -ae *f* boat

V

"Neptūnus frāter maria rēget. Ipsī
fluctūs maris oboedient mandātīs
ejus. Nautae Neptūnum adōrābunt.
Sī nautae eum rīte colent, Neptūnus
vicissim eōrum nāvēs per
tempestātēs tūtē dūcet.

rēg·ō -ěre rēxī rēctus to rule **ipsī** the very
fluct·us -ūs *m* wave **oboediō -īre -īvī** (*or*
-iī) **-ītum** (+ *dat*) to obey **mandāt·um -ī** *m*
order **rīte** duly, properly **colō -ěre -uī
cultus** to worship **vicissim** in turn **tūtē**
safely

VI

"Sī hominēs mē et aliōs deōs
deāsque rīte colent, ego eīs vītam
beātam et pācem dabō. Hic erit
novus ōrdō."

homin·ēs -um *mpl* people

beāt·us -a -um happy **erit** (it) will be

D. Choose the best answer from A, B, C, or D.

   I 1. The gods lived A) in Mt. Olympus; B) at the foot of Mt.
        Olympus; C) on Mt. Olympus; D) near Mt. Olympus.
     2. The Titans' battle with the Olympian gods was A) short and
        sweet; B) fierce but fair; C) both unfair and swift; D) long and
        bitter.
     3. The Titans attempted A) to take over Mt. Olympus; B) share
        Mt. Olympus; C) abandon Mt. Olympus; D) rule from Mt.
        Olympus.

4. The word **dēnique** *(line 4)* is A) an adjective; B) an adverb; C) a conjunction; D) a pronoun.

II 5. According to the new order the Titans will live A) in the lower world; B) on earth; C) on earth and in the lower world; D) on the earth and in the sky

6. The chief residence of Jupiter will be A) in the sky; B) in the sky and on earth; C) on Mt. Olympus; D) everywhere.

7. Jupiter will indicate his wishes by A) rain; B) earthquakes; C) thunder; D) thunder and lightning.

III 8. Jupiter will reign in heaven A) by himself; B) with the Titans; C) with the sun and moon; D) with two other deities.

IV 9. The sentence **Ibi mānēs habitābunt** is best translated A) Pluto will have the ghosts; B) they will have ghosts; C) there will be ghosts; D) the ghosts will dwell there.

10. The hound Cerberus will A) hound the ghosts; B) guard the entrance; C) serve as Pluto's bodyguard; D) serve as Pluto's pet.

11. The River Styx will flow A) around Tartarus; B) near Tartarus; C) through Tartarus; D) into Tartarus.

12. The ghosts will A) wade across the Styx; B) ride a boat across the Styx; C) float across the Styx; D) swim across the Styx.

13. Mercury will A) act as a guide to the river bank; B) drive the ghosts away from the Styx; C) pay the fare to the ferrryman; D) comfort the ghosts on the way to the Styx.

V 14. Neptune will rule A) the ocean; B) the rivers; C) the seas; D) the streams.

15. If sailors worship Neptune properly, he will A) free them from fear of the sea; B) supply them with seaworthy ships; C) guide their ships safely in stormy weather; D) eliminate bad weather.

VI 16. Jupiter promises people a happy life and peace if they A) offer sacrifices to him and the other gods; B) adore him above all the other gods; C) properly worship him and the other gods; D) recognize the difference between him and the other gods.

E. Latīnē respondē ad quaestiōnēs.

I 1. Ubi deī deaeque initiō habitābant?

2. Quis initiō in terrā habitābant?

3. Quis cum deīs Olympiīs pugnābant?
4. Erantne Titānī victōrēs?

II 5. Quandō Iuppiter novum ōrdinem prōclāmāvit?
6. Ubi Titānī nunc vīvent?
7. Ubi Iuppiter rēgnābit?
8. Quis pluviam dē caelō dēmittet?
9. Quōmodo Iuppiter voluntātem suam indicābit?

III 10. Quis est dea lūnae?
11. Quid illa dea illūminābit?
12. Quis terram interdiū illūminābit?
13. Quōmodo ille deus terram calefaciet?

IV 14. Quis in Tartarō rēgnābit?
15. Quis iānuam Tartarī custōdiet?
16. Quot capita iste canis habet?
17. Quis deus mortuōs ad rīpam Stygis dūcet?
18. Quis mānēs trāns Stygem trānsportābit?

V 19. Cuī deō fluctūs maris oboedient?
20. Quem Neptūnus per tempestātēs dūcet?

VI 21. Quid Iuppiter hominibus dabit, sī homīnēs deōs deāsque rītē
colent?

F. Change the verb from the imperfect to the future tense.

1. Familia mea larārium in ātriō habēbat.
2. Familia mea Larēs et Penātēs colēbat.
3. Virginēs Vestālēs ignem perpetuum cūrābant.
4. Deī in Monte Olympō habitābant.
5. Iuppiter in thronō aureō sedēbat.
6. Omnēs aliī deī circum Iovis thronum stābant
7. Via aurea ad Olympum dūcēbat.
8. Phoebus Apollō terram radiīs suīs calefaciēbat.
9. Omnēs homīnēs Iovem rītē colēbant.
10. Ipsī fluctūs maris Neptūnō oboediēbant.

G. Change the verb from the future to the present tense.

1. Omnēs Plūtōnem timēbunt.
2. Nautae Neptūnum adōrābunt.
3. Flūmen Styx circum Tartarum fluet.
4. Trīceps Cerberus iānuam Tartarī custōdiet.
5. Mānēs in Tartarō obscūrō semper manēbunt.

6. Charōn mānēs mortuōrum trāns Stygem trānsportābit.
7. Mercurius mānēs mortuōrum ad rīpam Stygis dūcet.
8. Iuppiter nōbīs vītam beātam dabit.
9. Iuppiter hominēs tonitrū et fulguribus terrēbit.
10. Iuppiter inquit: Ego "novum ōrdinem" prōclāmābō.
11. Timēbisne Cerberum, istum ferōcem canem Tartarī?
12. Nōs omnēs rēgnum Plūtōnis timēbimus.

WORD
POWER

H. Supply the Latin source for each of the following English derivatives. If the Latin source word is a verb, give the infinitive; if it is a noun or adjective, give the nominative singular.

1.	obscure	____	7.	obedience	____
2.	illuminate	____	8.	radial	____
3.	custodian	____	9.	solar	____
4.	fluctuate	____	10.	edifice	____
5.	mandate	____	11.	beatitude	____
6.	voluntary	____	12.	lunatic	____

WORD
SEARCH

I. First identify the following. Then search for and circle the Latin words for the English clues. Words may run horizontally, vertically or diagonally, but not backward.

1. Rome's greatest lawyer.
2. Brother of Romulus.
3. God of the sea.
4. Sky god, grandfather of Jupiter.
5. Founder of Alba Longa.
6. Pyramus's girlfriend.
7. The Hound of Hell.
8. Goddess of the moon.
9. City from which Aeneas set out.
10. First name of Porsenna.
11. Ferryman of the lower world.
12. Messenger of the gods.
13. God of agriculture, father of Jupiter.
14. River of the lower world.
15. King of the lower world.
16. God of the sun.
17. Reception room (with **impluvium**) of a Roman house.

18. First name of Cocles who fought at the bridge.
19. Father of Ascanius.
20. Mountain on which the gods dwelled.
21. Capital of Turnus' Rutulians.

```
L Q K X A E Q S K Y O R
A L Y N B O U S Z A L E
R T A S R R U S E A Y M
S I I E E I U D M S M U
D H C B T N R K E C P S
T I R A R A A M R A U Y
C E R U C Y N M C N S A
C O T Y H K U G U I T P
H A S Z A I S T R U R O
S V X Q R V P H I S O L
P L U T O E M Q U M I L
K Q A E N E A S S Q A O
```

CHAPTER 21

Irregular Verbs

esse, posse, īre, velle, nōlle, ferre

| Quī nōn est hodiē, crās minus aptus erit. | One who is not ready today will be less ready tomorrow. |

The following irregular verbs have unusual forms in the present, imperfect, and future tenses as well as in the infinitive. However, they are extremely important verbs, since they occur so frequently. They simply have to be memorized.

PRESENT TENSE					
sum esse	possum	eō īre īvī	volō velle	nōlō nōlle	ferō ferre
fuī futūrus	posse potuī	*or* iī itūrus	voluī	nōluī	tulī lātus
to be	to be able	to go	to want	not to want	to bear, bring
sum	possum	eō	volō	nōlō	ferō
es	potes	īs	vīs	nōn vīs	fers
est	potest	it	vult	nōn vult	fert
sumus	possumus	īmus	volumus	nōlumus	ferimus
estis	potestis	ītis	vultis	nōn vultis	fertis
sunt	possunt	eunt	volunt	nōlunt	ferunt

NOTE

Although these forms are irregular, the personal endings **-ō** *or* **-m, -s, -t, -mus, -tis, -nt** follow the pattern of regular verbs, except that **sum** and its compounds, such as **possum**, have **m** as the ending of the first person instead of ō.

1. **Posse** is a compound of **pot-** (meaning *able*) and **esse** (meaning *to be*). Wherever a form of the verb **esse** begins with an **s**, the **t** of **pot-** changes to **s: pot-sum** becomes **possum**). This change is called *assimilation*. The word means "making similar."

There are several important compounds of **esse,** besides **posse,** that occur frequently:

absum abesse āfuī āfutūr·us -a -um (**ab** + *abl*) to be absent (from)
adsum adesse adfuī adfutūr·us -a -um (+ *dat* or **ad** + *acc*) to be present (at)
dēsum dēësse dēfuī dēfutūr·us -a -um to be lacking, missing; (+ *dat)* to fail (someone)
praesum praeesse praefuī praefutūr·us -a -um (+ *dat)* to be in charge of

2. Here are some common compounds of **īre:**

abeō abīre abīvī *or* **abiī abitūrus** to go away, depart
adeō adīre adīvī *or* **adiī aditus** to go to, approach
exeō exīre exīvī *or* **exiī exitūrus** to go out
praetereō praeterīre praeterīvī *or* **praeteriī praeteritus** to go by, pass
redeō redīre redīvī *or* **rediī reditūrus** to go back, return
trānseō trānsīre trānsīvī *or* **trānsiī trānsitus** to cross over

NOTE

The Romans put a **d** in **redeō** to avoid pronouncing two **e**'s in a row, just as we say **an apple** rather than **a apple** because we don't like to pronounce two **a**'s in a row.

IMPERFECT TENSE

sum esse fuī futūrus to be	possum posse potuī to be able	eō īre īvī *or* iī itūrus to go	volō velle voluī to want	nōlō nōlle nōluī not to want	ferō ferre tulī lātus to bear, bring
eram	poteram	ībam	volēbam	nōlēbam	ferēbam
erās	poterās	ībās	volēbās	nōlēbās	ferēbās
erat	poterat	ībat	volēbat	nōlēbat	ferēbat
erāmus	poterāmus	ībāmus	volēbāmus	nōlēbāmus	ferēbāmus
erātis	poterātis	ībātis	volēbātis	nōlēbātis	ferēbātis
erant	poterant	ībant	volēbant	nōlēbant	ferēbant

NOTE

The personal endings of the irregular verbs in the imperfect, **-m, -s, -t, -mus, -tis, -nt** are the same as for the regular verbs. Except for **esse** and **posse,** the sign of the imperfect, **-ba,** occurs as well.

FUTURE TENSE

sum esse fuī futūrus to be	possum posse potuī to be able	eō īre īvī *or* iī itūrus to go	volō velle voluī to want	nōlō nōlle nōluī not to want	ferō ferre tulī lātus to bear, bring
erō	poterō	ībō	volam	nōlam	feram
eris	poteris	ībis	volēs	nōlēs	ferēs
erit	poterit	ībit	volet	nōlet	feret
erimus	poterimus	ībimus	volēmus	nōlēmus	ferēmus
eritis	poteritis	ībitis	volētis	nōlētis	ferētis
erunt	poterunt	ībunt	volent	nōlent	ferent

IMPERATIVE				
	sum esse fuī futūrus to be	eō īre īvī *or* iī itūrus to go	nōlō nōlle nōluī not to want	ferō ferre tulī lātus to bear, bring
SINGULAR	es	ī	nōlī (+ *inf*)	fer
PLURAL	este	īte	nōlīte (+ *inf*)	ferte

1. The imperative is used for positive commands. For negative commands, **nōlī** plus the infinitive of a verb is used for the singular, and **nōlīte** plus infinitive for the plural.

Example

SINGULAR	**cōnsīdĕ!** Sit down!	**Nōlī cōnsīdĕre!** Don't sit down!
PLURAL	**cōnsīdite!** Sit down!	**Nōlīte cōnsīdĕre!** Don't sit down!

2. **Irregular imperatives.** The verbs **dīcĕre, dūcĕre, facĕre** and **ferre** have the irregular imperatives **dīc, dūc, fac, fer.** Notice that they are lacking the final **e.** Their plural forms are regular: **dīcite, dūcite, facite.** However, the plural imperative of **ferre** is **ferte,** not **ferite.** These irregular forms were used because if the **e** were retained, the meaning would be ambiguous; for example, **dūce** could mean both "lead!" (an imperative) and "by the leader" (a noun), **face** could mean both "do!" (an imperative) and "with a torch" (a noun), etc.

EXERCISES

A. First read each sentence carefully. Then change the verb from the present to the future, keeping the same person and number.

Example

Sacerdōs ad templum *it.*	The priest *is going* to the temple.
Sacerdōs ad templum *ībit.*	The priest *will go* to the temple.

1. Ego ad forum *eō.*
2. Nōs ex urbe *exīmus.*
3. Cūr vōs domum meam *praeterītis?*
4. Hospitēs domum *redeunt.*
5. Nōnne tū ad Circum Maximum *adīs?*

B. Read carefully; then change the positive to a negative command, keeping the same person and number.

Example Mārcia, *sedē* prope mē.   Marcia, *sit* near me.
Mārcia, *nōlī sedēre* prope mē.   Marcia, *don't sit* near me.

1. Magister, menda mea *corrige*.
2. Discipulī, librōs vestrās nunc *prōmite*.
3. Magister, *docē* mē Latīnē.
4. Māter, *eme* mihi novam stolam.
5. Discipulī, *surgite* ex subselliīs vestrīs.
6. Diāna, *fer* amīcam tuam ad scholam.
7. Senātōrēs, *cōnsīdite*.
8. Mī amīce, *venī* ad mē hodiē.
9. Commīlitēs, *trānsīte* Pontem Sublicium mēcum.
10. Servī, *ferte* aquam ex cisternā.
11. Pater, *dūc* mē hodiē in forum.
12. Puer, *dīc* mihi nōmen magistrī tuī.
13. Magistrī, *facite* nōbīs tabulās ex lignō.

C. Change the negative command to a positive command.

Example Lārentia, *nōlī īre* ad Tiberim.   Larentia, *don't go* to the Tiber.
Lārentia, *ī* ad Tiberim.   Larentia, *go* to the Tiber.

VOCABULARY

exspectāre to wait for

1. Thisbē, *nōlī exspectāre* mē sub mōrō.
2. Pȳramē et Thisbē, *nōlīte currĕre* ex urbe.
3. Coriolāne, *nōlī dēfendĕre* Volscōs.
4. Lāvīnia, *nōlī nūbĕre* istī Turnō.
5. Horātī Coclēs, *nōlī trānsnatāre* Tiberim.
6. Māter, *nōlī ferre* cibum in trīclīnium.
7. Rutulī, *nōlīte pugnāre* cum Trōiānīs.
8. Anchīsē, *nōlī nāvigāre* cum Aenēā trāns mare.
9. Cōnsulēs, *nōlīte venīre* in cūriam hodiē.
10. Mī filī, *nōlī ferre* meum librum in tablīnum.
11. Cloelia, *nōlī trānsīre* ad istum Etrūscum rēgem.
12. Coriolāne, *nōlī facĕre* impetum in oppidum.
13. Clōdia, *nōlī dūcĕre* istōs virōs ad Palātīnum.
14. Virginēs Vestālēs, *nōlīte incendĕre* flammam in templō.
15. Praetōrēs, *nōlīte inīre* in basilicam sine cōnsulibus.

D. Change the statement to an imperative. If the statement contains **nōn,** use the negative imperative.

Examples

Discipulī dīligenter *student.*	The students study hard.
Discipulī, dīligenter *studēte.*	Students, study hard!
Aedīlis novam basilicam *nōn aedificat.*	The aedile *is not building* a new courthouse.
Aedilis, *nōlī aedificāre* novam basilicam!	Aedile, *do not build* a new courthouse.

1. Servae aquam ex cisternā nōn *hauriunt.* Servae, ____ aquam ex cisternā.
2. Māter mihi cēnam nōn *coquit.* Māter, ____ ____ mihi cēnam.
3. Senātōrēs in cūriā *adsunt.* Senātōrēs, in cūriā ____ .
4. Pater tēctum hodiē nōn *reficit.* Pater, tēctum ____ ____ .
5. Sorōrēs mihi dē tabernā vestiāriā nōn *nārrant.* Sorōrēs, ____ ____ mihi dē tabernā vestiāriā.
6. Rōmulus pācem ad patriam suam *fert.* Rōmule, ____ pācem ad patriam tuam.
7. Cicerō causam excellentem hodiē *agit.* Cicerō, ____ causam excellentem hodiē.
8. Sacerdōtēs populum ad templum *dūcunt.* Sacerdōtēs, ____ populum ad templum.
9. Augur voluntātem deī populō *dīcit.* Augur, ____ voluntātem deī populō.
10. Androclēs leōnem ferōcem nōn *timet.* Androclē, ____ ____ leōnem ferōcem.
11. Discipulī nihil dē magistrā in classe *dīcunt.* Discipulī, ____ nihil dē magistrā in classe.
12. Mārcus canem suum in ātrium nōn *dūcit.* Mārce, ____ ____ canem tuum in ātrium.

E. Here is a series of questions. Why don't you be contrary and answer them all in the negative? Change the verb to the first person singular.

Example

Amāsne grammaticam?	Do you like grammar?
Minimē, grammaticam nōn amō.	No, I don't like grammar.

1. Potesne legĕre?
2. Vīsne mēcum venīre?
3. Potesne silēre in scholā?
4. Ībisne hodiē in balneum?

5. Vīsne mē adiuvāre?
6. Potesne natāre trāns illud flūmen?
7. Tūne vīs grammaticam discěre?
8. Abībisne mox?
9. Tūne praeterībās Ardeam?
10. Ferēsne dōna ad magistram tuam?
11. Nōnne respondēbis magistrae tuae?
12. Manēbisne sub illā mōrō?

Roman Baths

Most people in Rome lived in one or two rooms in apartment buildings that had no bathrooms. In fact, Seneca (4 B.C.-A.D. 65), Nero's private tutor, tells us that the early Romans took a bath only once a week. Of course, they could take a dip in the Tiber in warm weather. In early times, public baths were small and dingy, and were used by the lower classes for a small fee. Only the homes of the wealthy had a bathroom (**balne·um -ī** *n).*

It was the Roman emperors who sought to gain popularity by building huge bathing establishments (**therm·ae -ārum** *fpl).* One of them, built by Emperor Diocletian in A.D. 306 in the heart of Rome, still exists in part today. It could accommodate 30,000 people at one time. The admission fee was a fraction of a penny. The hours in the morning were reserved for women; the afternoons were reserved for men. Imagine yourself as a Roman going from your gloomy two-room apartment to the **thermae** where you could swim in the pool (**piscīn·a -ae** *f),* stroll around and have fun with friends in the enclosed park (**hort·ī -ōrum** *mpl),* eat in a small restaurant (**popīn·a -ae** *f),* exercise or play ball in the exercise yard surrounded by a colonnade (**palaestr·a -ae** *f),* get a rubdown in the massage room (**ūnctōri·um -ī** *n),* watch a play in the theater (**theātr·um -ī** *n),* or read books in the public library (**bibliothēc·a -ae** *f).* You could have your pick of a hot bath (**caldāri·um -ī** *n),* a warm bath (**tepidāri·um -ī** *n),* or, on a very hot day, the cold bath (**frīgidāri·um -ī** *n).* You could even enjoy a steam bath in the sauna (**lacōnic·um -ī** *n).*

Now read a letter that Marcus wrote from Rome to his cousin Aulus who will be coming for the first time to the big city of Rome from his isolated farm in the country.

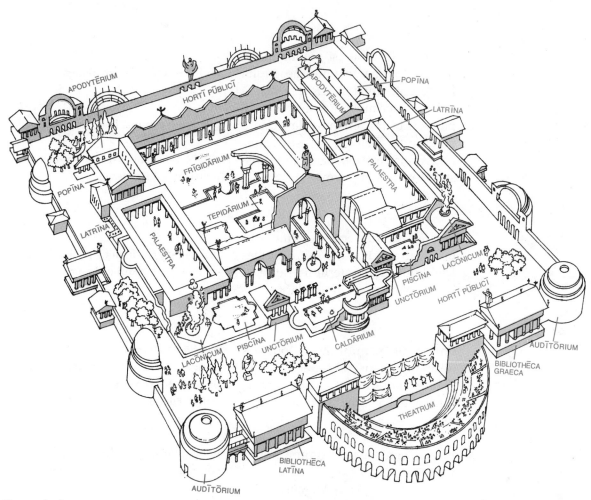

Roman baths

Mārcus Aulō cōnsōbrīnō suō salūtem dīcit.
Marcus sends greetings to his cousin Aulus.

I

Ego adventum tuum vix exspectāre possum. Mox ūnā erimus. Multa mīrifica loca in urbe vīsĕre poterimus. Sī volēs, poterimus īre ad Circum Maximum aut forum. In Colossēō poterimus spectāre gladiātōrēs aut vēnātiōnēs.

cōnsōbrīn·us -ī *m* cousin **salūtem dīcō -ĕre dīxī dictus** (+ *dat*) to send greetings to **advent·us -ūs** *m* arrival **ūnā** together **loc·us -ī** *m* place **vīs·ō -ĕre -ī** to go to see **mīrific·us -a -um** interesting **gladiātor gladiātōr·is** *m* gladiator **vēnātiō vēnātiōn·is** *f* wild-animal hunt **spectāre** to watch

II

Sed nihil in urbe est melius quam nostrae thermae magnificae. Multa facĕre poterimus in illīs thermīs. Sī volēs, poterimus nōs exercēre in palaestrā. Ibi etiam pilā lūdĕre poterimus. Deinde, sī ēsuriēmus, poterimus emĕre pānem et sapidissima tomācla in popīnā.

mult·a -ōrum *npl* many things

pilā lūd·ō -ĕre lūsī lūsūrus to play ball

pān·is -is *m* bread **sapid·us -a -um** tasty **tomācl·um -ī** *n* sausage

III

Sī diēs calidus erit, poterimus in piscīnam in frīgidāriō salīre. Sī diēs frīgidulus erit, poterimus salīre in piscīnam quae est in tepidāriō.

piscīn·a -ae *f* swimming pool **sal·iō -īre -uī** to jump **frīgidul·us -a -um** cool

IV

Post natātiōnem, in hortīs publicīs dēambulābimus, ubi puellās convenīre poterimus. Mihi credē, puellae in hāc urbe sunt formōsissimae.

natātiō natātiōn·is *f* swim **dēambulāre** to walk around **conveni·ō -īre convēnī conventus** to meet **mihi crēde** believe me **formōs·us -a -um** beautiful

Itaque, venī quam prīmum. Nunc valē.

            Tuus Mārcus.

itaque and so **quam prīmum** as soon as you can **nunc valē** goodbye for now

---

F. Now answer the following questions.

   I 1. What are the first places of interest that Marcus mentions?
       2. What events can they see in the Colosseum?

  II 3. Of all the places in the city, which does Marcus prefer?
       4. What two things can they do in the exercise yard?
       5. Where can they go if they get hungry?
       6. What two items does Marcus suggest they buy?

 III 7. What can they do after exercising?

IV 8. What can they do after swimming?

9. What is the chief attraction in the park?

G. Change the positive to the negative, keeping the same person, number, and tense.

Example

| In piscīnam salīre *volō*. | I *want* to jump into the pool. |
| **Nōlō in piscīnam salīre.** | I *don't want t*o jump into the pool |

1. Vīs legĕre librōs in bibliothēcā.
2. In lacōnicō sedēre volumus.
3. Volō ad popīnam īre.
4. Natāre possum.
5. Nōs in thermās ībimus.
6. Cūr vultis in Colossēum īre?
7. Cōnsōbrīnī meī natāre volunt.
8. In hortīs pūblicīs dēambulāre potes.

H. Change the verb from the present to the imperfect tense, keeping the same person and number.

Example

| Natāre *volō*. | I *want* to swim. |
| **Natāre *volēbam*.** | I *wanted* to swim. |

1. Ad Colossēum ītis.
2. Gladiātōrēs spectāre volumus.
3. Cōnsōbrīnī ad Colossēum īre nōlunt.
4. Ego ipse vēnātiōnēs spectāre nōlō.
5. Sed ad thermās saepe īmus.
6. Vīsne nōbīscum urbem vīsĕre?

I. Pick out the cultural misfit. Then give the reason for your choice.

Example

amīcī soccī vicīnī cōnsōbrīnī **soccī**
Reason: All are people except **soccī** (dress shoes).

MISFIT

1. frīgidārium piscīna impluvium palaestra
2. Apollō Mercurius Neptūnus Faustulus
3. Tartarus Styx Tiberis Plūtō
4. cubiculum oppidum vēstibulum tablīnum
5. ānulus monīle armilla taberna
6. ātrium culīna thermae trīclīnium

J. Pick out the grammatical misfit in each set. Then give the reason for your choice.

1. natāre   mare   narrāre   amāre
2. audiō   veniō   natātiō   saliō
3. vix   vox   mox   saepe
4. ībam   volēbam   poteram   popīnam
5. surge   nāve   dēfende   cōnsīde
6. ferēs   volēs   nōlēs   sedēs
7. īta   īte   nōlīte   ferte
8. dīc   sīc   dūc   fac
9. erimus   volēmus   summus   ferēmus
10. possum   nōlō   ferō   subitō

K. SCRAMBLED SENTENCES. Unscramble the sentences. Remember that the endings give you a clue as to what words belong together.

1. in piscīnam parvae saliunt calidam puellae.
2. ea in ego et puella volumus hortīs dēambulāre pūblicīs.
3. thermās ad volunt amīcī novās īre meī.
4. ad nōvas cōnsōbrīnus venīre thermās vult mēcum meus.
5. multa amīcī hāc loca meī in vīsēre mīrifica volunt urbe.
6. emĕre omnēs in puellae volunt popīnā tomācla calida.

L. Solve the following analogies, based on grammar. For examples and directions, see Chapter 4, Exercises **G** & **H**.

1. fers	:	fertis	::	es	:	_____
2. eram	:	erāmus	::	ībam	:	_____
3. dūcite	:	dūc	::	ferte	:	_____
4. est	:	sunt	::	it	:	_____
5. vīs	:	nōn vīs	::	vult	:	_____
6. sum	:	esse	::	nōlō	:	_____
7. dīc	:	dīcite	::	_____	:	nōlīte
8. sum	:	fuī	::	ferō	:	_____
9. possum	:	potes	::	volō	:	_____
10. eō	:	īre	::	ferō	:	_____

WORD
POWER

M. Supply the Latin source word for the following English derivatives. If it is a noun or adjective, give the nominative; if it is a verb, give the infinitive.

1. thermal   ____
2. advent   ____
3. expectation   ____
4. Formosa   ____

5. locality   ____
6. exit   ____
7. convention   ____

CHAPTER 22

Perfect Tense Active

THOUGHT
FOR
TODAY

Ūsus est optimus magister. Experience is the best teacher.

I. FORMS

PERFECT TENSE				
I	**II**	**III**	**III-iō**	**IV**
amō amāre	**doceō docēre**	**scrībō scrībĕre**	**capiō capĕre**	**audiō audīre**
amāvī amātus	**docuī doctus**	**scrīpsī scrīptus**	**cēpī captus**	**audīvī audītus**
to love	to teach	to write	to take	to hear
amāv *ī*	**docu** *ī*	**scrīps** *ī*	**cēp** *ī*	**audīv** *ī*
amāv *istī*	**docu** *istī*	**scrīps** *istī*	**cēp** *istī*	**audīv** *istī*
amāv *it*	**docu** *it*	**scrīps** *it*	**cēp** *it*	**audīv** *it*
amāv *imus*	**docu** *imus*	**scrīps** *imus*	**cēp** *imus*	**audīv** *imus*
amāv *istis*	**docu** *istis*	**scrīps** *istis*	**cēp** *istis*	**audīv** *istis*
amāv *ērunt*	**docu** *ērunt*	**scrīps** *ērunt*	**cēp** *ērunt*	**audīv** *ērunt*

1. ENDINGS. The perfect endings are the same for all verbs, regular and irregular. But notice that, as there was a present stem, so there is a perfect stem. For example, the perfect stem of **amāre** is **amāv-**. The perfect endings are added to the perfect stem.

PERFECT ENDINGS

PRONOUN	ENDING		EXAMPLE
ego	*-ī*	amāv*ī*	I loved, have loved
tū	*-istī*	amāv*istī*	you loved, have loved
is, ea, id	*-it*	amāv*it*	he, she, it loved, has loved
nōs	*-imus*	amāv*imus*	we loved, have loved
vōs	*-istis*	amāv*istis*	you loved, have loved
eī, eae, ea	*-ērunt*	amāv*ērunt*	they loved, have loved

2. The perfect stem is the **third principal part** of a verb. There were two previous principal parts: the present tense and the present infinitive. Principal parts are important because various tenses are formed on the principal parts. The present stem forms the basis for the present, imperfect, and future tenses. The perfect stem forms the basis for the perfect tense, and the next two tenses that we will study: the pluperfect and the future perfect.

In English there are three principal parts of a verb. For example, *sing, sang, sung.* In Latin there are normally four principal parts. For example,

amō I love   **amāvī** I loved, have loved
amāre to love   **amātus** (having been) loved

We will see later what forms are derived from the second principal part (the present active infinitive) and the fourth principal part (the past passive participle). You needn't worry about those right now.

To make sure that you get the principal parts right, you need to memorize them. There are certain typical patterns to be noticed in the formation of the perfect tense.

In the first conjugation, the perfect stem of most verbs ends in **-āv.**

cēnō cēnāre cēn*āv*ī cēnātus to dine, eat dinner
vocō vocāre voc*āv*ī vocātus to call; to invite

In the second conjugation, the perfect stem of most verbs ends in **-u.**

> **moneō monēre mon*u*ī monitus** to warn; to remind
> **teneō tenēre ten*u*ī tentus** to hold

In the third conjugation, the perfect stem of many verbs ends in **-s** or **-ss** or **-x.**

> **cōnspiciō cōnspicĕre cōnspe*x*ī cōnspectus** to catch sight of, spot, see
> **mittō mittĕre mī*s*ī missus** to send
> **gerō gerĕre ge*ss*ī gestus** to carry, to wear (*clothes*); to carry on (*war*); to hold (*office*)

In the third **-iō** conjugation, most verbs form their perfect stem by changing the **-a** or **-i** of the present stem to **-ē.**

> **faciō facĕre fē*c*ī factus** to do; to make
> **reficiō reficĕre refē*c*ī refectus** to redo, repair

In the fourth conjugation, the perfect stem ends in **-īv** or **-i.** Whether to have **-īv** or **-i** is simply a matter of the writer's choice.

> **audiō audīre aud*īv*ī** or **aud*i*ī audītus** to hear
> **custōdiō custōdīre custōd*īv*ī** or **custōd*i*ī custōdītus** to guard

---

PITFALL

There are many exceptions to the above guidelines, but they are helpful nevertheless. Remember that they are only guidelines, that is, they offer helpful clues but not to all verbs. If in doubt, check the vocabulary in the back of the book or your dictionary.

II. MEANING OF THE PERFECT TENSE

The term "perfect" comes from the Latin word meaning "completed." The perfect tense tells you something that happened in the past and indicates a single past act, not a continuous or repeated act. You will remember in the discussion of the imperfect tense it was said that the imperfect is like a motion picture, while the perfect tense is like a snapshot. It can be translated in two ways, as you saw above: **amāvī** can mean *I loved* or *I have loved*. However, almost always it needs to be translated as a simple past tense in English.

Only occasionally may the Latin perfect be translated with "have" or "has." When? Well, when the action happened in the immediate past and has an influence on the present. For example: **"Cēnāvistīne?" "Etiam. Cēnāvī."** "Have you eaten dinner? Yes, I have"; **studuī,** I have studied (and therefore I am now prepared).

III. COMMON VERBS

The following are the principal parts of some of the verbs that you have encountered in previous lessons or that will occur in the story below.

FIRST CONJUGATION
amō amāre amāvī amātus to love
dēmōnstrō dēmōnstrāre dēmōnstrāvī dēmōnstrātus to point out
properō properāre properāvī properātus to rush
pugnō pugnāre pugnāvī pugnātus to fight

SECOND CONJUGATION
doceō docēre docuī doctus to teach
habeō habēre habuī habitus to have
obsideō obsidēre obsēdī obsessus to besiege, blockade
prohibeō prohibēre prohibuī prohibitus to prohibit, prevent
respondeō respondēre respondī respōnsus to answer
videō vidēre vīdī vīsus to see

THIRD CONJUGATION
dēfendō dēfendĕre dēfendī dēfēnsus to defend
dīcō dīcĕre dīxī dictus to say
dūcō dūcĕre dūxī ductus to lead, take, guide
iungō iungĕre iūnxī iūnctus to join

THIRD -**iō** CONJUGATION
accipiō accipĕre accēpī acceptus to receive
capiō capĕre cēpī captus to take; to capture
cōnspiciō cōnspicĕre cōnspexī cōnspectus to catch sight of, spot
faciō facĕre fēcī factus to make
iniciō inicĕre iniēcī iniectus to throw in, throw on

Fourth Conjugation

custōdiō custōdīre custōdīvī *or* **custōdiī custōdītus** to guard
audiō audīre audīvī *or* **audiī audītus** to hear
hauriō haurīre hausī haustus to draw
veniō venīre vēnī ventūrus to come

EXERCISES

A. Which of these endings are found only in the perfect tense?

1. -imus	4. -istis	7. -istī	9. -ērunt
2. -it	5. -ō	8. -ī	10. -t
3. -tis	6. -m		

B. Change the verbs from the tense shown to the corresponding perfect tense.

Example | vocābāmus *vocāvimus*

1. rēgnābat	docēbō	dīcīs	faciam
2. pugnant	habēs	gerēbant	capiēmus
3. properō	vidētis	dēfendunt	cōnspicit
4. mōnstrābis	respondēbat	dūcam	veniēbat
5. amātis	vidēbimus	dīcēbam	audient

C. Complete the following sentences, using the perfect tense of the verb given in parentheses.

1. (facĕre) Ancus Mārcius, rēx quārtus Rōmae, Pontem Sublicium ____.
2. (custōdīre) Horātius Coclēs Pontem Sublicium ____.
3. (pugnāre) Lars Porsenna cum Rōmānis ante Pontem Sublicium ____.
4. (gerĕre) Rōmānī bellum contrā Volscōs magnā cum glōriā ____.
5. (obsidēre) Cūr Rōmānī oppidum Coriolōs ____.
6. (dūcĕre) Cūr, Coriolāne, exercitum contrā Rōmam ____.
7. (dīcĕre) Quid Faustulus et Lārentia geminīs _____?
8. (habēre) Quot rēgēs Rōma ōlim ____?
9. (respondēre) Quid Trōiānī Dīdōnī ____?
10. (properāre) Cūr, Aenēā, tū ex Āfricā in Italiam ____?
11. (custōdīre) Horātius et commīlitēs Pontem Sublicium ____.

12. (natāre)   Cloelia, fortissima puella, trāns Tiberim ___.
13. (exīre)   Cūr, Thisbē, tū sola ex urbe ___.
14. (convenīre) Num, Pȳrame, Thisbēn sub illā mōrō extrā moenia
                 urbis ___?

D. Pick out the grammatical misfit. A hint: not everything you'll see is perfect. Then give the reason for your choice.

1. docuit capit audīvit scrīpsit
2. mōvī monuī manuī mansī
3. cēpērunt habuērunt docuērunt cōnspiciunt
4. dīcimus fēcimus gessimus dūximus
5. pugnāvī nāvī amāvī properāvī
6. vēnī mōvī vīdī ibi
7. fēcistī istī dīxistī iniēcistī
8. habuimus animus dīximus mōvimus
9. monēre tenēre probibēre iungĕre
10. geris audīs mittis iungis
11. gessērunt dīxērunt dēfendunt dūxērunt
12. docuit capit scrīpsit fēcit

Now read the story of a girl who, according to Roman tradition, betrayed her city to the enemy, the Sabines, because of her love of jewelry. There have been many heroines in the history of Rome, but Tarpeia was definitely not one of them. At an early time, the Sabines became friends with Rome and were admitted to Roman citizenship. In fact, Numa Pompilius, second king of Rome, was a Sabine.

Perfida Tarpēia
The Disloyal Tarpeia

I

Sabīnī hostīlēs erant Rōmānīs, et bellum contrā eōs gessērunt. Sabīnī in urbem Rōmam ipsam iter fēcērunt. Illō tempore Tarpēius, pater Tarpēiae et dux Rōmānus, Capitōlium custōdīvit. Nam

Sabīn·ī -ōrum *mpl* Sabines (*living to the east of Latium*) **hostīl·is -is -e** (+ *dat*) hostile to **bellum gerĕre** to carry on a war **iter facĕre in** (+ *acc*) to march against

Tarpeia leading the Sabines to the Capitol

armilla

Capitōlium tum erat arx Rōmae.
Magnō in perīculō erat Rōma, quod
hostēs urbem obsīdēbant. Magna
erat inopia cibī et aquae intrā moenia.

quod because

inopi·a -ae *f* scarcity **moen·ia -ium** *npl*
walls

II

Cotīdiē Tarpēia prīmā lūce ex
moenibus properāvit ad fontem,
quī in cōnspectū hostium erat.
Mīlitēs Sabīnī puellam miseram
cōnspexērunt et eam cēpērunt.

cotīdiē daily **prīmā lūce** at dawn
fōns font·is *m* spring
cōnspect·us -ūs *m* sight

cōnspic·iō -ěre cōnspexī cōnspectus to
catch sight of, spot, see

III

Deinde Titus Tatius, rēx
Sabīnōrum, Tarpēiae dīxit:
"Dēmōnstrā nōbis, puella, viam in

Capitōlium. Sī viam nōbis dēmōnstrābis, praemium magnam accipiēs. Tarpēia vīdit armillās aureās, quās Sabīnī in bracchiīs gessērunt. Haec ōrnāmenta puella valdē dēsīderāvit. Tarpēia ergō respondit: "Dā ea quae mīlitēs in sinistrīs bracchiīs gerunt." "Tū vērō ea quae dēsīderās habēbis," dīxit Rēx Titus Tatius.

praemi·um -ī *n* reward

armill·a -ae *f* bracelet *(worn on upper arm)*
bracchi·um -ī *n* arm **ōrnāment·um -ī** *n* ornament; *(pl)* jewelry **valdē** very much

vērō all right

IV

Sine morā Tarpēia viam occultam in Capitōlium dēmōnstrāvit. Sīc Tarpēia patrem et patriam trādidit. Tum autem omnēs Sabīnī scūta gravia, quae quoque in bracchiīs gerēbant, in puellam iniēcērunt. Hōc modō mortua est puella perfida. Propter eius perfidiam, hostēs Capitōlium cēpērunt.

mor·a -ae *f* delay **occult·us -a -um** hidden
trā·dō -děre -didī -ditus to betray
tum autem but then **scūt·um -ī** *n* shield
grav·is -is -e heavy **quoque** too
mod·us -ī *m* way, manner

perfid·us -a -um disloyal **perfidi·a -ae** *f* disloyalty

Tarpeia's reward

E. Some words are missing from the following Latin passage, which is based on the story that you have just read. First read the entire story to get its meaning. Then complete each of the blanks with one Latin word, chosen from the word pool that is supplied. Look for contextual clues to help you supply the missing words.

WORD POOL

aquam	Capitōlium	fīliam	perfidiam
arx	cēpērunt	fontem	scūta
bellum	fēcērunt	hostēs	Tarpēius

Sabīnī et Rōmānī ōlim __1__ erant. Sabīnī saepe cum Rōmānīs __2__ gessērunt. Sabīnī ad urbem Rōmam iter __3__. Dux Rōmānōrum erat __4__. Dux __5__ habēbat, cui nōmen erat Tarpēia. Ille dux et mīlitēs Rōmānī __6__ custōdīvērunt. Illō tempore Capitōlium erat __7__ Rōmae.

Cotīdiē Tarpēia ad __8__ extrā moenia properāvit. Ibi Tarpēia __9__ ex fonte hauriēbat. Sed mīlitēs Sabīnī Tarpēiam cōnspexērunt et __10__. Sabīnī gravia __11__ sua in miseram puellam iniēcērunt. Propter __12__ puellae, Sabīnī facile Capitōlium cēpērunt.

F. Pick out the cultural misfit; then give the reason for your choice.

1. mīles   bellum   scūtum   cubiculum
2. ōrnāmentum   armilla   pōns   inaurēs
3. oppidum   moenia   porta   fōns
4. caput   praemium   bracchium   oculī
5. Tarpēia   Ardea   Lārentia   Rhēa Silvia

G. Supply the Latin source word for the following English derivatives. If the source word is a noun or adjective, give the nominative singular. If it is a verb, give the infinitive.

1. capitol	____	6. demonstrate	____
2. fountain	____	7. hostility	____
3. ornament	____	8. grave (serious)	____
4. perfidy	____	9. occult	____
5. mode	____	10. premium	____

Perfect Tense of Irregular Verbs

Sum quod eris; fuī quod es. I am what you will be; I was what you are. (Inscription on a Roman tombstone)

I. FORMS

PERFECT TENSE

sum esse fuī futūrus to be	possum posse potuī to be able	eō īre īvī *or* iī itūrus to go	volō velle voluī to want	nōlō nōlle nōluī not to want	ferō ferre tulī lātus to bear, bring
fuī	potuī	īvī *or* iī	voluī	nōluī	tulī
fuistī	potuistī	īvistī	voluistī	nōluistī	tulistī
fuit	potuit	īvit	voluit	nōluit	tulit
fuimus	potuimus	īvimus	voluimus	nōluimus	tulimus
fuistis	potuistis	īvistis	voluistis	nōluistis	tulistis
fuērunt	potuērunt	īvērunt	voluērunt	nōluērunt	tulērunt

NOTES

1) In Chapter 21 we saw the present, imperfect, future, and imperative forms of these irregular verbs. As you can see, the endings of the perfect tense for these irregular verbs are the same as the perfect endings of all verbs. It would be a good idea to review Chapter 21 before doing the exercises of the present chapter.

2) DEFECTIVE VERBS: We have verbs in English that lack certain parts; for example, the verb "must" does not have a past tense. Such verbs are called *defective*. There are some defective Latin verbs that have no present tense; the perfect tense of those verbs may have a present meaning.

coepī coepisse to begin

nōvī nōvisse to know, be familiar with (**sciō** is used in connection with facts, while **nōvī** is used in connection with persons and places.) The verb **nōsc·ō -ĕre nōvī nōtus** means "to get to know." The perfect tense **nōvī** means "I have gotten to know" and therefore "I know."

ōdī ōdisse to hate

A. First read the sentence carefully. Then change the verb to the perfect tense.

1. Tarpēius *praeerat* mīlitibus in Capitōliō.
2. Rōmulus et Remus geminī *sunt*.
3. Ego et Faustulus geminōs servāre *volumus*.
4. Faustulus, num geminōs ad Lārentiam *fers*?
5. Nōnne Lārentia in casā *adest*?
6. Nōnne, Aemūlī, rēgnāre *volēbās*?
7. Sabīnī cum Rōmānīs pugnāre *volunt*.
8. Aenēās ad Rēgem Latīnum *ībat*.
9. Servī, cūr cibum nōn in trīclīnium *fertis*?
10. Nōs Tarpēiam nōn culpāre *volumus*.
11. Ego in cūriā illō diē *aderam*.
12. Rōmānī *volēbant* esse amīcī cum Sabīnīs.
13. Cūr tū mēcum lūdĕre *nōlēbās*?

14. Cicerō, cūr tam diū ab urbe *aberās*?
15. Coriolānus domum *redībat*.
16. Cōnsul et praetōrēs ā cūriā *absunt*.
17. Familia mea per Viam Appiam ad oppidum Brundisium *it*.
18. Lars Porsenna Rōmam oppugnāre *vult*.
19. Lars Porsenna *est* rēx Etrūscus.
20. Horātius Coclēs in castra Lartis Porsennae *ībat*.

B. Translate into Latin, putting the verbs in italics into the perfect tense.

1. I *wanted* to be present.
2. Marcus *was* not *able* to go.
3. We *wanted* to go out.
4. All *wanted* to be absent.
5. I *did not want* to go away.
6. You (*pl*) *brought* no presents.
7. Who *was* not *able* to go in?
8. The Romans *were* near the bridge.
9. We *were* in town.
10. You (*sing*) *did not want* to go out.

C. Complete the following sentences by translating the English verbs.

1. Amūlius (*hates*) Numitōrem frātrem.
2. Cūr Rōmānī (*hate*) Tarquinium Superbum?
3. Ego ipse istum rēgem nōn (*know*).
4. Ille (*began*) rēgnāre post Servium Tullium.
5. Rōmānī (*do not hate*) rēgēs.

D. Scrambled sentences. Put the following sentences into a reasonable order by putting together the words that belong together. Place verbs at the end; place the adverbs directly before the verbs.

1. in natāre puerī meā voluērunt multī semper piscīnā.
2. potuī verba ego difficilia prōnūntiāre numquam Latīna.
3. diū meī mēcum in amīcī ātriō nōluērunt meō lūdĕre.
4. novum fundāre Monte in Rōmulus oppidum voluit pulchrum Palātīnō.
5. voluērunt perīculōsum trāns Aenēās nāvigāre et sociī mare.
6. parvō hodiē in nōluērunt cōnsōbrīnī meō meī dormīre cubiculō.

E. Read over each sentence, carefully noting the subject; then translate the verb into Latin in the perfect tense.

1. My younger sister, my mother, and I *went* to the clothing store.
2. My older sister Jessica *was* not at home.
3. In fact, she *was absent* for days.
4. My mother *brought* the money.
5. I *wanted* to buy a tunic.
6. I *was able* to buy two tunics.
7. My mother *wanted* to buy a gown (*stola*).
8. My sister *did* not *want* to buy new clothes.
9. We *went out* of the clothing store with new clothes.
10. Jessica, *did* you *not want* to go shopping with us?
11. The consuls *were in charge of* the senate.
12. Why *did* you *fail* your friends?

F. First translate each verb form as given. Give the infinitive of each verb. You have met all of these verbs in this chapter or in the previous ones.

1. nōluistī	5. nōvērunt	9. rediit	13. potuistis
2. exīvērunt	6. potuī	10. tulērunt	14. coepit
3. adfuī	7. voluistis	11. praefuistī	15. dēfuit
4. āfuimus	8. īvit	12. nōvit	16. ōdērunt

II. OVERVIEW AND REVIEW OF VERBS IN THE PERFECT TENSE

The verbs are listed according to patterns of perfect stems. This is a good time not only to see patterns of the perfect but also to review the verbs that you have encountered in the previous chapters. A few of the verbs will occur in the reading passage of this chapter.

1. Perfect ending in **-vī**

I	**amāvī**	**am·ō -āre amāvī amātus** to love (and most verbs of the first conjugation)
II	**dēlēvī**	**dēl·eō -ēre dēlēvī dēlētus** to destroy; to wipe out
	flēvī	**fleō flēre flēvī flētus** to cry, weep
III	**nōvī**	**nōsc·ō -ĕre nōvī nōtus** to get to know, become familiar with

III-iō	cupīvī	cup·iō -ĕre cupīvī (or -iī) cupītus to wish (for), desire
	petīvī	pet·ō -ĕre petīvī (or -iī) petītus to look for; to head for; to chase
IV	audīvī	aud·iō -īre audīvī (or -iī) audītus to hear
	custōdīvī	custōd·iō -īre custōdīvī (or -iī) custōdītus to guard
	scīvī	sciō scīre scīvī scītus to know

2. Perfect ending in -uī

I	sonuī	son·ō -āre sonuī sonitūrus to sound; (+ abl) to resound with
II	docuī	doc·eō -ēre docuī doctus to teach
	tenuī	ten·eō -ēre tenuī tentus to hold
	timuī	tim·eō -ēre timuī to fear, be afraid (of)
III	posuī	pōn·ō -ĕre posuī positus to place, put
IV	aperuī	aper·iō -īre aperuī apertus to open
	saluī	sal·iō -īre saluī saltūrus to jump

3. Perfect ending in sī

II	ārsī	ārd·eō -ēre ārsī ārsūrus to burn, be on fire; to catch fire
	mānsī	man·eō -ēre mānsī mānsūrus to stay, remain
III	invāsī	invād·ō -ĕre invāsī invāsus to attack, strike; to invade
	mīsī	mitt·ō -ĕre mīsī missus to send
	gessī	ger·ō -ĕre gessī gestus to carry; to wear (clothes); to carry on (war)
	prōcessī	prōcēd·ō -ĕre prōcessī prōcessūrus to proceed
	scrīpsī	scrīb·ō -ĕre scrīpsī scrīptus to write
	sumpsī	sūm·ō -ĕre sūmpsī sūmptus to take; to assume

| IV | assēn*s*ī | **assent·iō -īre assēnsī assēnsūrus** (+ *dat*) to agree with |
| | sēn*s*ī | **sent·iō -īre sēnsī sēnsus** to feel; to realize |

4. Perfect ending in -xī

II	au*x*ī	**aug·eō -ēre auxī auctus** to increase
III	dī*x*ī	**dīc·ō -ĕre dīxī dictus** to say
	flū*x*ī	**flu·ō -ĕre flūxī flūxūrus** to flow
	īnstrū*x*ī	**īnstru·ō -ĕre īnstrūxī īnstrūctus** to draw up, deploy (*troops*)
	iūn*x*ī	**iung·ō -ĕre iūnxī iūnctus** to join
	vī*x*ī	**vīv·ō -ĕre vīxī vīctūrus** to live, be alive
III-iō	aspe*x*ī	**aspic·iō -ĕre aspexī aspectus** to look at
	cōnspe*x*ī	**cōnspic·iō -ĕre cōnspexī cōnspectus** to catch sight of, spot

5. Perfect ending in -ī (with lengthened vowel in the stem)

II	mōvī	**mov·eō -ēre mōvī mōtus** to move
	vīdī	**vid·eō -ēre vīdī vīsus** to see
III	lēgī	**leg·ō -ĕre lēgī lēctus** to read
III-iō	cēpī	**cap·iō -ĕre cēpī captus** to take; to capture
	fēcī	**fac·iō -ĕre fēcī factus** to do; to make
	incēpī	**incip·iō -ĕre incēpī inceptus** to begin
IV	vēnī	**ven·iō -īre vēnī ventūrus** to come

6. Perfect ending in -i (with unchanged verb stem)

II	respondī	**respond·eō -ēre respondī respōnsūrus** to answer
III	ascendī	**ascend·ō -ĕre ascendī ascēnsūrus** to climb up
	dēfendī	**dēfend·ō -ĕre dēfendī dēfēnsus** to defend

7. Perfect ending in **-ī** (with reduplication of the stem)

I	**dedī**	**dō dare dedī datus** to give
	stetī	**stō stāre stetī statūrus** to stand
III	**cecidī**	**cad·ō -ĕre cecidī cāsūrus** to fall
	didicī	**disc·ō -ĕre didicī** to learn

Now read a story, beautifully told by the poet Ovid (43 B.C.-A.D. 18), about the interaction between father and son. According to the myth, Phaëthon was the son of Clymene, a mortal woman, and Phoebus Apollo, the sun god. It should be noted that once a god had sworn to keep a promise, he could never break it. If you need help with verbs in this passage, be sure to look them up in the review list above.

Phaethōn Currum Sōlis agitat.
Phaëthon Drives the Chariot of the Sun.

I

Phaëthon fuit fīlius Phoebī Apollinis, deī sōlis, quī equōs per caelum cotīdiē agitāvit. Quōdam diē, amīcī eius Phaëthontī dīxērunt: "Tū es tam superbus, sed deus nōn est tuus pater." Haec verba Phaëthontem commōvērunt. Itaque prīmā lūce properāvit ad regiōnēs, in quibus Sōl habitāvit. Splendida fuit rēgia Sōlis. Phaëthon domum patris inīvit et ad thronum Sōlis prōcessit. Propter splendōrem lūcis, Phaëthon vix patrem suum aspicĕre potuit.

Phaëthon Phaëthont·is *m* Phaëthon

agitāre to drive

commov·eō -ēre commōvī commōtus to upset **regi·ō -ōnis** *f* region
splendid·us -a -um dazzling, brilliant

ineō inīre inīvī *or* **iniī initūrus** to enter
thron·us -ī *m* throne **splend·or -ōris** *m* brilliance **aspic·iō -ĕre aspexī aspectus** to look at

II

Sōl iuvenem aspexit oculīs, quibus tōtam orbem terrārum aspicit.

iuven·is -is *m* young man
orb·is -is *m* **terrārum** the world

Phaëthon airborne

"Quae est causa huius itineris, mī fīlī?" rogāvit pater. "Dā, mī pater, certum signum, quō omnēs hōminēs scient mē esse fīlium tuum." "Rogā," respondit Apollō, "et ego id tibi dabō." "Dā mihi currum sōlis, quem cotīdiē agitās. Ego illōs equōs ūnum diem agitāre volō."

caus·a -ae *f* (+ *gen*) reason for

cert·us -a -um sure, unmistakable
sign·um -ī *n* sign
rogāre to ask
curr·us -ūs *m* chariot

III

Tum trīstis pater respondit: "Ego quidem fidem servābō. Maximō cum perīculō agitābis illōs equōs, quī flammās ex ōribus expīrant." Deinde sollicitus pater radiōs sōlis in capite fīlī posuit, et Phaëthōn in currum avidē ascendit.

trīst·is -is -e sad **quidem** of course
fidem servāre to keep (one's) word

flamm·a -ae *f* flame **ōs ōr·is** *n* mouth
expīrāre to breathe (out) **sollicit·us -a -um** worried **radi·us -ī** *m* ray
avidē eagerly **ascend·ō -ěre -ī ascēnsus** to climb up

IV

Prīmō, Phaëthōn per caelum fēlīciter volāvit. Equī tamen novum agitātōrem ignōrāvērunt, et in hōrās vēlōcitātem auxērunt. Territus Phaëthōn in omnēs partēs volāre incēpit. Nunc prōperāvit ad altās regiōnēs deōrum; nunc prope terram volāvit. Multās urbēs inflammāvit. Flūmina, ārida nunc propter magnum calōrem, nōn iam flūxērunt. Silvae ubique ārsērunt.

prīmō at first **fēlīciter** happily
volāre to fly **tamen** however
agitāt·or -ōris *m* driver **ignōrāre** to not know **in hōrās** from hour to hour
vēlōcit·ās -ātis *f* speed **aug·eō -ēre auxi auctus** to increase **territ·us -a -um** frightened **part·ēs -ium** *fpl* directions **incip·iō -ěre incēpī inceptus** to begin **nunc . . . nunc** first . . . then **inflammāre** to set on fire **ārid·us -a -um** dry **nōn iam** no longer **calor calōr·is** *m* heat **magn·us -a -um** intense **ubique** everywhere **ārd·eō -ēre arsī arsūrus** to burn, be on fire

V

Dēnique Iuppiter perīculum terrārum sēnsit; fulmine currum dēlēvit. Corpus miserī Phaëthontis in flūmen Ēridanum cecidit.

perīcul·um -ī *n* (+ *dat*) danger to **sent·iō -īre sēnsī sēnsus** to sense, realize **fulmen fulmin·is** *n* bolt of lightning **Ēridan·us -ī** *m* Po (so called by the Greeks)

G. Answer in English the following questions based on the story of Phaëthon.

I 1. Why did Phaëthon feel compelled to go to the palace of Phoebus Apollo?
2. How does Phaëthon show the urgency of settling his problem?
3. Why did Phaëthon find it difficult to face his father?

II 4. What favor does Phaëthon ask of Apollo?
5. What does Phaëthon want to prove by the "sign"?
6. Do you blame Phaëthon for making the request of his father? Explain.

III 7. How does the father feel about the request?
8. What prediction does he make about the ride?
9. Should the father have allowed his son to take the ride? Explain.

IV 10. How did Phaëthon do in the first part of the ride?
11. What effect do you think this had on him?
12. What confused the horses?
13. What did they do as a result?
14. When Phaëthon lost control, what two extreme paths did he take?
15. What happened on earth when he flew too close to it?

V 16. What did Jupiter do to end the wild ride?
17. Why did Jupiter end the ride?
18. What happened to Phaëthon in the end?

H. Fill in the missing principal parts and the conjugation number.

Example | **aspicĕre**
aspiciō (III-io) aspicĕre aspexī aspectus

1. scrībĕre	7. respondī	13. servāre
2. mōvī	8. dēfendī	14. ascēnsūrus
3. videō	9. inīre	15. iūnxī
4. factus	10. cāsūrus	16. auxī
5. dedī	11. expīrāre	17. mittĕre
6. dīcĕre	12. incipiō	18. lēctus

I. Expand your command of Latin vocabulary. And it's easy to do. Let the principal parts of verbs give you your clue. If you take the fourth principal part, drop the ending, and simply add **-iō,** you know yet another Latin word, as well as an English word. For example, **maneō manēre mānsī mānsūrus** *(to stay)*. Take the fourth principal part, namely, **mānsūrus;** drop the ending **-ūrus,** and you have the stem **māns + iō = mānsiō mānsiōn·is** *f* a stopover, "a place where one stays," or a "stopping place on a journey." Because such stopping places had many rooms for guests, "mansion" got to mean a private home with many rooms. Use the following example as your model.

Example

PRINCIPAL PARTS OF THE VERB **dēleō dēlēre dēlēvī dēlētus**
LATIN NOUN *dēlēt·iō -iōnis f*   ENGLISH TRANSLATION *deletion*

1. petō
2. pōnō
3. invādō
4. mittō
5. prōcēdō
6. dīcō
7. augeō
8. īnstruō
9. moveō
10. videō
11. ascendō
12. stō
13. expīrō
14. īnflammō
15. incipiō
16. commoveō

WORD POWER

J. Supply the Latin source word from which the following English derivatives come. If the source word is a noun or adjective, give the nominative singular; if it is a verb, give the infinitive.

1. aperture ____
2. arson ____
3. missile ____
4. process ____
5. assent ____
6. sentiment ____
7. aspect ____
8. fluent ____
9. instruct ____
10. juncture ____
11. fact ____
12. lecture ____
13. response ____
14. defense ____
15. ascend ____
16. status ____
17. regional ____
18. certain ____
19. signal ____
20. initial ____
21. expire ____
22. sollicitous ____
23. velocity ____
24. arid ____
25. calorie ____
26. ardent ____
27. deleterious ____
28. inflame ____
29. agitate ____
30. inception ____

CHAPTER **24**

Pluperfect and Future Perfect Tenses Active

**THOUGHT
FOR
TODAY**

Iniūria nōn excūsat iniūriam. One wrong does not excuse another.

PLUPERFECT TENSE (REGULAR VERBS)				
I	**II**	**III**	**III-iō**	**IV**
amō amāre	**doceō docēre**	**scrībō scrībĕre**	**capiō capĕre**	**audiō audīre**
amāvī amātus	**docuī doctus**	**scrīpsī scrīptus**	**cēpī captus**	**audīvī audītus**
to love	to teach	to write	to take	to hear
amāv_eram_	**docu**_eram_	**scrīps**_eram_	**cēp**_eram_	**audīv**_eram_
amāv_erās_	**docu**_erās_	**scrīps**_erās_	**cēp**_erās_	**audīv**_erās_
amāv_erat_	**docu**_erat_	**scrīps**_erat_	**cēp**_erat_	**audīv**_erat_
amāv_erāmus_	**docu**_erāmus_	**scrīps**_erāmus_	**cēp**_erāmus_	**audīv**_erāmus_
amāv_erātis_	**docu**_erātis_	**scrīps**_erātis_	**cēp**_erātis_	**audīv**_erātis_
amāv_erant_	**docu**_erant_	**scrīps**_erant_	**cēp**_erant_	**audīv**_erant_

PLUPERFECT TENSE (IRREGULAR VERBS)

sum esse fuī futūrus to be	possum posse potuī to be able	eō īre īvī *or* iī itūrus to go	volō velle voluī to want	nōlō nōlle nōluī not to want	ferō ferre tulī lātus to bear, bring
fu*eram* fu*erās* fu*erat*	potu*eram* potu*erās* potu*erat*	īv*eram* īv*erās* īv*erat*	volu*eram* volu*erās* volu*erat*	nōlu*eram* nōlu*erās* nōlu*erat*	tul*eram* tul*erās* tul*erat*
fu*erāmus* fu*erātis* fu*erant*	potu*erāmus* potu*erātis* potu*erant*	īv*erāmus* īv*erātis* īv*erant*	volu*erāmus* volu*erātis* volu*erant*	nōlu*erāmus* nōlu*erātis* nōlu*erant*	tul*erāmus* tul*erātis* tul*erant*

PLUPERFECT ENDINGS

PRONOUN	ENDING	EXAMPLE	
ego	*-eram*	amāv*eram*	I had loved
tū	*-erās*	amāv*erās*	you had loved
is, ea, id	*-erat*	amāv*erat*	he, she, it had loved
nōs	*-erāmus*	amāv*erāmus*	we had loved
vōs	*-erātis*	amāv*erātis*	you had loved
eī, eae, ea	*-erant*	amāv*erant*	they had loved

1. The pluperfect (also called past perfect) is formed in the same way for all verbs, regular and irregular. It is formed by adding the imperfect forms of **sum**, that is, **eram, erās, erat, erāmus, erātis, erant,** to the perfect stem.

2. The pluperfect tense indicates **an action that was completed in the past before another past action took place** that is stated or implied. It is always translated with the helping word *had.* For example, if we say "He was frying the fish that he *had* caught" it is obvious that the action of catching the fish took place before he was frying it. One might call the pluperfect a "double past." The Latin word **plūsquamperfectum** has the same idea; "more than completed."

Dux Tarpēium vīsit, quī Capitōliō praefuerat.   The general went to see Tarpeius who had been in charge of the Capitoline.

Ego cōnsulem numquam anteā vīderam.   I had never seen a consul before.

The first sentence suggests that Tarpeius was no longer in charge of the Capitoline. In the second sentence, in which the previous action is implied, the word "before" suggests something like "before I saw this consul."

3. The pluperfect tense is used with defective verbs. See **II** note **3.**

EXERCISES

A. The following verbs are all in the perfect tense. Give the pluperfect form for each verb in the same number and person. Then translate it.

Example | **fēcī**   *fēceram*   I had done

1. rīsī
2. accēpistis
3. nōluī
4. dīxit
5. didicimus
6. cēnāvērunt
7. aspexistī
8. tulimus
9. īvistis
10. cōnsēdimus

B. Give the pluperfect form of the verb in the same number and person; then translate it. To arrive at the pluperfect form, it is best to run the principal parts of each verb through your mind; then zero in on the third principal part (the perfect tense), drop off the ending **-ī**. You now have the perfect stem. Add the appropriate form (**eram, erās,** etc.) to the perfect stem.

Example | **ambulābam**   *ambulāveram*   I had walked

1. cantat
2. errābant
3. fabricābis
4. vocās
5. rīdent
6. vidēbās
7. tenētis
8. facimus
9. accipiam
10. discitis
11. dīcimus
12. fertis
13. venīmus
14. sciunt
15. nōlō

C. Translate the English words into Latin.

1. Phaëthōn (*had never driven*) currum.
2. Phaëthōn (*had never seen*) rēgiam sōlis.

3. Apollō (*had lived*) in rēgiā in caelō.
4. Phaëthōn (*had not been able*) aspicĕre patrem.
5. Phaëthōn (*had asked for*) certum signum ā patre suō.
6. Equī sōlis (*had breathed out*) flammās ex ōribus.
7. Prīmō Phaëthōn (*had not feared*) agitāre currum.
8. Sed mox equī (*had increased*) vēlōcitātem.
9. Mox Phaëthōn (*had rushed*) in omnēs partēs.
10. Iuppiter ipse (*had destroyed*) currum.
11. Phaëthōn (*had fallen*) in flūmen Ēridanum.
12. Phaëthōn (*had been*) agitātor malus.

FUTURE PERFECT TENSE (REGULAR VERBS)

I	II	III	III-iō	IV
amō amāre	doceō docēre	scrībō scrībĕre	capiō capĕre	audiō audīre
amāvī amātus	docuī doctus	scrīpsī scrīptus	cēpī captus	audīvī audītus
to love	to teach	to write	to take	to hear
amāv*erō*	docu*erō*	scrīps*erō*	cēp*erō*	audīv*erō*
amāv*eris*	docu*eris*	scrīps*eris*	cēp*eris*	audīv*eris*
amāv*erit*	docu*erit*	scrīps*erit*	cēp*erit*	audīv*erit*
amāv*erimus*	docu*erimus*	scrīps*erimus*	cēp*erimus*	audīv*erimus*
amāv*eritis*	docu*eritis*	scrīps*eritis*	cēp*eritis*	audīv*eritis*
amāv*erint*	docu*erint*	scrīps*erint*	cēp*erint*	audīv*erint*

FUTURE PERFECT TENSE (IRREGULAR VERBS)

sum esse	possum	eō īre īvī	volō velle	nōlō nōlle	ferō ferre
fuī futūrus	posse potuī	*or* iī itūrus	voluī	nōluī	tulī lātus
to be	to be able	to go	to want	not to want	to bear, bring
fu*erō*	potu*erō*	īv*erō*	volu*erō*	nōlu*erō*	tul*erō*
fu*eris*	potu*eris*	īv*eris*	volu*eris*	nōlu*eris*	tul*eris*
fu*erit*	potu*erit*	īv*erit*	volu*erit*	nōlu*erit*	tul*erit*
fu*erimus*	potu*erimus*	īv*erimus*	volu*erimus*	nōlu*erimus*	tul*erimus*
fu*eritis*	potu*eritis*	īv*eritis*	volu*eritis*	nōlu*eritis*	tul*eritis*
fu*erint*	potu*erint*	īv*erint*	volu*erint*	nōlu*erint*	tul*erint*

FUTURE PERFECT ENDINGS

PRONOUN	ENDING		EXAMPLE
ego	*-erō*	**amāv** *erō*	I shall have loved
tū	*-eris*	**amāv** *eris*	you will have loved
is, ea, id	*-erit*	**amāv** *erit*	he, she, it will have loved
nōs	*-erimus*	**amāv** *erimus*	we shall have loved
vōs	*-eritis*	**amāv** *eritis*	you will have loved
eī, eae, ea	*-erint*	**amāv** *erint*	they will have loved

1. The future perfect of all verbs, both regular and irregular, is formed by adding the future forms of **sum,** that is **erō, eris, erit, erimus, eritis, erunt,** to the perfect stem. Notice, however, that the third person plural of the future perfect is not **-erunt,** but **-erint.**

2. The future perfect tense is practically never used in English; it is only slightly more common in Latin. It is used to indicate **an action completed before a given time in the future.** Here is an example of its use in English: "By the time that you (will) return, the mechanic *will have finished* repairing your car."

Example | **Scrībam epistulam cum redieris.** | I'll write the letter when you return. (*lit:* when you shall have returned)

3. In Latin, the future perfect is also used with *defective verbs,* for example, **coepī coepisse** *to begin,* **nōvī nōvisse** *to know,* **ōdī ōdisse** *to hate.* We call these verbs defective because they do not have a present form. When the perfect form has a present meaning, the pluperfect form has an imperfect meaning, and the future perfect has a simple future meaning. (See Chapter 23, **I.** Note 2).

Examples | PERFECT FORM WITH PRESENT MEANING:
Omnēs Rōmānī ōdērunt rēgēs. | All Romans hate kings.

PLUPERFECT FORM WITH IMPERFECT MEANING:
Omnēs Rōmānī ōdērant rēgēs. | All Romans hated kings.

FUTURE PERFECT FORM WITH FUTURE MEANING:
Omnēs Rōmānī ōdērint rēgēs. | All Romans will hate kings.

D. Complete the sentences by translating the English verbs with defective Latin verbs.

1. (*I am beginning*) Latīnē intellegere.
2. (*I began*) ambulāre.
3. Puerī (*will begin*) lūdĕre.
4. Cūr, Mārce, (*do you hate*) scholam?
5. (*We hated*) bellum.
6. Rōmānī (*will hate*) Tarquinium Superbum.
7. (*I do not know*) hanc partem urbis.
8. Mūcius Scaevola (*did not know*) rēgem Porsennam.
9. Mīlitēs Sabīnī (*did not hate*) Tarpēiam.
10. Illī mīlitēs (*did not know*) Tarpēiam.
11. Sed Tarpēia (*will know*) illōs Sabīnōs.
12. Tarpēia vidētur (*to know*) mīlitēs.

E. SCRAMBLED SENTENCES. Now that you're an expert on the myth of Phaëthon, you should have no trouble unscrambling these sentences.

1. ante timidus cārum patrem steterat benignum Phaëthōn.
2. splendidā habitāverat in Apollō rēgiā.
3. radiīs tōtam suīs illūmināverat deus sōlis terram splendidīs.
4. capite radiōs pater cārī splendidōs in posuerat fīliī sollicitus.
5. validōs celerēs aurīga ferōcēs per agitāverat caelum equōs.
6. magnās montēs et urbēs altōs potuerat ex vidēre currū Phaëthōn.
7. timidus fēcerat omnēs in partēs perīculōsum aurīga iter caelī.
8. celerēs novum equī ignōrāverant agitātōrem.
9. fulmine omnipotēns miserum ūnō Iuppiter necāverat Phaëthontem.
10. dē mortuus currū dēnique celerī flūmen in ceciderat Ēridanum iuvenis.

F. Complete the following analogies. For explanations and examples, see Chapter 4, Exercises **G** and **H**.

1. Apollō	:	sōl	::	Diāna	: _____
2. Trōia	:	Aenēās	::	Ardea	: _____
3. Italia	:	Tiberis	::	Tartarus	: _____
4. Tarpēius	:	Tarpēia	::	Numitor	: _____
5. Plūtō	:	Tartarus	::	Neptūnus	: _____
6. stola	:	fēmina	::	toga	: _____
7. calor	:	calidus	::	frīgus	: _____

8.	bonus	:	malus	::	parvus	:	_____
9.	dexter	:	sinister	::	brevis	:	_____
10.	cōnsōbrīnus	:	puer	::	cōnsōbrīna	:	_____
11.	oculī	:	vidēre	::	aurēs	:	_____
12.	diēs	:	nox	::	pāx	:	_____
13.	coqua	:	culīna	::	tabernārius	:	_____
14.	gladiātōrēs	:	Colossēum	::	agitātōrēs	:	_____
15.	pater	:	fīlius	::	magister	:	_____
16.	trīclīnium	:	cēnāre	::	cubiculum	:	_____
17.	ānulus	:	digitus	::	armilla	:	_____
18.	inīre	:	exīre	::	dōnāre	:	_____
19.	librī	:	bibliothēca	::	flōrēs	:	_____
20.	agitātor	:	currus	::	nāvigātor	:	_____

Read this story carefully, and then answer the questions below that are based on the story.

Thēseus Pugnat cum Mīnōtaurō.
Theseus Fights the Minotaur.

I

Daedalus, architectus nōtus, in īnsulā Crētā magnum labyrinthum aedificāverat. Labyrinthus erat plēnus viārum flexuōsārum. In hōc labyrinthō mōnstrum, taurus partim, partim homō, habitāvit. Hoc mōnstrum hominēs iam dēvorāverat. Nōmen mōnstrō fuit Mīnōtaurus, nam rēx Crētae erat Mīnōs.

architect·us -ī *m* architect **nōt·us -a -um** well-known **labyrinth·us -ī** *m* labyrinth

flexuōs·us -a -um twisting
mōnstr·um -ī *n* monster **partim** partly
taur·us -ī *m* bull
iam already
dēvorāre to devour

Mīnōs Minō·is *m* Minos

II

Quotannīs populus Athēnārum dēbēbat mittĕre septem puerōs et septem puellās ad hunc labyrinthum, ubi Mīnōtaurus eōs dēvorābat.

quotannīs every year
dēb·eō -ēre -uī -itus to be obliged to, have to
ubi where

The Minotaur, Theseus, and Ariadne in the labyrinth

III

In victimīs miserīs quondam erat Thēseus, rēgulus Athēniēnsis, iuvenis validus et fortis. Quamquam magnum perīculum sēnserat, Thēseus tamen cum cēterīs iuvenibus nāvigāre dēbuit.

in (+ *abl*) among **victim·a -ae** *f* victim **quondam** once **Thēse·us -ī** *m* Theseus **rēgul·us -ī** *m* prince **Athēniēns·is -is -e** Athenian **quamquam** although **sent·iō -īre sēnsī sēnsus** to realize, sense **tamen** nevertheless **cēter·ī -ae -a** the rest of the

IV

Ariadnē, autem, fīlia rēgis, pulchrum iuvenem rēgālem prīmō aspectū adamāvit. Ariadnē fīlum longum et gladium Thēseō occultē dederat. Thēseus fīlum ad iānuam alligāverat antequam labyrinthum inīvit.

Ariadn·ē -ēs *f* Ariadne **pulcher pulchr·a -um** handsome **prīmō aspectū** at first sight **fīl·um -ī** *n* thread **gladi·us -ī** *m* sword **occultē** secretly **iānu·a -ae** *f* entrance **alligāre** to tie (to) **antequam** before

V

Mīnōtaurus, ubi Thēseum vīdit, iuvenem necāre temptāvit. Thēseus autem erat parātus; sine morā, mōnstrum gladiō necāvit. Deinde exitum labyrinthī fīlō facile invēnit et cēterōs iuvenēs līberāvit.

ubi when

mor·a -ae *f* delay

exit·us -ūs *m* way out, exit **līberāre** to free

VI

Deinde Thēseus cum Ariadnē et cēterīs iuvenibus trāns mare fūgit. Vespere ad īnsulam Naxum advēnērunt. Hīc, autem, mediā nocte Thēseus, ingrātus iuvenis, puellam fīdam et amantem, dēseruit, et sine illā ad patriam suam rediit.

vespere in the evening **hīc** here **mediā nocte** at midnight **ingrāt·us -a -um** ungrateful **fīd·us -a -um** loyal **amans amant·is** loving **dēser·ō -ĕre -uī -tus** to desert

G. Choose the best answer from A, B, C, or D.

I 1. Daedalus A) was the king of the island of Naxos; B) knew the architect of the labyrinth; C) tried to leave the island of Crete; D) had constructed the labyrinth on Crete.

   2. The labyrinth was built A) as a palace for the king; B) to give the Minotaur an interesting home; C) to restrain the dangerous beast; D) to keep out the curious crowds.

II 3. The people of Athens sent boys and girls to Crete A) to give them a vacation; B) to see the Minotaur; C) because they were somehow forced to; D) because the Athenians were friendly with the king of Crete.

III 4. Theseus went along because A) he just had the misfortune of being selected; B) because he was a prince; C) because he didn't think it dangerous; D) he had slain some of the victims.

IV 5. Ariadne helped Theseus because A) her father ordered her to do so; B) she became romatically involved with Theseus; C) the Minotaur had once threatened to devour her; D) she wanted to see what the Minotaur was like.

   6. Ariadne gave Theseus a long thread A) to tie up his broken sword; B) to tie up the Minotaur; C) to find his way out of the labyrinth; D) to tie up the door so that the Minotaur could not escape.

V 7. When the Minotaur first saw Theseus, it A) ran for the exit; B) tried to kill Theseus; C) tried to hide; D) pretended to be tame.

   8. After Theseus had slain the beast, A) he tried at first to save himself; B) he had trouble finding his way out; C) he freed his companions and escaped; D) he gave up his companions for dead.

VI 9. After their departure from Crete, Theseus A) lost his way in the dark of night; B) stopped off on an island and left Ariadne there; C) made Naxos his new fatherland; D) abandoned his unfaithful friends.

   10. This story is meant to show that: A) all princes are brave and handsome; B) even a prince can be lacking in gratitude; C) royalty is more important in life than loyalty; D) Theseus, a prince, could not marry a girl of the common people.

H. Translate the following sentences into Latin.

1. Daedalus had built a twisting labyrinth.
2. The Minotaur had lived in that labyrinth.
3. This monster had devoured boys and girls.
4. Theseus had gone into the labyrinth.
5. Ariadne had fallen in love with Theseus.
6. Ariadne had given thread to Theseus.

WORD POWER

I. Give the Latin source word for the following English derivatives. If the Latin source word is a noun or adjective, give the nominative singular; if it is a verb, give the infinitive.

1. monstrosity	____	7. liberation	____
2. debit	____	8. ingratitude	____
3. noted	____	9. desertion	____
4. victimize	____	10. odious	____
5. aspect	____	11. ingrate	____
6. occult	____	12. exit	____

CHAPTER 25

Present, Imperfect, and Future Passive

THOUGHT
FOR
TODAY

| **Tempora mūtantur et nōs mūtāmur in illīs.** | Times change and we change with them. |

I. FORMS

Latin does not use helping verbs, as we do in English, to form the present, imperfect, or future of the passive voice. The passive forms of the present, imperfect, and future tenses use the same stems as the active forms and add the passive personal endings, which are summarized below. Notice that in the first person singular of the present, the final **ō** is retained, making the ending **-or.** It would be a good idea to review the formation of the future and imperfect tenses of verbs in the active voice in Chapters 19 and 20.

ACTIVE AND PASSIVE PERSONAL ENDINGS OF THE PRESENT, IMPERFECT, AND FUTURE

SINGULAR			PLURAL		
PRONOUN	ACTIVE	PASSIVE	PRONOUN	ACTIVE	PASSIVE
ego	*-ō , -m*	*-r*	**nōs**	*-mus*	*-mur*
tū	*-s*	*-ris*	**vōs**	*-tis*	*-minī*
is, ea, id	*-t*	*-tur*	**eī, eae, ea**	*-nt*	*-ntur*

PRESENT PASSIVE VOICE				
I	**II**	**III**	**III-iō**	**IV**
amō amāre	doceō docēre	scrībō scrībĕre	capiō capĕre	audiō audīre
amāvī amātus	docuī doctus	scrīpsī scrīptus	cēpī captus	audīvī audītus
to love	to teach	to write	to take	to hear
am *or*	doce *or*	scrīb *or*	capi *or*	audi *or*
amā *ris*	docē *ris*	scrībe *ris*	cape *ris*	audī *ris*
amā *tur*	docē *tur*	scrībi *tur*	capi *tur*	audī *tur*
amā *mur*	docē *mur*	scrībi *mur*	capi *mur*	audī *mur*
amā *minī*	docē *minī*	scrībi *minī*	capi *minī*	audī *minī*
ama *ntur*	doce *ntur*	scrību *ntur*	capiu *ntur*	audiu *ntur*

IMPERFECT PASSIVE VOICE				
amā *bar*	docē *bar*	scrībē *bar*	capiē *bar*	audiē *bar*
amā *bāris*	docē *bāris*	scrībē *bāris*	capiē *bāris*	audiē *bāris*
amā *bātur*	docē *bātur*	scrībē *bātur*	capiē *bātur*	audiē *bātur*
amā *bāmur*	docē *bāmur*	scrībē *bāmur*	capiē *bāmur*	audiē *bāmur*
amā *bāminī*	docē *bāminī*	scrībē *bāminī*	capiē *bāminī*	audiē *bāminī*
amā *bantur*	docē *bantur*	scrībē *bantur*	capiē *bantur*	audiē *bantur*

FUTURE PASSIVE VOICE				
amā *bor*	docē *bor*	scrīb *ar*	capi *ar*	audi *ar*
amā *beris*	docē *beris*	scrīb *ēris*	capi *ēris*	audi *ēris*
amā *bitur*	docē *bitur*	scrīb *ētur*	capi *ētur*	audi *ētur*
amā *bimur*	docē *bimur*	scrīb *ēmur*	capi *ēmur*	audi *ēmur*
amā *biminī*	docē *biminī*	scrīb *ēminī*	capi *ēminī*	audi *ēminī*
amā *buntur*	docē *buntur*	scrīb *entur*	capi *entur*	audi *entur*

NOTE

In the second person singular of the present of third and third -**iō** conjugation verbs, the final **e** of the present stem is kept and not changed to **i** as in the active voice.

1. You have seen that a verb in the active voice indicates something that the subject does. A verb in the passive voice indicates something that is done to the subject.

Example

ACTIVE VOICE	**Parentēs līberōs *amant*.**	Parents *love* their children.
PASSIVE VOICE	**Līberī ā parentibus *amantur*.**	Children *are loved* by their parents.

In sentences with a passive verb, you will often find the preposition **ā**, **ab** with the ablative to indicate *by whom* the action is performed. This is called the *ablative of personal agency*. In the conversion from the active to the passive in the above example, note that **līberōs,** the direct object of the verb of the first sentence, becomes the subject of the second sentence; and **parentēs**, the subject of the first sentence, becomes the object of the preposition **ā.** Take a good look at these two sentences because a little later you will have to convert some sentences from the active to the passive and vice versa.

A verb in the present passive indicates something that is being done to the subject; a verb in the imperfect passive indicates something that was being done to the subject; a verb in the future passive indicates something that will be done to the subject.

Examples

PRESENT	**Pōns ab Horātiō dēfenditur.**	The bridge *is (being) defended* by Horatius.
IMPERFECT	**Pōns ab Horātiō dēfendēbātur.**	The bridge *was (being) defended* by Horatius.
FUTURE	**Pōns ab Horātiō dēfendētur.**	The bridge *will be defended* by Horatius

The verb **dēfenditur** can be translated as *is defended* or *is being defended*. Only the context can indicate which translation is required. The same holds true for the imperfect form **dēfendēbātur.**

2. It is important to know the passive voice well because Latin uses the passive much more frequently than we do in English. This fondness for the passive voice is a characteristic of Latin. Since most of Latin literature is of an historical nature, the third person singular and plural occur much more frequently than the first and second person; they also happen to be the easiest forms to remember.

Many transitive verbs get to have *an intransitive sense* in the passive. Consider the saying at the beginning of this chapter: **Tempora mūtantur et nōs mūtāmur in illīs.** If we translate it literally, we would say: "Times are changed and we are changed in them." But to the Roman it sounded like: "Times change and we change with them". Why? Because **mūtāre** is a transitive verb in Latin; when the Romans heard **mūtant,** they would think "change whom or what?" By using the passive of such a transitive verb, the verb acquired an intransitive sense to the Roman mind. (By the way, we say "We change *with* the times" and the Romans said "We change *in* the times."

III. DEPONENT VERBS

There are some Latin verbs that are passive in form and active in meaning. Such verbs are called deponent verbs. Here are some of the common ones.

admīror admīrārī admīrātus (-a -um) sum to admire; to wonder at
loquor loquī locūt·us (-a -um) sum to speak
morior morī mortu·us (-a -um) sum to die
nāscor nāscī nāt·us (-a -um) sum to be born
sequor sequī secūt·us (-a -um) sum to follow
ūtor ūtī ūs·us (-a -um) sum (+ *abl*) to use

EXERCISES

A. Translate the following sentences, paying particular attention to the verbs, all of which are deponents.

VOCABULARY
īnfāns īnfant·is *mf* infant, baby   **pauc·ī -ae -a** few

1. Multī mīlitēs bellō morientur.
2. Cōnsul cum sacerdōtibus loquitur.
3. Senātōrēs cōnsulēs in cūriam sequentur.
4. Pater cum hospitibus loquēbātur.
5. Nōnne Cloeliam admīrāris?
6. Ego tē, Cloelia, sequar.
7. Admīrārisne, Cloelia, Scaevolam?
8. Cūr, senātōrēs, cum Porsenna loquēminī?
9. Omnēs Rōmānī thermīs ūtēbantur.
10. Loquēris, Vetūria, cum fīliō tuō?

11. Paucī īnfantēs in Palātīnō nāscēbantur.
12. Hae discipulae multā chartā ūtuntur.
13. Vōsne admīrāminī vestram magistram?
14. Ego et amīca rārō dē scholā loquēbāmur.
15. Ego et Phyllis librīs nostrīs ūtēmur.

B. Learn to recognize the tenses of verbs in the passive voice. Indicate the tense of the following verbs in the passive voice, that is, whether they are in the present, imperfect, or future tense. Then translate.

Example | **Litterae scrībentur.** *future* The letter will be written.

1. Ad cēnam vocāmur.
2. Illī trīstēs videntur.
3. Animālia trāns pontem dūcentur.
4. Soror dē tē loquēbātur.
5. Compositiō melior scrībētur.
6. Nōmen meum in librō scrībitur.
7. Ante merīdiem exspectābimur.
8. Hī puerī puellās sequentur.
9. Cūr Aenēān admīrāris?
10. Sabīnī dīcuntur fortēs esse.
11. Etrūscī Rōmā mox expellentur.
12. Cūr tam celeriter loqueris?
13. Per tōtum theātrum audiēris.
14. Vōs semper meā piscīnā ūtiminī!

C. Identify the *ablatives of personal agency*. Not every sentence contains one. You can get the correct answer only by understanding the complete sentence.

1. Senātōrēs ā forō veniēbant.
2. Nāvēs ab ōrā cōnspiciēbantur.
3. Geminī ā Faustulō servābuntur.
4. Tarquinius Superbus ā thronō expellēbātur.
5. Mūrus Rōmae ā Rōmulō aedificābātur.
6. Haec verba ab omnibus audientur.
7. Pȳramus ā Thisbē amābātur.
8. Rōma nōn procul ā Tiberī flūmine est.
9. Capitōlium ā Tarpēiā hostibus trādēbātur.

10. Thēseus ā Crētā cum Ariadnē nāvigāvit.
11. Exercitus ab urbe Rōmā ad mare iter fēcit.
12. Sabīnī ab arce Rōmae cōnspiciēbantur.

D. Change the following verbs in the present tense from the active to the passive.

Example | vocant **vocantur**

1. rogant	docētis	scrībit	accipiunt	audiō
2. amō	tenēs	dīcunt	īnvitātis	aperit
3. vocāmus	moveō	dūcitis	incipimus	hauriunt
4. dēdicātis	vidēs	expellō	dēcipis	custōdīs
5. exspectās	timent	mittimus	recipit	sciunt

E. Change the following verbs in the imperfect tense from the active to the passive.

1. cantābat	vidēbat	agēbant	capiēbant
2. servābās	movēbam	dīcēbat	recipiēbam
3. clāmābam	tenēbant	dūcēbāmus	accipiēbat
4. ēmendābat	vidēbās	mittēbam	cupiēbātis
5. vocābās	tenēbātis	pōnēbās	incipiēbat
6. rogābāmus	vidēbāmus	dūcēbātis	inspiciēbās

F. Change the following verbs in the future tense from the passive to the active. Translate the passive.

1. dabitur	10. tenēbiminī	18. capiēminī
2. dabuntur	11. mittētur	19. īnspiciēminī
3. servābuntur	12. dūcar	20. accipiēmur
4. vocāberis	13. dīcentur	21. audientur
5. vocābiminī	14. pōnentur	22. hauriētur
6. vidēbor	15. dūcēmur	23. scientur
7. movēbitur	16. accipiar	24. sciēris
8. movēberis	17. recipiētur	25. audiēminī
9. monēbuntur		

G. Change the following sentences from the passive to the active. The fol-

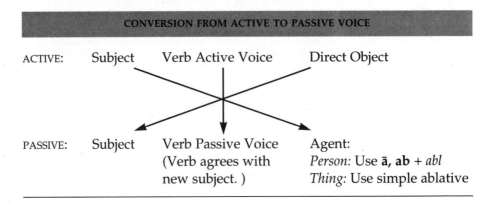

	CONVERSION FROM ACTIVE TO PASSIVE VOICE

ACTIVE: Subject   Verb Active Voice   Direct Object

PASSIVE: Subject   Verb Passive Voice   Agent:
(Verb agrees with   *Person:* Use **ā, ab** + *abl*
new subject.)   *Thing:* Use simple ablative

Example   **Faustulus geminōs servābat.**   Faustulus saved the twins.
Geminī ā Faustulō servābantur.   The twins were saved by Faustulus.

1. Lārentia geminōs ēducābat.
2. Rōmulus Rōmam fundābat.
3. Aenēās Ascanium amat.
4. Aenēās lēgātos ad Latīnum mittet.
5. Sabīnī Capitōlium capient.
6. Mīlitēs Tarpēiam necābunt.
7. Aenēās Dīdōnem dēserēbat.
8. Pȳramus Thisbēn amābat.
9. Nūma Pompilius templa dēdicābat.
10. Rōmāni statuam Scaevolae in forō ponent.

H. The verb **videō** *to see* generally means *to seem* in the passive voice, although it can possibly have the sense of *to be seen*. Complete the following Latin sentences by supplying the correct form of the verb in the present or imperfect in the sense of *to seem*.

Example   Puella laeta esse (*seems*).
Puella laeta esse *vidētur.*
The girl seems to be happy.

1. Mucius Scaevola (*seemed*) magnam virtūtem habēre.
2. Rōma (*seems*) esse urbs quam ōmnēs admīrantur.

3. Vōs (*seem*) esse discipulae studiōsae.
4. Patriciī Rōmānī (*seemed*) admīrārī Cicerōnem.
5. Ego (*seem*) habēre plūs pecūniae quam tū.

I. Similarly, supply the correct form of **dīcō** in the following sentences.

Example | Claudia (*is said*) esse in dēliciīs magistrae.
Claudia *dīcitur* esse in dēliciīs magistrae.
Claudia is said to be the teacher's pet.

1. Etrūscī (*were said*) ācriter pugnāre.
2. Porsenna (*is said*) rēx Etrūscus esse.
3. Tū, Horātī, (*will be said*) fortissimus esse.
4. Etiam commīlitēs tuī (*are said*) fortēs esse.
5. Ego quoque (*am said*) tē, Horātī, admīrārī.

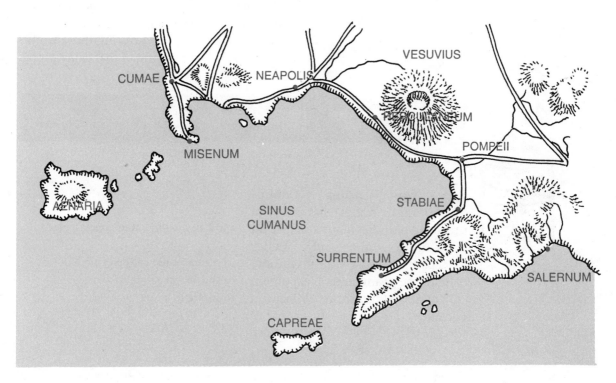

Map of Vesuvius environs

Of all the natural catastrophes that occurred within Roman memory, by the far the most awesome was the eruption of the volcano on Mount Vesuvius, which is located about seven miles inland from the Bay of Naples (**sin·us -ūs** *m* **Neāpolītānus**). The eruption began on August 24, A.D. 79, at the height of the vacation season, when hordes of vacationers from Rome and other big cities crowded the resort towns and beaches of the Bay of Naples. Just before and during the eruption there were earth tremors; wagons in which people tried to escape were knocked from one side of the road to the other. Thick ashes and hot gravel fell over a wide area and covered everything. A strong odor of sulphur made breathing difficult. The sun was completely blocked out. The darkness was not that of night but like the darkness in a room with no doors or windows. Blinded by the volcanic dust and gases, people lost their way. The terror lasted for three days.

A teenager, Gaius Plinius Secundus, whom we call Pliny and who happened to be staying at a villa in Misenum (**Mīsēn·um -ī** *n*), has left us a short but vivid eyewitness account of what happened during those frightful three days in August. Now read carefully a retelling of that catastrophe.

Ēruptiō Montis Vesuviō
The Eruption of Mount Vesuvius

I

Ego sum Gāius Plīnius, duodēvīgintī annōs nātus. Nōn procul ab hāc vīllā nātus sum. Apud avunculum ego et māter manēbāmus, cuius vīlla in summō colle prope ōram sinūs Neāpolītānī collocātur. Oppidum Mīsēnum vocātur.

apud avunculum at my uncle's place

in summō colle on top of a hill
coll·is -is (*gen pl:* **-ium**) *m* hill
collocāre to locate

II

Quōdam diē mēnsis Augustī, ego forte legēbam et studēbam. Subitō nūbēs inūsitāta trāns sīnum

mēns·is -is (*gen pl:* **-ium**) *m* month
forte by chance **subitō** suddenly
nūb·ēs -is (*gen pl:* **-ium**) *f* cloud
inūsitāt·us -a -um unusual

Vesuvius seen from the
villa at Misenum

vidēbātur. Ego et tōta familia ascendimus summum collem, ex quō illud mīrāculum cōnspicī poterat. Fūmus et cinis ēmittēbantur ex summō Monte Vesuviō.

mīrācul·um -ī *n* strange sight
cōnspicī to be visible
fūm·us -ī *m* smoke cin·is -eris *m* ashes
ēmitt·ō -ĕre ēmīsī ēmissus to send out

III

Tum tremor terrae sentiēbātur, et cinis dē caelō cadĕre incipiēbat. Paulātim cinis calidiōr et dēnsiōr cadēbat. Mox diēs mūtābātur in noctem. Arborēs et aedificia propter cālīginem obscūrābantur. Omnēs oppidānī terrēbantur. Clāmōrēs virōrum fēminārumque et vagītūs parvulōrum audiēbantur. Nōs ipsī ā villā per obscūrās viās Mīsēnī fūgimus.

trem·or -ōris *m* tremor sent·iō -īre sēnsī
sēnsus to feel
paulātim little by little dēns·us -a -um
dense

cālīg·ō -inis *f* dense atmosphere
obscūrāre to obscure
vagīt·us -ūs *m* cry
parvul·ī -ōrum *mpl* little ones, children
obscūr·us -a -um dark

IV

Dēnique tertiō diē, lūx paulātim redit. Sed omnia mūtantur. Omnia cinere teguntur. Nūntiī adveniunt et dīcunt: "Duo oppida, Pompēiī et Herculāneum ex tōtō dēlentur."

teg·ō -ĕre tēxī tēctus to cover nūnti·us -ī
m messenger ex tōtō totally dēl·eō -ēre
-ēvī -ētus to destroy

J. Choose the best answer from A, B, C, or D.

I 1. At the time of the event, Pliny's age was A) twenty; B) nineteen; C) eighteen; D) twenty-two.
2. It is implied that A) Pliny and his mother owned the villa; B) his mother and his uncle owned the villa; C) Pliny and his mother were guests at the villa; D) all were guests at the villa.
3. **Oppiduum Mīsēnūm vocātur** is best translated A) Misenus called the town; B) the town is called Misenum; C) Misenus was summoned by the town; D) the town was calling Misenus.
4. The villa is described as A) an inland villa; B) a villa on a hill by the shore; C) a villa far from the shore; D) a villa close to Vesuvius.

II 5. Pliny shows that, at the time of the eruption, he was A) fun-loving; B) taking it easy; C) working; D) studious.

6. The family members climbed up to a place where they could A) escape the danger; B) get a better look at the cloud; C) escape the smoke and ashes; D) be more easily seen by rescuers.

7. The first thing that they saw was A) fire; B) ashes; C) fumes; D) an unusually shaped cloud.

8. Mt. Vesuvius is said to be located A) across the Bay of Naples from them; B) near the villa; C) near the shoreline; D) somewhere between the villa and the sea.

III 9. **Tum tremor terrae sentiēbātur** is best translated: A) I felt the earth tremble; B) the tremor felt for the earth; C) a tremor was felt by the earth; D) then an earth tremor was felt.

10. **Mox diēs mūtābātur in noctem** implies A) that the eruption started at sunset; B) the day lasted throughout the night; C) the sun was blocked out by the murky atmosphere; D) the high trees and buildings blocked out the rays of the sun.

11. The terror and confusion of the people is shown by A) their shouts; B) the darkness all around; C) the anger of the men toward the women; D) the light traffic in the streets of the town.

12. Pliny and his mother A) tried to calm the crowds; B) pretended that there was nothing to fear; C) took refuge in their villa; D) fled for safety like the rest.

IV 13. When the sun came out again, Pliny was struck by A) the brightness of the sun; B) the desolate scene; C) the calm of the people; D) the good news from Pompeii and Herculaneum.

WORD POWER

K. Give the Latin source word for the following English derivatives. If the source word is a verb, give the present infinitive; if it is a noun or adjective, give the nominative singular.

1. avuncular	____	6. sinuses	____
2. emissions	____	7. incinerate	____
3. collocation	____	8. emit	____
4. miracle	____	9. obscure	____
5. fumigate	____	10. fumes	____

CHAPTER 26

Perfect, Pluperfect, and Future Perfect Passive

THOUGHT
FOR
TODAY

Rōma nōn ūnō diē condita est. Rome was not built in a single day.

PERFECT PASSIVE VOICE				
I	II	III	III-iō	IV
amō amāre	doceō docēre	scrībō scrībĕre	capiō capĕre	audiō audīre
amāvī amātus	docuī doctus	scrīpsī scrīptus	cēpī captus	audīvī audītus
to love	to teach	to write	to take	to hear
amātus sum	doctus sum	scrīptus sum	captus sum	audītus sum
amātus es	doctus es	scrīptus es	captus es	audītus es
amātus est	doctus est	scrīptus est	captus est	audītus est
amātī sumus	doctī sumus	scrīptī sumus	captī sumus	audītī sumus
amātī estis	doctī estis	scrīptī estis	captī estis	audītī estis
amātī sunt	doctī sunt	scrīptī sunt	captī sunt	audītī sunt

amātus eram	doctus eram	scrīptus eram	captus eram	audītus eram
amātus erās	doctus erās	scrīptus erās	captus erās	audītus erās
amātus erat	doctus erat	scrīptus erat	captus erat	audītus erat
amātī erāmus	doctī erāmus	scrīptī erāmus	captī erāmus	audītī erāmus
amātī erātis	doctī erātis	scrīptī erātis	captī erātis	audītī erātis
amātī erant	doctī erant	scrīptī erant	captī erant	audītī erant

FUTURE PERFECT PASSIVE VOICE

amātus erō	doctus erō	scrīptus erō	captus erō	audītus erō
amātus eris	doctus eris	scrīptus eris	captus eris	audītus eris
amātus erit	doctus erit	scrīptus erit	captus erit	audītus erit
amātī erimus	doctī erimus	scrīptī erimus	captī erimus	audītī erimus
amātī eritis	doctī eritis	scrīptī eritis	captī eritis	audītī eritis
amātī erunt	doctī erunt	scrīptī erunt	captī erunt	audītī erunt

1. **The perfect passive** of a verb is formed with the fourth principal part (i.e., the perfect passive participle) plus the present tense of **esse** (*to be*). The fourth principal part has masculine, feminine, and neuter endings. Like an adjective, the participle agrees in gender and number with the subject.

Examples

Rōma ā Rōmulō condita est.   Rome was founded by Romulus.

Geminī ā Faustulō et Lārentiā ēducātī sunt.   The twins were raised by Faustulus and Larentia.

Faustulus et Lārentia ā geminīs amātī sunt.   Faustulus and Larentia were loved by the twins.

In the first sentence, **condita** has a feminine singular ending because the subject **Rōma** is feminine singular. In the second sentence, **ēducātī** has a masculine plural ending because the subject **geminī** is masculine plural. If there are two subjects, one of them masculine and the other feminine, the masculine plural is to be used in the verbs, as in the third example (**amātī**).

2. The pluperfect passive of a verb is formed with the fourth principal part of the verb plus the imperfect tense of the verb **esse**.

Examples

Rōma ā Romulō condita erat.   Rome had been founded by Romulus.

Geminī ā Faustulō et Lārentiā ēducātī erant.   The twins had been raised by Faustulus and Larentia.

3. The future perfect passive of a verb is formed with the fourth principal part of the verb plus the future tense of the verb **esse**. As stated in the previous chapter, the future perfect, active and passive, rarely occurs.

PITFALL

In the perfect and pluperfect, and future perfect passive, the forms of the verb **esse** are helping verbs. Do not translate them as main verbs.

Example   **Pyramus ā Thisbē amātus est.**
WRONG: Pyramus *is loved* by Thisbe.
CORRECT: Pyramus *was loved* by Thisbe.

WORD ORDER

At times in Roman authors, the form of the verb **esse** can and does come before the perfect passive participle.

Tarquinius Superbus ex urbe ā populō Rōmānō est expulsus.   Tarquinius Superbus was driven out of the city by the Roman people.

Here the auxiliary (helping) verb **est** comes before the perfect passive participle **expulsus.**

EXERCISES

A. Remember that the subject determines the ending of the perfect passive participle in the perfect and pluperfect passive. Select the verb form that agrees with the subject. Remembering the stories that you read in previous chapters will help you to make the right choices.

VOCABULARY
rēg·ō -ĕre rēxī rēctus to rule

1. Mercurius ā Iove ad Aenēān ____.
   a) missus est b) missī sunt c) missum est
2. Cūr Coriolī ab Rōmānīs ____?
   a) oppugnātum est b) oppugnātī sunt c) oppugnāta est

3. Cūr oppidum Coriolī ab Rōmānīs ___?
a) captī sunt b) captum est c) capta est

4. In omnibus bellīs mīlitēs ___.
a) captī erant b) captīs erant c) captus erat

5. Rōma ipsa ōlim ā rēgibus ___.
a) rēcta erat b) rēctus erat c) rēctī erant

6. Pōns Sublicius ab Horātiō ___.
a) dēfēnsus erat b) dēfēnsum erat c) dēfēnsa erat

7. Aenēās ā mātre ___.
a) amātās est b) amāta est c) amātus est

8. Thisbē ā Pȳramō saepe ___.
a) vocātē est b) vocāta est c) vocātae sunt

9. Nōs senātōrēs in forum ___.
a) ductōs erāmus b) ductī erant c) ductī erāmus

10. Equī sōlis ā Phaëthonte ___.
a) agitātī erant b) agitātīs erant c) agitātōs erant

B. Here's a slightly different twist. Select the correct subject to be placed at the beginning of each sentence and make sure it agrees with the verb. Remembering the stories narrated in previous chapters will again help in your selection.

1. ___ ā Cicerōne scrīptae erant.
a) epistolae b) verba c) librī

2. ___ ā Faustulō servātī sunt.
a) lupa b) Rōmulus et Remus c) uxor

3. ___ ā mātre sunt doctae.
a) līberī b) fīliī c) fīliae

4. ___ ab hostibus dēlēta sunt.
a) urbēs b) urbs c) moenia

5. ___ in Capitōlium ā Tarpēiā dēmōnstrāta est.
a) via b) viae c) Sabīnī

6. ___ bracchiīs sinistrīs Sabīnōrum gesta sunt.
a) perfidia b) puella c) scūta

7. ___ ā Sabīnīs est captum.
a) Rōma b) arx c) Capitōlium

8. ___ ā mīlitibus Sabīnīs cōnspecta erat.
a) Tarpēia b) armillae c) praemia magna

9. ___ ā Iove dē caelō dēmissa sunt
a) pluvia b) tonitrūs c) fulmina

10. ___ ā Phaëthonte est agitātus.
a) equī b) aurīga c) currus

11. ____ Tartarī ā Cerberō custōdīta erat.
   a) iānua b) saxa c) fundāmenta
12. ____ ab Apolline est amāta.
   a) Anchīsēs b) Daphnē c) Ascanius

C. Convert the following verbs from the active to the passive voice, keeping the same tense, number, and person. The gender is indicated in parentheses.

Examples | cōnspeximus *(f)*   **cōnspectae sumus**
           | docueram *(f)*   **docta eram**

1. vocāvī *(f)*
2. rēgnāvērunt *(f)*
3. mīsimus *(m)*
4. cēperant *(n)*
5. dēfenderās *(f)*
6. audīvistī *(f)*
7. dedimus *(m)*
8. mōverat *(f)*
9. scrīpsērunt *(m)*
10. agitāverat *(m)*
11. gessērunt *(n)*
12. vīderās *(f)*
13. exspectāvistis *(m)*
14. posuimus *(f)*
15. scīvit *(n)*

D. Give the corresponding active form of each of the following passive verbs. Then translate the active form.

Example | vocātī sunt *vocāvērunt* they called

1. capta est
2. scīta sunt
3. commōtī erāmus
4. gestī erant
5. audītus sum
6. vocātus es
7. cōnspectī erātis
8. scrīptum est
9. acceptus sum
10. monitī estis
11. custōdīta es
12. doctae sunt

E. In the following sentences, the verb is in the present tense, passive voice. Supply the perfect and pluperfect passive in each sentence. You need not repeat the entire sentence as is done in the following examples; just supply the verbs.

Examples | Geminī ā Faustulō inveniuntur.   The twins are found by Faustulus.
           | **Geminī ā Faustulō *inventī sunt*.**   The twins *were found* by Faustulus.
           | **Geminī ā Faustulō *inventī erant*.**   The twins *had been found* by

con·dō -děre -didī -ditus to found

1. Urbs ā Coriolānō capitur.
2. Mūrus ā Rōmulō aedificātur.
3. Ego (*Tullia*) ad cēnam invitor.
4. Trōiānī ab Aenēā dūcuntur.
5. Templa ā Numā Pompiliō dēdicantur.
6. Iānua casae ā Faustulō reficitur.
7. Nōs puellae ā puerīs petimur.
8. Verba Dīdōnis ab Aenēā nōn audiuntur.
9. Alba Longa ab Ascaniō conditur.
10. Trōia ā Graecō exercitū dēlētur.
11. Tōta urbs ex arce vidētur
12. Numitor ab Amūliō expellitur.
13. Tū, Dīdō, ab Aenēā dēseritur.
14. Ego (*Helena*) et Hecuba capimur.
15. Alia pars urbis oppugnātur.

F. REVIEW OF THE PASSIVE IN ALL TENSES. Supply the passive form in the imperfect, future, perfect, and pluperfect. The principal parts of the verbs in the sentences are provided for your convenience. You need not repeat the entire sentences; just supply the verbs.

Example

amō amāre amāvī amātus to love	
Rōmulus ab omnibus amātur.	Romulus is loved by all.
Rōmulus ab omnibus *amābātur*.	Romulus used to be loved by all.
Rōmulus ab omnibus *amābitur*.	Romulus will be loved by all.
Rōmulus ab omnibus *amātus est*.	Romulus was loved by all.
Rōmulus ab omnibus *amātus erat*.	Romulus had been loved by all.

1. **dēfendō dēfenděre dēfendī dēfēnsus** to defend
   Rōma ā mīlitibus Rōmānīs dēfenditur.
2. **vēndō vēnděre vēndidī vēnditus** to sell
   Vestīmenta ā tabernāriō vēnduntur.
3. **vincō vincěre vīcī victus** to conquer
   Volscī ab Rōmānīs dēnique vincuntur.
4. **hauriō haurīre hausī haustus** to draw
   Aqua ex fonte extrā moenia ā Tarpēiā hauritur.
5. **cōnspiciō cōnspicěre cōnspexī cōnspectus** to see
   Misera Thisbē ā Pȳramō nōn cōnspicitur sub illā mōrō.
6. **invītō invītāre invītāvī invītātus** to invite
   Nōs fēminae ad cēnam numquam invītāmur.

7. **dūcō dūcĕre dūxī ductus** to take, lead
Ego (f) ā parentibus meīs ad thermās dūcor.
8. **dīcō dīcĕre dīxī dictus** to say
Haec verba āb Aeneā Dīdōnī dīcuntur.
9. **culpō culpāre culpāvī culpātus** to blame
Cūr vōs semper ab aliīs discipulīs culpāminī?
10. **dēserō dēserĕre dēseruī dēsertus** to desert
Ariadnē ā Thēseō in īnsulā Naxō dēseritur.
11. **condō condĕre condidī conditus** to found
Rōma ā Rōmulō conditur.
12. **nōminō nōmināre nōmināvī nōminātus** to call, name
Ego ā Rōmānīs nōminor Scaevola.

G. Give the imperfect, future, perfect, and pluperfect of the following deponents. You need not repeat the entire sentences; just supply the verb.

1. Magistra nostra saepe dē historiā *loquitur*.
2. Nōs omnēs fortitūdinem Scaevolae *admīrāmur*.
3. Ego semper cōnsilium (*advice*) parentium meōrum *sequor*.
4. Rōmānī saepissimē ōrāculō Apollinis *ūtuntur*.

H. SCRAMBLED SENTENCES. With the endings of words as a clue, rebuild these scrambled words into good Latin sentences.

1. territī Monte multī sunt Vesuviō Rōmānī.
2. Monte ex Vesuviō dēlēta tōtō oppida sunt duo.
3. labyrinthus in Daedalō īnsulā est ā flexuōsus Crētā aedificātus.
4. iste fortī et validō Mīnōtaurus necātus est ā Thēseō saevus.
5. sine patriam sōlus nāvigāvit miserā Thēseus ad Ariadnē.
6. voluērunt in hāc discipulī Latīnē discĕre omnēs scholā.
7. magnus et equus est Graecīs ex lignō cavus ā mīlitibus factus.
8. est fulmine Phaëthōn necātus Iovis miser.

Now read the story of Orion the hunter, who, on his death, was changed into the Constellation Orion, which appears in the sky in November, the beginning of the rainy season in the Mediterranean area. He is depicted carrying a club and a hunting knife.

Constellation of Orion

GEMINI

Aldebaran

Betelgeuse

Rigel

TAURUS

CANIS
MINOR

ORION

Sirius

CANIS
MAJOR

Ōrīōn et Diāna
Orion and Diana

I

Dea Diāna ab Ōrīōne vēnātōre amābātur. Apollō autem, frāter Diānae, Ōrīōnem nōn cūrābat. "Ōrīōn," sēcum dīxit Apollō, "est pulcher et ingēns vēnātor, sed ego eum tolerāre nōn possum. Numquam meam sorōrem cāram in mātrimōnium dūcet."

Ōrīōn Ōrīōn·is *m* Orion **vēnāt·or -ōris** *m* hunter
cūrāre to care for, like
sēcum dīcěre to say to oneself **pulcher pulchr·a -um** handsome **ingēns ingent·is** mighty, huge **tolerāre** to stand, tolerate **cār·us -a -um** dear

II

Quōdam diē Apollō et soror Diāna per ōram maritimam ambulābant. Deus et dea arcūs et sagittās gerēbant. Ōrīōn procul in marī natābat.

per (+ *acc*) along **arc·us -ūs** *m* bow
sagitt·a -ae *f* arrow
ger·ō -ěre gessī gestus to bear, carry

III

Apollō eum cōnspexit et dīxit: "Ecce, Diāna, mōnstrum marīnum in aquīs longinquīs. Istud mōnstrum necāre volō, sed sagittās meās tam longē mittěre nōn possum."

Ecce! look! **marīn·us -a -um** (of the) sea
longinqu·us -a -um distant

tam longē so far **mitt·ō -ěre mīsī missus** to shoot, send

IV

"Manēdum!" respondit Diāna. "Ego istud mōnstrum vidēre possum. Porrō hās sagittās tam longē mittěre facile possum. Spectā mē."

manēdum! wait a minute!

porrō moreover
spectāre to watch

V

Sagitta in caput mōnstrī cito missa est. Sed rē nōn caput mōnstrī sed caput Ōrīōnis erat. Ōrīōn nēcātus est, et corpus eius ad ōram mariti-

cito quickly **rē** in reality

Orion shot by Diana

mam fluctibus portātum est. Nunc multae lacrimae ā miserā Diānā fūsae sunt.

lacrim·a -ae *f* tear
fund·ō -ĕre fūdī fūsus to shed

VI

Ōrīōn autem ā Iove in caelō positus est. Ōrīōn nōn iam vēnātor in silvīs erat sed stella in caelō. Nunc "imbrifer" vocātur, quia stella Ōrīōnis imbrem indicat.

nōn iam no longer
stell·a -ae *f* constellation, star
imbrif·er -erī *m* rain-bringer
imber imbr·is *m* rain

I. Indicate whether the following statements are true or false. If they are false, correct them.

I 1. Orion was in love with the goddess Diana.
   2. Apollo was not fond of Orion.
   3. Apollo kept his feelings to himself.
   4. Apollo was protective of his sister Diana.
   5. The last sentence of this paragraph implies some sort of threat.

II 6. Apollo and Diana were hunters.
   7. From the weapons they carry, one can see that they were going fishing.
   8. Orion was deep-sea fishing.

III 9. Orion spotted Apollo walking on the shore.
   10. Apollo claimed to see a sea monster.
   11. The sea monster was close to the shore.
   12. Apollo said that he should shoot the sea monster but didn't have the heart to do so.

IV 13. Diana volunteers to shoot what she thinks is a sea monster.
   14. Diana displays confidence in her ability to shoot.

V 15. Diana's first shot just misses the target.
   16. Diana hits Orion in the head.
   17. Orion is hurt but swims to shore.
   18. Orion dies of exhaustion from swimming as he reaches the shore.
   19. Diana cries when she realizes that she shot Orion.
   20. Apollo meant to protect his sister but actually did her a disfavor.

WORD POWER

J. Supply the Latin source word for each English derivative. If the Latin source word is a noun or adjective, give the nominative singular; if it is a verb, give the infinitive.

1. arch	___	7. tolerate	___
2. Sagittarius	___	8. expectation	___
3. marine	___	9. monstrous	___
4. lacrimose	___	10. desertion	___
5. stellar	___	11. invincible	___
6. convince	___	12. vendor	___

APPENDIX

B.C.

1184	Fall of Troy; Aeneas lands in Italy.
1154	Ascanius founds Alba Longa.
	14 Alban kings. Last Alban king: Numitor
753	**Founding of Rome by Romulus**

THE MONARCHY

Kings: 1) Romulus; 2) Numa Pompilius; 3) Tullus Hostilius; 4) Ancus Marcius; 5) Tarquinius Priscus; 6) Servius Tullius; 7) Tarquinius Superbus

THE REPUBLIC

509	The Romans expel Tarquinius Superbus and his entire clan, and establish the Republic. Legendary heroes of Rome: Coriolanus; Horatius; Mucius Scaevola; Cincinnatus
494	First revolt of the Plebeians against the Patricians
451-450	Laws of the Twelve Tables (the foundation of all Roman law)
445	Canuleian law permits marriage between Patricians and Plebeians.
390	Battle of Allia; Rome sacked by Gauls
343-290	Rome fights successful wars against Samnites and Latins.
312	Appian Way, Rome's first highway, is built. Also the first aqueduct
300	First barber comes to Rome from Sicily.
287	Second plebeian revolt against the Patricians
281-272	Pyrrhic Wars. Rome wins two wars against Pyrrhus, king of Epirus.
270-266	War with Etruscans and Umbrians; Rome supreme in Italy
264	First gladiatorial games at Rome
264-241	First Punic War, fought against the Carthaginians. Rome acquires Sicily (first Roman province) and Sardinia and Corsica (second Roman province).
284-204	Livius Andronicus, founder of Roman drama
251-184	Plautus, writer of Roman comedies
239-169	Ennius, father of Latin Poetry
224-222	Conquest of Northern Italy (Cisalpine Gaul)
218-201	Second Punic War. Hannibal crosses the Alps into Italy.
201	Spain becomes a Roman Province.
153	Year begins January 1 instead of March 1.
150	Scipio Africanus begins fashion of daily shaving.

149-46	Third Punic War; Carthage and Corinth are destroyed.
133	Tiberius Gracchus, tribune of the people, is asssassinated for attempting to introduce socialism. Pergamum willed to Rome
122	Gaius Gracchus, tribune of the people, meets his brother's fate.
111-105	Jugurthine War against Jugurtha, king of Numidia, in North Africa
106-43	Cicero, orator and statesman
90-88	Social War. Rome reconquers its Italian allies.
84-54	Catullus, lyric poet
82-80	Sulla is dictator.
73-71	Slave revolt under Spartacus at the gladiatorial school in Capua
70-19	Vergil, Roman poet (The Aeneid)
65-08	Horace, Roman poet
63	Octavian (the later Augustus) is born near Naples; consulship of Cicero; Catilinarian conspiracy
60	First Triumvirate (Caesar, Crassus, Pompey)
59	Caesar's consulship; beginning of Gallic War
55	Julius Caesar invades Britain.
50-A.D.17	Livy, Roman historian
49-46	Civil war: Caesar vs. Pompey and senatorial order
48	Battle of Pharsalus; death of Pompey. Caesar confirms Cleopatra as queen of Egypt.
44	Death of Caesar on March 15 at hand of Brutus and Cassius and twenty-three senators
43	Second Triumvirate (Octavian, Marc Antony, Lepidus)
43-A.D.17	Ovid, Roman poet (Metamorphoses)
42	Battle of Philippi; death of Brutus and Cassius
31	Battle of Actium: Octavian defeats Antony and Cleopatra
31	**THE EMPIRE**
27-A.D.14	Reign of Augustus

A.D.

14-37	Reign of Tiberius
23-79	Elder Pliny, author of Natural History
37-41	Reign of Caligula
38-100	Quintilian, Roman educator
41-54	Reign of Claudius

54-68	Reign of Nero
	Tacitus, Roman historian
55-120	Pliny the Younger, author of Letters
61-112	Rome burns; persecution of Christians
64	Year of three emperors (Galba, Otho, Vitellius)
68-69	Reign of Vespasian
69-79	Suetonius, biographer of emperors
69-140	Jerusalem destroyed by Titus; construction of Colosseum begun
70	Destruction of Pompeii and Herculaneum by Vesuvius eruption
79	Reign of Titus
79-81	Colosseum is dedicated with 100 days of gladiatorial fights and fights with wild
80	animals (5,000 wild animals were killed).
	Reign of Domitian
81-96	Reign of Nerva
96-98	Reign of Trajan
98-117	Reign of Hadrian; 73-mile wall built in Britain
117-138	Reign of Antoninus Pius
138-161	Reign of Marcus Aurelius
161-180	Growing disorder: 60 emperors
235-284	Reign of Diocletian
284-305	Reign of Constantine
307-337	Freedom of worship for Christians
313	Constantine moves to Byzantium and calls it Constantinople.
330	Division into West Roman Empire and East Roman Empire
395	Abandonment of Britain by Rome
409	Visigoths loot Rome
410	Rome is sacked by the Vandals.
455	End of Roman Empire as Germanic tribes overthrow the last Roman emperor,
476	Romulus Augustulus. Beginning of the Byzanthine Empire that will survive until 1453

NOTE: in the case of phrases, grammatical information is placed in parentheses in order not to break up the expression; e.g., desk **mēns·a (-ae** *f)* **scrīptōria**

VOCABULARY

absent **abs·ēns -ent***is*; to be absent **absum abesse āfuī āfutūr·us**

adjective **adiectīv·um -ī** *n*

adverb **adverbi·um -ī** *n*

aloud **clārē**

answer **respōns·um -ī** *n*; to give someone an answer **alicui respōnsum redd·ō (reddĕre reddidī)**

ask the teacher a question **magistram [magistrum] interrogāre**

assign **assignāre**

assignment **pēns·um -ī** *n*; *(written)* **praescrīpt·um -ī** *n*

attend school **scholam frequentāre**

blackboard **tabul·a (-ae** *f)* **ātra**

book **lib·er -rī** *m*

call roll **catalogum recitāre, nōmina recitāre**

chalk **crēt·a -ae** *f*

chapter **cap·ut -it***is* *n*

class **class·is -is** *(gen pl:* **-ium)** *f*

college **collēgi·um -ī** *n*

composition **compositi·ō -ōn***is* *f*

computer **computāt·or -ōr***is* *m*

conjunction **coniūncti·ō -ōn***is* *f*

copy **exscrīb·ō -ĕre exscrīpsī exscrīptus** (from **ex** + *abl) (in order to cheat)* **fūrtim exscrībĕre**

correct *adj* **rēct·us -a -um** *(opp:* **prāv·us -a -um);** *(free from faults)* **ēmendāt·us -a -um**; to correct *tr (esp. mistakes in writing)* **ēmendāre;** *(a person or mistake)* **corrig·ō -ĕre corrēxī corrēctus**

correctly **rēctē** *(opp:* **perperam)**

deal with *(a topic or person)* **tractāre**

desk **mēns·a(-ae** *f)* **scrīptōria**

dictionary **dictiōnāri·um -ī** *n*

discuss **disputāre dē (+** *abl)*

end **dēsin·ō -ĕre** *(e.g.,* **puella** ends in an a: **puella in a litteram desinit)**

ending *(of a word)* **termināti·ō -ōn***is* *f*

eraser **ērās·or -ōr***is* *m*

error **errāt·um -ī** *n*; *(in writing)* **mend·um -ī** *n*

essay **tractāt·us -ūs** *m*

examination **exāmināti·ō -ōn***is* *f*

exercise *(written)* **exerciti·um -ī** *n*; *(practice)* **exercitāti·ō -ōn***is* *f*

explain **explānāre, explicāre**

explanation **explānāti·ō -ōn***is* *f,* **explicāti·ō -ōn***is* *f*

form *(of a word)* **figūr·a -ae** *f*; to form **fac·iō -ĕre fēcī factus**

flunk a test **cad·ō (-ĕre cecidī cāsūrus) in probātiōne**

freshman **tīr·ō -ōn*is*** *m/f*

get (*to understand*) **ten·eō -ēre -uī;** now I get it **iam teneō**

grade (*papers*) **notāre**

grade **grad·us -ūs** *m;* (*for perfor-mance*) **not·a -ae** *f*

hand in **trād·ō -ĕre trādidī trāditus**

history **histori·a -ae** *f*

homework **pēns·um (-ī** *n)* **domes-ticum;** (*written*) **praescrīpt·um (-ī** *n)* **domesticum**

incorrect **mendōs·us -a -um, vitiōs·us -a -um, prāv·us -a -um**

incorrectly **perperam**

instruct **īnstit·uō -uĕre -uī -ūtus**

instruction **īnstitūti·ō -ōn*is*** *f;* (*direc-tion*) **mandāt·um -ī** *n*

instructor **doc·ēns -ent*is*** *m/f*

intelligent **intellig·ēns -entis**

interjection **interiecti·ō -ōn*is*** *f*

jot down **annotāre**

junior **iūni·or -ōr*is*** *m/f*

late **tard·us -a -um, sēr·us -a -um;** to come late **sērō ven·iō -īre vēnī**

Latin (*to know, read, speak, translate, understand, write*) **Latīnē**

learn **disc·ō -ĕre didicī**

learner **disc·ēns -ent*is*** *m/f*

line (*of poetry or verse*) **vers·us -ūs** *m*

memorize **ēdisc·ō -ĕre ēdidicī**

mistake **mend·um -ī** *n;* to make a mistake **errāre, mendum fac·iō (-ĕre fēcī factus)**

note **not·a -ae** *f;* to take notes **com-mentāriōs confic·iō (-ĕre confēcī confectus)**

notebook **libell·us -ī** *m*

note pad **pugillār·ēs -ium** *mpl*

noun **nōm·en -in*is*** *n*

page **pāgin·a -ae** *f;* at the bottom (top) of the page **in īmā [summā] pāginā**

paper **chart·a -ae** *f*

pass a test (examination) **probātiōnem [exāminātiōnem] sustin·eō (-ēre -uī)**

passage (*in a text*) **loc·us -ī** *m*

pay attention **animum** (*or if applied to several:* **animōs) attend·ō (-ĕre -ī)** to pay attention to **animadvert·ō -ĕre -ī**

pen **penn·a -ae** *f*

pencil **stil·us -ī** *m*

practice **exerc·eō -ēre -uī -itus**

preposition **praepositi·ō -ōn*is*** *f*

present: to be present **adsum adesse adfuī adfutūrus**

pronoun **prōnōm·en -in*is*** *n*

pronounce **prōnūntiāre**

question **interrogāt·um -ī** *n*

read **leg·ō -ĕre lēgī lēctus**

recess **intermissi·ō -ōn*is*** *f*

recite **recitāre**

repeat **repet·ō -ĕre -īvī -ītus**

review **retractāti·ō -ōn*is*** *f;* to review **retractāre**

scan (*poetry*) **scand·ō -ĕre**

school (*elementary*) **lūd·us -ī** *m;* (*advanced*) **schol·a -ae** *f*

seat **subselli·um -ī** *n*

senior **seni·or -ōr*is*** *m/f*

sentence **sententi·a -ae** *f*

sheet **sched·a -ae** *f*

silence **silenti·um -ī** *n*

slow **tard·us -a -um**

slowly **tardē, lentē** (*opp:* **cito**)

sophomore **sophomōr·us -ī** *m,* **sophomōr·a -ae** *f*

spell **scrīb·ō -ěre scrīpsī scrīptus**

spelling **orthographi·a -ae** *f*

student **stud·ēns -ent***is* *m/f,* **discipul·us -ī** *m,* **discipul·a -ae** *f*

studies **studi·a -ōrum** *npl*

study period **spati·um (-ī** *n)* **studiōsum**

subject *(a course taken in school)* **disciplīn·a -ae** *f; (topic)* **argūment·um -ī** *n*

subject matter **māteri·a -ae** *f*

take down *(notes)* **excip·iō -ěre excēpī exceptus**

teach *(w. double acc)* **doc·eō -ēre -uī -tus**

teacher **magist·er -rī** *m,* **magistr·a -ae** *f*

test **probāti·ō -ōn***is* *f*

textbook **lib·er (-rī** *m)* **scholāris**

theme *(topic)* **argūment·um -ī** *n;* *(essay)* **tractāt·us -ūs** *m*

topic **māteri·a -ae** *f*

translate **(con)vert·ō -ěre -ī (con)versus; red·dō -děre -didī -ditus;** to translate from Latin to English **ex Latīnō in Anglicum (con)vertěre** *(or* **redděre)**

understand **intelleg·ō -ěre intellēxī intellēctus**

verb **verb·um -ī** *n*

vocabulary **vocābul·a -ōrum** *npl*

word **vocabul·um -ī** *n,* **verb·um -ī** *n*

write **scrīb·ō -ěre scrīpsī scrīptus;** to write down **dēscrīběre;** to write out **perscrīběre**

writing **scrīptūr·a -ae** *f;* writings **scrīpt·a -ōrum** *npl*

COMMANDS

answer me **respondē [respondēte] mihi**

answer my question **respondē [respondēte] ad meum interrogātum**

be silent **tacē [tacēte]; silentium tenē [tenēte]**

blackboard: go to the blackboard **accēde [accēdite] ad tabulam ātram;** write the sentence on the blackboard **scrībe [scrībite] sententiam in tabulā ātrā**

collect the papers **collige [colligite] scrīpta**

continue (reading, writing, speaking, translating) **perge [pergite] (legěre, scrīběre, loquī, vertěre)**

don't speak English **nōlī [nōlīte] Anglicē loquī**

explain this construction [form] **explicā [explicāte] hanc cōnstrūctiōnem [figūram]**

get out your books **librōs prōme [prōmite]**

get up **surge [cōnsurgite]**

go back to your seat(s) **reverte ad subsellium [revertite ad subsellia]** go to the blackboard **accēde [accēdite] ad tabulam ātram**

hand in your papers [homework] **trade [tradite] chartās [pēnsum domesticum]**

listen carefully **audī [audīte] dīligenter**

open your book(s) to page . . . **aperī librum [aperīte librōs] ad pāginam . . .**

pay attention **animum attende [animōs attendite];** pay attention to what I am saying **animadverte [animadvertite] dīcta mea**

put your book[s] away **dēpōne librum [dēpōnite librōs]**

raise your hand[s] **attolle manum [attollite manūs]**

read the next sentence **lege [legite] sententiam proximam**

read slower [faster, louder, with inflection of the voice] **lege [legite] lentius [celerius, clārius, flexū vōcis]**

repeat what you just said **repete [repetite] quid modo dīxeris [dīxeritis]**

silence, please **silentium, quaesō**

sit down, please **cōnsīde [cōnsīdite], quaesō**

stand up **surge [cōnsurgite];** *(esp. as a mark of respect)* **assurge [assurgite]**

take down *(write down)* **excipe [excipite]**

take your seat[s] **reverte ad subsellium [revertite ad subsellia]**

translate literally **redde [reddite] verbum prō verbō**

translate this sentence from English to Latin **converte [convertite] hanc sententiam ex Anglicō in Latīnum**

translate this sentence from Latin to English **converte [convertite] hanc sententiam ex Latīnō in Anglicum**

use your dictionary **ūtĕre [ūtiminī] dictiōnāriō**

write the following words **scrībe [scrībite] haec verba**

SAMPLE DIALOGUE

MAGISTRA: **Silentium, quaesō. Catalogum recitāre velim. Cynthia! recitāre velim. Cynthia!**

TEACHER: Silence, please. I'd like to take rollcall. Cynthia!

CYNTHIA: **Adsum.**

CYNTHIA: Present.

MAGISTRA: **Anna!**
CYNTHIA: **Abest. (Tarda est)**

TEACHER: Anne!
CYNTHIA: She's absent. (She's late.)

MAGISTRA: **Quam ob rem?**
CYNTHIA: **Aegrōta est.**

TEACHER: Why?
CYNTHIA: She's sick.

MAGISTRA: **Mārce!**
PETRUS: **Mārcus sērō venit.**

TEACHER: Mark!
PETER: Mark is late.

MAGISTRA:	Vōs omnēs, promite vestram grammāticam (librum scholārem).	TEACHER:	All of you, get out your grammar (textbook).
DEBRA:	Vīsne etiam īnspectāre praescrīpta domestica?	DEBRA:	Do you also want to look at our homework?
MAGISTRA:	Ita vērō. Iōannēs, ubi est tuum prasescrīptum domesticum?	TEACHER:	Yes, indeed. John, where is your homework?
IŌANNĒS:	In libellō meō.	JOHN:	In my notebook.
MAGISTRA:	Prome libellum tuum et lege sententiam prīmam.	TEACHER:	Get out your notebook and read your first sentence.
IŌANNĒS:	Mē paenitet, sed nōn possum Latīnē legĕre.	JOHN:	Sorry, but I can't read Latin.
MAGISTRA:	Francēsca, lege illam prīmam sententiam.	TEACHER:	Frances, read that first sentence.
FRANCĒSCA:	Magistra, ego praescrīptum domesticum nōn fēcī.	FRANCES:	Teacher, I didn't do my homework.
MAGISTRA:	Quidnī?	TEACHER:	Why not?
FRANCĒSCA:	Mihi tempus nōn erat.	FRANCES:	I didn't have time.
MAGISTRA:	Iennifer, lege illam prīmam sententiam.	TEACHER:	Jennifer, read that first sentence.
IENNIFER:	Mē paenitet, sed ego pēnsum meum domī relīquī.	JENNIFER:	I'm sorry, but I left my homework at home.
MAGISTRA:	Iāson, animum attende!	TEACHER:	Jason, pay attention!
IĀSON:	Animum attendō. Quid vīs?	JASON:	I am. What do you want?
MAGISTRA:	Converte prīmam sententiam in Latīnum.	TEACHER:	Translate the first sentence into Latin.
IĀSON:	Illam prīmam sententiam nōn omīnō intellēxī. Multa menda fēcī. Tam aliēnum ōrdinem verbōrum!	JASON:	I didn't understand that first sentence at all. I made a lot of mistakes. Such a strange word order!
MAGISTRA:	Quālem classem! Quālem diēm!	TEACHER:	What a class! What a day!

ab ōvō ad māla from beginning to end [*lit:* from egg to apples, *i.e.,* from appetizer to dessert]

ab urbe conditā from the founding of the city

ad hoc for this (occasion): *e.g.,* an **ad hoc** committee

ad impossibilia nēmō tenētur no one is held to (do) the impossible

ad īnfīnītum endlessly

ad libitum at pleasure

ad nauseam to (the point of) disgust

alma māter one's college [nourishing mother]

alter ego (one's) other self

amīcus cūriae friend of the court

ante bellum before the war

argūmentum ad hominem personal attack [instead of attacking issues]

ars artis grātiā art for art's sake

audī et alteram partem hear the other side too

aut Caesar aut nullus either Caesar or no one [*i.e.,* either the best leader or no leader]

ā verbīs ad verbera from words to blows

bonā fide in good faith

carpe diem seize the opportunity [*lit:* the day]

cavē canem beware of the dog

corpus dēlictī facts proving a crime has been committed [in a murder case **corpus dēlictī** is not just the body of the victim, but the fact that the victim has been murdered]

cui bonō? to whose benefit? [*lit:* to whom for good]

cum laude with honors

cum grānō salis with a grain of salt

dē eādem fidēliā duōs parietēs dealbāre to kill two birds with one stone [*lit:* to whitewash two walls from one bucket]

dē factō in fact; actual(ly): *e.g.,* there is **dē factō** segregation

dē gustibus nōn disputandum est you can't argue about taste

dē jūre by right, legally

dē mortuīs nīl nisi bonum (speak) nothing but good about the dead

dē novō anew [*lit:* from a new (start)]

Deō grātiās thanks be to God

Deō volente God willing

dīvide et imperā divide and rule

Dominus prōvidēbit the Lord shall provide

dramatis persōnae cast of characters

ductāre aliquem labiīs to lead someone by the nose [*lit:* by the lips]

dulce est dēsipĕre in locō a bit of foolishness is O.K. in its place

dulce et decōrum est prō patriā morī it is sweet and noble to die for one's country

dum spīrō spērō while there's life there's hope [*lit:* as long as I breathe, I hope]

ē plūribus ūnum one out of many [*lit:* one out of more]

errāre hūmānum est to err is human

esse quam vidērī to be rather than to seem [motto of the state of North Carolina]

et aliī and other (co-authors)

et tū, Brute! even you, Brutus! [dismay that even your best friend has "stabbed you in the back"]

ex abundantiā cordis ōs loquitur from the abundance of the heart the mouth speaks

ex animō from the heart

ex cathedrā with absolute authority

exceptiō rēgulam probat the exception tests the rule [commonly mistranslated: the exception proves the rule]

excitāre fluctōs in simpulō to stir up a tempest in a teapot [lit: to stir up waves in a ladle]

exemplī grātiā for example, for instance

ex librīs from the books (of) [often written on the cover of a book]

ex officiō by virtue of office: e.g., John Doe, chairman ex officiō

ex parte on (one) side

experientia docet experience teaches

ex post factō (enacted) after the fact; retroactive

ex tempore on the spur of the moment

facta, nōn verba deeds, not words

festīnā lentē make haste slowly

fortēs Fortūna adiuvat Fortune helps the brave

Fortūna caeca est (Lady) Fortune is blind

iacta est ālea the die is cast

ignōrantia lēgis nēminem excūsat ignorance of the law doesn't excuse anyone

in absentiā in absence: e.g., to be condemned in absentiā

in articulō mortis at the point of death

in generālibus versātur error error thrives in generalities

in locō parentis in the place of a parent

in mediās rēs into the midst of things [to plunge into the middle of a story]

in memoriam in memory (of)

in perpetuum forever [lit: into perpetuity]

inter alia among other things

in tōtō entirely

ipse dīxit he himself said it

ipsō factō by the very fact itself, thereby

labor vincit omnia effort overcomes everything

lāpsus linguae a slip of the tongue

lēx dubia nōn obligat a doubtful law does not obligate

lupus in fābulā talk of the devil [said when talking of someone and that person shows up]

magnā cum laude with high honors

magnum opus a major work, masterpiece

manus lavat manum one hand washes another

mēns sāna in corpore sānō a sound mind in a sound body

mīrābile dictū strange to say

modus operandī method of operation

multum in parvō much in little [to say much in a few words]

nē plūs ultrā you can't beat it [*lit:* no more beyond]

nē quid nimis nothing to excess

nōlō contendĕre I don't wish to contest (the charge)

nōn compos mentis not all there [*lit:* not in control of one's mind]

notā bene mark well

obiter dictum said off the cuff [said by the way]

Ō tempora! Ō mōrēs! Oh the times! Oh the morals!

parēs cum paribus facillimē congregantur birds of a feather flock together [*lit:* equals very easily gather with equals)

pater patriae father of his country

pāx tēcum peace be with you

per annum annually, by the year

per capita per person (*lit:* by heads)

per diem per day, for each day

per sē by itself

persōna nōn grāta an unwelcome person

post mortem (examination) after death

post scrīptum written afterwards

prīmā faciē on first appearance

prīmus inter parēs first among equals

prō and con for and against

prō bonō (pūblicō) for the common good [generally, legal work done free of charge]

prō Deō et patriā for God and country

prō formā (merely) for form, as a mere formality

prō tempore for the time being, temporary

quid prō quō something (in exchange) for something (else)

rāra avis a rare bird, unusual person

requiēscat in pāce may (he or she) rest in peace

rēs ipsa loquitur the situation speaks for itself

salūs populī suprēma est lēx the safety of the people is the supreme law

semper fidēlis ever faithful (motto of the Marine Corps)

semper parātus always prepared (motto of boyscouts)

sēsquipedālia verba big words [words a foot and a half long]

sīc itur ad astra such is the way to immortality

sīc semper tyrannīs thus ever to tyrants [motto of the state of Virginia]

sīc trānsit glōria mundī thus passes the glory of the world

sine quā nōn without which something cannot (be), indispensable

status quō the (existing) state (of affairs) in which (things now are)

subpoenā under penalty (of the law)

sub rosā privately [*lit:* under the rose]

summā cum laude with highest honors

summum bonum the highest good

tangis ulcus you've hit a sore spot
[*lit:* you are touching a sore]

tempus fugit time flies

terra incognita unfamiliar territory
[*lit:* unknown land]

terra firma solid ground

timeō Danaōs et dōna ferentēs I fear
the Greeks even bringing gifts

vāde mēcum go with me [said of
someone or something you always
take with you]

vae victīs woe to the vanquished

vānitās vānitātum et omnia vānitās
vanity of vanities and all is vanity

vēnī, vīdī, vīcī I came, I saw, I conquered

verbātim word for word

verbum sapientī satis est a word to
the wise is sufficient

vēritās vōs līberābit the truth will
set you free

viā by way of

vice versā the other way around

vīvā vōce by word of mouth, from
the voice of a living person [as
opposed to something written]

vīvat rēx! long live the king!

vōx populī the voice of the people

STATE MOTTOES

(Not all States have Latin mottoes)

Alabama	**Audemus iūra nostra dēfendĕre** We dare defend our rights.	
Arizona	**Dītat Deus.** God enriches.	
Arkansas	**Rēgnat populus.** The people rule.	
Colorado	**Nīl sine nūmine.** Nothing without the Deity.	
Connecticut	**Quī trānstulit sustinet.** He who transplanted [true faith] sustains [us].	
Idaho	**Estō perpetua.** May she endure forever.	
Kansas	**Ad astra per aspera.** To the stars through difficulties.	
Maine	**Dīrigō.** I direct.	
Maryland	**Scūtō bonae voluntātis corōnāstī nōs.** With the shield of Thy goodwill Thou hast covered us.	
Massachusetts	**Ēnse petit placidam sub lībertāte quiētem.** With the sword she seeks peace under liberty.	
Michigan	**Sī quaeris pēnīnsulam amoenam, circumspice**. If you seek a pleasant peninsula, look around you.	
Mississippi	**Virtute et armis.** By valor and arms.	
Missouri	**Salūs populī suprēma lēx estō.** Let the welfare of the people be the supreme law.	

New Mexico	**Crēscit eundō.**	It grows as it goes.
New York	**Excelsior.**	Higher.
North Carolina	**Esse quam vidērī.**	To be rather than to seem.
Oklahoma	**Labor omnia vincit.**	Effort conquers all.
Oregon	**Ālīs volat propriīs.**	She flies with her own wings.
South Carolina	**Animīs opibusque parātī.**	Ready in mind and resources.
Virginia	**Sīc semper tyrannīs.**	Thus ever to tyrants.
West Virginia	**Montānī semper līberī.**	Mountaineers (are) always free.
Wyoming	**Cēdant arma togae.**	Let arms yield to the toga.

LATIN WORD ORDER

While an English sentence derives its meaning from the order of the words, a Latin sentence is dependent for its meaning more on word endings than on word order. In all sentences, the beginning and the end are the points of emphasis. Although Latin word order is very flexible, even in one and the same author, there are still some observations that can be made about Latin word order in general that can prove helpful in writing and reading Latin.

1. Usually, the *subject* stands at the beginning of a sentence. But when conjunctions like **sed** (but) or **nam** (for, since) occur, they take first place. Certain adverbs never take first place; for example, **autem** (however).

   Senātōrēs [*qui* in cūriā tum *sedēbant*] **senātūs cōnsultum fēcērunt.**
   The senators [*who were sitting* in the chamber at that time] passed a senatorial decree.

2. The *direct object* usually comes before the *indirect object*.
   Fidem tibi dō. I give you my word.

   In compound tenses, the auxiliary verb generally comes after the main verb.
   Mīnōtaurus ā Thēseō interfectus est. The Minotaur was killed by Theseus.

3. Where *two or more pronouns* occur in the same sentence, Roman writers are fond of placing them next to each other.
   ut ego tibi saepe dīxī as I often told you

   However, the order is quite frequently reversed. Here's an example from Cicero.
   Variē sum affectus tuīs litterīs. I was variously affected by your letter.

4. The *verb* often, but by no means always, comes at the end of a sentence. The verb of a subordinate clause comes at the end of that clause, and the subordinate conjunction or relative pronoun stands at the beginning of the clause. Thus one can tell where the subordinate clause begins and ends.

5. No general rule can be laid down about the position of *adjectives*. On the whole, they precede the noun oftener than they follow it.
   a) *adjectives of quantity* (including numerals) regularly precede the noun they modify.
      omnēs hominēs all men
      quīnque nāvēs five ships

b) *the adjectives* **Rōmānus** *and* **Latīnus** regularly follow.
populus Rōmānus the Roman people
lingua Latīna the Latin language

c) *when two adjectives modify a noun,* they are either connected by **et** or one adjective precedes the noun and the other comes after the noun.
vir honestus et doctus an honorable and learned man
or **honestus vir doctus** an honorable and learned man

d) *demonstrative adjectives* usually precede the noun.
ille homō that man
eōdem tempore at the same time

e) however, **ille** in the sense of *that famous* or emphatic *the* usually comes after the noun.
Alexander ille that famous Alexander [*the* Alexander]

f) *possessive adjectives* can come before or after a noun.
meā sententiā in my opinion
verba tua your words

g) *noster* coming before a proper name often has the sense of *our friend* . . .
noster Pūblius our friend Publius

h) *indefinite adjectives* usually follow the noun.

homō quīdam a certain man
mulier aliqua some woman

6. *Adverbs* usually precede the word they modify.
valdē irrātus very angry
ut saepe dīxī as I have often said
paulō post a little later

The adverbs **autem** (however), **igitur** and **ergō** (then, therefore), are the second elements in a sentence.
The adverb **itaque** (and so) regularly comes first.
The adverbs **quidem** (indeed) and **dēmum** (finally) and **quoque** (too) follow the words that they emphasize.
The adverb **etiam** (also) precedes the word it emphasizes.

7. *Prepositions* usually precede the words they govern.
post multōs cāsus after many adventures

When a noun is modified by an adjective, the adjective is often placed before the preposition.
summā cum laude with highest honors

hanc ob rem because of this factor

A noun or phrase in the genitive normally comes between the preposition and the noun it governs.
ex culpae meae recordātiōne from the recollection of my mistake

The preposition **cum** (with) is sometimes attached to a pronoun as an enclitic.

mēcum with me; **vōbīscum** with you; **quibuscum** with whom

8. The *vocative* usually follows one or more words.

    Scrībe, Quīnte, ad mē tuō commodō. Quintus, write me at your convenience.

9. The word order of *nouns in apposition*, such as "my brother Quīntus,"is the reverse of the English word order. In other words, Latin will say "Quintus my brother": **Quīntus frāter,** or "Cornelius uncle" instead of "uncle Cornelius": **Cornēlius avunculus.**

10. When a *noun is the subject* of the main clause as well as of a subordinate clause, that noun will come before the conjunction. Note the difference in the following two sentences. In the first sentence, the noun is the subject of both the main clause and the subordinate clause; in the second sentence, the noun of the subordinate clause is different from that of the main clause.

    Terentius, quandōcumque me videt, semper subrīdet.
    Whenever Terence sees me, he always smiles.

    Quandōcumque Mārs bellum incitat, Iuppiter īram exhibet.
    Whenever Mars stirs up war,

Jupiter shows his anger.

11. *Conjunctions.* The conjunctions **nam** and **enim** (for, since), regularly stand in second place in the sentence.

12. Words and phrases *referring to the preceding sentence* or to some part of it, regularly stand first.

    Id **ut audīvit, Cicerō continuō litterās ad Caesarem mīsit.**
    When Cicero heard *that*, he immediately sent a letter to Caesar.

13. *Interrogative pronouns, adjectives, and adverbs* come first in interrogative sentences.

    Quis **hoc dīxit?** *Who* said this?
    Quid **imperātor dē obsidibus fēcit?** *What* did the general do about the hostages?
    Quae **scelera pēiōra esse possunt quam haec?** *What* crimes can be worse than these?
    Ubi **terrārum sumus?** *Where* in the world are we?

    If the interrogative sentence is not introduced by such a pronoun, adjective, or adverb, *the enclitic -ne* is attached to the first word of the sentence, which is usually the verb, sometimes a pronoun.

    Audīvistīne **mandāta ducis?** Did you hear the instructions of the general?
    Tūne **vērō praemium exspectās?** Do you really expect a reward?

    The interrogatives **nōnne,** expecting a positive answer, and **num,** expecting a negative answer, are placed first.

Nōnne sentīs tē sōlum in culpā esse? You realize, don't you, that you alone are at fault?

Num hinc abībis? You're not leaving, are you?

14. In English the *participle* comes at the beginning of its phrase. In Latin the participle comes at the end of its phrase.

Servus, dominum crūdēlem *timēns*, fūgit. The slave, *fearing* his cruel master, ran away.

Amōre Thisbēs *adductus*, Pȳramus eam extrā urbem clam convēnit. *Induced* by love for Thisbe, Pyramus met her secretly outside the city.

If we were to use the Latin word order in English, it would sound like this:

The slave, his cruel master fearing, ran away.

By love for Thisbe induced, Pyramus her outside the city secretly met.

ablative case: it is used

a) as ablative of *accompaniment* with the preposition **cum**; it answers the question "with whom?": - **Faustulus *cum Lārentiā* habitāvit.** (Faustulus lived *with* Larentia.)

b) as ablative of *comparison* instead of using **quam**: - **Alba Longa est vestutior *Rōmā*.** (Alba Longa is older *than* Rome.)

c) as ablative of *degree of difference*: - *multō* **celerior** (*much* faster, *lit:* faster by much]

d) as ablative of *manner*, which answers the question "in what way was it done?" The preposition **cum** is optional if the noun in the ablative is modified by an adjective: -**Rōmulus *magnā (cum) glōriā* rēgnāvit** (Romulus reigned *with* great glory.)

e) as ablative of *quality*, when modified by an adjective: - **Cātō est vir magnā prudentiā.** (Cato is a man of great wisdom.)

f) as ablative of *means or instrument*, which answers the question "by means of what?" No preposition is used: - **Thisbē sē *sīcā* fodicāvit.** (Thisbe stabbed herself *with* a dagger.)

g) as ablative of *personal agent*: - **Rōma *ab Rōmulō* condita est.** (Rome was founded *by* Romulus)

h) as ablative of *place from which* with the preposition **ex** : - **Senātōrēs *ex cūriā* veniunt**. (The senators are coming *out of* the senate building). But no preposition is used with names of towns and small islands: - *Rōmā* **dēcessit.** (He withdrew *from* Rome). - **Thēseus sōlus *Naxō* revertit.** (Theseus returned alone *from* Naxos).

i) as ablative of *place in which* with the preposition **in**. It answers the question "where does it happen?" The preposition **in** can mean "in" or "on." : - **Cicerō *in forō* est.** (Cicero is *in* the forum.) - **Remus *in mūrō* sedēbat.** (Remus was sitting *on* the wall.)

j) as ablative of *time when* or *within which* with or without the preposition **in,** but more frequently without a preposition.

   (1) *time when*: - **tertiā hōrā** (at the third hour); **tertiō annō** (in the third year); but: **ter in annō** (three times in the course of the year)

   (2) *time within which*: - **decem annīs** (within ten years)

k) with some common Latin prepositions: **dē** (down from; about, concerning); **sine** (without); **sub** (under); but when motion is shown, **sub** takes the accusative.

l) with the adjectives **dignus** and **indignus** :- **dignus honōre** (worthy of honor)

accusative case: also called "objective case"; it is used

a) as *direct object* of a verb: - **Populus *Rōmulum* amāvit.** (The people loved *Romulus*).

b) in apposition with a noun in the objective case: - **Omnēs**

Rōmulum, prīmum *rēgem* Rōmae, amāvērunt. (All loved Romulus, the first *king* of Rome).

c) as object of a preposition: *trāns* **mare** (*across* the sea) *ad* **forum** (*to* the forum)

d) to show *place to which* with names of towns and small islands: - *Rōmam* **vēnī.** (I came *to* Rome), *Dēlum* **īvī.** (I went *to* Delos).

e) to show extent of time: **Rōmulus** *multōs annōs* **rēgnāvit.** (Romulus reigned (*for*) many years.)

active voice: when the subject is the doer of the action of the verb, we call the verb active: - **Horātius pontem** *dēfendit.* (Horatius *defended* the bridge.) Here the subject **Horātius** did the defending, and so the verb is said to be in the active voice. The opposite of active voice is *passive* voice.

adjective: a word that modifies a noun or pronoun: - *bonus* **fīlius** (a *good* son). The adjective must agree with its noun in number, gender, and case. There are adjectives of the first and second declensions: - **bon·us -a -um** (good), and adjectives of the third declension: - **facil·is -is -e** (easy).

adverb: a word that modifies **a)** a verb: - *lentē* **ambulant** (they walk *slowly*), **b)** an adjective: - *longē* **melior** (*far* better); **c)** another adverb: - *nimis* **cito** (*too* quickly); or **d)** an entire clause: - *vidēlicet* **id ignōrābant** (*obviously*, they didn't know about it).

agreement: *Adjectives*: In English, an adjective does not change form, regardless of whether the noun it modifies is singular or plural, sub-jective or objective case. In Latin, an adjective must agree with the noun it modifies in number, gender, and case; and it shows agreement by changing its ending. This does not mean that noun and adjective must have identical endings; this is especially true when the noun and its adjective belong to different declensions: - **bonus pater** (good father); here we have a masculine adjective of the second declension, modifying a masculine noun of the third declension.

Pronouns must agree with their antecedents in number and gender; however, their case depends on how they function within their own clause: - *senātor quem* **populus honōrāvit erat Cicerō.** (The senator *whom* the senate honored was Cicero). Here the pronoun **quem**, while agreeing with its antecedent **senātor,** is in the accusative case because within its own clause (**quem populus honōrāvit)** it is the direct object of the verb **honōrāvit.**

antecedent: a word to which a pro-noun refers: - **Ubi est** *cōnsul* **quī illam ōrātiōnem habuit?** (Where is the *consul* who gave that speech?) "Antecedent" means "(the word) going before." In this example, **quī** is the pronoun and **cōnsul** is its antecedent. One must be especially careful with pronouns that refer to things, since in Latin things can be masculine, feminine, or neuter: - **Cicerō ōrātiōnem heri habuit. Mē in** *eā* **nōmināvit.** (Cicero gave a speech yesterday. He mentioned me by name in *it.*) Because "it" refers to the antecedent **ōrātiōnem,**

which happens to be feminine, the feminine pronoun *eā* must be used.

apposition: a noun is said to be "in apposition" to another noun when it is placed next to another noun which it identifies. *(See* appositive) It means literally "being placed next to."

appositive: a noun that follows another noun and identifies it: - **Priamus,** *rēx* **Trōiae** (Priam, the *king* of Troy.)

assimilation: changing a letter to make it similar to the letter that follows: - *ad* **cēdĕre** becomes **accēdĕre;** *ad* **gressiō** becomes **aggressiō;** *ob* **pugnāre** becomes **oppugnāre**

articles: in English we have two articles: the definite article *the,* and the indefinite article *a* or *an.* Latin has no articles. Therefore, **puella** can mean *a girl* or *the girl.* You have to judge from the context which one is to be used in translation.

auxiliary verb: also called "helping verb": - **Carthāgō dēlēta** *est.* Carthage *has been* destroyed. We often use helping verbs where the Latin does not: - **Canēs lātrant.** The dogs *are* barking.

base: the form of a noun without any ending, found by dropping the genitive singular ending, for example, **corpor-** (from **corpus corpor***is n* body*)*

case: the form of a noun, pronoun, or adjective which indicates by the ending its relationship to other parts of its clause. The basic Latin cases are: nominative, genitive, dative, accusative, ablative, vocative. The locative is a special case

and is not listed in the declension of nouns. *See* **locative** below. In English, the order of the words in a sentence indicates the function of nouns and shows the meaning of the sentence as a whole. In Latin, the endings of nouns (therefore their case) show how they function in the sentence rather than the order of the words.

clause: a group of words acting as a unit and containing a subject and predicate. A clause is called *independent* if it can stand alone: - **Catō diū vīxit.** (Cato lived a long time). A clause is called *dependent* or *subordinate* if it depends on another clause to make complete sense: - **Cicerō,** *dum vīvit,* **multās ōrātiōnēs habuit.** (*While he was alive,* Cicero gave many speeches.*)*

cognates: words related to each other because they come from the same root or stem: - **amāre** to love, **amor amōris** *m* love, **amātor amātōris** *m* lover, **amābil·is -is -e** lovable, etc. *Amorous, amiable,* and *amateur* are English cognates, derived from the Latin word **amō.**

collective noun: a noun that is singular in number but refers to several persons, places, or things: - **populus** people,- **turba** crowd,- **exercitus** army. Because collective nouns are singular in form, they take singular verbs: - **populus multōs deōs coluit** (the people worshipped many gods).

comparison: it refers to changes in the form of an adjective or adverb to show greater degree of quality or intensity than the simple word. There are three degrees of comparison: positive, comparative, and superlative: **fortis fortior fortissimus** (brave braver bravest)

complementary infinitive: an infinitive that completes the meaning of the verb with which it is used: -*Discēdĕre* **volō**. (I want *to leave*).

complex sentence: *see* **sentence.**

compound sentence: *see* **sentence.**

conjugation: arrangement of verb forms in regular order according to the subject: - **amō, amās, amat,** etc. (I love, you love, she or he loves, etc). In Latin there are four conjugations, distinguished from one another by a vowel in the ending of the present active infinitive:

CONJUGATION	I	II	III	IV
INFINITIVE ENDING	**-āre**	**-ēre**	**-ĕre**	**-īre**
DISTINGUISHING VOWEL	**ā**	**ē**	**ĕ**	**ī**
EXAMPLE	**amāre**	**docēre**	**scrībĕre**	**audīre**
MEANING	to love	to teach	to write	to hear

NOTE: We also speak of a **III -iō** conjugation to which belong such verbs as **capiō capĕre cēpī captus** *to take;* verbs of this conjugation are really hybrid, sharing some forms with the fourth conjugation, but essentially with endings typical of the third conjugation.

conjunction: a word that joins other words, phrases, or clauses.

A *coordinate* conjunction joins grammatically equal elements: - two nouns: **senātus populus***que* **Rōmānus** (the senate *and* the Roman people); two prepositional phrases: - **in forō** *et* **in senātū** (in the forum *and* in the senate); two similar clauses :- **ego sum homō**

novus, *sed* **Claudius est vetus patricius.** (I am a newcomer, *but* Claudius is an old patrician.)

A *subordinate* conjunction joins grammatically unequal elements, for instance a main clause and a subordinate clause: - **Claudicō** *cum* **ambulō. (**I limp *when* I walk.) Like adverbs and prepositions, conjunctions never change in form, that is, they do not have number, gender, case, or tense.

consonant: any of the letters of the alphabet except the vowels **a, e, i, o, u, y,** namely, **b, c, d, f, g, h, i, k, l, m, n, p, q, r, s, t, v, x, z:-** se̲na̲to̲r̲ se̲na̲to̲r̲ contains four consonants. Notice that **y** is not a consonant in Latin, but a vowel. Latin has a consonantal **i** which is pronounced as a **j**.

dative case: it is used

a) as *indirect object,* that is, to indicate to whom something is given or said: - **Imperātor corōnam mūrālem** *Coriolānō* **dedit.** (The general gave *Coriolanus* a mural crown.) - **Vir nihil** *puerō* **dīxit.** (The man said nothing *to the boy.)*

b) with *intransitive* verbs: - **Leō** *Androclae* **nōn nocuit.** (The lion did not hurt Androcles.)

c) with *certain adjectives* such as: friendly, unfriendly, similar, equal, near, related to, etc.: - **Fīlia est cāra** *mātrī*. (The daughter is dear *to the mother.)*

d) to indicate *possession*:- *Mihi* **multī amīcī sunt.** (I have many friends (*lit:* many friends are *to me*).

declension: the classification of nouns, adjectives, and pronouns, arranged in regular order according to case, number, and gender. Latin has five declensions (or classes) of nouns:

declension I:- **porta** *f* (gate) (gen. **-ae**)
declension II:- **amīcus** *m* (friend), **puer** *m* (boy), **bellum** *n* (war) (genitive **-ī**)
declension III:- **canis** *mf* (dog), **uxor** *f* (wife), **corpus** *n* (body) (genitive **-is**)
declension IV:- **exercitus** *m* (army), **manus** *f* (hand; gang), **genū** *n* (knee) (genitive **-ūs**)
declension V:- **diēs** *m* (day), **rēs** *f* (thing) (genitive **-ēī** or **-ĕī**)

defective verb: a verb is said to be defective when it lacks certain forms. In English, the verb *must* is defective, since it has only a present tense: - *I must leave.* It has no past tense. In Latin, verbs like **coepī** (to begin) and **ōdī** (to hate) have the form of the perfect tense, but have a present meaning. These verbs lack the forms of the present, imperfect, and future. (*See* Chapter 23) Instead of using those verbs we can use another verb, such as **incipiō** instead of **coepī,** which has the same sense and can be formed in all tenses.

demonstrative adjective: a word used to point out a person, place, or thing: - *illa* **fēmina** (*that* woman); -*hī* **virī** (*these* men); -*istud* **oppidum** (*that* town).

demonstrative pronoun: replaces a noun which has been mentioned before. It is called "demonstrative"

because it points out a person, place, or thing. In English we use *this (one)* to refer to persons, places, or things that are close to the speaker, and *that (one)* to refer to those that are farther away from the speaker: - *Hoc* **cupiō.** (I want *this (one)*; -*Illud* **cupiō** (I want *that (one)*.

deponent verb: a verb that is passive in form but active in meaning:- **loquor loquī locūtus sum** *to speak.* **Locūt·us sum** means *I have spoken. See* Chapter 25.

derivative: a word that has its source in a Latin word for example, *document* from Latin **documentum.**

diphthong: a sound produced by pronouncing two vowels together quickly in one syllable: **ae, au, eu, oe, ui: ros***ae* (roses); *aut***em** (however); **Orph***eus* (Orpheus); *poen***a** (punishment); **q***uī* (who).

expletive: the word "there" serving as formal subject to anticipate the real subject. Latin does not have an expletive, but the idea of the expletive is generally indicated by initial position: - *Erant* **multī accūsātōrēs in iūdīciō.** (*There were* many prosecutors in the courtroom.)

gender: the grouping of nouns into classes: masculine, feminine, neuter. In English, persons are masculine or feminine, and things are neuter. But in Latin, things can be masculine, feminine, or neuter: - **digitus** *m* (finger); **coma** *f* (hair); **caput** *n* (head) Here we have three parts of the body, each with a different gender. You simply have to memorize the gender and use the guidelines.

genitive case: it is used

a) to show *possession*: - **tēctum *domūs*** (the roof *of the house*), - **benevolentia *mātris*** (*the mother's* kindness)

b) after certain adjectives: - **via plēna *hominum*** (a street full *of people*)

c) to indicate *material* of which something is made: - **mūrus *saxī*** (a wall *of stone*)

d) to show *a quality:* - **fēmina *magnae benevolentiae*** (a woman *of great kindness*)

e) The *partitive genitive* denotes the whole, of which something forms a part: - **pars Galliae** (a part of Gaul); **multī mīlitum** (many of the soldiers). In these instances, **Galliae** and **mīlitum** indicate the whole, of which **pars** and **multī** form a part. The partitive genitive has a special form only with the pronouns **nōs** and **vōs**: - **multī nostrum** (many of us); **multī vestrum** (many of you)

imperfect tense: indicates an action or state as *continued* or *repeated* in the past and can be translated as follows: - **dormiēbam** I was sleeping *(continued);* I slept *(simple);* I used to sleep *(repeated or habitual).*

Sometimes the action, by its very nature, didn't happen just for an instant and therefore is translated into English by a simple past: - **Ego avum et aviam *amābam.*** (*I loved* my grandfather and grandmother.) Remember, the perfect tense is like a snapshot; the imperfect tense is like a motion picture.

infinitive: a form of a verb without person or number, e.g., **amāre** (to love). "Infinitive" comes from the Latin, meaning "not limited," that is, not limited to a specific person or number. In contrast, a finite verb, e.g., **portō**, is limited to the first person singular. In English, the infinitive is generally composed of two words, "to" plus verb: to go, to hide, to be. The "to" is called the sign of the infinitive. Latin does not have the sign of the infinitive. The present infinitive can be active: **amāre** (to love), or passive: **amārī** (to be loved). The perfect infinitive can also be active: **amāvisse** (to have loved), or passive: **amāt·us -a -um esse** (to have been loved*).* In English there is no future infinitive, but Latin has a future infinitive: - **amātūr·us -a -um esse** (to be about to love). In Latin, the infinitive is never used to show purpose. We can say: "He said this *to impress* the audience." In Latin, purpose is expressed by **ut** and the subjunctive or **ad** with the gerund or gerundive (constructions that are explained in Book II).

inflection: a term that includes both *declining* nouns, pronouns, and adjectives and *conjugating* verbs. Thus, we can speak of inflecting nouns and inflecting verbs. Inflection in this grammatical sense is to be distinguished from *inflection of the voice*, whereby we raise and lower the pitch of the words as we speak in order to assist in the communication of ideas.

intensive pronoun: a pronoun that emphasizes the identity of a noun: - **Cicerō *ipse* lēgem tulit.** (Cicero himself *[and not someone else]* proposed the law.) In English, the intensive and reflexive pronouns have identical forms, ending in *-self*, and therefore the two can easily be confused. In Latin there is a special form for each. The Latin intensive form for masculine singular is **ipse** *himself;* the reflexive pronoun for the masculine singular is **sē** *himself.*

interjection: exclamatory word or phrase without grammatical connection: - **heus!** (hey*!*)

interrogative: an adjective, adverb, or pronoun that introduces a question:

adjective: - *quā* **viā?** by what way?

adverb: - **cūr?** why?

pronoun: - **quis?** who? **quid?** what?

An interrogative sentence may also be introduced by the particles **-ne** (expecting a positive or negative answer), **nōnne** (expecting a positive answer) or **num** (expecting a negative answer).

The interrogative adjective "whose" is translated by **cuius** when "whose" refers to one person: - *Cuius* **sententia est optima?** (*Whose* opinion is best?) and **quōrum, quārum, quōrum** when "whose" refers to several individuals: - *Quōrum* **iūra violāta sunt?** (*Whose* rights were violated?)

intransitive: a verb is said to be intransitive when it does not take a direct object in the objective case: **stāre** (to stand), **sedēre** (to sit). Verbs that take the dative case rather than the accusative case are also said to be intransitive: **Nihil illī virō** *placet.* (Nothing *pleases* that man). The word "intransitive" means in Latin "not going over" (from the subject that is the doer to the object that is the receiver of the action of the verb). Note that verbs

such as "to please" are transitive in English, but because they require the dative case in Latin, they are considered intransitive verbs.

locative case: in most instances, the preposition **in** (+ *abl*) shows location; in some instances, such as names of towns and small islands, as well as the words for *home* and *country*, a special form, the locative, is used: **Rōmae** (in Rome); **domī** (at home); **rūrī** (in the country.)

mood: form of a verb that shows whether the action or state being expressed is regarded as fact or as possibility, wish, or command: the *indicative mood* indicates fact: - **amant** (they love); the *subjunctive mood* indicates possibility or wish: - **ament** (they may love, may they love); the *imperative mood* indicates a command: - **silēte!** (be quiet!) Another word for "mood" is "*mode,*" the manner in which a statement is made, but the word "mood" has become traditional.

nominative case: The subject of a verb, as well as a noun in apposition with the subject or a predicate noun or adjective, is in the nominative case.

noun: the name of a person, place, or thing. *Common noun:* (general name, shared by several): - **imperātor** (general); *proper noun* (name of a specific person, place or thing): **Caesar** (Caesar); *concrete noun* (name of something that can be touched): - **mēnsa** (table); *abstract noun* (name of something that can't be touched): - **vēritās** (truth); *collective noun* (name that is singular in form but designating a number of individuals): - **turba**

(crowd); **populus** (the people).

number: the form of a noun, pronoun, adjective, or verb that shows it to be singular or plural; singular: **dux** (leader); plural: **ducēs** (leaders).

participle: a verbal adjective. As an adjective it modifies a noun or pronoun; as a "verbal," it can take an object: **servus patinam** *tenēns* (the servant *holding* a plate); **patina ā servō** *portāta* (a plate *carried* by the servant). A participle can be used as a noun: **am·āns -ant***is* *mf* lover. Notice that in English, the present active participle ends in *-ing:* the *whistling* wind; the past passive participle generally ends in *-ed*, less often in *-t* or *-en:* a *completed* task; a toga, *bought* in the Subura; a speech *given* in the senate.

partitive genitive: *See* **genitive.**

parts of speech: the classification of words according to their function. There are eight parts of speech: noun, pronoun, adjective, verb, adverb, preposition, conjunction, interjection.

passive voice: a) A verb is said to be in the passive voice when the action of the verb is not performed by the subject, but is done to the subject: - **Duo cōnsulēs ā populō quotannīs** *creātī sunt.* **(**Two consuls *were elected* yearly by the Roman people.)

b) The passive voice is also used to convert a transitive verb into an intransitive verb: - **Tempora** *mūtāntur.* (Times *are changing.*) The word "passive" in Latin means "undergoing, suffering"; that is,

the subject of the sentence "undergoes" the action of the verb.

perfect tense: the third principal part of a verb, indicating an action that was completed in the past: - **scrīpsī** (I wrote, I have written). Although in English we can use the helping verb *have,* the Latin perfect active verb does not use a helping verb. The word "perfect" in Latin means "completed." The perfect active tense is formed by adding **-ī, -istī, it, -imus, -istis, -ērunt** to the perfect stem. The perfect passive tense is formed by adding the present forms of **sum** to the perfect participle: **amātus sum, amātus es,** etc.

person: the classification of pronouns and verb forms to distinguish between the speakers (first person: **ego** I, **nōs** we*),* the ones spoken to (second person: **tū, vōs** you*),* and persons or things spoken about (third person: **is** he, **ea** she, **id** it, **eī,** **eae, ea** they*).*

phrase: a group of words serving as a unit, without subject or predicate: - **sine timōre** (without fear)

pluperfect tense: indicates an action that was completed in the past *before* some other action in the past. It might be called a "double past." The word "pluperfect" in Latin means "more than completed." The pluperfect active tense is formed with the perfect stem plus the forms of the imperfect of **sum: amāv- + eram = amāveram (**I had loved). The pluperfect passive tense is formed with the perfect participle, the fourth principal part, plus the imperfect forms of **sum: amātus eram, amātus erās,**

etc.

positive degree: *see* **comparison**

possessive adjective: indicates possession or ownership: *mea* **māter** (*my* mother); *tuum* **oppidum** (*your* town). The gender of the possessive adjective is determined by the noun that it modifies, not by the gender of the possessor. The reflexive adjective is used when the possessive adjective refers to the subject of the sentence: - **Brūtus Caesarem manū** *suā* **interfēcit.** (Brutus killed Caesar with *his own* hand.)

predicate: a verb and any other words used with it to say or ask something about the subject: - **puer** *Latīnē ēmendātē loquitur.* (The boy *speaks Latin correctly.*)

predicate adjective: an adjective that follows a form of **esse** or similar linking verbs and refers to the subject: - **Puella est/vidētur** *callida.* (The girl is/seems *smart*). In English, the predicate adjective always comes after the verb; an adjective that modifies a noun and occurs before the verb is called an *attributive* adjective; for example, a *good* student studies hard. It should be noted that the terms "attributive" and "predicate" refer strictly to the position of adjectives in an English sentence. Since the sense of a sentence in Latin is determined by the endings of words rather than by their position, the terms "attributive" and "predicate" really don't apply to Latin grammar. Look at the Latin sentence above. It could be stated **puella** *callida* **est/***vidētur* and the meaning of the sentence would not change; it would still mean: the girl is/seems *smart*.

predicate noun: a noun which follows a form of **esse** or similar linking verbs and refers to the subject: - **Vir est** *praetor.* (The man is a *praetor.*) The word order could be: **Vir** *praetor* **est;** the word **praetor** is still the predicate noun. But note the distinction between English and Latin grammar that is described under "predicate adjective."

prefix: a preposition attached to the beginning of a word: - *inter***venīre** (to come between, intervene.) Certain prefixes do not occur independently: *re-, sē-:* **recēdĕre** (to go back); **sēdūcĕre** (to take aside.)

preposition: an indeclinable word that establishes a link between the noun or pronoun that is the object of the preposition and some other word in the sentence. The noun or pronoun associated with the preposition is said to be its object: - **Homō** *sub* **arbore est Pūblius.** (The man *under* the tree is Publius.) Here the preposition shows the relationship between "man" and "tree." Latin prepositions govern either the accusative case: - *ad* **forum** (*to* the forum); or the ablative case: - *prō* **patriā** (*for* one's country); or both: *in* **forum** (*into* the forum); *in* **forō** (*in* the forum). A preposition with object and any modifiers is called a prepositional phrase.

principal parts: the key forms of a verb from which all other forms can be derived. The typical Latin verb has four principal parts: 1) first person singular present tense;

2) present infinitive; 3) first person singular perfect tense active; 4) perfect passive participle: **amō amāre amāvī amātus** (I love, to love, I loved, [having been] loved.)

pronoun: a word substituted for a noun: - **Senātōrem vīdī et** *eum* **statim recognōvī.** (I saw the senator and immediately recognized *him*.) The word for which the pronoun is substituted is called the "antecedent." *See* **antecedent.**

reflexive: a pronoun or adjective is said to be reflexive when it refers specifically to the subject of the clause or sentence. **a)** *reflexive pronoun*: - **Puella** *sē* **lāvit.** (The girl washed *herself*.) In such cases we also say that the *verb* is reflexive; **b)** *reflexive adjective*: - **Brūtus Caesarem** *suā* **manū interfēcit.** (Brutus killed Caesar with *his own* hand.) The gender of the adjective depends on the noun it modifies, not on the gender of the antecedent. Thus, **suā** is feminine because it modifies the feminine noun **manū.** *See* **intensive pronoun.**

relative pronoun: a pronoun that refers to a previously mentioned noun (antecedent) in the same sentence: - **Puella** *quem* **vīdī subrīdēbat.** (The girl *whom* I saw was smiling.) The relative pronoun introduces a subordinate clause (*quem* **vīdī**), called a relative clause. The pronoun agrees with is antecedent **(puella)** in number and gender; but its case depends on how it is used within its own clause (here *quem* is the direct object of the verb **vīdī**).

sentence: a word or group of words grammatically complete and making complete sense. It can consist of a single word or many words: - **Apage!** (Scram!) - **Mea amīca rosās omnīnō adōrat.** (My girlfriend absolutely adores roses.) A sentence can be *simple*, consisting of only one main clause; or it can be *compound*, consisting of two main clauses; or it can be *complex*, consisting of one main clause and one or more dependent clauses; or it can be *compound complex*, consisting of two or more main clauses and one or more dependent clauses.

stem: the unchanging part of a verb to which the connecting vowel and the personal endings are added. There are three stems in a Latin verb: the present stem (e.g., **am-**), the perfect stem (e.g., **amāv-**) and the participial stem (e.g., **amāt-**). We use the term "stem" when speaking of verbs, and "base" when speaking of nouns. Both terms indicate the part of a word to which endings are added.

The *present stem* is used to form: **a)** the present, imperfect, and future tenses; **b)** the present infinitive; **c)** the imperative; **d)** the present participle; **e)** the gerund and gerundive.

The *perfect stem* is used to form: **a)** the perfect, pluperfect, and future perfect active tenses; **b)** the perfect active infinitive.

The *participial stem* is used to form: **a)** the perfect, pluperfect, and future perfect passive tenses; **b)** the perfect passive infinitive; **c)** the perfect passive participle.

subject: the person, thing, or idea about which a statement is made or a question is asked. *Rōmulus* **dīcitur Rōmam condidisse.** (*Romulus* is said to have founded Rome.) **Ubi iam sunt illī** *agricolae* **dūrī?** (Where are those tough *farmers* now?)

syllable: a part of a word uttered in a single breath impulse; a Latin word has as many syllables as it has vowels or diphthongs: **aes·ti·mā·ti·ō** esteem.

tense: the form of a verb that indicates the time of an action or condition. Latin has six tenses: present, imperfect, future, perfect, pluperfect, and future perfect: **portō** (I carry, am carrying); **portābam** (I was carrying, I used to carry); **portābō** (I shall carry); **portāvī** (I carried, have carried); **portāveram** (I had carried); **portāverō** (I shall have carried).

transitive: a verb is transitive when it takes a direct object: *Ōdī* **ōrātiōnēs longās.** (I *hate* long speeches.) Some verbs that are transitive in English are intransitive in Latin, because in Latin some verbs take the dative rather than the accusative case: **Līberī bonī parentibus** *oboediunt.* (Good children *obey* their parents.) "Obey" is transitive in English, but the Latin verb for "obey" takes the dative and therefore is intransitive.

verb: a word expressing an act, occurrence, or state of being: - **Rōmānī Latīnē** *loquuntur.* (The Romans *speak* Latin.); **Deī** *exsistunt* (Gods *exist.*); **Parvulī fēlīcēs** *sunt* (The children *are* happy.)

vocative: the case used in addressing a person or thing: - **quid, Mārce, facis?** (*Mark,* what are you doing?) - **Quid,** *mī fīlī,* **vīs?** (*My son,* what do you want?) The vocative case is the same as the nominative case of all nouns except masculine nouns of the second declension, as illustrated above. In English, the word in the vocative case is generally the first element of a sentence; in Latin, it is generally the second element in a sentence.

voice: the form of the verb indicating whether the subject is doing or receiving the action of the verb. The verb can be *active:* - **Parentēs meī mē** *amant.* (My parents *love* me). Or the verb can be *passive:* - **Ego ā parentibus meīs** *amor.* (I am *loved* by my parents.)

vowel: a speech sound allowing relatively free passage through the mouth and nose: **a, e, i, o, u, y.** Notice that the letter **y** is a vowel in Latin; in English it is a consonant. Latin vowels can be long or short. In this book, long vowels are marked by a macron above them: - **cōnsulēs** (consuls). In addition, the **e** of the infinitive of the third conjugation is marked short (**ĕ**) to distinguish it from the infinitive of the second conjugation: **facĕre** *to do, make;* **movēre** *to move.*

The four conjugations are distinguished by a different connecting vowel which links the stem and the endings of the verb forms. They are: **ā** for the first conjugation, **ē** for the second, **ĕ** for the third, and **ī** for the fourth.

FORMS

NOUNS

FIRST DECLENSION / SECOND DECLENSION

	FEMININE		MASCULINE	NEUTER
	via *f* road, street		**amīcus** *m* friend	**oppidum** *n* town

SINGULAR				
NOM.	**vi·***a*	the road	**amīc·***us*	**oppid·***um*
GEN.	**vi·***ae*	of the road	**amīc·***ī*	**oppid·***ī*
DAT.	**vi·***ae*	to, for the road	**amīc·***ō*	**oppid·***ō*
ACC.	**vi·***am*	the road	**amīc·***um*	**oppid·***um*
ABL.	**vi·***ā*	from, by, with the road	**amīc·***ō*	**oppid·***ō*

PLURAL				
NOM.	**vi·***ae*	the roads	**amīc·***ī*	**oppid***a*
GEN.	**vi·***ārum*	of the roads	**amīc·***ōrum*	**oppid·***ōrum*
DAT.	**vi·***īs*	to, for the roads	**amīc·***īs*	**oppid·***īs*
ACC.	**vi·***ās*	the roads	**amīc·***ōs*	**oppid·***a*
ABL.	**vi·***īs*	from, by, with the roads	**amīc·***īs*	**oppid·***īs*

MASCULINE NOUNS OF THE SECOND DECLENSION IN *-er* AND *-ir*

	puer *m* boy		**ager** *m* field	**vir** *m* man

SINGULAR				
NOM.	**puer**	the boy	**ager**	**vir**
GEN.	**puer·***ī*	of the boy	**agr·***ī*	**vir·***ī*
DAT.	**puer·***ō*	to, for the boy	**agr·***ō*	**vir·***ō*
ACC.	**puer·***um*	the boy	**agr·***um*	**vir·***um*
ABL.	**puer·***ō*	from, by, with the boy	**agr·***ō*	**vir·***ō*

PLURAL				
NOM.	**puer·***ī*	the boys	**agr·***ī*	**vir·***ī*
GEN.	**puer·***ōrum*	of the boys	**agr·***ōrum*	**vir·***ōrum*
DAT.	**puer·***īs*	to, for the boys	**agr·***īs*	**vir·***īs*
ACC.	**puer·***ōs*	the boys	**agr·***ōs*	**vir·***ōs*
ABL.	**puer·***īs*	from, by, with the boys	**agr·***īs*	**vir·***īs*

MASCULINE AND FEMININE NOUNS OF THE THIRD DECLENSION
(CONSONANT STEM)   (i-STEM)

	dux *m* leader	**soror** *f* sister	**mons** *m* hill	**nāvis** *f* ship
	SINGULAR			
NOM.	dux	soror	mons	nāv·*is*
GEN.	duc·*is*	sorōr·*is*	mont·*is*	nāv·*is*
DAT.	duc·*ī*	sorōr·*ī*	mont·*ī*	nāv·*ī*
ACC.	duc·*em*	sorōr·*em*	mont·*em*	nāv·*em*
ABL.	duc·*e*	sorōr·*e*	mont·*e*	nāv·*e*
	PLURAL			
NOM.	duc·*ēs*	sorōr·*ēs*	mont·*ēs*	nāv·*ēs*
GEN.	duc·*um*	sorōr·*um*	mont·*ium*	nāv·*ium*
DAT.	duc·*ibus*	sorōr·*ibus*	mont·*ibus*	nāv·*ibus*
ACC.	duc·*ēs*	sorōr·*ēs*	mont·*ēs*	nāv·*ēs*
ABL.	duc·*ibus*	sorōr·*ibus*	mont·*ibus*	nāv·*ibus*

NEUTER NOUNS OF THE THIRD DECLENSION
(CONSONANT STEM)

	nōmen *n* name	**corpus** *n* body	**genus** *n* kind, sort
	SINGULAR		
NOM.	nōmen	corpus	genus
GEN.	nōmin·*is*	corpor·*is*	gener·*is*
DAT.	nōmin·*ī*	corpor·*ī*	gener·*ī*
ACC.	nōmen	corpus	genus
ABL.	nōmin·*e*	corpor·*e*	gener·*e*
	PLURAL		
NOM.	nōmin·*a*	corpor·*a*	gener·*a*
GEN.	nōmin·*um*	corpor·*um*	gener·*um*
DAT.	nōmin·*ibus*	corpor·*ibus*	gener·*ibus*
ACC.	nōmin·*a*	corpor·*a*	gener·*a*
ABL.	nōmin·*ibus*	corpor·*ibus*	gener·*ibus*

NEUTER NOUNS OF THE THIRD DECLENSION ENDING IN -e, -al, -ar (i-STEM)

	mare *n* sea	**animal** *n* animal	**exemplar** *n* example; copy
	SINGULAR		
NOM.	**mar·e**	**animal**	**exemplar**
GEN.	*mar·is*	*animāl·is*	*exemplār·is*
DAT.	**mar·ī**	**animāl·ī**	**exemplār·ī**
ACC.	**mar·e**	**animal**	**exemplar**
ABL.	**mar·ī**	**animāl·ī**	**exemplār·ī**
	PLURAL		
NOM.	**mar·ia**	**animāl·ia**	**exemplār·ia**
GEN.	*mar·ium*	*animāl·ium*	*exemplār·ium*
DAT.	**mar·ibus**	**animāl·ibus**	**exemplār·ibus**
ACC.	**mar·ia**	**animāl·ia**	**exemplār·ia**
ABL.	**mar·ibus**	**animāl·ibus**	**exemplār·ibus**

	FOURTH DECLENSION			**FIFTH DECLENSION**	
	MASCULINE	FEMININE	NEUTER	FEMININE	MASCULINE
	sinus *m* bay	**manus** *f* hand	**genū** *n* knee	**rēs** *f* thing; affair	**diēs** *m* day
	SINGULAR				
NOM.	**sin·us**	**man·us**	**gen·ū**	**r·ēs**	**di·ēs**
GEN.	*sin·ūs*	*man·ūs*	*gen·ūs*	*r·eī*	*di·eī*
DAT.	**sin·uī**	**man·uī**	**gen·ū**	**r·eī**	**di·ēī**
ACC.	**sin·um**	**man·um**	**gen·ū**	**r·em**	**di·em**
ABL.	**sin·ū**	**man·ū**	**gen·ū**	**r·ē**	**di·ē**
	PLURAL				
NOM.	**sin·ūs**	**man·ūs**	**gen·ua**	**r·ēs**	**di·ēs**
GEN.	*sin·uum*	*man·uum*	*gen·uum*	*r·ērum*	*di·ērum*
DAT.	**sin·ibus**	**man·ibus**	**gen·ibus**	**r·ēbus**	**di·ēbus**
ACC.	**sin·ūs**	**man·ūs**	**gen·ua**	**r·ēs**	**di·ēs**
ABL.	**sin·ibus**	**man·ibus**	**gen·ibus**	**r·ēbus**	**di·ēbus**

GREEK NOUNS: FIRST DECLENSION

	Aenēās *m* Aeneas	**Anchīsēs** *m* Anchises	**Daphnē** *f* Daphne
NOM.	Aenē·*ās*	Anchīs·*ēs*	Daphn·*ē*
GEN.	Aenē·*ae*	Anchīs·*ae*	Daphn·*ēs*
DAT.	Aenē·*ae*	Anchīs·*ae*	Daphn·*ae*
ACC.	Aenē·*ān*	Anchīs·*ēn*	Daphn·*ēn*
ABL.	Aenē·*ā*	Anchīs·*ē*	Daphn·*ē*
VOC.	Aenē·*ā*	Anchīs·*ē*	Daphn·*ē*

GREEK NOUNS: SECOND DECLENSION THIRD DECLENSION

	Tenedos *f* Tenedos	**Īlion** *n* Ilium (Troy)	**Dīdō** *f* Dido
NOM.	Tened·*os* *or* -*us*	Īli·*on* *or* -*um*	Dīdō
GEN.	Tened·*ī*	Īli·*ī*	Dīdōn·*is*
DAT.	Tened·*ō*	Īli·*ō*	Dīdōn·*ī*
ACC.	Tened·*on* *or* -*um*	Īli·*ōn* *or* -*um*	Dīdōn.em
ABL.	Tened·*ō*	Īli·*ō*	Dīdōn·*e*
VOC.	Tened·*ō*	Īli·*on* *or* -*um*	Dīdō

ADJECTIVES

ADJECTIVES: FIRST AND SECOND DECLENSIONS

	MASCULINE	FEMININE	NEUTER	MASCULINE	FEMININE	NEUTER

bon·us -a -um good

	SINGULAR			PLURAL		
NOM.	bon·*us*	bon·*a*	bon·*um*	bon·*ī*	bon·*ae*	bon·*a*
GEN.	bon·*ī*	bon·*ae*	bon·*ī*	bon·*ōrum*	bon·*ārum*	bon·*ōrum*
DAT.	bon·*ō*	bon·*ae*	bon·*ō*	bon·*īs*	bon·*īs*	bon·*īs*
ACC.	bon·*um*	bon·*am*	bon·*um*	bon·*ōs*	bon·*ās*	bon·*a*
ABL.	bon·*ō*	bon·*ā*	bon·*ō*	bon·*īs*	bon·*īs*	bon·*īs*

miser· -a -um poor, pitiful

	SINGULAR			PLURAL		
NOM.	miser	miser·*a*	miser·*um*	miser·*ī*	miser·*ae*	miser·*a*
GEN.	miser·*ī*	miser·*ae*	miser·*ī*	miser·*ōrum*	miser·*ārum*	miser·*ōrum*
DAT.	miser·*ō*	miser·*ae*	miser·*ō*	miser·*īs*	miser·*īs*	miser·*īs*
ACC.	miser·*um*	miser·*am*	miser·*um*	miser·*ōs*	miser·*ās*	miser·*a*
ABL.	miser·*ō*	miser·*ā*	miser·*ō*	miser·*īs*	miser·*īs*	miser·*īs*

āter ātr·a -um black

	SINGULAR			PLURAL		
NOM.	āter	ātr·*a*	ātr·*um*	ātr·*ī*	ātr·*ae*	ātr·*a*
GEN.	ātr·*ī*	ātr·*ae*	ātr·*ī*	ātr·*ōrum*	ātr·*ārum*	ātr·*ōrum*
DAT.	ātr·*ō*	ātr·*ae*	ātr·*ō*	ātr·*īs*	ātr·*īs*	ātr·*īs*
ACC.	ātr·*um*	ātr·*am*	ātr·*um*	ātr·*ōs*	ātr·*ās*	ātr·*a*
ABL.	ātr·*ō*	ātr·*ā*	ātr·*ō*	ātr·*īs*	ātr·*īs*	ātr·*ī*

THIRD DECLENSION: TWO ENDINGS

	MASC. & FEM.	NEUTER

THIRD DECLENSION: THREE ENDINGS

	MASCULINE	FEMININE	NEUTER

facilis easy   **ācer** sharp, shrill

	MASC. & FEM.	NEUTER	MASCULINE	FEMININE	NEUTER
SINGULAR					
NOM.	facil·*is*	facil·*e*	ācer	ācr·*is*	ācr·*e*
GEN.	facil·*is*	facil·*is*	ācr·*is*	ācr·*is*	ācr·*is*
DAT.	facil·*ī*	facil·*ī*	ācr·*ī*	ācr·*ī*	ācr·*ī*
ACC.	facil·*em*	facil·*e*	ācr·*em*	ācr·*em*	ācr·*e*
ABL.	facil·*ī*	facil·*ī*	ācr·*ī*	ācr·*ī*	ācr·*ī*
PLURAL					
NOM.	facil·*ēs*	facil·*ia*	ācr·*ēs*	ācr·*ēs*	ācr·*ia*
GEN.	facil·*ium*	facil·*ium*	ācr·*ium*	ācr·*ium*	ācr·*ium*
DAT.	facil·*ibus*	facil·*ibus*	ācr·*ibus*	ācr·*ibus*	ācr·*ibus*
ACC.	facil·*ēs*	facil·*ia*	ācr·*ēs*	ācr·*ēs*	ācr·*ia*
ABL.	facil·*ibus*	facil·*ibus*	ācr·*ibus*	ācr·*ibus*	ācr·*ibus*

THIRD DECLENSION: ONE ENDING

fēlīx lucky; happy   **prūdēns** prudent, wise   **vetus** old

	MASC. & FEM.	NEUTER	MASC. & FEM.	NEUTER	MASC. & FEM.	NEUTER
SINGULAR						
NOM.	fēlīx	fēlīx	prūdēns	prūdēns	vetus	vetus
GEN.	fēlīc·*is*	fēlīc·*is*	prūdent·*is*	prūdent·*is*	veter·*is*	veter·*is*
DAT.	fēlīc·*ī*	fēlīc·*ī*	prūdent·*ī*	prūdent·*ī*	veter·*ī*	veter·*ī*
ACC.	fēlīc·*em*	fēlīx	prūdent·*em*	prūdens	veter·*em*	vetus
ABL.	fēlīc·*ī*	fēlīc·*ī*	prūdent·*ī*	prūdent·*ī*	veter·*e*	veter·*e*
PLURAL						
NOM.	fēlīc·*ēs*	fēlīc·*ia*	prūdent·*ēs*	prūdent·*ia*	veter·*ēs*	veter·*a*
GEN.	fēlīc·*ium*	fēlīc·*ium*	prūdent·*ium*	prūdent·*ium*	veter·*um*	veter·*um*
DAT.	fēlīc·*ibus*	fēlīc·*ibus*	prūdent·*ibus*	prūdent·*ibus*	veter·*ibus*	veter·*ibus*
ACC.	fēlīc·*ēs*	fēlīc·*ia*	prūdent·*ēs*	prūdent·*ia*	veter·*ēs*	veter·*a*
ABL.	fēlīc·*ibus*	fēlīc·*ibus*	prūdent·*ibus*	prūdent·*ibus*	veter·*ibus*	veter·*ibus*

COMPARISON OF REGULAR ADJECTIVES AND ADVERBS

| POSITIVE | | COMPARATIVE | | SUPERLATIVE | |
ADJECTIVE	ADVERB	ADJECTIVE	ADVERB	ADJECTIVE	ADVERB
altus	altē	alt*ior*	alt*ius*	alt*issimus*	altissim*ē*
fortis	fortiter	fort*ior*	fort*ius*	fort*issimus*	fortissim*ē*
ācer	ācriter	āc*rior*	āc*rius*	acer*rimus*	acerrim*ē*
facilis	facile	facil*ior*	facil*ius*	facil*limus*	facillim*ē*
prudens	prūdenter	prūdent*ior*	prūdent*ius*	prūdent*issimus*	prūdentissim*ē*

DECLENSION OF THE COMPARATIVE

alt·us -a -um high; deep

| | **SINGULAR** | | **PLURAL** | |
	MASC. & FEM.	NEUTER	MASC. & FEM.	NEUTER
NOM.	altior	altius	altiōr·*ēs*	altiōr·*a*
GEN.	altiōr·*is*	altiōr·*is*	altiōr·*um*	altiōr·*um*
DAT.	altiōr·*ī*	altiōr·*ī*	altiōr·*ibus*	altiōr·*ibus*
ACC.	altiōr·*em*	altius	altiōr·*ēs*	altiōr·*ēs*
ABL.	altiōr·*e*	altiōr·*e*	altiōr·*ibus*	altiōr·*ibus*

IRREGULAR COMPARATIVE FORMS

MASC. FEM. NEUTER	MASC. & FEM. NEUTER	MASC. FEM. NEUTER
POSITIVE	**COMPARATIVE**	**SUPERLATIVE**
bon·us *-a -um* good	**mel*ior* mel*ius*** better	**optim·us** *-a -um* best
mal·us *-a um* bad	**pē*ior* pē*ius*** worse	**pessim·us** *-a -um* worst
parv·us *-a -um* small	**min*or* min*us*** smaller	**minim·us** *-a -um* smallest
magn·us *-a -um* big	**mā*ior* mā*ius*** bigger	**maxim·us** *-a -um* biggest
mult·us *-a -um* much	**plūs** *(neut. noun)* more	**plūrim·us** *-a -um* most
mult·ī *-ae -a* many	**plūr·ēs** *-a* more	**plūrim·ī** *-ae -a* most
īnfer·us *-a -um* below	**īnfer*ior* īnfer*ius*** lower	**īnfim·us** *-a - um* lowest
		īm·us *-a -um* lowest
super·us *-a -um* above	**super*ior* super*ius*** higher	**suprēm·us** *-a -um* highest
		summ·us *-a -um* highest
vetus, veter·is old	**vetust*ior* vetust*ius*** older	**veterrim·us** *-a -um* oldest
	pr*ior* pr*ius* former	**prīm·us** *-a -um* first
	prop*ior* prop*ius* nearer	**proxim·us** *-a -um* nearest, next
	ulter*ior* ulter*ius* farther	**ultim·us** *-a -um* farthest

DECLENSION OF NUMERALS

ūnus one   duo two

	SINGULAR			PLURAL ONLY		
	MASCULINE	FEMININE	NEUTER	MASCULINE	FEMININE	NEUTER
NOM.	ūnus	ūna	ūnum	duo	duae	duo
GEN.	ūnīus	ūnīus	ūnīus	duōrum	duārum	duōrum
DAT.	ūnī	ūnī	ūnī	duōbus	duābus	duōbus
ACC.	ūnum	ūnam	ūnum	duōs	duās	duo
ABL.	ūnō	ūnā	ūnō	duōbus	duābus	duōbus

trēs three   mīlle thousand   mīlia thousand(s)

	PLURAL ONLY		INDECLINABLE	PLURAL ONLY
	MASC. & FEM.	NEUTER	MASC., FEM., NEUTER	NEUTER
NOM.	trēs	tria	mīlle	mīlia
GEN.	trium	trium	mīlle	mīlium
DAT.	tribus	tribus	mīlle	mīlibus
ACC.	trēs	tria	mīlle	mīlia
ABL.	tribus	tribus	mīlle	mīlibus

PRONOUNS

DECLENSION OF PERSONAL PRONOUNS

	FIRST PERSON		SECOND PERSON		THIRD PERSON					

SINGULAR

NOM.	**ego**	I	**tū**	you	**is**	he	**ea**	she	**id**	it
GEN.	**meī**		**tuī**		**eius**		**eius**		**eius**	
DAT.	**mihi**		**tibi**		**eī**		**eī**		**eī**	
ACC.	**mē**		**tē**		**eum**		**eam**		**id**	
ABL.	**mē**		**tē**		**eō**		**eā**		**eō**	

PLURAL

NOM.	**nōs**	we	**vōs**	you	**eī**	they	**eae**	they	**ea**	they
GEN.	**nostrum**		**vestrum**		**eōrum**		**eārum**		**eōrum**	
	nostrī		**vestrī**							
DAT.	**nōbīs**		**vōbīs**		**eīs**		**eīs**		**eīs**	
ACC.	**nōs**		**vōs**		**eōs**		**eās**		**ea**	
ABL.	**nōbis**		**vōbis**		**eīs**		**eīs**		**eīs**	

DECLENSION OF REFLEXIVE PRONOUNS

	FIRST PERSON		SECOND PERSON		THIRD PERSON
	SINGULAR	PLURAL	SINGULAR	PLURAL	SINGULAR AND PLURAL
NOM.					
GEN.	**meī**	**nostrum**	**tuī**	**vestrum**	**suī**
DAT.	**mihi**	**nōbīs**	**tibi**	**vōbīs**	**sibi**
ACC.	**mē**	**nōs**	**tē**	**vōs**	**sē**
ABL.	**mē**	**nōbis**	**tē**	**vōbis**	**sē**

DECLENSION OF INTENSIVE PRONOUNS

	MASCULINE		FEMININE		NEUTER	
SINGULAR						
NOM.	ipse	himself	ipsa	herself	ipsum	itself
GEN.	ipsīus		ipsīus		ipsīus	
DAT.	ipsī		ipsī		ipsī	
ACC.	ipsum		ipsam		ipsum	
ABL.	ipsō		ipsā		ipsō	
PLURAL						
NOM.	ipsī	themselves	ipsae	themselves	ipsa	themselves
GEN.	ipsōrum		ipsārum		ipsōrum	
DAT.	ipsīs		ipsīs		ipsīs	
ACC.	ipsōs		ipsās		ipsa	
ABL.	ipsīs		ipsīs		ipsīs	

DECLENSION OF RELATIVE PRONOUNS

	MASCULINE	FEMININE	NEUTER	MASCULINE	FEMININE	NEUTER
	SINGULAR			PLURAL		
NOM.	quī	quae	quod	quī	quae	quae
GEN.	cuius	cuius	cuius	quōrum	quārum	quōrum
DAT.	cui	cui	cui	quibus	quibus	quibus
ACC.	quem	quam	quod	quōs	quās	quae
ABL.	quō	quā	quō	quibus	quibus	quibus

DECLENSION OF INTERROGATIVE PRONOUNS

	MASC. & FEM.	NEUTER	MASCULINE	FEMININE	NEUTER
	SINGULAR		PLURAL		
NOM.	quis	quid	quī	quae	quae
GEN.	cuius	cuius	quōrum	quārum	quōrum
DAT.	cui	cui	quibus	quibus	quibus
ACC.	quem	quid	quōs	quās	quae
ABL.	quō	quō	quibus	quibus	quibus

DECLENSION OF DEMONSTRATIVES

	MASCULINE	FEMININE	NEUTER	MASCULINE	FEMININE	NEUTER
	SINGULAR			PLURAL		

hic this

Nom.	hic	haec	hoc	hī	hae	haec
Gen.	huius	huius	huius	hōrum	hārum	hōrum
Dat.	huic	huic	huic	hīs	hīs	hīs
Acc.	hunc	hanc	hoc	hōs	hās	haec
Abl.	hōc	hāc	hōc	hīs	hīs	hīs

ille that

	SINGULAR			PLURAL		
Nom.	ille	illa	illud	illī	illae	illa
Gen.	illīus	illīus	illīus	illōrum	illārum	illōrum
Dat.	illī	illī	illī	illīs	illīs	illīs
Acc.	illum	illam	illud	illōs	illās	illa
Abl.	illō	illā	illō	illīs	illīs	illīs

īdem the same

	SINGULAR			PLURAL		
Nom.	īdem	eadem	idem	eīdem	eaedem	eadem
Gen.	eiusdem	eiusdem	eiusdem	eōrundem	eārundem	eōrundem
Dat.	eīdem	eīdem	eīdem	eīsdem	eīsdem	eīsdem
Acc.	eundem	eandem	idem	eōsdem	eāsdem	eadem
Abl.	eōdem	eādem	eōdem	eīsdem	eīsdem	eīsdem

First Conjugation -āre
amō amāre amāvī amātus to love

ACTIVE VOICE		*PASSIVE VOICE*	
SINGULAR	PLURAL	SINGULAR	PLURAL

INDICATIVE MOOD

PRESENT

am*ō* I love	am**ā***mus* we love	am**or**	am**ā***mur*
am**ā***s* you love	am**ā***tis* you love	am**ā***ris*	am**ā***minī*
am*at* he, she, it loves	am*ant* they love	am**ā***tur*	am*antur*

IMPERFECT

amā*bam*	amā*bāmus*	amā*bar*	amā*bāmur*
amā*bās*	amā*bātis*	amā*bāris*	amā*bāminī*
amā*bat*	amā*bant*	amā*bātur*	amā*bantur*

FUTURE

amā*bō*	amā*bimus*	amā*bor*	amā*bimur*
amā*bis*	amā*bitis*	amā*beris*	amā*biminī*
amā*bit*	amā*bunt*	amā*bitur*	amā*buntur*

PERFECT

amā*vī*	amā*vimus*	amātus sum	amātī sumus
amā*vistī*	amā*vistis*	amātus es	amātī estis
amā*vit*	amā*vērunt*	amātus est	amātī sunt

PLUPERFECT

amā*veram*	amā*verāmus*	amātus eram	amātī erāmus
amā*verās*	amā*verātis*	amātus erās	amātī erātis
amā*verat*	amā*verant*	amātus erat	amātī erant

FUTURE PERFECT

amā*verō*	amā*verimus*	amātus erō	amātī erimus
amā*veris*	amā*veritis*	amātus eris	amātī eritis
amā*verit*	amā*verint*	amātus erit	amātī erunt

IMPERATIVE MOOD

PRESENT

amā	amāte

Second Conjugation: -ēre
doceō docēre docuī doctus to teach

ACTIVE VOICE		*PASSIVE VOICE*	
SINGULAR	PLURAL	SINGULAR	PLURAL

INDICATIVE MOOD

PRESENT

doceō I teach	**docē***mus* we teach	**doce***or*	**docē***mur*
doce*s* you teach	**docē***tis* you teach	**docē***ris*	**docē***minī*
doce*t* he, she, it teaches	**doce***nt* they teach	**docē***tur*	**doce***ntur*

IMPERFECT

doc**ē***bam*	docē*bāmus*	docē*bar*	docē*bāmur*
docē*bās*	docē*bātis*	docē*bāris*	docē*bāminī*
docē*bat*	docē*bant*	docē*bātur*	docē*bantur*

FUTURE

docē*bō*	docē*bimus*	docē*bor*	docē*bimur*
docē*bis*	docē*bitis*	docē*beris*	docē*biminī*
docē*bit*	docē*bunt*	docē*bitur*	docē*buntur*

PERFECT

docu*ī*	docu*imus*	doctus sum	doctī sumus
docu*istī*	docu*istis*	doctus es	doctī estis
docu*it*	docu*ērunt*	doctus est	doctī sunt

PLUPERFECT

docu*eram*	docu*erāmus*	doctus eram	doctī erāmus
docu*erās*	docu*erātis*	doctus erās	doctī erātis
docu*erat*	docu*erant*	doctus erat	doctī erant

FUTURE PERFECT

docu*erō*	docu*erimus*	doctus erō	doctī erimus
docu*eris*	docu*eritis*	doctus eris	doctī eritis
docu*erit*	docu*erint*	doctus erit	doctī erunt

IMPERATIVE MOOD

PRESENT

docē	**docē***te*

Third Conjugation: -ĕre
scrībō scrībĕre scrīpsī scrīptus to write

ACTIVE VOICE		PASSIVE VOICE	
SINGULAR	PLURAL	SINGULAR	PLURAL

INDICATIVE MOOD

PRESENT

scrībō I write	scrībimus we write	scrībor	scrībimur
scrībis you write	scrībitis you write	scrīberis	scrībiminī
scrībit he, she, it writes	scrībunt they write	scrībitur	scrībuntur

IMPERFECT

scrībēbam	scrībēbāmus	scrībēbar	scrībēbāmur
scrībēbās	scrībēbātis	scrībēbāris	scrībēbāminī
scrībēbat	scrībēbant	scrībēbātur	scrībēbantur

FUTURE

scrībam	scrībēmus	scrībar	scrībēmur
scrībēs	scrībētis	scrībēris	scrībēminī
scrībet	scrībent	scrībētur	scrībentur

PERFECT

scrīpsī	scrīpsimus	scrīptus sum	scrīptī sumus
scrīpsistī	scrīpsistis	scrīptus es	scrīptī estis
scrīpsit	scrīpsērunt	scrīptus est	scrīptī sunt

PLUPERFECT

scrīpseram	scrīpserāmus	scrīptus eram	scrīptī erāmus
scrīpserās	scrīpserātis	scrīptus erās	scrīptī erātis
scrīpserat	scrīpserant	scrīptus erat	scrīptī erant

FUTURE PERFECT

scrīpserō	scrīpserimus	scrīptus erō	scrīptī erimus
scrīpseris	scrīpseritis	scrīptus eris	scrīptī eritis
scrīpserit	scrīpserint	scrīptus erit	scrīptī erunt

IMPERATIVE MOOD

PRESENT

scrībe	scrībite

Third Conjugation: -iō
capiō capĕre cēpī captus to take

	ACTIVE VOICE		PASSIVE VOICE	
	SINGULAR	PLURAL	SINGULAR	PLURAL

INDICATIVE MOOD

PRESENT

capiō I take	capimus we take	capior	capimur
capis you take	capitis you take	caperis	capiminī
capit he, she, it takes	capiunt they take	capitur	capiuntur

IMPERFECT

capiēbam	capiēbāmus	capiēbar	capiēbāmur
capiēbās	capiēbātis	capiēbāris	capiēbāminī
capiēbat	capiēbant	capiēbātur	capiēbantur

FUTURE

capiam	capiēmus	capiar	capiēmur
capiēs	capiētis	capiēris	capiēminī
capiet	capient	capiētur	capientur

PERFECT

cēpī	cēpimus	captus sum	captī sumus
cēpistī	cēpistis	captus es	captī estis
cēpit	cēpērunt	captus est	captī sunt

PLUPERFECT

cēperam	cēperāmus	captus eram	captī erāmus
cēperās	cēperātis	captus erās	captī erātis
cēperat	cēperant	captus erat	captī erant

FUTURE PERFECT

cēperō	cēperimus	captus erō	captī erimus
cēperis	cēperitis	captus eris	captī eritis
cēperit	cēperint	captus erit	captī erunt

IMPERATIVE MOOD

PRESENT

cape	capite

Fourth Conjugation: -īre
audiō audīre audīvī audītus to hear

ACTIVE VOICE		*PASSIVE VOICE*	
SINGULAR	PLURAL	SINGULAR	PLURAL

INDICATIVE MOOD

PRESENT

audiō I hear	**audīmus** we hear	**audior**	**audīmur**
audīs you hear	**audītis** you hear	**audīris**	**audīminī**
audit he, she, it hears	**audiunt** they hear	**audītur**	**audiuntur**

IMPERFECT

audiēbam	**audiēbāmus**	**audiēbar**	**audiēbāmur**
audiēbās	**audiēbātis**	**audiēbāris**	**audiēbāminī**
audiēbat	**audiēbant**	**audiēbātur**	**audiēbantur**

FUTURE

audiam	**audiēmus**	**audiar**	**audiēmur**
audiēs	**audiētis**	**audiēris**	**audiēminī**
audiet	**audient**	**audiētur**	**audientur**

PERFECT

audīvī	**audīvimus**	**audītus sum**	**audītī sumus**
audīvistī	**audīvistis**	**audītus es**	**audītī estis**
audīvit	**audīvērunt**	**audītus est**	**audītī sunt**

PLUPERFECT

audīveram	**audīverāmus**	**audītus eram**	**audītī erāmus**
audīverās	**audīverātis**	**audītus erās**	**audītī erātis**
audīverat	**audīverant**	**audītus erat**	**audītī erant**

FUTURE PERFECT

audīverō	**audīverimus**	**audītus erō**	**audītī erimus**
audīveris	**audīveritis**	**audītus eris**	**audītī eritis**
audīverit	**audīverint**	**audītus erit**	**audītī erunt**

IMPERATIVE MOOD

PRESENT

audī	**audīte**

Conjugation of *sum*
sum esse fuī futūrus to be

SINGULAR	PLURAL	SINGULAR	PLURAL

INDICATIVE MOOD

PRESENT		FUTURE	
sum	sumus	erō	erimus
es	estis	eris	eritis
est	sunt	erit	erunt

IMPERFECT		FUTURE PERFECT	
eram	erāmus	fuerō	fuerimus
erās	erātis	fueris	fueritis
erat	erant	fuerit	fuerint

PERFECT		PLUPERFECT	
fuī	fuimus	fueram	fuerāmus
fuistī	fuistis	fuerās	fuerātis
fuit	fuērunt	fuerat	fuerant

Conjugation of *possum*
possum posse potuī to be able

SINGULAR	PLURAL	SINGULAR	PLURAL

INDICATIVE MOOD

PRESENT		FUTURE	
possum	possumus	poterō	poterimus
potes	potestis	poteris	poteritis
potest	possunt	poterit	poterunt

IMPERFECT		FUTURE PERFECT	
poteram	poterāmus	potuerō	potuerimus
poterās	poterātis	potueris	potueritis
poterat	poterant	potuerit	potuerint

PERFECT		PLUPERFECT	
potuī	potuimus	potueram	potuerāmus
potuistī	potuistis	potuerās	potuerātis
potuit	potuērunt	potuerat	potuerant

Conjugation of *eō*
eō īre īvī *or* iī itūrus to go

SINGULAR	PLURAL	SINGULAR	PLURAL

INDICATIVE MOOD

PRESENT		FUTURE	
eō	īmus	ībō	ībimus
īs	ītis	ībis	ībitis
it	eunt	ībit	ībunt

IMPERFECT		FUTURE PERFECT	
ībam	ībāmus	īverō	īverimus
ībās	ībātis	īveris	īveritis
ībat	ībant	īverit	īverint

PERFECT		PLUPERFECT	
īvī *or* iī	īvimus *or* iimus	īveram	īverāmus
īvistī *or* īstī	īvistis *or* īstis	īverās	īverātis
īvit *or* iit	īvērunt *or* iērunt	īverat	īverant

Conjugation of *volō*
volō velle voluī to want

SINGULAR	PLURAL	SINGULAR	PLURAL

INDICATIVE MOOD

PRESENT		FUTURE	
volō	volumus	volam	volēmus
vīs	vultis	volēs	volētis
vult	volunt	volet	volent

IMPERFECT		FUTURE PERFECT	
volēbam	volēbāmus	voluerō	voluerimus
volēbās	volēbātis	volueris	volueritis
volēbat	volēbant	voluerit	voluerint

PERFECT		PLUPERFECT	
voluī	voluimus	volueram	voluerāmus
voluistī	voluistis	voluerās	voluerātis
voluit	voluērunt	voluerat	voluerant

Conjugation of *nōlō*
nōlō nōlle nōluī not to want

SINGULAR	PLURAL	SINGULAR	PLURAL

INDICATIVE MOOD

PRESENT | | **FUTURE** |
nōlō	nōlumus	nōlam	nōlēmus
nōn vīs	nōn vultis	nōlēs	nōlētis
nōn vult	nōlunt	nōlet	nōlent

IMPERFECT | | **FUTURE PERFECT** |
nōlēbam	nōlēbāmus	nōluerō	nōluerimus
nōlēbās	nōlēbātis	nōlueris	nōlueritis
nōlēbat	nōlēbant	nōluerit	nōluerint

PERFECT | | **PLUPERFECT** |
nōluī	nōluimus	nōlueram	nōluerāmus
nōluistī	nōluistis	nōluerās	nōluerātis
nōluit	nōluērunt	nōluerat	nōluerant

Conjugation of *ferō*
ferō ferre tulī lātus to bear, bring

SINGULAR	PLURAL	SINGULAR	PLURAL

INDICATIVE MOOD

PRESENT | | **FUTURE** |
erō	ferimus	feram	ferēmus
fers	fertis	ferēs	ferētis
fert	ferunt	feret	ferent

IMPERFECT | | **FUTURE PERFECT** |
ferēbam	ferēbāmus	tulerō	tulerimus
ferēbās	ferēbātis	tuleris	tuleritis
ferēbat	ferēbant	tulerit	tulerint

PERFECT | | **PLUPERFECT** |
tulī	tulimus	tuleram	tulerāmus
tulistī	tulistis	tulerās	tulerātis
tulit	tulērunt	tulerat	tulerant

A centered period indicates the point at which endings are attached. The nominative and genitive endings and the gender are given for nouns: **amīc·us -ī** *m*, **mater matr·is** *f.* The masculine, feminine, and neuter forms are given for adjectives: **clār·us -a -um, facil·is -is -e.** Adjectives of the third declension with one ending are followed by the genitive singular: **vetus veter·is.** For nouns and adjectives of the third declension, when the genitive form is not given in full, the ending *is* is italicized: **equ·es -it*is*** *m,* **adiac·ēns -ent*is*.** The following abbreviations occur:

abl	=	ablative	*E.*	=	East(ern)	*N.*	=	North(ern)
acc	=	accusative	*f*	=	feminine	*n*	=	neuter
adj	=	adjective	*gen*	=	genitive	*pl*	=	plural
adv	=	adverb	*indecl*	=	indeclinable	*prep*	=	preposition
conj	=	conjunction	*m*	=	masculine	*pron*	=	pronoun
dat	=	dative	*m/f*	=	masc. or fem.	*S.*	=	South(ern)

ā, ab *prep* (+ *abl*) from, away from; by; *(with name)* after

abeō abīre abīvī *or* **abiī abitūrus** to go away

abhinc *adv* from now; ago; **abhinc trēs annōs** three years ago

absum abesse āfuī āfutūrus (ab + *abl*) to be absent (from)

ac *conj* and

accēd·ō -ĕre accessī accessūrus (ad + *acc*) to go up to, approach

accip·iō -ĕre accēpī acceptus to accept; to receive

acclām·ō -āre -āvī -ātus to yell to

accol·a -ae *m/f* neighbor

ācer ācr·is ācr·e bitter, sharp; harsh; shrill; stern

ācerrimē *adv* very sharply

Achāt·ēs -ae *m* Achates *(Aeneas's right-hand man)*

aciēs aci·ēī *f* troops *(in battle formation),* battleline

ācriter *adv* hard, fiercely; bitterly; harshly; sternly

ad *prep* (+ *acc*) to, toward; at; on; to

the house of; **ad mē** to my house

adam·ō -āre -āvī -ātus to fall in love with

addūc·ō -ĕre addūxī adductus to take (to), lead (to)

adeō adīre adīvī *or* **adiī aditūrus** to go to, approach

adhūc *adv* still

adiac·ēns -ent*is* adjacent

adit·us -ūs *m* approach

admīrābil·is -is -e astonishing; admirable

admīrāti·ō -ōn*is* *f* admiration

admīr·or -ārī -ātus sum to admire; to be surprised at; to wonder at

adōr·ō -āre -āvī -ātus to adore

adsum adesse adfuī adfutūrus (+ *dat or* **ad** + *acc*) to be present (at)

adven·iō -īre advēnī adventūrus to come to, arrive

advent·us -ūs *m* arrival

advocāt·us -ī *m* defense lawyer

aedifici·um -ī *n* building

aedific·ō -āre -āvī -ātus to build

aedīl·is -is *m* aedile *(minister of public works)*

aegrē *adv* with difficulty

Aegypt·us -ī *f* Egypt

Aenē·ās -ae *(acc:* **Aenēān)** *m* Aeneas

aequ·or -or*is* *n* sea

aetern·us -a -um eternal

afflict·ō -āre -āvī -ātus to afflict, strike

Āfric·a -ae *f* Africa

ager agr·ī *m* field

agitāt·or -ōr*is* *m* driver

agit·o -āre -āvī -ātus to drive

agnōm·en -in*is* *n* nickname, honorary name

agō agĕre ēgī āctus to do; to drive; to spend *(time, life);* to plead *(cases in court)*

agricultūr·a -ae *f* agriculture, farming

āl·a -ae *f* wing

Alb·a Long·a -ae *f* Alba Longa *(mountain town S. of Rome)*

Albān·us -a -um Alban

alb·us -a -um white

aliēn·us -ī m alien, foreigner

aliquandō adv someday

aliquot indecl some

ali·us -a -ud other, another; alius
. . . ex aliō one . . . after another

allig·ō -āre -āvī -ātus to tie (to)

Alp·ēs -ium fpl the Alps

alt·er -era -erum the other (one); a
second (one)

alt·us -a -um high; deep

amābil·is -is -e lovable, loving

am·āns -antis adj loving; m/f lover;
m boyfriend; f girlfriend

Amāt·a -ae f Amata (wife of King
Latinus)

amāt·or -ōris m lover

ambul·ō -āre -āvī to walk

amīc·us -ī m friend

am·ō -āre -āvī -ātus to love

amoen·us -a -um pleasant

amor amōr·is m love

amplissim·us -a -um on a grand
scale

Amūli·us -ī m Amulius (brother of
Numitor and granduncle of
Romulus and Remus)

Anchīs·ēs -ae m Anchises (father of
Aeneas by Venus)

Anc·us Mārci·us -ī m Ancus
Marcius (fourth king of Rome)

Androcl·ēs -ae m Androcles (lion's
friend)

anim·al -ālis (gen pl -ium) n animal

anim·us -ī m mind; attention;
courage; heart (as seat of emo-
tions); animī attention (of several
people); in animo in mind

ann·us -ī m year

ante prep (+ acc) in front of; before

anteā adv before, previously

antequam conj before

antīqu·us -a -um ancient, old

Anti·um -ī n Antium (Volscan
town, modern Anzio, on Latium's
seacoast)

ānul·us -ī m ring

an·us -ūs f old lady

anxiē adv anxiously

Āpennīn·us -ī m the Apennines

aper·iō -īre -uī -tus to open

apertē adv obviously

Apoll·ō -inis m Apollo (god of the
sun and prophecy)

applaud·ō -ĕre applausī
applausus to applaud

apprehen·dō -dĕre -dī
apprehēnsus to apprehend,
arrest

approb·ō -āre -āvī -ātus to
approve of

appropinqu·ō -āre -āvī (+ dat or ad
+ acc) to approach

apt·us -a -um (+ dat) suitable;
ready

apud (prep + acc) near; in the writing of; at the home of; before, in
the presence of (a judge, magistrate); apud mē at my house

Āpūli·a -ae f Apulia (district of SE.
Italy)

aqu·a -ae f water

aquil·a -ae f eagle

Arachn·ē -ēs f Arachne (girl turned
into a spider by Minerva)

architect·us -ī m architect

arc·us -ūs m bow

Arde·a -ae f Ardea (Rutulian capital
city in Latium)

ārd·eō -ēre ārsī ārsūrus to burn, be
on fire; to catch fire

Ariadn·ē -ēs f Ariadne (daughter of

Minos, king of Crete)

ārid·us -a -um dry

arm·a -ōrum npl arms, weapons

armāri·um -ī n clothes chest

armāt·us -a -um armed

armill·a -ae f bracelet (worn on the
upper arm)

Arpīn·um -ī n Arpinum (birthplace
of Cicero and Marius)

arrog·āns -antis arrogant

arx arc·is (gen pl -ium) f citadel;
(fortified) hill

Ascani·us -ī m Ascanius (son of
Aeneas)

ascend·ō -ĕre -ī ascēnsus to climb
up; to rise

Asi·a -ae f Asia (Asia Minor)

aspect·us -ūs m sight

asper· -a -um rough

aspic·iō -ĕre aspexī aspectus to
look at

assent·iō -īre assēnsī assēnsūrus
(+ dat) to agree with

assign·ō -āre -āvī -ātus to assign

assūm·ō -ĕre -psī -ptus to assume;
to begin to wear

astr·um -ī n star

astūt·us -a -um shrewd

āter ātr·a -um black; dark

Athēn·ae -ārum fpl Athens

Athēniēns·is -is -e Athenian

āthlēt·a -ae m/f athlete

ātrāment·um -ī n ink

ātri·um -ī n atrium (central room),
reception hall

atrōx atrōc·is atrocious, cruel

audāx audāc·is bold

aud·iō -īre -īvī or -iī -ītus to hear

aug·eō -ēre auxī auctus to increase

aure·us -a -um gold, golden

aurīg·a -ae m charioteer

aur·um -ī *n* gold

auscult·ō -āre -āvī -ātus to listen to

aut *conj* or

autem *adv* however; now

auxili·um -ī *n* help

Aventīn·us -ī *m* Aventine (Hill)

avidē *adv* eagerly, avidly

avid·us -a -um eager, avid

av·is -is (*gen pl* **-ium**) *f* bird

avuncul·us -ī *m* uncle

av·us -ī *m* grandfather

balneol·um -ī *m* (small) bath

balne·um -ī *n* bathroom; (public) bath

basilic·a -ae *f* courthouse

bāsi·um -ī *n* kiss

beāt·us -a -um happy; blessed

bellicōs·us -a -um warlike

bell·um -ī *n* war

benĕ *adv* well

benevol·ēns -entis benevolent, kind-hearted

benevolenti·a -ae *f* kindness

benignē *adv* kindly, warmly

benign·us -a -um kind, benign

bēsti·a -ae *f* wild beast; **ad bēstiās dare** to condemn (*someone*) to be thrown to the wild beasts

bibliothēc·a -ae *f* library

bis *adv* twice

blandīment·um -ī *n* act of endearment

bon·us -a -um good

brac·ae -ārum *fpl* pants, trousers

bracchi·um -ī *n* arm

Brundisi·um -ī *n* Brundisium (*port town at end of the Appian Way*)

būbō būbōn·is *m* owl

bull·a -ae *f* locket

cad·ō -ĕre cecidī cāsūrus to fall

caed·ēs -is *f* the kill, slaughter; bloodshed

cael·um -ī *n* sky

Calabri·a -ae *f* Calabria (*district of Italy*)

calamitōs·us -a -um disastrous, calamitous

calam·us -ī *m* reed, "pencil"

calce·us -ī *n* shoe (*worn with toga*)

caldāri·um -ī *n* hot bath

calefac·iō -ĕre calefēcī calefactus to warm

cālīg·ō -inis *f* dense atmosphere

callid·us -a -um clever

calor calōr·is *m* heat

Campāni·a -ae *f* Campania (*district of Italy S. of Latium*)

Capitōlīn·us -a -um Capitoline

camp·us -ī *m* plain

can·is -is *m/f* dog

Cann·ae -ārum *fpl* Cannae (*town in S. Italy where the Romans suffered a major military defeat*)

cantic·um -ī *n* song

cant·ō -āre -āvī -ātus to sing

cap·iō -ĕre cēpī captus to take; to capture; to hold

Capitōli·um -ī *n* Capitoline Hill

capt·ō -āre -āvī -ātus to capture

Capu·a -ae *f* Capua (*city in Campania*)

caput capit·is *n* head; capital, chief city; source (*of a river*)

cārē *adv* dearly

cārissimē *adv* very dearly

cārius *adv* more dearly

Carthāg·ō -inis *f* Carthage

cār·us -a -um (+ *dat*) dear (to)

cas·a -ae *f* cottage, hut

castr·a -ōrum *npl* camp

cās·us -ūs *m* adventure

cathedr·a -ae *f* (teacher's) chair

Catilīn·a -ae *m* Catiline (*notorious politician*)

Catō -ōnis *m* Cato (*famous as a conservative*)

caud·a -ae *f* tail

caus·a -ae *f* cause; (+ *gen*) reason for; (legal) case; **causās agĕre** to plead cases, serve at the bar

cav·us -a -um hollow

cēd·ō -ĕre cessī cessūrus to go, come

celer -is -e swift, fast

celeriter *adv* fast, swiftly

celerius *adv* faster, more speedily

celerrimē *adv* fastest, very fast

cell·a -ae *f* storeroom; servant's room

cēn·a -ae *f* dinner

cēnācul·um -ī *n* apartment

cēn·ō -āre -āvī to eat dinner; to dine

centum *indecl* hundred

cerāt·us -a -um wax-; **tabula cerāta** wax tablet

Cerber·us -ī *m* Cerberus (*dog guarding the gates of the lower world*)

certām·en -inis *n* contest; (single) combat, duel

cert·ō -āre -āvī to fight, compete

cert·us -a -um certain; sure, unmistakable

cēter·us -a -um (*rarely sing*) other, the rest of

Char·ōn -ontis *m* Charon (*ferryman on the Styx*)

chart·a -ae *f* paper

cib·us -ī *m* food; meal

Cicer·ō -ōnis *m* Cicero (106-43 B.C.)

cinis ciner·is *m* ashes

Circ·ē -ēs *f* Circe (*an enchantress or witch*)

circiter *adv* approximately, about

circum *prep* (+ *acc*) around

Cisalpīn·us -a -um Cisalpine ("*this side, i.e., Roman side, of the Alps*")

cistern·a -ae *f* cistern

cito *adv* quickly

cīv·is -is (*gen pl* -ium) *m/f* citizen

clam *adv* secretly

clām·ō -āre -āvī -ātus to shout; to cheer

clārē *adv* aloud

clārit·ās -āt*is f* clarity; fame

clār·us -a -um famous; clear

class·is -is (*gen pl* -ium) *f* class

claudic·ō -āre -āvī to limp

claud·us -a -um lame

clēm·ēns -ent*is* clement, mild

cliēns client·is *m/f* client

clīvōs·us -a -um hilly

Cloeli·a -ae *f* (*brave girl who escaped from Etruscan captivity*)

Clūsi·um -ī *n* Clusium (*Etruscan town ruled by Lars Porsenna, about 90 miles N. of Rome*)

Cocl·ēs -it*is m* Horatius Cocles (*hero at the Sublician bridge*)

coep·ī -isse (*defective verb*) to begin; amāre coepisse to fall in love

cogit·ō -āre -āvī -ātus to think

cognōm·en -in*is n* family name, last name; honorary name; nickname

cognōsc·ō -ĕre cog/nōvī cognitus to find out, learn

cohors cohort·is *f* cohort

coll·is -is (*gen pl* -ium) *m* hill

colloc·ō -āre -āvī -ātus to locate

col·ō -ĕre -uī cultus to worship

colōni·a -ae *f* colony

columb·a -ae *f* dove

com·a -ae *f* hair

commīl·es -it*is m* fellow soldier

commod·us -a -um nice, obliging

commōt·us -a -um touched, moved; upset

commov·eō -ēre commōvī commōtus to touch, move; to upset

compar·ō -āre -āvī -ātus to get together, assemble

compluvi·um -ī *n* skylight (*to let in light and rain*)

compōn·ō -ĕre composuī compositus to write (*a book, etc.*)

compositi·ō -ōn*is f* composition

comprim·ō -ĕre compressī compressus to suppress, quash, crush

conclāv·e -is (*gen pl* -ium) *n* room

condici·ō -ōn*is f* condition; terms (*of an agreement*)

con·dō -dĕre -didī -ditus to found

confici·ō -ĕre confēcī confectus to accomplish

confīd·ēns -ent*is* confident, self-assured

confīd·ō -ĕre confīsus sum (+ *dat*) to trust

coniugāti·ō -ōn*is f* conjugation

cōnsīd·ō -ĕre cōnsēdī cōnsessūrus to sit down; to settle (*in a place*)

cōnsili·um -ī *n* plan; idea; cōnsilium capĕre to form a plan

cōnsist·ō -ĕre cōnstitī to stop, come to a stop

cōnsōbrīn·us -ī *m* cousin

cōnspect·us -ūs *m* sight; in cōnspectum venīre (+ *gen*) to come within sight (of)

cōnspic·iō -ĕre cōnspexī cōnspectus to catch sight of, spot

cōnspīrāti·ō -ōn*is f* conspiracy

cōnstitu·ō -ŭere -uī -ūtus to decide

cōnst·ō -āre cōnstitī to cost (*often with abl*)

cōnsul consul·is *m* consul

cōnsulār·is -is -e of consular rank

cōnsūm·ō -ĕre -psī -ptus to spend (*time*)

continuō *adv* immediately

continu·us -a -um continuous

contrā *prep* against, in opposition to

conven·iō -īre convēnī conventus *tr & intr* to come together with, meet

convert·ō -ĕre -ī conversus to turn, draw, attract

convīvi·um -ī *n* party

cōpi·a -ae *f* supply; copiae *fpl* troops, forces

cōpiōs·us -a -um abundant, copious

coqu·a -ae *f* cook

coqu·ō -ĕre coxī coctus to cook, bake

coqu·us -ī *m* cook

cor cord·is *n* heart

Corinthi·us -a -um Corinthian

Corinth·us -ī *f* Corinth

Coriol·ī -ōrum *mpl* Corioli (*town in Latium*)

Cornēli·us -ī *m* Cornelius (*Roman middle name*)

corn·ū -ūs *n* horn

corōn·a -ae *f* wreath; crown; corōna mūrālis mural crown (*awarded to the soldier first to penetrate the enemy's walls*)

corōn·ō -āre -āvī -ātus to crown

corpus corpor·is *n* body

corrig·ō -ĕre corrēxī corrēctus to correct

cotīdiē *adv* daily

crās *adv* tomorrow

crass·us -a -um thick

crēd·ō -ĕre crēdidī crēditūrus (+ *dat*) to believe, trust

cre·ō -āre -āvī -ātus to make, elect, appoint

crescō -ĕre crēvī crētūrus to grow

crūdēl·is -is -e cruel

cruent·us -a -um bloody

cubicul·um -ī *n* bedroom

culīn·a -ae *f* kitchen

culp·a -ae *f* fault, blame; **in culpā esse** to be at fault

culp·ō -āre -āvī -ātus to blame

cum *prep* (+ *abl*) with; against; **cum** *conj* when; since, because; **cum primum** *conj* as soon as

Cum·ae -ārum *fpl* Cumae (*seat of prophecy, located just N. of the Bay of Naples*)

Cupīd·ō -in*is* *m* Cupid

cup·iō -ĕre -īvī -ītus to wish for, desire, want

cūr *adv* why

cūri·a -ae *f* senate building

cūr·ō -āre -āvī -ātus to take care of, look after; to care for, like

curr·ō -ĕre cucurrī cursūrus to run

curr·us -ūs *m* chariot

curs·us -ūs *m* course; **cursus honōrum** political career

custōd·iō -īre -i/vī *or* **-iī -ītus** to guard

Cythēr·a -ōrum *npl* Cythera (*Greek island off the S. Peloponnese*)

Daphn·ē -ēs *f* Daphne (*woodland nymph, loved by Apollo*)

dē *prep* (+ *abl*) down from; from; about, concerning

de·a -ae *f* goddess

dēambul·ō -āre -a/vī to walk around, stroll

deb·eō -ēre -uī -itus (+ *inf*) to be obliged to, have to; to owe

decem *indecl* ten

dēcid·ō -ĕre -ī to fall down

decim·us -a -um tenth

dēcip·iō -ĕre dēcēpī dēceptus to deceive

dēclīnāti·ō -ōn*is* *f* declension

dēdic·ō -āre -āvī -ātus to dedicate

dēfend·ō -ĕre -ī dēfēnsus to defend

dēfess·us -a -um tired out, exhausted

dein(de) *adv* then

deinceps *adv* then, after that, from then on

dēlectāti·ō -ōn*is* *f* (source of) delight

dēlectāt·us -a -um delighted

dēlect·ō -are -āvī -ātus to delight; to entertain

dēlect·us -a -um *adj* select, choice

dēl·eō -ēre -ēvī -ētus to destroy; to wipe out

dēlici·ae -ārum *fpl* (source of) delight; pet

Delph·ī -ōrum *mpl* Delphi (*Greek religious site*)

dēmitt·ō -ĕre dēmīsī dēmissus to drop; to send down

dēmōnstr·ō -āre -āvī -ātus to point out, show

dēnāri·us -ī *m* denarius (*silver coin*)

dēnique *adv* finally

dēns dēnt·is (*gen pl* **-ium**) *m* tooth

dēns·us -a -um dense

dēscend·ō -ĕre dēscendī dēscēnsūrus to descend, come down

dēscrīb·ō -ĕre dēscrīpsī dēscrīptus to describe

dēser·ō -ĕre -uī -tus to desert

dēsīder·ō -āre -āvī -ātus to wish, desire

dēsil·iō -īre -uī to jump down

dēspērāt·us -a -um desperate

dēstru·ō -ĕre dēstrūxī dēstrūctus to destroy, tear down

dēsum dēĕsse dēfuī dēfutūrus to be lacking, be missing; (+ *dat*) fail (someone)

dēteg·ō -ĕre dētēxī dētēctus to uncover, detect

dētrah·ō -ĕre dētrāxī dētractus to take off, pull off (*clothes, shoes, ring*)

de·us -ī *m* god

dēven·iō -īre dēvēnī dēventūrus to come down

dēvor·ō -āre -āvī -ātus to devour

dext·er -(e)ra -(e)rum right; **ā dext(e)rā** on the right (side)

dīc·ō -ĕre dīxī dictus to say; **sēcum dīcĕre** to say to oneself

Dīdō Dīdōn·is *f* Dido (*Phoenician queen who founded Carthage*)

diēs, di·ēī *m* day; *f* time

difficil·is -is -e difficult

dignē *adv* deservedly, worthily

dignissimē *adv* very deservedly

dignius *adv* more deservedly

dign·us -a -um (+ *gen or abl*) worthy (of), deserving (of)

dīlig·ēns -ent*is* diligent, careful

dīmitt·ō -ĕre dīmīsī dīmissus to dismiss, let go

discēd·ō -ĕre discessī discessūrus to depart

discipul·a -ae *f* student

discipul·us -ī *m* student

disc·ō -ĕre didicī to learn

disput·ō -āre -āvī -ātus (dē + *abl*) to discuss

dissimil·is -is -e dissimilar, unlike

diū *adv* for a long time

diūtissimē *adv* for a very long time

diūtius *adv* longer; **nōn diūtius** no longer

dīvīnitus *adv* by divine agency

do dare dedī datus to give

doc·eō -ēre -uī doctus to teach

dolor dolōr·is *m* pain; grief

domestic·us -a -um home-, of a home; **domesticī** *mpl* domestics, servants

domicili·um -ī *n* home

domin·a -ae *f* owner, mistress, lady of the house

domin·us -ī *m* owner, master

dom·us -ūs *f* home; palace

dōn·um -ī *n* gift

dors·um -ī *n* back

ducent·ī -ae -a two hundred

dūc·ō -ĕre dūxī ductus to take, lead, guide

dulc·is -is -e sweet

dum *conj* as long as; while

duo duae duo two

duodecim *indecl* twelve

duodēvīgintī *indecl* eighteen

dūr·us -a -um tough, hardy

dux duc·is *m/f* general; leader

ē, ex *prep* (+ *abl*) out of; of; from

... on; by

ea *pron* she

ecce! look!, lo and behold!

ēd·ō ēdĕre ēdidī ēditus to edit; to produce, put on (*public entertainment*)

ēduc·ō -āre -āvī -ātus to raise (*children, animals, crops*)

ēdūc·ō -ĕre ēdūxī ēductus to lead out

effug·iō -ĕre effūgī effūgitūrus to escape

ego *pron* I

eius (*gen of* is, ea, id) his, her, its

ēleg·āns -antis elegant

ēleganter *adv* elegantly

ēmend·ō -āre āvī -ātus to emend, correct

ēmin·ēns -entis eminent, outstanding

ēmitt·ō -ĕre ēmīsī ēmissus to send out

em·ō -ĕre ēmī ēmptus to buy

enim *conj* for; *adv* indeed

eō *adv* there, to that place

eō īre īvī or iī ītūrus to go

epistul·a -ae *f* letter

equ·es -itis *m* equestrian, knight

equidem *adv* indeed

equ·us -ī *n* horse

ergō *adv* therefore

Ēridan·us -ī *m* Po River (*called Eridanus by the Greeks*)

err·ō -āre -āvī -ātūrus to roam

error errōr·is *m* mistake

ērump·ō -ĕre ērūpī ēruptum to break out, rush out

ēsur·iō -īre to be hungry

et *conj* and; **et ... et** both ... and

etiam *adv* also; even; (*in answer*) yes

Etrūri·a -ae *f* Etruria (*district of Italy N. of Latium*)

Etrūsc·us -a -um Etruscan

Eurydic·ē -ēs *f* Eurydice (*wife of Orpheus*)

ēven·iō -īre ēvēnī ēventūrus to come out, emerge; to turn out

ex *prep* (+ *abl*) out of; of; from; from ... on; by

exanimāt·us -a -um fainting

exanim·us -a -um out of breath, breathless

excell·ēns -entis excellent; outstanding

excell·ō -ĕre -uī to excel

excip·iō -ĕre excēpī exceptus to welcome; to except, exclude

excit·ō -āre -āvī -ātus to excite

exempl·ar -āris *n* copy; example

exeō exīre exīvī or exiī exitūrus to go out, exit

exerc·eō -ēre -uī -itus to practice; to train

exerciti·um -ī *n* exercise (*esp. written*)

exercit·us -ūs *m* army

exit·us -ūs *m* way out, exit

expell·ō -ĕre expulī expulsus drive out, expel

expīr·ō -āre -āvī -ātus to breathe out

exprim·ō -ĕre expressī expressus to express

expugn·ō -āre -āvī -ātus to storm, capture

expuls·us -a -um (having been) expelled (*see* expellō)

exscrīb·ō -ĕre exscrīpsī exscrīptus (ex + *abl*) to copy (from); **fūrtim exscrībĕre** to cheat

exspect·ō -āre -āvī -ātus to wait for; to expect

extrā *prep* (+ *acc*) outside; beyond

exu·ō -ĕre -ī exūtus to take off (*clothes*)

fab·er -rī *m* craftsman; **faber ferrārius** blacksmith

fabric·ō -āre -āvī -ātus to make, put together, construct

fābul·a -ae *f* story

faci·ēs -ēī *f* face

facile *adv* easily

facil·is -is -e easy

fac·iō -ĕre fēcī factus to make; to do; **negōtium facĕre** to do, carry on business

fact·um -ī *n* deed

falsō *adv* falsely

fals·us -a -um false

Faustul·us -ī *m* Faustulus (*shepherd who found Romulus and Remus*)

fav·eō -ēre fāvī fautūrus (+ *dat*) to favor

fēlīciter *adv* happily

fēlīx fēlīc·is happy; lucky; successful

fēmin·a -ae *f* woman

fer·a -ae *f* wild animal

fermē *adv* about, approximately

ferō ferre tulī lātus to bring, bear

ferōci·a -ae *f* ferocity

ferōcissimē *adv* very fiercely

ferōciter *adv* fiercely

ferōcius *adv* more fiercely

fer·ōx -ōcis fierce

fer·us -a -um wild, fierce

fēst·us -a -um festive; **diēs fēstus** holiday

fībul·a -ae *f* safety pin, clasp (*to pin the toga, stola, etc.*)

fid·ēs -ēī *f* faith, trust; word (of honor); **fidem servāre** to keep

one's word

fīd·us -a -um loyal, trusty, faithful

fīli·a -ae *f* daughter

fīliol·a -ae *f* little daughter

fīli·us -ī *m* son

fīl·um -ī *n* thread

fīn·is -is (*gen pl* **-ium**) *m* end

fīō fierī factus sum to become; to take place

firmiter *adv* firmly

firm·us -a -um firm

flamm·a -ae *f* flame

flāv·us -a -um yellow

fleō flēre flēvī flētus to cry, weep

flexuōs·us -a -um winding, twisting

Flōrenti·a -ae *f* Florence (*town in N. Italy*)

flōs flōr·is *m* flower

fluct·us -ūs *m* wave

flūm·en -inis *n* river

flu·ō -ĕre flūxī flūxūrus to flow

fluvi·us -ī *m* river

fodic·ō -āre -āvī -ātus to stab

foli·um -ī *n* leaf

fōns font·is *m* spring

forīs *adv* outside, out of doors

formōs·us -a -um beautiful, shapely

forte *adv* by chance; **forte esse** to happen to be; **forte vidēre** to happen to see

fortitūd·ō -inis *f* gallantry

fort·is -is -e brave

fortissimē *adv* very bravely

fortiter *adv* bravely

fortius *adv* more bravely

for·um -ī *n* forum, marketplace

frag·or -ōris *m* crash, noise

frāter frātr·is *m* brother

fremit·us -ūs *m* roar

frequent·ō -āre -āvī -ātus to attend (*school*)

frīgidāri·um -ī *n* cold bath

frīgidul·us -a -um cool

frīgid·us -a -um cold

frūstrā *adv* in vain

fug·iō -ĕre fūgī fugitūrus to flee

fuī *see* **sum**

fulgur fulgur·is *n* flash of lightning

fulmen fulm·inis *n* bolt of lightning

fūm·us -ī *m* smoke

fundāment·um -ī *n* foundation

fund·ō -āre -āvī -ātus to found, establish

fund·ō -ĕre fūdī fūsus to shed (*tears*)

fund·us -ī *m* farm

fūrtim *adv* secretly, on the sly, stealthily

futūr·a -ōrum *npl* the future

Gāi·a -ae *f* Gaia (*female name*)

Gāi·us -ī *m* Gaius (*Roman first name*)

gale·a -ae *f* helmet

Galli·a -ae *f* Gaul (*now modern France*)

gaudi·um -ī *n* joy

gemin·ī -ōrum *mpl* twins

gemm·a -ae *f* jewel

gemmāri·us -ī *m* jeweler

gem·ō -ĕre -uī -itūrus to sigh

gener·ō -āre -āvī -ātus to father, have, produce

gēns gēnt·is *f* clan, extended family; people, nation, country

gen·ū -ūs *n* knee

genus gener·is *n* kind, sort

Germāni·a -ae *f* Germany

gerō gerĕre gessī gestus to wear *(clothes)*; to carry, bear; to hold *(office)*

gladiāt·or -ōr*is* *m* gladiator

gladi·us -ī *m* sword

glōri·a -ae *f* glory, fame

gradātim *adv* gradually, step by step

Graeci·a -ae *f* Greece

Graec·us -a -um Greek

grammatic·a -ae *f* grammar

grammatic·us -ī *m* teacher *(of literature and literary criticism)*

grāt·us -a -um attractive, pleasing

gravid·us -a -um heavy

grav·is -is -e heavy

graviter *adv* seriously

hab·eō -ēre -uī -itus to have

habit·ō -āre -āvī to live, dwell

hāctenus *adv* thus far; **haec hāctenus** enough of this

haec *pro & adj* this

haur·iō -īre hausī haustus to draw

Hecub·ē -ēs *(or* **·a -ae)** *f* Hecuba *(wife of Priam, king of Troy)*

Helen·ē -ēs *(or* **·a -ae)** *f* Helen *(wife of Menelaus, king of Sparta)*

herb·a -ae *f* grass

hic haec hoc *pron & adj (gen* **huius)** this; the latter

hiems hiem·is *f* winter

histori·a -ae *f* history

hoc *pron & adj* this

hodiē *adv* today; **hodiē māne** this morning

Homēr·us -ī *m* Homer

homō homin·is *m* person; **hominēs** *mpl* people

honor honōr·is *m* honor; (high) office

hōr·a -ae *f* hour **in hōrās** from hour to hour

hort·us -ī *m* garden; **hortī** *mpl* park

hosp·es -it*is* *m/f* guest

hospiti·um -ī *n* guest room

hostīl·is -is -e (+ *dat*) hostile (to)

host·is -is *m* enemy

hūc *adv* here, to this place

hūmāniter *adv* humanly; humanely, kindly

hūmān·us -a -um human; humane, kind

humil·is -is -e low

iac·eō -ēre -uī to lie, be located

iam *adv* already; now; **iam diū** for a long time; **iam dūdum** long ago; **nōn iam** no longer

iānu·a -ae *f* entrance, door

id *pron* it

īdem eadem idem *pron & adj* the same

identidem *adv* again and again

idōne·us -a -um (+ *dat*, **ad** + *acc*, **in** + *acc*) suitable, fit (for)

Īd·ūs -uum *fpl only* the Ides

igitur *adv* and so, therefore

ign·is -is (*gen pl* **-ium**) *m* fire

ignōr·ō -āre -āvī -ātus not to know

ignōsc·ō -ĕre ignōvī (+ *dat*) to pardon, forgive

īlicō *adv* on the spot, in (his, her, its) tracks

Īli·on -ī *(or* **·um -ī)** *n* Ilion *(another name for Troy)*

ill·e -a -ud *pron & adj* that; **ille . . . hic** the former . . . the latter

illūmin·ō -āre -āvī -ātus to illuminate

illustr·is -is -e famous, illustrious

imāg·ō -in*is* *f* bust; statue; picture

imber imbr·is *m* rain

imbrifer··ī *m* rain-bringer

immigr·ō -āre -āvī -ātūrus to move into *(a home, a place)*; to immigrate

immin·ēns -ent*is* imminent

immortāl·is -is -e immortal

imper·ō -āre -āvī imperātūrus (+ *dat*) command, order

impet·us -ūs *m* attack; **impetum facĕre** to mount an attack

implōr·ō -āre -āvī -ātus to implore, beg for

impluvi·um -ī *n* rain basin *(built into the floor of the atrium)*

impūnē *adv* safely

īm·us -a -um lowest

in *prep* (+ *acc*) into; to; against; (+ *abl*) in; on; among

inaur·ēs -ium *fpl* earrings

incend·ō -ĕre -ī incēnsus to set on fire

incip·iō -ĕre incēpī inceptus to begin

incol·a -ae *m/f* inhabitant

incolum·is -is -e unharmed

inde *adv* from there

indign·us -a -um (+ *gen or abl*) unworthy (of)

īnf·āns -ant*is* *m/f* infant, baby

īnferi·ae -ārum *fpl* funeral rites

īnfer·ior -ior -ius lower, inferior

īnfer·us -a -um below

īnfest·us -a -um hostile

īnfim·us -a - um lowest

īnfirm·us -a -um weak

īnflamm·ō -āre -āvī -ātus to set on fire

īnfrā *prep* (+ *acc*) below; south of

ing·ēns -ent*is* huge, mighty

ingrāt·us -a -um ungrateful

inic·io -ĕre iniēcī iniectus to throw in, throw on; to thrust in

inimīc·us -a -um unfriendly; **inimīcus** *m* (personal) enemy

initiō *adv* in the beginning, initially

innoc·ēns -ent*is* innocent; harmless

innocenter *adv* innocently; harmlessly

inopi·a -ae *f* lack; scarcity

inquīr·ō -ĕre inquīsīvī inquīsītus to ask

inquit he/she says (*used with direct quotations*)

inru·ō -ĕre -ī to rush in

inspic·iō -ĕre īnspexī īnspectus to look at, inspect

īnstru·ō -ĕre īnstrūxī īnstrūctus to draw up, deploy (*troops*)

īnsul·a -ae *f* island; apartment building (*so called because taking up a whole block*)

intelleg·ō -ĕre intellēxī intellēctus to understand

intellig·ēns -ent*is* intelligent

inter *prep* (+ *acc*) between, among; during

interdiū *adv* during the day

interdum *adv* sometimes

interim *adv* meanwhile

interrogāt·um -ī *n* question

interrog·ō -āre -āvī -ātus to ask, question

inter·sum -esse -fuī -futūrus (+ *dat*) to attend

interven·iō -īre intervēnī interventūrus to come between, intervene

intrā *prep* (+ *acc*) within, inside

intr·ō -āre -āvī to enter

intrō·dūcō -dūcĕre -dūxī -ductus

to bring in, introduce

intus *adv* inside

inūsitāt·us -a -um unusual

invād·ō -ĕre invāsī invāsus to attack, strike; to invade

inven·iō -īre invēnī inventus to come upon, find, discover

inventi·ō -ōn*is* *f* discovery

invīt·ō -āre -āvī -ātus to invite

ips·e -a -um *pron* himself, herself, itself; (*placed before the word*) the very . . .

īr·a -ae *f* ire, rage

irrēp·ō -ĕre -sī -tūrus to sneak in

is ea id *pron & adj* that; (*as simple pron*) he, she, it

ist·e -a -ud *pron* that

ita *adv* so

Ital·ī -ōrum *mpl* Italians

Itali·a -ae *f* Italy

itaque *adv* and so, therefore

iter itiner·is *n* trip, journey; way (*military*) march; **iter facĕre** to travel; (**in** + *acc*) to march against, into

iterum *adv* again

iub·eō -ēre iussī iussus to order, tell, bid

iucund·us -a -um pleasant

iung·ō -ĕre iūnxī iūnctus to join

Iūni·us -a -um June, of June

Iūnō Iūnōn·is *f* Juno (*queen of the gods, wife of Jupiter*)

Iuppiter Iov·is *m* Jupiter (*king of the gods*)

iūs iūr·is *n* law, right(s)

iussū *n* (*abl*) (+ *gen*) at the order of

iuven·is -is *m/f* youngster; *m* young man, youth; *f* young woman

iūxtā *prep* (+ *acc*) next to

labyrinth·us -ī *m* labyrinth

lacern·a -ae *f* cape

lacōnic·um -ī *n* sauna

lacrim·a -ae *f* tear

laet·us -a -um happy

lamb·ō -ĕre -ī -itus to lick

lani·ō -āre -āvī -ātus to tear up

larāri·um -ī *n* shrine *or* altar to the household gods

Lārenti·a -ae *f* Larentia (*wife of Faustulus*)

Lars Lart·is Porsenn·a -ae *m* Lars Porsenna (*Etruscan king of Clusium*)

lat·eō -ēre -uī to hide

Latīnē *adv* (in) Latin

Latīn·us -a -um Latin

Latīn·us -ī *m* Latinus (*king of Latium*)

Lati·um -ī *n* Latium (*district of Italy S. of Etruria*)

latrīn·a -ae *f* latrine, toilet

lāt·us -a -um wide

laur·us -ī *f* laurel tree

laus laud·is *f* praise

Lāvīni·a -ae *f* Lavinia (*daughter of King Latinus*)

lav·ō -āre lāvī lautus to wash

lectul·us -ī *m* (little) bed

lect·us -ī *m* bed

lēgāt·us -ī *m* ambassador

legiō legiōn·is *f* legion, division (*about 5000 men*)

leg·ō -ĕre lē/gi lēctus to read

leō leōn·is *m* lion

lepus lepor·is *m* hare

lēv·is -is -e *adj* smooth

lēx lēg·is *f* law

libenter *adv* gladly, willingly

liber libr·ī *m* book

līberāl·is -is -e liberal, generous

līber·ō -āre -āvī -ātus to free

librāri·a -ae *f* bookstore

lign·um -ī *n* wood

litter·a -ae *f* letter *(of alphabet)*; litterae letter *(in correspondence)*

litterāt·or -ōris *m* elementary
school teacher

lītus lītor·is *n* shore

loc·us -ī place (loc·a -ōrum *npl)*;
passage *(in a book)* (loc·ī -ōrum
mpl)

longinqu·us -a -um distant

long·us -a -um long

loqu·or -ī locūtus sum to speak,
say

Lūcāni·a -ae *f* Lucania *(district in S.
Italy)*

lūd·ō -ĕre lūsī lūsus to play

lūd·us -ī *m* play; school; lūdus
scaenicus stage play

lup·a -ae *f* wolf

lūx lūc·is *f* light; prīmā lūce at
dawn

magis *adv* more; rather; magis
magisque more and more

magist·er -rī *m* teacher; lūdī magister school teacher

magistr·a -ae *f* teacher

magistrat·us -ūs *m* office, magistracy; magistrate, official

magnific·us -a -um magnificent

magnitūd·ō -inis *f* size

magnopere *adv* greatly

magn·us -a -um big; great; loud
(sound); intense *(heat, light)*

mā·ior -ior -ius bigger; māior nātū
older

māiōr·ēs -um *mpl* ancestors

male *adv* badly

mal·us -a -um bad

māl·us -ī *f* apple tree

mandāt·um -ī *n* order, instruction

manēdum! wait a minute!

man·eō -ēre mānsī mānsūrus to
stay, remain

mānēs mān·ium *mpl* ghosts

Mantu·a -ae *f* Mantua *(town in N.
Italy)*

man·us -ūs *f* hand; band, group

Mārc·us -ī *m* Marcus, Mark

mar·e -is *(gen pl* -ium) *n* sea

margarīt·a -ae *f* pearl

marīn·us -a -um sea-, of the sea

marīt·us -ī *m* husband

Mār·s -tis *m* Mars *(god of war)*

māter mātr·is *f* mother

mātrimōni·um -ī *n* marriage; in
mātrimōnium dare to give in
marriage in mātrimōnium
dūcĕre to marry

maximē *adv* very much; most,
especially; very loudly

maxim·us -a -um biggest, largest;
greatest

mē *pron* me *(acc & abl)*

mediā nocte at midnight

meī *pron (gen of* ego) of me

mel·ior -ior -ius better

melius *adv* better

mem·or -oris *adj (+ gen)* mindful of

mend·um -ī *n* error, mistake *(esp.
in writing)*; mendum facĕre to
make a mistake

mēns ment·is *f* mind

mēns·is -is *(gen pl* -ium) *m* month

Mercuri·us -ī *m* Mercury *(messenger of the gods)*

merīdi·ēs -ēī *m* midday

me·us -a -um my

migr·ō -āre -āvī to move *(from one
residence to another)*

mihi *pron (dat of* ego) to me

mīles milit·is *m* soldier

mīlit·ō -āre -āvī to serve *(as a soldier)*, be in the army

mille *indecl* thousand; duo milia
(+ gen) two thousand

Minerv·a -ae *f* Minerva *(goddess of
wisdom)*

minimē *adv* least; not at all;
minimē vērō not at all

minim·us -a -um smallest, least;
youngest

min·or -or -us less; younger;
minor nātū younger

Mīn·ōs -ōis *m* Minos *(king of Crete)*

Mīnōtaur·us -ī *m* Minotaur

minus *adv* less

mīrācul·um -ī *n* strange sight

mīrific·us -a -um interesting, surprising

mīr·us -a -um wonderful; strange

Mīsēn·um -ī *n* Misenum *(town
near Naples)*

miser· -a -um poor, pitiful, miserable

mitt·ō -ĕre mīsī missus to send; to
shoot *(an arrow)*

modo *adv* just now

mod·us -ī *m* way, manner

moen·ia -ium *npl* the walls *(of a
town or fortress)*

mon·eō -ēre -uī -itus to warn; to
remind

monīl·e -is *n* necklace; monīle
bacātum pearl necklace

mōns mont·is *(gen pl* -ium) *m*
mountain, hill

mōnstr·ō -āre -āvī -ātus to show

mōnstr·um -ī *n* monster

montān·us -a -um mountainous

mor·a -ae *f* delay

more *prep* (+ *abl*) like, in the manner of

mor·ior -ī mortuus sum to die

mors mort·is (*gen pl* **-ium**) *f* death; **ad mortem dare** to put to death

mortu·us -a -um *adj* dead; **mortuī** *mpl* the dead

mōr·us -ī *f* mulberry tree

mov·eō -ēre mōvī mōtus to move; to cause, stir; to wag (*the tail*)

mox *adv* soon; (*in a series*) then, next

Mūci·us -ī *m* Mucius (*first name of Mucius Scaevola*)

mult·a -ōrum *npl* many things, much

mult·ī -ae -a many

multō *adv* (by) much

multum *adv* much, a lot

mult·us -a -um much

mūn·us -eris *n* gift; show (*esp. gladiatorial*)

mūrāl·is -is -e wall-, mural; **corōna mūrālis** mural crown (*military award for being the first to penetrate the enemy's wall*)

mūr·us -ī *m* wall

mūs mūr·is (*gen pl* **-ium**) *m* mouse

mūt·ō -āre -āvī -ātus to change

mūtu·us -a -um mutual

nam *conj* for, since

nārr·ō -āre -āvī -ātus to tell, relate

nāscor nāscī nātus sum to be born

natāti·ō -ōnis *f* swimming

nat·ō -āre -āvī to swim

naut·a -ae *m* sailor

nāvicul·a -ae *f* boat

nāvigi·um -ī *n* boat

nāvig·ō -āre -āvī to sail

nāv·is -is (*gen pl* **-ium**) *f* ship

ne *interrog. particle expecting yes or no*

Neāpolītān·us -a -um of Naples

nec·ō -āre -āvī -ātus to kill

negleg·ēns -entis negligent, careless, indifferent

neg·ō -āre -āvī -ātus to say no

negōti·um -ī *n* business; **negōtium gerĕre** to do business

nēm·ō -inis *m* no one

nep·ōs -ōtis *m* grandson

Neptūn·us -ī *m* Neptune (*god of the sea*)

neque . . . neque neither . . . nor

nesc·iō -īre -īvī *or* **-iī -ītus** not to know

nihil *indecl* nothing

nimis *adv* too

nix niv·is (*gen pl* **-ium**) *f* snow

nōbil·is -is -e noble

noc·eō -ēre -uī (+ *dat*) to harm

noctū *adv* at night, by night

nōlō nōlle nōluī to be unwilling, not want

nōm·en -inis *n* name; clan name, middle name (*of Roman citizen*)

nōmin·ō -āre -āvī -ātus to call (*by name*); to mention by name; to name

nōn *adv* not; **nōn iam** no longer

nōnāgintā *indecl* ninety

nōndum *adv* not yet

nōngent·ī -ae -a nine hundred

nōnne *adv* (*interrog. expecting a positive answer*) isn't it true that?

nōn·us -a -um ninth

nōs (*pron*) we; us

nōscit·ō -āre -āvī to recognize

nōsc·ō -ĕre nōvī nōtus to get to know, become familiar with

nos·ter -tra -trum our

not·ō -āre -āvī -ātus to notice

nōt·us -a -um well-known

novem *indecl* nine

nōv·ī -isse (*defective verb*) to know, be familiar with; **nōvistīne?** do you know?

nov·us -a -um new

nox noct·is (*gen pl* **-ium**) *f* night; **ad multam noctem** until late at night

nūb·ēs -is (*gen pl* **-ium**) *f* cloud

nūb·ō -ĕre nupsī nuptum to marry (*of a woman*)

nūll·us -a -um no

num *adv* (*interrog. expecting a negative answer*) it isn't, is it?

Num·a -ae Pompili·us -ī *m* Numa Pompilius (*second king of Rome*)

nūm·en -inis *n* supernatural power, deity, god

Numit·or -ōris *m* Numitor (*last Alban king, grandfather of Romulus and Remus*)

numquam *adv* never

nunc *adv* now; **nunc . . . nunc** now . . . now, first . . . then

nūnti·ō -āre -āvī -ātus to announce

nūnti·us -ī *m* messenger

nūper *adv* recently

nūperrimē *adv* most recently

nymph·a -ae *f* nymph

ob *prep* (+ *acc*) because of; for

obēdi·ēns -entis obedient

obēd·iō -īre -īvī (*or* **-iī**) **-ītūrus** (+ *dat*) obey

obscūr·ō -āre -āvī -ātus to obscure

obscūr·us -a -um dark

obsecr·ō -āre -āvī -ātus to beg, entreat

observ·ō -āre -āvī -ātus to watch

obses obsid·is *m/f* hostage

obsid·eō -ēre obsēdī obsessus to besiege, blockade

occīd·ō -ĕre -ī occīsus to kill

occultē *adv* secretly

occult·us -a -um hidden

occup·ō -āre -āvī -ātus to occupy

ōcean·us -ī *m* ocean

octāv·us -a -um eighth

octingent·ī -ae -a eight hundred

octō *indecl* eight

octōgintā *indecl* eighty

ocul·us -ī *m* eye

ōd·ī -isse (*defective verb*) to hate

offend·ō -ĕre -ī offēnsus to offend

officīn·a -ae *f* workshop

ōlim *adv* once (upon a time)

Olympi·us -a -um Olympian

Olymp·us -ī *m* Olympus (*mountain in N. Greece*)

omnipot·ēns -ent*is* omnipotent, almighty

omn·is -is -e every, all

oppidān·ī -ōrum *mpl* townspeople

oppid·um -ī *n* town

oppugn·ō -āre -āvī -ātus to attack, assault

optimē *adv* best

optim·us -a -um best

opt·ō -āre -āvī -ātus to wish, desire

opus oper·is *n* task, job, work

ōr·a -ae *f* coast; ōra maritima seacoast, coastline

ōrācul·um -ī *n* oracle

ōrāti·ō -ōn*is* *f* speech; ōrātiōnem habēre to give a speech

orb·is -is *m* globe; orbis terrārum the world

ōrd·ō -in*is* *m* order

Ōrīōn Ōrīōn·is *m* Orion (*gigantic hunter*)

ōrnāment·um -ī *n* ornament; ōrnāmenta jewels

ōrnāt·us -ūs *m* outfit, uniform

ōs ōr·is *n* mouth

ōscul·um -ī *n* kiss

Ōsti·a -ae *f* Ostia (*port town of Rome*)

ōsti·um -ī *n* doorway; door; mouth (*of a river*)

ōti·um -ī *n* leisure; in ōtium venīre to retire (*from office or job*)

Pad·us -ī *m* Po (River)

paene *adv* nearly, almost

paenīnsul·a -ae *f* peninsula

paenul·a -ae *f* (hooded) raincoat

palaestr·a -ae *f* exercise yard, palestra

pall·a -ae *f* wrap (*often colorful, worn over the stola*)

pallid·us -a -um pale

pānicul·us -ī *m* roll, bun

pān·is -is *m* bread

parāt·us -a -um prepared, ready

parc·ō -ĕre pepercī *or* parsī parsūrus (+ *dat*) to spare

par·ēns -ent*is* *m/f* parent

par·eō -ēre -uī (+ *dat*) obey

pari·ēs -et*is* *m* wall

par·iō -ĕre peperī partus to give birth to

par·ō -āre -āvī -ātus to prepare

pars part·is (*gen pl* -ium) *f* part; direction; in omnēs partēs in all directions; partēs role

partim *adv* partly

parum *adv* (too) little, not enough; (*sometimes as a simple negative*) not

parvō *adv* (by) a little

parvul·us -ī *m* little one, baby, child

parv·us -a -um small; young

pass·us -ūs *m* pace, step; mille passūs a mile

pāst·or -ōr*is* *m* shepherd

pat·ēns -ent*is* open

pater patr·is *m* father

pati·ēns -ent*is* patient

patri·a -ae *f* country, native land; native city

patrici·us -a -um patrician; *m* patrician

patrōn·a -ae *f* patroness

pauc·ī -ae -a few

paulātim *adv* little by little, gradually

paulisper *adv* for a little while

paulō *adv* a little, by a little

Paul·us -ī *m* Paul

pauper pauper·is poor

pavīment·um -ī *n* floor, pavement

pāv·ō -ōn*is* *m* peacock

pāx pāc·is *f* peace

pect·us -or*is* *n* chest, breast

pē·ior -ior -ius worse

pēius *adv* worse

Pēnelop·ē -ēs *f* Penelope (*wife of Odysseus*)

Pēnē·us -ī *m* Peneus (*river god*)

peperī *see* pariō

per *prep* (+ *acc*) through; throughout; along (*e.g., a road*); during; through the agency of

per- *prefix* very

peracūt·us -a -um very sharp

percip·iō -ĕre percēpī perceptus to perceive, notice; to understand

per·dō perdĕre perdidī perditus to lose

perfect·us -a -um perfect

perfic·iō -ěre perfēcī perfectus to finish

perfidi·a -ae *f* disloyalty, treachery

perfid·us -a -um disloyal, treacherous

perfod·iō -ěre perfōdī perfossus to stab

perfug·iō -ěre perfūgī to take refuge, run for help

pergul·a -ae *f* porch

perīculōs·us -a -um dangerous

pericul·um -ī *n* danger

perinde ac *conj* just as, just like

peristȳli·um -ī *n* courtyard (*surrounded by a colonnaded walk*)

pernoct·ō -āre -āvī to spend the night

perperam *adv* mistakenly

perpetu·us -a -um perpetual; **in perpetuum** forever

persuād·eō -ēre persuāsī persuāsūrus (+ *dat*) to persuade

perterr·eō -ēre -uī -itus to terrify

perturb·ō -āre -āvī -ātus to upset

Perusi·a -ae *f* Perugia (*modern Perugia in N. Italy*)

perven·iō -īre pervēnī perventūrus (+ **ad** *or* **in** + *acc*) to arrive at, reach

pēs ped·is *m* foot

pessimē *adv* worst

pessim·us -a -um worst

pestilenti·a -ae *f* pestilence

petas·us -ī *m* hat

pet·ō -ěre -īvī -ītus to ask for; to seek; to head for; to chase after

Phaëth·ōn -ontis *m* Phaëthon (*drove the chariot of the sun*)

philosophi·a -ae *f* philosophy

Phoeb·us -ī *m* Phoebus (*epithet of Apollo as sun god*)

Pīcēn·um -ī *n* Picenum (*district in E. central Italy*)

pictūr·a -ae *f* painting

pil·a -ae *f* ball; **pilā lūděre** to play ball

Pīs·ae -ārum *fpl* Pisa (*coastal town in N. Italy*)

piscīn·a -ae *f* swimming pool

pīst·or -ōris *m* baker

pīstrīn·a -ae *f* bakery

plac·eō -ēre -uī -itūrus (+ *dat*) to please

placidē *adv* calmly, peacefully

plān·us -a -um flat

plēbs plēb·is *f* the common people, the plebeians

plēn·us -a -um (+ *gen or abl*) full (of)

plūr·ēs -ēs -a more

plūrimum *adv* most (of all); mostly

plūrim·us -a -um most

plūs *n* (+ *gen of the noun*) more

plūs *adv* more

Plūt·ō -ōnis *m* Pluto (*brother of Jupiter and god of the lower world*)

pluvi·a -ae *f* rain

Pompēi·ī -ōrum *mpl* Pompeii (*town in S. Italy*)

Pompēi·us -ī *m* Pompey (the Great)

pōn·ō -ěre posuī positus to put, place; to station **castra poněre** to encamp

pōns pont·is *m* bridge

popīn·a -ae *f* restaurant, cafe

popul·us -ī *m* people

porrō *adv* moreover

port·a -ae *f* gate

portic·us -ūs *f* portico, porch

portit·or -ōris *m* ferryman

port·ō -āre -āvī -ātus to carry

possum posse potuī to be able, can

post *prep* (+ *acc*) after; behind

posteā *adv* later, after that, afterwards

poster·us -a -um following, next

postquam *conj* after

postrēmō *adv* finally

postrīdiē *adv* on the following day

postul·ō -āre -āvī -ātus to call for, demand

potēns potēnt·is powerful

potissimum *adv* especially

potius *adv* rather

pot·ō -āre -āvī -atus *or* **pōtus** to drink; **pōtus et cēnāt·us -a -um** having wined and dined

praecipuē *adv* especially

praedīc·ō -ěre praedīxī praedictus to predict

praemi·um -ī *n* reward

praenōm·en -inis *n* first name

praescrīpt·um -ī *n* **domestic·um** (*written*) homework

praesēns praesent·is present

praesertim *adv* especially

prae·sum -esse -fuī -futūrus (+ *dat*) to be in charge of

praeter *prep* (+ *acc*) above, beyond; past, by (*a place*); besides

praevtereā *adv* especially

praeter·eō -īre -īvī *or* **-iī -itus** to go by, pass

praet·or -ōris *m* praetor (*minister of justice*)

pretiōs·us -a -um precious

prex prec·is *m* prayer, entreaty

Priam·us -ī *m* Priam (*king of Troy*)

prīmō *adv* at first, in the beginning

prīmōr·ēs -um *mpl* leading men, "big shots"

prīmum *adv (in a series)* first

prīm·us -a -um first; **prīmā lūce** at first light, at dawn; **prīmō aspectū** at first sight

pr·ior -ior -ius former

Prīsc·us -ī *m* Tarquinius Priscus *(fifth king of Rome)*

prius *adv* previously; sooner; rather

prīvātim *adv* privately

prō *prep (+ abl)* in front of; for (the sake of); on behalf of; instead of

probāti·ō -ōn*is* *f* test

prōcēd·ō -ēre prōcessī prōcessūrus to proceed

prōclām·ō -āre -āvī -ātus to proclaim

procul *adv* from far off; **procul ab** (+ *abl*) far from

prōdit·or -ōr*is* *m* betrayer

proeli·um -ī *n* battle

profectō *adv* as a matter of fact, indeed

prohib·eō -ēre -uī -itus to prohibit, prevent, hinder

prōmitt·ō -ēre prōmīsī prōmissus to promise

prōm·ō -ēre -psī -ptus to get out

prope *adv* almost, nearly

prope *prep* (+ *acc*) near

proper·ō -āre -āvī to rush

prophētic·us -a -um prophetic

prop·ior -ior -ius closer

propter *prep* (+ *acc*) because of; for the sake of

Proserpīn·a -ae *f* Persephone *(queen of the lower world)*

prōvocāti·ō -ōn*is* *f* challenge

proxim·us -a -um nearest; next;

following; last, latest; (+ *dat*) near, next to

prūd·ēns -ent*is* prudent

prūdentissimē *adv* very prudently

prūdentius *adv* more prudently

puer puer·ī *m* boy

pugn·ō -āre -āvī -ātus to fight

pulch·er -ra -rum beautiful; handsome

pūr·us -a -um pure

Pȳram·us -ī *m* Pyramus *(boyfriend of Thisbe)*

quadrāgintā *indecl* forty

quadringent·ī -ae -a four hundred

quae *pron* who; which, that

quaest·or -ōr*is* *m* quaestor *(financial officer)*

quam *adv* how; *(with comparatives)* than; **quam celerrimē** as quickly as possible; **quam prīmum** as soon as possible

quamobrem *adv* for that reason, that's why

quamquam *conj* although

quandō *adv* when

quantī how much?; **quantī cōnstat?** how much does it cost?

quāpropter *adv* wherefore, for that reason

quārt·us -a -um fourth

quasi *conj* as if

quattuor *indecl* four

quattuordecim *indecl* fourteen

-que *conj (joins the word to which it is attached to the previous word)* and

quī *pron* who

quia *conj* because

quid *pron* what?; **quid agis?** How are you?; **quid aliud?** what else?

quīdam quaedam quoddam *pron* a certain, a particular; **quōdam dīe** one day

quidem *adv* of course, indeed

quīndecim *indecl* fifteen

quīngent·ī -ae -a five hundred

quīnquāgintā *indecl* fifty

quīnque *indecl* five

quīnt·us -a -um fifth

quis *pron* who?

quō magis . . . eō magis the more . . . the more

quod *pron* which, that

quod *conj* because

quondam *adv* once, one day

quoque *adv* too *(always comes after the word it modifies)*

quot *indecl adj* how many?

quotannīs *adv* every year

radi·us -ī *m* ray

rām·us -ī *m* branch

rārō *adv* rarely

rār·us -a -um rare, sparse

rātiō rātiōn·is *f* policy

rē *adv* in reality, really

rebell·ō -āre -āvī to rebel

recēd·ō -ēre recessī recessūrus to withdraw, recede

recēns recēnt·is recent; fresh

recip·iō -ēre recēpī receptus to get back; to recapture, regain; to receive, make welcome

recit·ō -āre -āvī -ātus to recite, read aloud; **nōmina recitāre** to call roll

rēct·us -a -um straight

record·ō -āre -āvī -ātus to recall

recuper·ō -āre -āvī -ātus to regain

recūs·ō -āre -āvī -ātus to turn down, reject

red·dō -děre -didī -ditus to give back, return

red·eō -īre -iī *or* **-īvī -itūrus** to return, come back, go back

refic·iō -ěre refēcī refectus to redo, repair

rēgi·a -ae *f* palace

rēgīn·a -ae *f* queen

regi·ō -ōnis *f* region

regi·us -a - um royal, the king's

rēgn·ō -āre -āvī -ātūrus to reign; **rēgnāre in** (+ *acc*) rule over

rēgn·um -ī *n* kingdom, throne, realm

reg·ō -ěre rēxī rēctus to rule

rēgul·us -ī *m* prince

reman·eō -ēre -sī -sum to stay behind

remitt·ō -ěre remīsī remissus to send back

Rem·us -ī *m* Remus

repentē *adv* suddenly

rēp·ō -ěre -sī rēptūrus to crawl; **fūrtim rēpěre** to sneak

requīr·ō -ěre requīsīvī requīsītus (**ex** + *abl*) ask of (*a person*)

respond·eō -ēre respondī respōnsus to answer

rēs reī *f* thing; affair **rēs pūblica** government, the State; politics

resist·ō -ěre restitī (+ *dat*) resist

respon·deō -děre -/di -sūrus to answer

respōns·um -ī *n* answer

retrō *adv* back, backwards

retund·ō -ěre ret(t)udī retūsus to blunt, break up (*an attack*)

reven·iō -īre revēnī to come back; to come again

rēx rēg·is *m* king

Rhē·a Silvi·a -ae *f* Rhea Silvia

(*mother of Romulus and Remus*)

rhēt·or -ōris *m* rhetorician, professor of public speaking

rhētōric·a -ae *f* rhetoric, art of public speaking

rhētōric·us -a -um rhetorical, dealing with public speaking

rīd·eō -ēre rīsī rīsus to laugh; to laugh at

rīp·a -ae *f* bank (*of a river*)

rītē *adv* duly, properly

rīvālit·ās -ātis *f* rivalry

robust·us -a -um robust, muscular

rogit·ō -āre -āvī -ātus to keep asking

rog·ō -āre -āvī -ātus to beg

Rōm·a -ae *f* Rome

Rōmān·us -a -um Roman

Rōmul·us -ī *m* Romulus

rōstr·a -ōrum *npl* rostrum, podium

rotund·us -a -um round

rupt·us -a -um broken

rūrāl·is -is -e rural, country-

rūrsus *adv* again

rūs rūr·is *n* country; **rūre** from the country; **rūrī** in the country

rūstic·us -a -um rustic; *m* rustic, hick

Rutul·ī -ōrum *mpl* Rutulians (*a native Italic tribe whose capital was Ardea*)

Sabīn·ī -ōrum *mpl* the Sabines (*living to the E. of Latium*)

sacer sacr·a -um holy, sacred

sacerd·ōs -ōtis *m* priest

sacr·a -ōrum *npl* sacred rites

saepĕ *adv* often

saepissimē *adv* very often

saepius *adv* more often

saev·us -a -um savage

sagitt·a -ae *f* arrow

sal·iō -īre -uī to jump

sal·ūs -ūtis *f* greetings; **salūtem dīcěre** (+ *dat*) to send greetings to

salve! hello!; **salvē et tū!** hello yourself

salv·us -a -um safe, unharmed

Samni·um -ī *n* Samnium (*district in central Italy*)

sandali·um -ī *n* sandal

sān·us -a -um healthy; sane

sapid·us -a -um delicious

sapienti·a -ae *f* wisdom

Sardini·a -ae *f* Sardinia

satell·es -itis *m* attendant, bodyguard

Sāturn·us -ī *m* Saturn (*father of Jupiter*)

sax·um -ī *n* stone

scaenic·us -a -um stage-, of the stage; **lūdus scaenicus** stage play

scaevol·us -a -um left-handed

schol·a -ae *f* school

sciō scīre scīvī scītus to know; to know how to

scop·ae -ārum *fpl* broom

scrīb·a -ae *m* scribe, secretary

scrīb·ō -ěre scrīpsī scrīptus to write

scūt·um -ī *n* (*oblong*) shield

secund·us -a -um second

sēcūr·us -a -um secure

sēdecim *indecl* sixteen

sed·eō -ēre sēdī sessūrus to sit

sēgreg·ō -āre -āvī -ātus to keep apart

semel *adv* once

semper *adv* always

senāt·or -ōris *m* senator

senāt·us -ūs *m* senate; senate session

sent·iō -īre sēnsī sēnsus to feel; to realize

septem *indecl* seven

septendecim *indecl* seventeen

septim·us -a -um seventh

septingent·ī -ae -a seven hundred

septuāgintā *indecl* seventy

sequor sequī secūtus sum to follow

serv·iō -īre īvī *or* **iī -ītum** to be a slave; to serve

serv·ō -āre -āvī -ātus to save; to keep

serv·us -ī *m* slave

sescent·ī -ae -a six hundred

sex *indecl* six

sexāgintā *indecl* sixty

sext·us -a -um sixth

sīc *adv* thus, so

sīc·a -ae *f* dagger

Sicili·a -ae *f* Sicily

sign·um -ī *n* sign

silenti·um -ī *n* silence

sil·eō -ēre -uī to be silent

simil·is -is -e similar, like

simul *adv* at the same time

sine *prep* (+ *abl*) without

sinist·er -ra -rum left

sin·us -ūs *m* bay

sit·iō -īre to be thirsty

sit·us -a -um located

socc·us -ī *m* low dress shoe

soci·us -ī *m* ally

sole·a -ae *f* sandal *(plain)*

sollicit·us -a -um worried

sōlum *adv* only; **nōn sōlum . . . sed etiam** not only . . . but also

sōl·us -a -um alone, only

son·ō -āre -uī -itūrus to sound; (+ *abl*) to resound with

sonōr·us -a -um loud, resounding

sor·or -ōris *f* sister

speci·ēs -ēī *f* appearance, looks

spectāt·or -ōris *m* spectator

spect·ō -āre -āvī -ātus to look at, watch

spēlunc·a -ae *f* cave

spēr·ō -āre -āvī -ātus to hope for

spēs sp·eī *f* hope

splendid·us -a -um dazzling, brilliant

splend·or -ōris *m* brilliance

statim *adv* immediately

stati·ō -ōnis *f* guard post, guard duty; **in statiōne esse** to be on guard (duty)

statu·a -ae *f* statue

stell·a -ae *f* constellation, star

stil·us -ī *m* stilus, "pen," "pencil"

stipendi·um -ī *n* (military) pay

stō stāre stetī status to stand

stol·a -ae *f* gown

strāment·um -ī *n* straw, thatch

strepit·us -ūs *m* noise

stud·eō -ēre -uī (+ *dat*) to study, pursue

Styx Styg·is *m* Styx *(river flowing around the lower world)*

sub *prep* (+ *acc*) under; toward, just before; at about; (+ *abl*) under; at the foot of *(a mountain); (when motion is shown,* **sub** *takes the accusative)*

subitō *adv* suddenly

subit·us -a -um sudden

subrīd·eō -ēre subrīsī subrīsūrus to smile

subselli·um -ī *n* seat, bench

subterrāne·us -a -um subterranean, below the earth

succēd·ō -ēre successī successūrus to succeed

suffic·iō -ĕre suffēcī suffectūrus to suffice

suggest·us -ūs *m* platform

sum esse fuī futūrus to be

summ·us -a -um highest; top of

sūm·ō -ĕre sūmpsī sūmptus to put on *(clothes)*; to take; to assume

super *prep* (+ *abl*) about, concerning

super·ior -ior -ius higher

super·ō -āre -āvī -ātus to defeat, conquer, vanquish

supplic·ō -āre -āvī -ātus to beg, supplicate

super·us -a -um above; **superī** *mpl* the gods above

suprā *prep* (+ *acc*) above, over; north of; beyond

suprēm·us -a -um highest

surg·ō -ĕre surrēxī surrēctūrus to get up, rise

sustin·eō -ēre -uī to stand up to *(an attack)*; to pass *(a test)*

susurr·ō -āre -āvī to whisper

sūtor sūtōr·is *m* shoemaker

sūtrīn·a -ae *f* shoemaker's shop

su·us -a -um *adj & pron* his, her, its, their (own)

tabern·a -ae *f* shop, store; **taberna vestiāria** clothing store

tabernāri·us -ī *m* shopkeeper

tablīn·um -ī *n* study, office

tabul·a -ae *f* writing tablet

taeni·a -ae *f* ribbon

tam *adv* such (a); **tam longē** so far; **tam . . . quam** as . . . as

tamen *adv* however

tamquam *conj* as if

tandem *adv* at last

tantummodo *adv* only

Tarpēi·a -ae *f* Tarpeia (*daughter of Tarpeius*)

Tarpēi·us -ī *m* Tarpeius (*commander of the garrison of the Capitoline*)

Tarquini·ī -ōrum *mpl* Tarquinia (*town in Etruria*)

Tarquini·us Prīsc·us -ī *m* Tarquinius Priscus (*fifth king of Rome*)

Tarquini·us Superb·us -ī *m* Tarquin the Proud (*seventh and last king of Rome*)

Tartar·us -ī *m* Tartarus, lower world

taur·us -ī *m* bull

tēct·um -ī *n* roof

teg·ō -ĕre tēxī tēctus to cover

tempest·ās -ātis *f* storm; time

templ·um -ī *n* temple

tempt·ō -āre -āvī -ātus to try

temp·us -or·is *n* time; **tempore** in time

Tened·os (*or* **·us**) **-ī** *f* Tenedos (*island off the coast of Troy*)

ten·eō -ēre -uī -tus to hold; to occupy; to understand; **nunc tenō** now I get it

tener ·tener·a -um tender

tenu·is -is -e shallow

tepidāri·um -ī *n* warm bath

terr·a -ae *f* land, country

terrific·us -a -um frightening

territ·us -a -um terrified, frightened, in terror

terti·us -a -um third

theātr·um -ī *n* theater

therm·ae -ārum *fpl* public bath

Thēse·us -ī *m* Theseus (*Athenian prince*)

Thessali·a -ae *f* Thessaly (*a district N of Greece*)

Thisb·ē -ēs *f* Thisbe (*girlfriend of Pyramus*)

Thrāci·a -ae *f* Thrace (*country NE of Greece*)

thron·us -ī *m* throne

Tiber·is -is (*acc:* **-im**) *m* Tiber (River)

tim·eō -ēre -uī to fear, be afraid (of)

timid·us -a -um timid, shy

tim·or -ōris *m* fear

Tītān·us -ī *m* Titan (*one of a race of gods who preceded the Olympians*)

tog·a -ae *f* toga; **toga pura** pure-white toga; **toga praetexta** purple-bordered toga; **toga virīlis** toga of manhood

toler·ō -āre -āvī -ātus to stand, tolerate

toll·ō -ĕre sustulī sublātus to lift (up)

tomācl·um -ī *n* sausage

tonitr·us -ūs *m* thunder

tōt·us -a -um whole, entire; **ex tōtō** totally

tract·ō -āre -āvī -ātus to treat, deal with

trā·dō -dĕre -dedī -ditus to betray

trah·ō -ĕre trāxī tractus to drag

trāns *prep* (+ *acc*) across

trāns·eō -īre -īvī *or* **-iī -itūrus** to cross (over)

trānsnat·ō -āre -āvī to swim across

trecent·ī -ae -a three hundred

tredecim *indecl* thirteen

trem·or -ōris *m* tremor

trēs trēs tria three

tribūn·us -ī *m* **plēbis** tribune of the people

trīceps trīcipit·is three-headed

trīclīni·um -ī *n* dining room

trid·ēns -ent·is (*gen pl* **-ium**) *m* trident

trienni·um -ī *n* three-year period, three years

trīgintā *indecl* thirty

trīst·is -is -e sad

Trōi·a -ae *f* Troy

Trōiān·us -a -um Trojan

tū *pron* you

tum *adv* then, at that time; **tum autem** but then

tunic·a -ae *f* tunic

turb·a -ae *f* crowd

Turn·us -ī *m* Turnus (*king of the Rutulians*)

tūtē *adv* safely

tūt·us -a -um safe

tu·us -a -um your(s)

ubi *adv* where; *conj* when

ubique *adv* everywhere

ūllus -a -um any

ulter·ior -ior -ius farther

ultim·us -a -um last, final; farthest

Umbri·a -ae *f* Umbria (*district of NE Italy*)

umquam *adv* ever

ūnā *adv* together; **ūnā cum** (+ *abl*) together with

ūnctōri·um -ī *n* massage room

ūndecim *indecl* eleven

ūndēvīgintī *indecl* nineteen

ūn·us -a -um one; alone

Ūran·us -ī *n* Uranus (*father of Saturn and grandfather of Jupiter*)

urbs urb·is (*gen pl* **-ium**) *f* city

ut *conj* as, when; **ut . . . sīc etiam** as . . . so also

utique *adv* at least

ūtor ūtī ūsus sum (+ *abl*) to use

utpote *adv* as you might expect, as is natural

utrimque *adv* on both sides

ux·or -ōris *f* wife

vagīt·us -ūs *m* cry (*of a baby*)

valdē *adv* very much

valē good-bye; **bene valē** good-bye; **nunc valē** good-bye for now

valid·us -a -um strong; powerful

vāstit·ās -ātis *f* huge size

vect·us -a -um having traveled

vehem·ēns -ent·is vehement, intense

veh·ō -ĕre vexī vectus to carry

vehor vehī vectus sum to be carried, ride; **equō (or vehiculō) vehī** to ride; **nāve vehī** to sail

Vēi·ī -ōrum *mpl* Veii (*Etruscan city*)

vēlām·en -inis *n* wrap

vēlōcit·ās -ātis *f* speed

vēl·um -ī *n* sail; **vēlum dare** to set sail

vēnāti·ō -ōnis *f* wild-animal show; hunting

vēnāt·or -ōris *m* hunter

ven·iō -īre vēnī ventūrus to come

Ven·us -eris *f* Venus

Venusi·a -ae *f* Venusia (*town in S. Italy*)

venust·us -a -um charming

verb·um -ī *n* word

Vergili·us -ī *m* Vergil (*poet of the Aeneid*)

vērit·ās -ātis *f* truth

vērō *adv* in fact, really; indeed, all right

Vērōn·a -ae *f* Verona (*town in N. Italy*)

vēr·um -ī *n* the truth; **vērum dīcis** you're right

vēr·us -a -um true, real

vespere *adv* in the evening

Vest·a -ae *f* goddess of the hearth

Vestāl·is -is (*gen pl:* -**ium**) Vestal, of Vesta

vester vest·ra -rum your(s)

vestiāri·us -a -um clothing-; **taberna vestiāria** clothing store

vēstibul·um -ī *n* entrance way, front hall

vēstīgi·um -ī *n* track, footstep

vestīment·a -ōrum *npl* clothes

veterrim·us -a -um oldest

vetul·us -a -um old

Vetūri·a -ae *f* Veturia (*mother of Coriolanus*)

vetus veter·is old

vetust·ior -ior -ius older

vi·a -ae *f* way, road, street

vīcēsim·us -a -um twentieth

vicīn·us -ī *m* neighbor

vicissim *adv* in turn

victim·a -ae *f* victim

vict·or -ōris *m* victor

vid·eō -ēre vīdī vīsus to see

vig·il -ilis *m* fireman, policeman

vigil·ō -āre -āvī to be awake

vīgintī *indecl* twenty

vinc·ō -ĕre vīcī victus to conquer, defeat

vīn·um -ī *n* wine

violēns violēnt·is violent

vir vir·ī *m* man

vīr·ēs -ium *fpl* strength

virg·ō -inis *f* young (unmarried) girl; virgin

virīl·is -is -e manly, of manhood

virt·ūs -ūtis *f* valor, courage

vīsit·ō -āre -āvī -ātus to visit

vīs·ō -ĕre -ī -us to go and see

vīt·a -ae *f* life

vīv·ēns -entis living, while alive

vīv·ō -ĕre vīxī vīctus to live, be alive

voc·ō -āre -āvī -ātus to call (on); to invite (*esp. to dinner*)

vol·ō -āre -āvī -ātūrus to fly

vol·ō velle voluī to want, wish, be willing

Volsc·us -a -um Volscan

voluntāri·us -a -um voluntary

volunt·ās -ātis *f* will, wishes

vōs *pron* you

vōx vōc·is *f* voice

Vulcān·us -ī *m* Vulcan

vulg·us -ī *n* general public

vulner·ō -āre -āvī -ātus to wound

vulnus vulner·is *n* wound

See also the Glossary of Grammatical Terms and the Forms in the Appendix for each entry (pp 344 to 374).

sion nouns 35; 4th declension nouns 52; 5th declension nouns 60; nouns ending in **-us** 52

genitive case 20, 34, 61, of material 20; of possession 20; of quality 20; with certain adjectives 20; with *plus* 121

Greek nouns 68-69

helping verb 207, 210, 248, 316

i-stem **nouns** 34-35, 43

imperative mood 1st, 2nd, 3rd conjugations 213; 3rd *-iō* and 4th conjugations 225; irregular verbs 260

intransitive verbs 206-207

īre 258-261, 280, 292, 294

locative 25-26, 80

name (with dative) 23

nōlle 258-261, 280, 292, 294

nominative case 4, 5-6

number (singular/plural) 4

numerals and numbers 188-191; declension 188; cardinals and ordinals 189-190

personal endings 205, 259-260; active and passive 302

posse 258-261, 280, 292, 294

predicate adjective 6; noun 5-6; whole predicate 6

prefixes 91, 226, 259

prepositional phrase 7, 79

prepositions 7, 27, 79-86

principal parts 206, 271

pronouns demonstrative 164-166; intensive 155-156; interrogative 180-181; personal 145-147, 210; possessive 153; reciprocal 152; reflexive 150-151, 154, 155; relative 176-177

stem 205, 270-272

subject 5

suffixes 115

superlative 116-117, 120, 121

tenses future active 247-248, 260, future passive 303; future perfect 294-295; future perfect passive 315-316; imperfect 238-239; 260; imperfect passive 303; perfect 270-273, 280-281; perfect passive 314-315; pluperfect 291-293; pluperfect passive 315-316; present imperative 213, 225; present 209-210, 224, 258; present passive 303

transitive verbs 206-207

typical vowel 205

velle 258-261, 280, 292, 294

verbs *See tenses and conjugations.* auxiliary/helping 207, 210; basic facts about verbs 205, 208; commonly used verbs 273-274; compound verbs 226; defective verbs 281-295; deponent verbs 305; interrogative forms 211-213; irregular verbs 258-261, 280, 292, 294; negative forms 211; overview of verbs in the perfect 283-286; passive forms 302-303; reflexive 151; transitive and intransitive 206-207; uses of the passive 304-305

vocative 28

voice, active and passive 206

word order 7, 81, 99, 156, 211, 316, 340-343

References do not include names occurring within the exercises.